## Praise for *Raisin' Cain*

"From Texas progressive to deep blues revivalist, from rock star highs to heroin lows, this story is a raucous good time, full of drama, and ultimately, an exciting personal triumph."

—Robert Gordon, author of
*Can't Be Satisfied: The Life and Times of Muddy Waters*

"'The road of excess leads to the palace of wisdom,' wrote William Blake. This book shows just how rocky that road can be, and how much a great blues artist has to work and endure to create the music. It'll remind you what a giant force Johnny Winter has been in blues and rock, both with his own music and for his work with Muddy Waters and others. It's all here—the sex, drugs, rock 'n' roll, heartbreaks, triumphs, and famous friends. What a wild, improbable, twisting tale!"

—Mark Hoffman, author of
*Moanin' at Midnight: The Life and Times of Howlin' Wolf*

"Incredibly detailed. . . . For those of us who are Johnny Winter fans, this is more information than anyone would ever need. Raises the bar when someone says they are writing an authorized biography."

—Bill Wax, Program Director and host of
*B. B. King's Bluesville* on Sirius/XM Satellite Radio

"Blues fans talk about 'real deal' blues. They also want a 'real deal' biography, too, with research and facts and not just a string of liner notes and record reviews. *Raisin' Cain* is the 'real deal.' The detail and completeness make this history, not just a cover version for the tourists. The next time someone asks Edgar Winter, 'Hey, where's your brother?' he can tell them to pick up a copy."

—Jay Sieleman, Executive Director
The Blues Foundation, Memphis, Tennessee

# Raisin' Cain

# Raisin' Cain

## The Wild and Raucous Story of Johnny Winter

Mary Lou Sullivan

Published in 2010 by Backbeat Books
4501 Forbes Boulevard, Suite 200
Lanham, Maryland 20706
www.rowman.com
800-462-6420



Book design by UB Communications

Library of Congress Cataloging-in-Publication Data is available upon request.

ISBN 978-0-87930-973-2

www.backbeatbooks.com

*To Lloyd J. Jassin,*
*whose wisdom, perseverance, and heart*
*made my dream come true*

*I am truly blessed to have you*
*as my agent,*
*attorney, and*
*friend*

# Contents

# Foreword

I love this book. It has everything. All the things that I wanted people to know, from how hard it was growing up in Texas being an albino, my career, the early days, my problems with drugs . . . it's excellent and very realistic—it's exactly what happened.

It's like reliving my life again. Reading things people said that I had forgotten. There were a few things that I didn't remember that really surprised me. I had forgotten about Salvador Dali wanting me to stick a microphone up my ass . . . that was ridiculous.

Reading this book was emotional—the good stuff was great and the bad stuff was really horrible. Some of the memories were painful, but I'm glad they're in the book. To try to whitewash my life would have been horrible, that wouldn't have been worth reading. I've always been very honest. You don't get the right picture if you're not honest.

Mary Lou did a fantastic job—it couldn't have been better. I don't think anybody else could have done such a good job or been as honest. I loved talking to her on all those Saturday nights. I was really open because I wanted my story to be told. She did an excellent job on research and really spent a lot of time on this book. It is perfect—there isn't anything left out.

I'm very glad I stayed true to the blues—I wouldn't have been nearly as happy if I stayed a *rock* star. It was just too much pressure. The life of a bluesman is a little easier than the life of a *rock* star. As a bluesman, I love what I'm doing; I'm not forcing anything. People seem to really love my music, and that feels good.

The blues is such an emotional music—it has so much feeling. There never was a point where I didn't want to play blues. You can't describe the blues; you just have to feel it. Some people say it's boring, but it sure isn't to me. I try to do it different every time I play.

Blues goes in and out of style, but it'll always be around because it's just too good to go away. There will always be people that love the blues and play the blues. Stations like Bluesville on XM radio really help the blues by exposing it to new people. I've influenced a lot of people too. People are always telling me if it wasn't for me they wouldn't be into the blues, and that makes me feel real good.

Most of today's blues isn't as good as it was back during Muddy's time. People used to live such hard lives. They grew up picking cotton, and people don't do that anymore. The passing of Muddy, John Lee Hooker, Gatemouth, and so many elder bluesmen certainly hurts because there are not as many good people coming up. There are still a few good people around though—Magic Slim, Derek Trucks, Little Ed, Eric Sardinas. . . .

I'm real glad to still be playing after all these years. I want to keep playing as long as I possibly can. I've been playing all over the U.S. and Europe and just came back from playing in Europe for three weeks. Having so many loyal fans is great. Now they bring their kids to the shows, and their kids like me. Playing live shows, you feed off all the energy from the people. The people make a lot of difference.

I really hope everybody enjoys this book as much as I did. I read it as soon as I got it and couldn't wait to see what happened next. Even though I knew, it was still fun to read. I've led a very interesting life. You can't make this stuff up.

Johnny Winter
November 29, 2008
Fairfield County, Connecticut

# Preface

*Raisin' Cain* is a book that Teddy Slatus, Johnny Winter's manager and business associate for thirty-five years, didn't want published, and a book I was determined to write. It has been a tumultuous twenty-five-year journey.

My quest to write Johnny's life story began in 1984, when I interviewed him for the *Hartford Advocate*. Impressed by his honesty, affinity for storytelling, philosophical approach to life, and tongue-in-cheek sense of humor, I felt an immediate kinship and wanted to know more. I set up a second interview for a Johnny Winter special on my WCCC radio show, and approached Slatus Management about writing his biography.

Although Slatus turned down my idea several times during the 1980s, I never abandoned my quest. During the '90s, Slatus consistently rejected requests for interviews, and eventually shut Johnny off from all media contact. But I was still determined to tell Johnny's story with *his* input during *his* lifetime, rather than leave it to biographers forced to rely on the often self-serving memories of peripheral players after he was gone.

Ironically, it was on the day before 9/11/2001 that Slatus and I entered into a handshake agreement to make me Johnny's biographer. It took another fifteen months before Slatus made it official. He said he had talked to other writers but chose me because "You have heart and you really care about Johnny."

In January 2003, I began interviewing Johnny in his home. By then his lifestyle had affected his memory, so I did an enormous amount of research prior to each meeting, compiling 400–450 questions each week to help jog his recollections. After Johnny and I had shared many a Saturday night strolling down memory lane, Slatus called in his attorney, stopped the project, and forbade Johnny from having any further contact with me. He had become threatened by my close friendship with Johnny, and frantic about what he may have told me.

Crushed that I could no longer see my new friend, but still determined to tell his tale, I embarked on a six-year journey to fill in the blanks and write a definitive biography. I interviewed Paul Oscher in a coffee shop in Memphis; and traveled to the Delta Blues Museum in Clarksdale, Mississippi, where a blown-up photo of Johnny, Muddy Waters, and Eric Clapton adorns the wall of the remains of Waters's Stovall Farms cabin. I conducted an in-depth interview with Alligator Records' president and founder Bruce Iglauer outside of Robinsonville, Mississippi, where Robert Johnson, another one of Johnny's influences, spent his childhood. I traveled with Howlin' Wolf biographer Mark Hoffman to Leland, Mississippi, to see the life-size mural honoring Johnny, Edgar, and other blues musicians, and to visit the birthplace of Johnny's father and grandfather, who had lived and worked there as cotton brokers.

I made several trips to Austin, Texas, where Uncle John Turner and Tommy Shannon regaled me with tales of their early struggles, adventures on LSD, rock festivals, and historic recording sessions. Austin artist Jim Franklin shared memories of his lifelong friendship with Johnny, Johnny's gigs with Muddy Waters and Freddie King, and some bizarre stories about Salvador Dali.

I interviewed Mark Epstein at a gig he played with Joe Bonamassa, and waited out a hurricane to talk to producer Terry Manning at Compass Point Studios in the Bahamas. I hooked up with Billy Branch and Jerry Portnoy at the North Atlantic Blues Festival in Rockland, Maine. I met Steve Paul backstage at B. B. King's in New York City, thanks to Johnny's new manager Paul Nelson, who brought the project and my friendship with Johnny back on track.

I gleaned a wealth of information about Johnny and had a ball speaking with people from throughout the United States and beyond: Edgar Winter in Los Angeles; Edwina Winter in Beaumont, Texas; Muddy's manager Scott Cameron, Dick Shurman, and Dennis Drugan in Chicago; Bobby Caldwell and Floyd Radford in Florida; Bob Margolin in North Carolina; Doug Brockie in New Jersey; Bobby T. in Connecticut; and Mike and Richard Vernon in Spain and the United Kingdom.

Yet my fondest memory is the night Johnny answered the door wearing the Homer Simpson slippers I had given him the week before. After our interview, he walked over to his CD player, his shirt open to display his trademark tattoos, wearing dark blue sweatpants and those bright yellow slippers with bulging white eyes. I had asked him to play me his fiery rendition of B. B. King's "It's My Own Fault" on the *Mike Bloomfield/Al Kooper Fillmore East: The Lost Concert Tapes 12/13/68* CD that had just been released. As I sat beside him on the couch, listening to that historic performance by this amazing guitarist with a wonderful heart, my only thought was, "It doesn't get any better than this."

December 2009

# ACKNOWLEDGMENTS

To Johnny Winter, who trusted me with his legacy and shared some amazing stories (and a lot of laughs) during our Saturday nights together.

To Susan Winter, a sweet and gracious lady, who shared her memories and Johnny's personal archives.

Warm thanks to the musicians, artists, producers, and music industry people who generously shared their time and memories: Andy Aledort, Bill Bentley, Billy Branch, Doug Brockie, Bobby Caldwell, Scott Cameron, Rick Derringer, Rick Dobbis, Dennis Drugan, Mark Epstein, Mark Erlewine, Dennis Ferrante, Jim Franklin, Josh Alan Friedman, Jeff Ganz, Steve Hecht, Styve Homnick, Bruce Iglauer, John Jackson, Wayne June, Vito Liuzzi, Jimmy Jo Longoria, Terry Manning, Bob Margolin, Val Minett, James Montgomery, Paul Nelson, Paul Oscher, Steve Paul, Jerry Portnoy, Floyd Radford, Pat Rush, Tommy Shannon, Dick Shurman, Teddy Slatus (who trusted me enough to start the ball rolling), Scott Spray, Bobby T. (Torello), Uncle John Turner, Mike Vernon, Richard Vernon, Edgar Winter, Edwina Winter, and John Wooler.

To the writers, researchers, and photographers who generously shared their work: Steve Banks, Thomas Brown, Charles Fitzsimmons, Bob Gruen, Tom Guerra, Charles Harbutt, Dennis Hickey, Nels Jacobson, John Nova Lomax, Sean McDevitt, Dan Muise, Paul Natkin, Jim Sherman, Lois Siegel, Jim Summaria, Burton Wilson, and Susan Winter. Special thanks to Jim Geuther from Switzerland, who developed and maintains "The Johnny Winter

Story," the ultimate fan website with 20,000 pages and several thousand photographs.

For his vision, passion, and dedication to the integrity of the project: Mike Edison, my editor at Backbeat.

For literary inspiration, advice, and expertise: Scott Bradfield, Scott Dirks, Robert Gordon, Tom Guerra, John Gustavson, Mark Hoffman, Jordan Pecile, Tom Smith, and Patrick Sullivan.

For transcribing and proofreading: Jessie Bradley, Chris Dimock, Wendy Merchant, Kelly Racine, Lisa Rau, and special thanks to Bev Canfield, who spent endless hours transcribing dozens of interviews.

For legal assistance and friendship above and beyond the call of duty: Vinny Cervoni. To the old friends and new friends who helped me on my journey: Dom Forcella, Andy (Drew Blood) Grzybowski, Steve Knauf, Tim Lee, Ron MacDonald, Neal Olderman, Jack Ortman, Steven Pearl, T. Bone Piazza, Walter Potter, Jim Quist, Les Strong, Josh Sullivan, Kerry Tilton, and members of the Johnny Winter Guitar Slinger Group.

To those warm and wonderful Texans who made me feel at home: Kumi Smedley, Morgan Turner, Jeanne Whittington, Leaa Mechling, Leland Parks, and Alan Haynes, whose amazing guitar virtuosity always makes a trip to Austin memorable.

And finally, a very special thanks to Johnny Georgiades, who offered moral support and encouragement, and believed in me and this book every step of the way.

# Introduction

## Madison Square Garden, June 1973

The smell of marijuana permeated Madison Square Garden. The 19,000-seat arena was sold out—filled with fans eagerly awaiting Johnny Winter's comeback concert after a nine-month hiatus in River Oaks Hospital in New Orleans. Chants of "John-ny, John-ny, John-ny" filled the smoky auditorium. The surreal glow of thousands of matches raised the level of excitement in the charged atmosphere. The house lights dimmed and the crowd jumped to its feet, wildly applauding the return of their guitar hero, who strutted onstage wearing a black velvet cape and brandishing a white Firebird guitar. Unlike his lover Janis Joplin and his friend Jimi Hendrix, Johnny Winter had triumphed over the excesses of a drug-filled lifestyle and lived to tell the tale.

A silver blizzard of tiny metallic photos floated from the rafters as Johnny tore into a blazing version of "Rock Me Baby," a fiery fusion of the rock that made him famous and the blues he loved. His long agile fingers raced across his guitar strings, cranking out the scorching guitar riffs that had become synonymous with his name. "Rock 'n' roll!" he yelled in a guttural voice, a combination rasp and holler emanating from his very soul, working the crowd into a fever pitch.

He teased the audience with an earthy pelvic thrust as he flung his cape aside to reveal an outfit as outrageous as his antics. New

York fashion designer Bill Witten had created his costume—a white spandex jumpsuit with silver-studded bellbottoms and suspenders, a studded collar, and an amethyst medallion reflecting the spotlight shining on his bare chest. The overhead spots created a halo on the translucent white hair flowing over his shoulders and bounced off the studded armbands adorned with silver streamers that draped down toward the floor.

Johnny's band—bassist Randy Jo Hobbs and drummer Richard Hughes—were joined by Jimmy Gillan, a second drummer, whose hard-pounding rhythm added to the intensity of the powerful trio. Susan Warford, a pretty blonde in a blue jumpsuit slit to her navel, pounded on a tambourine and danced to the music with wild abandon.

Wielding his power on a changing array of Firebird guitars, he whipped the audience into a frenzy, playing behind his back, over his head, and perched on his knees at the edge of the stage. He was a combination of Texas bluesman—who captivated the audience with his masterful slide, scorching guitar, and gritty vocals—and the quintessential rock star, who pounced across the stage in a wild celebration of raw sexuality and unbridled rock 'n' roll.

He took the audience on a musical journey to the Mississippi Delta and his Texas roots with "Black Cat Bone." Without missing a beat, he jumped back into rock with an elongated version of "Rock & Roll," an original that fused a driving rock tempo with blistering Texas slide guitar. His hands slithered around the frets during the blazing solo on his version of "Jumpin' Jack Flash," which appeared on *Johnny Winter And Live*, his first gold album. The Stones shared a mutual respect with Johnny, and had played one of his songs, "I'm Yours and I'm Hers," for an audience of 250,000 at their Hyde Park concert in London on July 5, 1969. Mick Jagger and Keith Richards, who leased rehearsal space next to his at S.I.R. (Studio Instrumental Rentals) in New York, had sent him two more songs for his latest album.

Columbia had released *Still Alive and Well*, his fifth album on that label, in March. The title track was his battle cry; the lyrics reflected the direction his life had taken in the past few years:

*"Did you ever take a look and see who's left around?*
*Everyone I thought was cool is six feet underground.*
*They tried to get me lots of times and now they're comin' after you.*
*I got out and I'm here to say, 'Baby, you can get out too.'*
*I'm still alive and well,*
*I'm still alive and well,*
*Every now and then I know it's kinda hard to tell,*
*But I'm still alive and well."*

The aura of death and destruction from drugs, alcohol, and the rock lifestyle wasn't about to leave him alone—within years, Hobbs would die of a cocaine overdose and Hughes would hook a hose to his car's exhaust pipe and commit suicide. But tonight Johnny was ecstatic and drug-free, playing the music he loved to thousands of adoring fans who hadn't deserted him.

After two heady encores, coaxed by the deafening sound of thousands of fans clapping their hands and stomping their feet, the lanky albino headed for the sleek stretch limo waiting outside. His manager Steve Paul and the Garden's bouncers pushed a path through the crowd hovering by the exit and surrounding the limousine. Still reeling from the adulation of a standing ovation, Johnny settled in the white leather seat with Susan, a glass of Jack Daniels in his hand, and a Kool dangling from his lips. The crush of the mob began rocking the limo, signaling to the chauffeur it was time to depart. He gunned the engine as a warning and drove off into the night.

It had been an incredible performance and Johnny was back in the game. He had come a long way from Beaumont, Texas, and the journey had only begun.

# PART I

# Albino in a Redneck Town

*"Beaumont is a workingman's town where everything smells bad—it's right in the middle of all these chemical plants, a great place to grow up. The population is about 100,000 to 125,000 people. Most of them work in the refinery. You can tell which way the wind blows by which kind of smell you're getting. That direction over there's a paper plant, over there's a sulfur plant, and there's the oil refinery. It's glorious."*

— JOHNNY WINTER

Beaumont was built on a fifty-acre tract of land on the Neches River bluff in southeast Texas in 1835. The earliest industries were lumber, rice, and ranching. On January 10, 1901, a gusher on Spindletop Hill turned it into the world's first oil boomtown. The Lucas Gusher was quickly joined by five more, and Spindletop's production of oil outstripped the total yield of the rest of the world.

When Johnny was born in 1944, Jim Crow laws were still in effect across the South; Beaumont's schools, buses, restaurants, restrooms, and water fountains were segregated. Blacks had their own stores, nightclubs, schools, neighborhoods, and social lives in another side of town. In fact, blacks were turned away from the 1944 Georgia Democratic primary polling booths and not allowed to vote. Drafted into the service during World War II, they were considered unfit for combat and segregated into all-black units.

By the time Johnny graduated from high school, the "Golden Triangle" region of Beaumont, Port Arthur, and Orange was the petrochemical complex of southeastern Texas. Beaumont's economy was dominated by the chemical, petroleum, shipbuilding, and oil-drilling industries. But Johnny knew long before high school that his destiny would take him far beyond the refineries of Beaumont, Texas.

Johnny's parents, Edwina Holland Winter, a native of Orange, Texas, and John Dawson Winter Jr., a Leland, Mississippi native, met on a blind date arranged by a mutual friend.

"John was in the Army National Guard," said Edwina Winter. "We hit it off pretty well. I was twenty-five and he was thirty-three when we got married about a year later on February 5, 1943. The National Guard was activated early in World War II but John did not go overseas until late 1943."

Edwina describes herself and her husband as "Americans" but Johnny delves deeper into the family genealogy. "Winter is English, German, and Scottish," he explains. "My father's family was from Mississippi as far as I can go back. Daddy was a cotton broker in Leland and my grandfather was too. He bought the cotton from the farmers and sold it to the cotton merchants in Manchester, England. It was my grandfather's company. Daddy wasn't very old when he started doing brokering. He did it for a while, then went to college at Virginia Military Institute and went into the army."

The Winters lived at Fort Sill in Oklahoma before John Jr. was sent overseas.

"John went from Oran in South Africa to Italy and then to Manila in the Philippines before he ever got home," Edwina said. "He was a colonel in the field artillery until he went overseas; then he was a quartermaster of black troops. John was not prejudiced because all his officers were black and he always had a very good relationship with them. Of course, John grew up in Mississippi, where most of the coloreds chopped the cotton. In fact, you didn't have help at certain times of the year because all the help went to chop the cotton. It was a different kind of life from anything you have now. Southern white people and black people have, as a rule, always had a very special relationship. There were bad white men who didn't treat their servants well, but the majority had very good relationships because they were in your home all the time."

Born John Dawson Winter III in Beaumont on February 23, 1944, Johnny was twenty-one inches and weighed a little over seven pounds. "Daddy was in the military when I was born, so my mother had to live with her parents in Beaumont," remembers Johnny. "It was just Momma, my grandfather Edgar Holland, my great-grandfather Ole Pa, and my great-grandmother. We lived in Ole Pa's house. My grandfather and Ole Pa were both lawyers."

When John Jr. was discharged from the service, he moved his family to Leland, Mississippi and worked as a cotton broker. The Winters lived in Leland about a year before buying a house and settling in Beaumont. For many years Johnny thought he was born in Leland; he wrote and recorded "Leland Mississippi Blues" on *Johnny Winter*, his 1968 debut album on Columbia Records. But he only lived in Leland for a brief period of time.

"We moved back to Beaumont when I was about four," says Johnny. "Daddy worked at an appliance store, and then he worked with a contractor, learned what the guy knew, and went out on his own. Most of the time I knew him he was a contractor who built houses—he had three or four people workin' for him.

"Daddy wasn't prejudiced. He told me he had a black guy working for him who got the clap and he talked to him about it. He'd had the clap a couple of times. Daddy asked him why he kept gettin' the clap and he said, 'Colonel Winter, I can stop doing a lot of things but young girls and women is one thing I can't stop, so I'll just keep gettin' the clap.'"

•◆•

Edwina sent her husband photographs of Johnny when he was overseas, but the elder Winter didn't know his son was an albino. "Johnny was born after John Jr. was sent overseas, so John didn't see Johnny till he was over two years old," she said. "I can't imagine what he thought."

"Daddy didn't know I was albino till he came home from the service," says Johnny. "He still didn't know what I was. He could tell I wasn't completely normal but he didn't know what it was or why I looked different. I don't think he had a problem with it—what could he do?"

The doctors told the Winters the chance of having another albino child was one in a million. So Edwina became pregnant again shortly after her husband returned to the States. Edgar was born on December 28, 1946.

"I was almost three when Edgar was born," says Johnny. "I remember eating downstairs and Momma being upstairs in bed and wanting her to come down. I was jealous, but I didn't try to hit him or anything, not yet—that was later on. When they discovered he was an albino too, they didn't know what to do about it."

Johnny's parents, like parents of most children born with albinism, had normal hair, skin, and eye color. There was no history of albinism in either family, but they both carried the recessive gene that gave them a one in four chance each child would be born with the condition.

Johnny has oculocutaneous albinism and little or no pigment in his eyes, hair, and skin. He was born legally blind, with blue eyes, white hair, and milky white skin. The vision problems associated with albinism are due to the lack of pigment in the retina, and an abnormal pattern of nerve connections between the eye and the brain. Doctors in Texas in the mid-'40s knew little about albinism, and neither did the general public. NOAH, the National Organization for Albinos and Hypopigmentation, an information and support organization, wouldn't be founded for almost forty years.

"None of the doctors even knew what the word albino meant," says Johnny. "They just knew we had some problems. They told my parents there wasn't anything that could be done about it. My mother had looked it up in our medical reference books, so she knew more about it than the doctors did."

"With albinism, the optic nerve does not develop properly," explained Edwina. "When your optic nerve is not developed, your sight is short circuited. In addition to the lack of ability to see, it results in a lateral astigmatism and they have trouble focusing. It wasn't a condition that there was any hope of improvement. In truth, Johnny and Edgar have done remarkably well. They both took art lessons and could go through a magazine and tell you every car in it. Whatever they saw wasn't what you and I were seeing, but they interpreted it so they knew what it was. We always hoped there would be glasses or something developed to give them more normal eyesight. But the glasses that have been developed have been so cumbersome."

Born with 20/400 eyesight in one eye and 20/600 in the other, Johnny has vivid memories of how his limited eyesight affected his years at Longfellow Elementary School. It was an all-encompassing handicap affecting his ability to complete assignments, take tests during class, fit in, and make friends.

"I couldn't even see the E on the eye chart unless I got right up on it," he says. "I tried eyeglasses but I hated them, so I didn't wear 'em.' I'd always lose them because they gave me headaches and they didn't help that much. I had to hold something close to read it. At school, I couldn't see the blackboard. I'd tell the teachers, but they didn't want to hear it. They'd just tell me to get up real close and copy it. When you had tests, teachers would usually write the questions on the board. Some teachers would give me the questions written out for me and some of 'em would let me get up in front of the whole class and read it. I got in everybody else's way; they'd be screamin' at me to sit down and I couldn't sit down. It was a big mess. I was a mediocre student because I couldn't see the blackboard."

Johnny attended Dick Dowling Junior High School, but transferred to Ballard Stevenson School in the eighth grade to take special-education classes.

"They used a special big-print book and they didn't do any board work at all," Johnny explains. "They were teaching a wide variety of ages and it wasn't just for people who couldn't see. They had a lot of different things: some spastics, some people that were slow. It was real weird; they put everybody in one room. Mostly it was people who had problems gettin' the work in regular school. I made great grades in that school but didn't like it. You'd go to dances and people would say, 'What school do you go to?' and I'd tell them the name of the school and they'd say, 'I never heard of that school.' I wouldn't volunteer any more information than that."

When Edwina took Johnny and Edgar to Belk Burns, a psychologist in Beaumont, to test their learning ability, she was relieved to learn albinism didn't affect intelligence. They took standard IQ tests, and both registered in the genius range.

"They never told me my IQ," says Johnny. "They said me and Edgar had the intelligence of the top ten percent. I can believe Edgar had it but I can't believe I was smart. I never felt very smart; I never made great grades in the regular schools."

Children are known for being cruel to anybody that is different and the children in Texas were no exception. Besides struggling with his vision and schoolwork, Johnny had to deal with the taunts of schoolmates and children in his neighborhood.

"Kids teased me in school for being albino," he says. "They called me 'Cotton' and 'Whitey.' There was a little kid in our neighborhood that ran around saying, 'You're an albino. You're an albino.' I said, 'No, I'm not.' I had never heard that word before. When I went and asked my parents about it, they said, 'Yes, you are an albino.' That they knew there was a word for our problem, for what we were. They used the word albino to describe me. It was really bad to find out about it in that way—to hear it from a neighborhood kid bothering me about it. I got in a lot of fights with kids for callin' me an albino. People bothered Edgar too. My parents tried to stay out of the way and let me be responsible for myself but they were always real supportive.

"It was kind of a drag that I couldn't fit in. I didn't really care about fitting in so much, but I didn't like not being liked. I guess I just wanted to be left alone and not bothered. I didn't have any idea why people had a hard time accepting anybody different from them—it's crazy, but it's a fact.

"They were pretty good at church; they didn't bother me as much. Having a brother who was also albino helped. I had somebody else who could understand what it was like to go through that. My parents would tell me I just had to put up with it. That I was okay being different and not to worry about it so much—that kids were just that way.

"I had some friends at school but not a whole lot. They didn't treat me well, so I didn't bother with them. People didn't know anything about it [albinism]. Sometimes people on the street treated you differently too. It never affected the way I felt about myself but it sure affected the way I felt about other people."

Johnny had a loving relationship with both parents, who were supportive and compassionate and provided their children with all the benefits of growing up in an upper-middle-class family—art classes, dance lessons, diction lessons, swimming lessons, summer camp, music lessons, as well as a playhouse in their backyard. Although Johnny's father didn't quite understand what it was like growing up as an albino in a redneck town, music forged the link that kept them close together.

"I had a pretty good relationship with my father growing up," says Johnny. "I always felt like he didn't know exactly what our problems were like, what it was like to be one of us. Sometimes he had a little problem with knowing how to relate to being an albino. I talked about it too, but it was hard to explain to somebody what it's like not to be able to see. Music definitely played a part in keeping me and Daddy close. We did a lot of musical things together.

"Daddy played saxophone, banjo, and ukulele, and had his own band in college. He stopped playing when he got out of school but still sang in barbershop quartets. The barbershop quartet practiced at our house, singing songs like 'Ain't She Sweet' and 'Bye Bye Blackbird.' Daddy sang hymns in the Episcopalian church choir too; he sang in the choir until he died. I don't think me and Edgar would have become musicians if it hadn't been for Daddy. He helped us but he didn't push us. I don't think he wanted us to be musicians; he wanted us to be doctors or lawyers—something like that. I really loved music from a very early age; there was never a point that I didn't want to be a musician. When I told them [my parents], they said they'd do anything they could to help out. They didn't think it was a great idea but they weren't gonna try to push us away from it either."

Like many first born sons, Johnny shared a special bond with his mother, who offered understanding, encouragement, and unconditional love. "I had a real good relationship with Momma," he said. "I was a lot closer to my mother than I was to my father. If I got into trouble at school—mostly doing things kids do, like flushing firecrackers down the toilet—I'd go to my mother because I could talk to her easier."

A ritual that strengthened the bond between Johnny and his mother was the time she spent reading to both sons before they went to bed. Not school textbooks, but books that touched their imaginations and expanded their horizons far beyond the city of Beaumont. She selected books that required a higher comprehension than typical children's books because she knew both boys had an understanding well above their grade level.

"Momma read to us all the time," Johnny says. "She read the *Hobbit* books—*Lord of the Rings. The Wizard of Oz* and the whole series of books about Oz. She usually read to us when we were goin' to sleep. She'd sit on the bed and read to me and Edgar."

Johnny also listened to "Talking Books," which his mother ordered from the Library for the Blind. "We got books on records," says Johnny. "Fairy tales, Disney stories. We got them until I was fifteen or sixteen. They came regularly in a pack. My mother told them what categories we liked, and they'd send us books—records—from that category. We had all kinds of different books. Me and Edgar listened to them when we were goin' to sleep."

Religion was an integral part of the Winter household. Edwina read the Bible to Johnny and Edgar every afternoon when they got home from school, and the family attended church services every Sunday. Beaumont was predominantly Baptist, and Edwina attended services at the Calder Baptist Church. John Jr. was Episcopalian and attended services at St. Mark's Episcopal Church. Johnny attended both churches when he was young, but when he was older, he was allowed to choose the church he wanted to attend. Johnny chose St. Mark's Episcopal Church, where his father, a high tenor, sang in the church choir. Johnny also joined the choir at St. Mark's, but his time in that ensemble was short-lived.

"Everybody else was so bad it pissed me off," he says. "Nobody else could sing. I sang real loud and they called me out for singing too loud. I said, 'Nobody else is singing loud enough so you can hear it.' That pissed me off, and I finally quit."

Despite his hostility toward the choir, Johnny still attended church every Sunday until he was nineteen years old. "I think it helped us, that we got something out of it," he says. "I believe in God. I've always believed there's something out there, something bigger than just people."

•◆•

Johnny grew up with a small extended family. George Holland Jr., his mother's brother, never married, and his father's two sisters, Roberta Winter and Mary Castleman, lived out of state, as did his fraternal grandmother, also named Roberta Winter. His childhood influences came from his mother's side of the family, particularly his great-grandfather George Holland Sr., who doted on him from the minute he was born.

"My grandfather was just wild about Johnny," remembered Edwina. "He loved him dearly. He always carried him around and talked to him."

"Ole Pa was in his nineties," says Johnny. "He didn't have a musical background but he tried to help me get into music. When my rabbit died, he bought me a ukulele to make me feel better. He bought me my first guitar, and started giving me money to learn particular songs. He really was a big force in me learning to play different kinds of music. I named my corporation after him—Ole Pa Enterprises. He was my businessman hero."

His grandfather Edgar Holland, who he called "Bompa," played bluegrass music on the violin. He played "Turkey in the Straw" and other bluegrass classics for Johnny and Edgar when they visited.

Although he never met John Dawson Winter Sr., his namesake and grandfather on his father's side, he has fond memories of his fraternal grandmother. "Daddy's mother was sweet, and real prim and proper," Johnny says. "She was born in Berryville, Virginia. We went down there for vacation—it was a long way from Beaumont—

a three-day drive. We saw her in the summer and I got to know her pretty well. She was a sweet old woman."

John Jr.'s older sister, Roberta Winter, was a drama instructor at Agnes Scott College in Decatur, Georgia. The college named a theater after her, but Johnny wasn't a fan.

"She was an old school marm—I think she was an old dyke really," says Johnny. "She didn't have any kids. I remember not likin' her at all; she tried to control us and that really made me mad. She threw a glass of water on me when I was just a little kid. I told her God didn't let her have kids because she didn't have sense enough to have any—to treat them like that. Instead of pickin' the glass up, I was slidin' it across the table. She threw it at me and she didn't have any business doin' that. It was in my parents' house, but they stayed out of it. That made me mad at them too. They should have said something to her."

Johnny had another aunt and three cousins in Kingsport, Tennessee. He didn't see them often, but when he spent time with them during a family vacation, his older cousin Tommy made a lasting impression.

"Daddy's younger sister, Mary Castleman, was real sweet," he says. "Aunt Mary had three children. I saw them for a month one summer when Aunt Roberta rented a beach house in Florida. There was one kid named Tommy who played the trombone. He was about twelve when he played it for us. I couldn't believe it. I loved it."

With the magic of Tommy's trombone still vivid in his memory, Johnny was captivated by *Pete Kelly's Blues*, a film he saw with his parents while vacationing in San Antonio. Released in 1955, *Pete Kelly's Blues* was a musical action drama about jazz musicians who have violent run-ins with mobsters while playing a speakeasy during prohibition. Set in Kansas City in 1927, the film starred Jack Webb as a cornet player in a struggling jazz band, and featured musical performances by Ella Fitzgerald and Peggy Lee. That film proved to be a turning point in Johnny's life.

"I remember that movie making me want to be a musician," Johnny says. "It was real bluesy music with songs I could relate to, a lot of the songs I had grown up singing. I didn't like Pete Kelly's part so much; the shootin' part of the movie didn't appeal to me. It was the music that got me. I didn't feel like I had a way to express myself, but after seein' that movie, I knew I could do it through my music."

Johnny's belief in himself and in his ability to do whatever he wanted to do was stronger than any liability fate had sent his way. Fearless as a child (a trait he never lost), Johnny never let his limited eyesight deter him from using a bicycle to explore his neighborhood, ride to school, and visit his grandparents, who lived about a ten-minute car trip from his home.

Johnny always had red bikes, but his favorite was "a real fancy red bike with chrome fenders." That bike could have cost him his life; instead it opened his eyes to an adult world of wives, girlfriends, and payoffs.

"My bike was in my friend's front yard and a guy who was drunk ran over it," he recalls. "The guy went up the front lawn, right over my bicycle, and up the front steps of the house. We went to the movies; if we'd been playin' in the yard, we would have been run over. That's why he paid me a good bit of money for wrecking my bike. The guy had a girlfriend in the car with him and it wasn't his wife. So he was willing to pay anything because he didn't want to get in trouble."

Johnny grew up in a big house on 275 West Caldwood Drive with a spacious yard, a double swing on the porch, and swings in the backyard. He remembers climbing high up a mulberry tree to play in a tree house his father built. During their early years, he and Edgar shared a small bedroom, where they slept in yellow bunk beds.

"I picked it so I was on the top bunk," says Johnny. "Edgar and I got along real fine. We're different and we had that in common. As kids, we played mostly music and cowboys. I was the good guy. At the movies, we'd see cowboy and Indian movies. Roy Rogers was my favorite. We played cowboys, space people, and pirates. Anything we wanted to be, we'd dress up like it. We'd put on cowboy hats one day, pirate outfits another day, and spacemen outfits another day."

Because of Johnny's fascination with space travel, his grandfather built him a spaceship. Constructed of plywood and shaped like a pyramid, the spaceship had portholes in the sides and radio equipment Johnny and Edgar used as a control board.

Their father bought a small standalone store that had gone out of business and moved it into the backyard as a playhouse. When Johnny was about ten or twelve, he formed a club called the Texas Golden Eagles; the playhouse became their clubhouse. As leader and president of the club, he made up "weird initiations" for new members and banned girls from joining.

As the oldest and more dominant brother, Johnny ruled the roost. He picked the games they would play and made the rules. He always won at Monopoly and other board games; chess was the only game where Edgar could beat his older brother.

Due to the lack of pigmentation characteristic of being albino, Johnny was told to cover up and stay out of the sun. But he never heeded that advice.

"There were a lot of beaches in Beaumont," he says. "Although I wasn't supposed to, I played outside in the sun anyway and went to the beach all the time. I'd get real red, real burned. I didn't blister though—just burned. We fished a little bit too. Me and Daddy fished off the pier in the Gulf of Mexico."

Another pastime Johnny shared with his father was learning how to shoot a gun, a rite of passage in Texas. Johnny remembers his grandfather and great-grandfather always keeping a gun handy, both in the house and in the glove compartment of their cars.

"Learning how to shoot a gun was the normal thing to do—people carry guns there a lot," says Johnny. "I was twelve when Daddy taught me how to shoot. I always had guns—shotguns and pistols too. We had a farm where we'd shoot beer cans in the water. We had a manmade lake and we'd throw them in and shoot at them." It would be another seven years before Johnny realized how dangerous carrying a gun could be.

During the summers of 1955 and 1956, Johnny spent five weeks each summer at Camp Rio Vista in Texas Hill Country near the Guadalupe River.

"It was a long time to be away from home," he says. "The first year I went by myself; I got homesick but ended up having a pretty good time. The second year Edgar went to the same camp with me, but was in a different age group. We played, went swimming, rode horses; they had all different games you could play."

Johnny's close friends, family, band members, and crew are well aware of his proclivity to go *au naturel*, but his tendency to sleep in the nude didn't go over well with the counselors at Camp Rio Vista.

"I don't usually wear a lot of clothes around the house," he explains. "When I was in school, in my mother's house in the winter, I'd do my homework without my clothes on. I'd keep the heater on in the bathroom to keep the room warm. When I was goin' to summer camp, they made me run around the whole track naked because I did the Pledge of Allegiance without any clothes on. I was late wakin' up and just ran out. They said their way of curing me was to make me run around the track. But that was fine with me. I'm more comfortable that way—I just don't like to wear clothes."

Johnny loved to swim. He had taken private lessons and lessons at the YMCA, so he enrolled in advanced swimming classes at summer camp.

"I started takin' lessons when I was a kid; I was seven or eight years old. I'm a pretty good swimmer—I used to swim for hours."

Summer camp gave Johnny the recognition and acceptance he craved. During his second year, he won two awards; one for musical talent and the other for popularity. The latter award touched his heart.

"I won one for singing two Homer and Jethro tunes. They were a country and western comedy team. I did 'Two Tone Shoes,' makin' fun of 'Blue Suede Shoes' and 'Heartbreak Motel' instead of 'Heartbreak Hotel.' I also won the Golden Arrows Award for getting along with everybody else, and being one of the most liked people. It was great because I wasn't liked in school at all.

"I was one of the most popular people at summer camp, but back in school I was a total reject. I couldn't play football or baseball. There wasn't anything I could do to be one of the gang. But in summer camp, I *was* one of the gang. I was liked a lot 'cause I could do things. They had archery, high jumps, broad jumps, the one-hundred-yard dash, boxing, canoeing, bowling—things I could do as well as anybody. I enjoyed summer camp a whole lot."

Although Johnny's limited eyesight affected his ability to play sports at school and made him feel like an outcast, he didn't let that discourage him.

"I made up my mind at a real early age, that things were gonna be real hard for me and I was gonna have to fight for anything I wanted to get," Johnny says. "Edgar was always more willing to sit back and observe what was goin' on. I wanted to jump right in the middle and feel what was goin' on."

Johnny broadened his social outlets by joining the Cub Scouts and the Boys Scouts, where he earned badges, went on camping trips, and achieved the rank of second-class scout.

"I never did get to be Eagle Scout," he says with a laugh. "You had to learn Morse code, and I just couldn't learn Morse code to save my life. That was the one thing that kept me from getting to be a first-class scout. What I remember most about the camping trips is being cold. Freezing my butt off. It was cold in the middle of March in Texas. We had campfires at every campsite and they put me in charge of keeping all the fires goin' for about two hours at a time. I could not keep all the fires going at once and I got whipped for that. I didn't think I did too badly, but I got whipped anyway. They hit ya in the butt."

When the South Texas State Fair came to Beaumont every October, Johnny and his friends breezed through the livestock and poultry exhibits and spent the day and their allowances on the carnival midway, eating candy apples and cotton candy, and going on all the rides. But even then, he was smart enough not to waste his money on carnival games that were rigged. His albinism had taught him the ways of the world at an early age, but it also gave him compassion for other people who didn't quite fit into society.

"I used to go to the freak shows with my friends," he says. "You'd go in a tent and they'd have gorilla man—a guy who had hair all over his body—tattooed men and women too, bearded lady, midgets. I felt sorry for them because I could relate to the people who were in there. I could do more where I wouldn't end up in a sideshow, but I definitely felt sorry for the people who had to go through that."

•◆•

Johnny's early memories include listening to a wooden console radio with his family in the evening. He loved "scary radio shows," especially *Inner Sanctum Mysteries* and *The Shadow*. Those shows made such an impression on him, he still occasionally listens to vinyl recordings of *Inner Sanctum Mysteries*, *The Shadow*, and *Lights Out*, a mid-1930s radio show billed as the "ultimate in horror."

Television was still in its infancy in the late 1940s, a luxury only the wealthy could afford. Johnny's grandparents bought an RCA Victor set before the Winters had a TV, so Johnny and his family watched the early television shows at their house. Johnny woke up early on Saturday mornings to go to his grandparents' house and watch children's shows. He didn't like cartoons, but never missed *Space Patrol*, a half-hour space show that debuted in 1950. He loved the adventures of the show's hero and still imitates the announcer's voice when he says, "Buzz Corry—commander in chief of the Space Patrol."

When Johnny's family finally bought a Philco television, he watched *The Howdy Doody Show*, *Roy Rogers*, and a local children's show called *Uncle Willie's*. Johnny appeared on *Uncle Willie's*, which began as a radio show and moved to TV.

"I was on *Uncle Willie's* on radio and TV," says Johnny. "I was just a little kid when I first went on. Uncle Willie read books and played little kids' records. The kids sat on a bench and we'd say our names. I'd say, 'I'm Johnny Winter and I want to say hello to my mother and my daddy and my grandparents.'"

Johnny's grandparents never missed *The Ed Sullivan Show*, so his family watched it with them on Sunday nights. Johnny wasn't impressed with the smorgasbord of jugglers, acrobats, animal acts, singers, comedians, puppeteers, ventriloquists, and plate spinners, but enjoyed Elvis Presley's debut appearance on September 9, 1956.

Elvis Presley was the *white* man with the black sound and feel that Sun Records owner Sam Phillips had been searching for, so it isn't surprising that four of Presley's five Sun Record singles were remakes of songs written and/or recorded by black blues artists. It was the blues feel of Elvis's records that appealed to Johnny.

Johnny was developing his taste for the blues, but had only heard homogenized versions deemed suitable for white audiences. Ironically, it was the upper-middle-class status of his parents and grandparents that introduced him to the real deal. Both families had black servants working in their homes, which would prove to be fortuitous in several ways. It made Johnny "colorblind" when it came to people and kept him from embracing the prejudice that was a way of life in Beaumont. It also exposed him to the music that would turn his life around.

"Servants were treated well, but nobody treated them normally—you wouldn't treat them like a friend," Johnny says. "You'd be nice to them and that was it. Sadie was my mother's maid. We called her Sainty—she was real sweet. She lived in the black side of town and came in twice a week. She ironed clothes, cleaned the house, did laundry. I treated Sadie like a real friend. I still have a picture of her daughter in high school. I stayed friendly with Sadie."

Johnny also befriended his great-grandfather's servants, who introduced him to raw earthy sounds of blues by black artists.

"Ole Pa had a guy named Ameal Martin who was Creole, a black Frenchman from Louisiana." Johnny says. "We called him Meal. He cleaned the yard, cut the grass, did chores around the house. Lilly, a black woman in her forties, was the maid. Lilly had the radio on all the time. She listened to KJET in the kitchen—the only black station in Beaumont. I was about ten or eleven and that was the first time I heard blues. It was real raw—completely different from the music my parents and grandparents listened to. I started listenin' to blues on KJET because I liked what I heard in the kitchen."

# Musical from Birth

Growing up in a family of musicians had a strong influence on both Johnny and Edgar.

"The boys were both musical from the time they were born," said Edwina. "Part of it was because they were legally blind and their acute hearing made up in part for their lack of sight. Music was always a part of their lives. When they were little, I would play with them and for them, and their Daddy would, too. When they were little tiny fellas, they could harmonize. They had a natural ear for music."

"I always wanted to be a musician from the time I was old enough to start singing, when I was three or four years old," says Johnny. "I liked performing—everybody got off on me and I liked to do it. Edgar and me learned to sing as soon as we could talk because Daddy was always involved in music. When I was just a little kid—maybe five or six, Momma would play piano in our living room and we started singing three-part harmonies with Daddy. Our first songs were 'Bye, Bye Blackbird,' 'Ain't She Sweet,' and 'Shine on Harvest Moon'—songs Daddy sang in the barbershop quartet. It was really nice."

Johnny's first instrument was ukulele. "I liked ukulele because it was something I could play and back my singing up," he says. Never too shy to perform in public, Johnny and Edgar began playing on a local TV program airing in Beaumont and Houston.

"We were on *Don Mahoney and the Kiddie Troopers* a lot for a long time," says Johnny. "Me and Edgar played ukuleles and sang harmony parts on Everly Brothers songs."

Playing in contests and talent shows came natural to the boys, who won awards, including cash prizes, in most of the competitions. Johnny and Edgar won their first talent contest playing ukuleles and singing harmony on UHF Channel 31 in Beaumont in 1953.

"We'd been on the show enough that we didn't have to audition," says Johnny. "Waitin' in the studio to go on was scary—it was hard waitin' to go on. There were other kids too and older acts. I was nine and Edgar was six. We won a seventy-dollar Bulova wristwatch and I traded Edgar my clarinet for his half of the watch. I got the watch because I was older. That was real bad. I was pretty awful to Edgar. He said he always looked up to me when we were little kids, but I didn't know it. I always gave him the hard way to go. He was my younger brother and always got the bad end of everything. Everything we did or played, he always came after me."

Winning the Beaumont talent contest made the boys eligible to audition for the nationally televised *Ted Mack and the Original Amateur Hour*, a talent contest broadcast from Radio City Music Hall. The family drove from Beaumont to New York City, a trip that took four days, traveling eight hours a day and staying in motels along the way.

"We went to Radio City Music Hall for the audition," says Johnny. "We had our ukuleles and were gonna sing in front of the judges. There was a large waiting room with all kinds of acts, mostly older acts. We didn't get called until probably eleven or twelve at night."

Johnny and Edgar played their hearts out despite the late hour and were sure they'd be chosen to perform on national television. It wasn't until they had returned to Texas that they learned they didn't make it.

"We didn't win the audition," says Johnny. "We always won too, so I couldn't believe it when we didn't win. It was the first time. It was a drag but there wasn't much you could do about it."

Rather than letting the boys wallow in defeat, Edwina encouraged them to learn another instrument. She signed them up for piano lessons with Hazel Bergman, a grand pianist who played in a swing band in Beaumont.

"I started piano as a kid because my mother wanted me to," says Johnny. "I took piano lessons two or three years—from about fourth to sixth grade. I didn't play very much piano—I learned enough to know it was something I didn't want to do. It didn't feel normal to me like guitar did. They tried to get me to learn how to read music but I didn't. Reading music didn't interest me because the music I wanted to learn—the popular stuff on the radio—wasn't available in sheet music and nobody knew how to play it anyway."

During the years Johnny was halfheartedly taking piano lessons, he was also learning to play the clarinet, an instrument with more appeal.

"I was in the fourth grade when I began playing clarinet," he says. "I played in the school band. I had a silver clarinet and learned by ear. I liked the way it sounded. I played it for a couple of years, but I had an overbite, and the orthodontist said playing the clarinet would make it worse. I had to stop playing when I was just startin' to get it down. When the orthodontist said I couldn't play anymore, I cried a long time about it. It was a real drag 'cause I loved playin' clarinet."

Determined to encourage his son's love of music and help him discover an instrument he enjoyed, John Jr. began teaching Johnny chords on the banjo and ukulele. Although he enjoyed playing songs from the '20s and '30s that were later popularized by Tiny Tim, embarking on a career as a ukulele player seemed like too much of a long shot.

"My daddy told me Arthur Godfrey and Ukulele Ike are the only ukulele players I ever heard of that made it, so maybe you ought to play guitar," says Johnny. "I was about eleven or twelve when I started playing guitar. My first guitar had belonged to my great-grandmother on my mother's side. It was an acoustic Spanish guitar in bad shape. The strings above the fret board were bad. It was too warped to really play. I just played around with it and learned a few chords on the bottom.

"I didn't play the acoustic guitar very long. Just long enough to know it was something I wanted to keep doing. All the rock songs on the radio had guitars in 'em so I talked my great-grandfather into buying me a real guitar—my first electric guitar in 1956. Ole Pa bought me an ES 125—a really nice guitar—at Jefferson Music in Beaumont. I loved it. I played it in my bedroom with a Fender Bassman, the best-soundin' amp around.

"I taught myself songs like 'Hound Dog,' whatever was on the radio at the time. A lot of songs Elvis did—I was a big Elvis fan. It was always pretty easy for me to hear it and then play it on the guitar. Music has always been easy for me."

Johnny took his first formal guitar lessons at age twelve from Luther Nallie, a country and western musician who worked at Jefferson Music Company. He took thirty-minute lessons once a week for a year and practiced six hours every day.

"Luther was twenty-two—about ten years older than me," says Johnny. "He was playin' around Beaumont when I was takin' lessons; later he played with the Sons of Pioneers with Roy Rogers. Mostly country and western songs—he didn't know any blues. I'd play a song for him and ask him how it was played. I learned a lot from him. He taught me how to finger pick, which was a style I wanted to learn how to play."

Nallie found Johnny to be a quick study and was impressed with his talent and enthusiasm. "Johnny had me scratching my head a lot of the time because he would soak up anything I taught him immediately, and I would have to think up something else real quick to show him," Nallie said in a 2001 interview in *Vintage Guitar.*

Johnny learned what he could from Nallie, then returned to Jefferson Music in late 1958 to take lessons from Seymour Drugan. A jazz guitarist, Drugan played with Paul Whiteman and other big bands in the 1930s and '40s before settling in Chicago in the early '40s to play on Don McNeill's *The Breakfast Club.*

"I learned a few jazz chords from him," says Johnny. "That didn't help much, but he did help me learn my chords. I quit after three months because I wasn't interested in jazz. I stopped taking lessons because there wasn't anybody that played what I wanted to play."

Although Johnny's lessons with Drugan were short-lived, it led to a friendship with Drugan's son Dennis, who said his father was amazed by Johnny's talent.

"My father told me, 'You won't believe the young fellow that came into the store. He's a really good guitar player and he learns very fast,'" said Dennis Drugan.

Johnny's talent led to a job at Jefferson Music Company teaching guitar on weekdays after school. "I was sixteen and seventeen when I gave guitar lessons," he says. "I had six or eight customers. We made two dollars a half an hour and I got one dollar a half an hour—half of what we made."

That job led to a meeting with Clarence Garlow, a Creole DJ who played blues and R&B on the *Bon Ton Roulette Show* at KJET.

"He was the main Texas guitar player who influenced me," says Johnny. "I was giving a lesson and he came in to buy strings. I could tell him by his voice. He had a really unique voice. I knew he was Clarence Garlow and I started playing one of his songs. He said, 'You know who I am, don't ya?' And I said, 'Yeah.' He was real nice to me after that."

Nocturnal by nature, Johnny still has what one of his sidemen called "a vampire schedule," staying up all night, going to bed at 6 or 7 AM, and sleeping late into the afternoon. His natural biorhythm as a night person began early in his childhood, and allowed him to indulge his love of the blues.

"I've always had that schedule," he says. "I slept late all the time. I never had a day job except for giving guitar lessons. I hated going to bed, even as a kid. I always stayed up late at night. Edgar was better than I was about going to bed. They'd tell us to go to bed—but I always got right back up. I'd get back up, come out of my room, go in my walk-in closet, and put my radio under my pillow. I'd put my ear up to the pillow, so I could hear it, but nobody else could.

"You had better reception at night, so you could get the stations from Nashville and Shreveport—great stations that played mostly blues. They had WLAC in Nashville. KWKH in Shreveport, Louisiana was another good station on late at night. They had Ernie's Record Shop, Buckley's Records, Stan's Record Shop—the record shops would sponsor the shows.

"Howlin' Wolf was one of the first blues artists I heard. I heard 'Somebody in My Home' on KWKH in Shreveport. It had a real bluesy feeling to it. I liked him—he appealed to me. His voice was real raw. I didn't ever see him perform but I heard he crawled up the curtains at a concert hall. There was another station, XERF, in Del Rio, Mexico. Their transmitter was in Mexico; the stations were in Texas. They played straight blues—Lightnin' Hopkins, Guitar Slim, Lazy Lester, Bobby Bland, Little Walter."

Growing up, Johnny listened to his parents' 78 rpm records—Artie Shaw, Benny Goodman, Tommy Dorsey, Glenn Miller, and Dinah Shore—on the family phonograph in the living room. When he started buying 45s in late 1955, Johnny had his own record player in his bedroom, a portable black RCA Victor designed like a small suitcase. His first singles were "Tutti Frutti" by Little Richard and "Sixteen Tons" by Tennessee Ernie Ford. "Sixteen Tons" was written by Merle Travis, another artist whose records he bought and influenced his style of playing.

"I bought some Merle Travis and Chet Atkins real early, before I bought blues," he says. "I first heard finger pickin' when I got a record by Merle Travis. He played country bluegrass. Merle Travis could play with his fingers and a thumb pick—I liked the sound of finger-style guitar. You could play by yourself; keep rhythm with your thumb, and play lead with your fingers. I started off using a plastic thumb pick and have never used any other picks. Chet Atkins played the same way. Luther Nallie played with a thumb pick too."

Johnny first started buying records through the mail from the record shops that sponsored the late night radio blues shows. Then he discovered the Gaylynn Record Store in Beaumont. He'd skip lunch at school and use his lunch money to buy 45s for "pretty close to a dollar, eighty-nine cents or something like that," he says. He also used the allowance money he earned for taking out the garbage and cutting the grass ("$1.25 for the front yard and $1.50 for the backyard").

The Gaylynn Record Store had a small blues section, so Johnny started shopping at the Harmony Shop. Although Beaumont was still segregated, the Harmony Shop catered to both a black and white clientele, and carried "race records," recordings by black artists on mostly white-owned labels marketed to black audiences. He had his choice of Kent, Duke, Excello, Federal, Checker, Chess, RPM, and Vee-Jay records.

"The lady there bought a lot of records for the black juke joints. Her husband put jukeboxes in black clubs so she had a good selection of blues artists. I bought literally every blues artist I could find, even if I didn't know who they were. The record stores had little record players where you could listen to 'em. I liked everything. I just really love them. It made my style broader because I literally bought everybody I could find so I didn't sound just like one person. I heard everybody."

Johnny's first blues single was Howlin' Wolf's "Somebody in My Home," released on Chess in 1957. His first Muddy Waters single was "She's Nineteen Years Old," featuring Little Walter Jacobs on harp, released on Chess Records in 1958. "Muddy's records probably are my favorites," he says. "I'd play the record, then listen to it, and learn how to do it. I would play it note for note when I first learned, but later I'd change it to my own style.

"I'd practice six or eight hours a day in my room after school. From the time I got home—with whatever my newest record was. I played so many different styles that they turned into my style. At first I'd try to learn how the artist played, and then I'd switch it around and play it my own way. I never did want to be like any particular artist—just learn from them. Listen and copy little parts of everybody's stuff."

Johnny's first album was B. B. King's *Singin' the Blues*, released in 1957; his second was *The Best of Muddy Waters*, released in 1958. That Muddy Waters's album was the first time Johnny heard a slide guitar; the sound perplexed and fascinated him at the same time.

"Muddy Waters was the first slide guitarist I ever heard," he says. "It was always really interesting and amazing to me when I heard it. I hadn't read anything about it and I didn't know what it was. I could tell the guy was fretting the guitar and sliding something. At first I thought it was the steel guitar until I realized he was a fretting it also. It was a mystery to me how you could do both. I was trying to figure out what was goin' on, and how it was being done. I had to listen, learn how he did it, and practice it. I had never seen anyone play a slide when I taught myself. I used the top of a lipstick holder for my first slide. Then I used my watch crystal. It sounded pretty good but it broke the watch. Then I had a test tube I bought at a drugstore. I cut it off and that worked pretty good. I was about fourteen when I started playing, but I didn't get real serious until I was about twenty-five.

"Robert Johnson knocked me out—he was a genius. As to him selling his soul to the devil; I don't know, it's hard to say about something like that. He sure was better than everybody else. Later on, I bought *Son House: Father of the Delta Blues*. Their styles were real different—it took me awhile to get used to 'em. They were more country sounding than the 45s I'd been buying. Most of 'em were just guitar and singer, recorded in hotel rooms. Both were big influences on my acoustic slide playing.

"Elmore James was also an influence on my slide playing. Elmore played the same licks on a lot of his songs. His one little lick that he played over and over again—I picked that up. Can't really describe it, but I liked him a lot. He was similar to Robert Johnson—his stuff sounds the same too a lot of times.

"Little Walter influenced my guitar playing too. I was good enough to be able to hear something and play it; I would play the same stuff on guitar that he played on harp. He was a great harp player. He played clear notes and did tongue blocking too. I liked everything Little Walter put out.

"Jimmy Reed was one of the guys I heard a lot around Texas. I bought a lot of his albums. He played guitar and harp and wrote a lot of songs. Nobody else sounded like Jimmy. He played a lot of high register notes on harp and he did songs I liked—'Baby, You Don't Have to Go,' 'A String to Your Heart,' 'Big Boss Man.' He was one of the first black blues artists who successfully crossed over to white audiences.

"It's important to listen to different styles of music when you're young—be exposed to them because you learn more. Listenin' to early blues artists—you can tell where it's all comin' from. You just want to know what came first and where it came from."

Although Johnny's early vocal influences came from his father's barbershop quartet and his harmonies with Edgar, he soon abandoned that musical style. He wanted to develop his own style and was impressed by the bluesy vocal renderings of Bobby "Blue" Bland and Ray Charles. When he was about ten or twelve, he created his own method of voice training to help him develop the scream that has become his trademark—especially on his battle cry of "rock 'n' roll!"

"Singing is something I really had to work at," he says. "I always had a good ear for music but my voice didn't have a lot of depth to it, especially the scream. The scream seemed like a better style to me—I was trying to get a sound like Bobby Bland and Ray Charles. I really had to practice that. I can remember when I was a kid putting a pillow over my mouth and putting my fingers in my ears so I could hear what was going on and nobody else could. I'd practice screaming into a pillow in my bedroom. I couldn't just start screamin' 'cause people would think we were getting killed or something. I really did practice a long time. At first it would sound like somebody hit me, just a yell. But a controlled scream, especially if you want to scream, get that riff, and use vibrato at the same time, took a lot of work. It didn't come natural."

Johnny's passion for blues wasn't shared by his friends or his brother. The sounds were too primitive for teenagers who grew up listening to country and western or Top Forty songs on the radio.

"When I first started playing blues, my friends didn't know what it was, and didn't like it," says Johnny. "They asked me what I would do with that kind of music—'Ain't nobody like it.' I said, 'It's good music.' My friends would just listen to whatever was on the radio, and Edgar's never been into blues that much. He just learned from me, from listening to my records."

Although Johnny is known as a Texas guitarist, he doesn't like to categorize himself, the music he plays, or the music he grew up listening to. The nuances are often subtle; and categories just can't capture or describe the music he loves.

"It's hard to say the difference between Mississippi Delta and Texas blues," says Johnny. "Delta blues is more slide. There wasn't much slide for Texas, but there was Blind Willie Johnson and he did church music. 'Dark Is the Night, Cold Is the Ground' is one of the best slide songs I've ever heard. He was an early Texas slide player, one of the first Texas bluesmen. His music had a whole lot less structure—he would play without any meter at all. He was totally different than anybody else. Definitely country blues.

"I don't consider myself 'Texas blues,' because I play a whole lot of different styles. Texas blues is influenced by country and western, jazz, and western swing. Generally, there are more instruments with Texas blues; but then again, there's Lightnin' Hopkins, and he plays mostly by himself. You can hear T-Bone Walker and Lightnin' Hopkins and there's no similarity between the two. There's so many guitar players from Texas and none of them sound the same. Albert Collins doesn't sound like anybody else; Gatemouth Brown didn't sound like anybody else either. He played a lot of styles: blues, jazz, zydeco. His styles were different from anybody else; his tuning was much different from other people too. In his early records he sounded just like T-Bone—note for note. That changed as he learned how to play his own stuff.

"T-Bone Walker played with a lot of horns. He's the father of the electric-blues style 'cause he's one of the first guys to play it. You could hear western swing and big bands of the '40s in some of his records. He had a lot of different records; he recorded prolifically. T-Bone was one of the best guitar players around. He knew more chords than most of the Mississippi players and it gave him a broader influence. Mississippi players only had to know but one or two chords.

"A lot of guys could play simple stuff that sounded great because it was very original. Like John Lee Hooker. You could always tell who John Lee Hooker was; he didn't sound like everybody else. Muddy's stuff was pretty similar. A musician doesn't have to be technically great to be a good blues artist. John Lee Hooker isn't a great guitar player but he's a great blues artist. It doesn't make much difference if a guy is technically good or not. You just gotta have feeling."

Feeling was the key element that attracted Johnny to the blues, a raw, earthy music that reflects the pain people endure as they experience the hardships life has tossed their way. A sensitive child, Johnny wasn't immune to the pain that came from being different, and found solace in music. Rather than dwelling on being ostracized by his classmates, he spent endless hours in his bedroom, pouring his energy into learning to play the blues. The old adage "you've got to live the blues to play the blues" is an apt description of his life.

"I've had enough blues in my life to where I don't think I need anymore," says Johnny. "Growin' up was the hardest part. Growin' up in school, I really got the bad end of the deal. People teased me and I got in a lot of fights. I was a pretty bluesy kid.

"When anybody would say albino—it depended on the way they said it. In Texas, they always said it the same way. 'You're weird and we don't like weird people here. Later for you.' There was a period for a year or so where I was telling people I was from Venus. I didn't know what was wrong—I didn't know why I was different. I know my parents felt guilty. They seemed to feel like it was something they had done that was wrong. Even though they tried to not let that show, it still came across. Some people are born with no arms or blind or whatever. Everybody has some kind of a problem—even if it's not something you can see. This is just one of the little problems life gives to you to see how you're gonna handle it."

Having to endure the cruel taunts for being albino, he felt a kinship with black blues artists. "We both had a problem with our skin being the wrong color," he says. "I never really wished I wasn't albino. I guess I would have rather been normal, but it's just one of those things you have to put up with. Edgar bein' albino made it nice to have somebody else who had some of the same problems."

"Regardless of what we go through in life, I know Johnny will always understand how I feel," said Edgar. "Stardom is a part of that because we experienced stardom in a different way than the average person. Growing up and in school, we both experienced the reaction of people for our unusual looks—as being albino. When we were kids, I remember him talking about how albinos were viewed in different cultures. In some primitive tribes, an albino might be killed as defective; in other tribes, an albino might be venerated as a god—all because of his unusual appearance. I've seen that demonstrated in everyday life. I have encountered people who thought I was beautiful and people who thought I was repulsive. When you have gone through that and suddenly become well known and respected, it is such a dichotomy. And it's an experience we share—unlike anyone else."

# Johnny B. Goode

The alienation Johnny and Edgar felt was mirrored to some extent by adolescents across the country. Spurred on by the earthy rhythms of Elvis Presley and rebelling against the music of their parents' generation, teenagers embraced the hot new phenomenon called rock 'n' roll. Johnny was twelve when radio turned him on to the raucous energy of this new musical genre.

"The Big Bopper had a good blues show on KTRM, but he also played rock 'n' roll as J. P. Richardson," Johnny says of the legendary Texas disc jockey. "He played Chuck Berry, Little Richard, Fats Domino, Buddy Holly, and Sun artists—Elvis Presley, Roy Orbison, Jerry Lee Lewis, and Carl Perkins."

Johnny loved the early rock 'n' rollers who captured the feeling of the blues. "I love Little Richard because it had a lot of feeling. I liked Fats Domino, 'Blue Suede Shoes' by Carl Perkins, and Jerry Lee Lewis too—he was a great musician, a good ole rock 'n' roller."

Johnny watched *American Bandstand,* a live dance music TV show hosted by Dick Clark that debuted in 1957. But *American Bandstand* never featured Johnny's favorite black rock 'n' roll performers. The show's racial barrier wasn't broken until 1960 with a performance by Chubby Checker, a nonthreatening black artist, whose stage name (a takeoff on Fats Domino) was suggested by Clark's wife.

The racism wasn't lost on Johnny, who loved Elvis Presley's "That's All Right Mama," the 1954 Sun single *Rolling Stone* called the first rock 'n' roll record. The combination of the sound of the blues and the acclaim Elvis generated from fanatical and adoring fans heightened Johnny's desire to live the life of a musician.

"Elvis could play blues like 'That's All Right Mama' and other songs that were bluesy because he was white," says Johnny. "He could do that, get away with it, and have people love him—mostly white women."

Johnny got his first chance to play rock 'n' roll for a live audience in 1959, when Anchor Bay Entertainment released *Go, Johnny, Go*, an early rock 'n' roll film featuring performances by Chuck Berry, Jackie Wilson, Richie Valens, the Cadillacs, Eddie Cochran, and others.

Movie theaters across the country held "Johnny Melody" contests to accompany the release of that film. KTRM jumped on the bandwagon, offering a recording session and a record deal as first prize. Johnny entered the contest as a solo artist.

"There were about ten of us; you could only play one song," says Johnny. "I played 'Johnny B. Goode.' Me and this other guy were the best out of the bunch, so they had a contest for the two of us to fight it out for the best singer. I won the contest and won a session at Bill Hall's Gulf Coast Recording Studio in Beaumont and a record deal for a single at Dart Records."

Johnny's rendition of "Johnny B. Goode" impressed the judges enough to catapult him into his first record deal, but his victory was marred by the audience's initial reaction. The crowd in the Beaumont movie theater laughed when he walked out onto the stage. That cruel reaction made a lasting impression, and he told the story almost twenty-five years later when he appeared on *Late Night with David Letterman* in May 1983.

"I'll never forget the first time I did 'Johnny B. Goode' for an audience," he told Letterman after playing a rousing live version of the song with Paul Shaffer and the Late Night Band. "I'll never forget walking out onstage and everybody laughed. Like, 'What is it?'.... People didn't know exactly what to think because there are not that many albinos around and especially that many years ago in the Deep South. Nobody knew quite what to think of us."

Now he's a bit more philosophical when he talks about the contest. "They thought it was funny to see a white-headed person up there, I guess," he says. "It bothered me but what could I do? All I could do was get up there and play good. That wiped them out anyway—they were sorry they laughed."

In late 1959, shortly before the contest, he formed his first band, Johnny and the Jammers, with a lineup that included Edgar on tenor guitar (and later piano), Dennis Drugan on bass, and David Holiday on drums. Later, he added Willard Chamberlain on saxophone.

"I wanted a band so I could play clubs," he says. "David Holiday wanted to be a guitar player; he called me up and asked questions about playin' the guitar. I didn't need another guitar player, so he got a drum set and taught himself drums. Dennis Drugan, who's still a good friend of mine, was my bass player. Dennis's daddy taught guitar lessons at Jefferson Music where I was teachin' too. He'd come down to see his dad and we got to be friends. We practiced once or twice a week in the room we had upstairs. My parents were great about it."

"Johnny got offers to play different functions, so he put the band together," said Drugan. "By then he had quit taking lessons with my father and pretty much picked up a lot himself by listening to records. He had hundreds of records in his house. He'd hear new songs on the radio and say, 'Let's learn these.' By the next week, he'd have 'em all down—memorized and then he'd play them in his own style. He was a quick learner."

Edgar always played in Johnny's early bands, but it wasn't because they were siblings.

"I always included Edgar in bands and on records because he was one of the few guys that could play everything," says Johnny. "Not because he was my brother; it was because he could play a lot of different instruments."

"I played bass for a while, drums, piano, even before electric piano," said Edgar. "In Johnny and the Jammers, I played a tenor guitar that was like a four-string electric, like the top four strings of the guitar. I played drums for a short while in Johnny and the Jammers—between David Holiday and Melvin Carpenter. That was when the band changed its name to the Crystaliers and we were playing the Black Cat Club in Port Arthur. I saw the movie *The Gene*

*Krupa Story* and had to have a set of drums. I got Slingerland drums—champagne sparkle—and set them up in my room."

By then, Johnny and Edgar had their own bedrooms. Their parents had renovated the attic into a bedroom for Edgar and a family room for rehearsals.

"We used to rehearse in the garage when we had bands," Edgar said. "When we started to have electric instruments with amplifiers, my parents decided to remodel the attic because everything was getting too loud and driving everybody crazy."

Johnny and the Jammers had only been together six weeks when they went into Bill Hall's Gulf Coast Recording Studio to cut their first record. Hall, a music producer, promoter, and publisher, had booked and eventually managed country artist George Jones. He had produced the Big Bopper's "Chantilly Lace" in 1958, and later joined forces with Sun Records engineer Jack Clements to form the Gulf Coast Recording Company.

Johnny penned two songs for his first record: "School Day Blues," a rocking number, and "You Know I Love You," a ballad for the flip side. Hall produced that single, with Johnny on guitar and vocals, Edgar on piano, Chamberlain on sax, Drugan on bass, and Holiday on drums.

The recording studio was primitive by today's standards, with egg crates on the walls to reduce the echo, and a mixing board in the same room where the musicians were recording. Still, it was a heady experience for Johnny and his band.

"I was pretty excited to be able to play in a recording studio," says Johnny. "We didn't go through the songs very many times—we got 'em pretty quick."

"They set up the players on the floor and microphones all over the place," said Drugan. "In those days, they just put a microphone in front of your speakers and adjusted it. They didn't record separately—everybody played at the same time. We did about five different takes. The mixing board was behind a glass in the same room. They'd open the door and holler out, 'Okay, take one,' and close the door. You'd watch 'em in the window but couldn't hear them; they'd make faces and point. When they point, you start playing.

Then they'd play it back through a little radio to see how it would sound. We thought we were real big time—making a record already."

Recording his brother's original songs, as well as spending time in a studio with a well-known engineer and professional musicians, made a strong impression on Edgar, who was twelve.

"Recording 'School Day Blues' was certainly a memorable experience for all of us," said Edgar. "At that time, I didn't know Johnny could write. I was so impressed when he came up with that song. I was amazed. All we had done was copy other people's music and when he came up with 'School Day Blues,' it was a real song. It was very exciting for a little kid—actually being in a recording studio and being able to listen back to what we had played."

Johnny's single was released on Dart Records, a small label in Houston owned by Pappy Daley. Although the record wasn't distributed to a broad market, it was available in all the Beaumont record stores and several stores in Houston.

"It was great seein' it in stores and hearin' it on the radio," says Johnny. "Ridin' around town with the radio blastin', playing your own music—that was great. I didn't make any money on my record. I only sold 200 copies, and we got twenty-five free copies. Ole Pa was real happy when I came home with the record. But my parents didn't want me to get into it too much. They wanted me to be sure to keep school first."

Drugan remembers hearing the single on KTRM radio, which included it on the station's favorite songs listing in February 1960.

"They put out a survey of 'Favorite Fifty Songs' with a lot of famous artists on the list," he said. "Ray Charles was number eleven with 'My Baby' and Johnny was number eight with 'School Day Blues.' For us to get number eight, we were on top of the world. We had made it already. We were also listed in 'Country Song Roundup,' a national country list that came out that July."

Their excitement at fever pitch, the teenagers began promoting their record at local radio stations. Sax player Willard Chamberlain drove the band to the stations.

"As soon as we got some extra records, we got in Willard's car and went around to the radio stations," said Drugan. "That's how you had to get your record played—you had to go to the stations and ask them to play your record. We knocked on the door, told 'em who we were, and asked them to play our record. They'd say, 'No problem,' and we'd sit down and talk on the radio for a while. Outside the radio station, there was a big tower broadcasting maybe eighty or one hundred miles around. The station would play our record and I'd run out to the car to see if it was on. We were so excited to hear our record played on the radio. As soon as we'd get on one station, another station in the local area would pick it up. Those were exciting days—the infancy of rock 'n' roll."

The airplay proved to be advantageous to Johnny's band. "When the record hit number eight on the Beaumont charts, we got a few more bookings and could make a little more money," says Johnny. "There were bigger bands in Beaumont, but we started getting a few jobs at dances."

To promote their gigs at dances and other school functions, they had posters printed and placed them around town. The posters read: Johnny and the Jammers—featuring guitarist and the voice of Johnny Winter, Beaumont, Texas's own Johnny Melody. Playing the Best of Rock 'N' Roll, Rhythm 'N' Blues. Lines for "Place" and "Time" were printed at the bottom so the band could customize the posters for specific shows.

"We'd go around three or four hours after school putting posters all over town, at where we were playing the next time, different soda shops and places where the kids would see them," said Drugan. "The more people we'd draw, the more money we'd make. In those days, they had a thing called the kitty. You'd put a box out and people would come up and request songs and put a dollar in the kitty. You'd also get money at the door—they'd charge maybe fifty cents. What you made depended on how many people came through the door rather than getting a set amount."

Early in their career, Johnny and the Jammers played social clubs and semiformal dances as the Johnny Winter Orchestra. They played a homecoming dance at the St. Anthony's High School auditorium, and a graduation dance at St. Ann's High School. Their first gig, a social event at the Beaumont Country Club, featured

Johnny on guitar, Edgar on tenor guitar, Chamberlain on sax, and Drugan on "silent guitar."

"That was my first job with Johnny," said Drugan. "Johnny was in junior high. He didn't have a bass player and there was no keyboard at that time. We wore white sports coats, black bow ties, and sunglasses. There was a group called the Shades at that time and they wore sunglasses. I wasn't quite good enough to play, so I played silent guitar. I was hooked up to an amp but didn't have any volume. He said, 'Just stand up there and look good.' He paid me for it too; he said, 'I'll give you five dollars for that job because you weren't hooked up.' They turned the volume up as I got better."

"I had him play silent guitar just for fun because I liked him," says Johnny. "He learned to play bass later on and really played in my band."

After the country-club gig, and Drugan's switch to bass, the band started playing more school functions, as well as teen dances called canteens, including several dances at the Park District Canteen.

"We played a lot of school functions—after the basketball games, sock hops, stuff like that," says Johnny. "They always liked us pretty good. Kids usually brought liquor into dances. The band drank too and we got away with it. We drank everything—vodka, Jack Daniels. I started smokin' cigarettes when I was fifteen too. I had different girlfriends—it was probably easier being in a band. I didn't date a lot in high school—it was more fucking than dating."

Johnny's introduction to the pleasures of the flesh began in the red light district of Beaumont, which like many Texas boomtowns, still had a thriving prostitution and gambling district in the late 1950s. Unfortunately for Johnny, it didn't last long. In 1960, the Texas House General Investigation Committee uncovered evidence of open prostitution in Beaumont and nearby Port Arthur. In 1961, the James Committee, a five-man panel headed by Dallas representative Tom James, held three days of televised hearings exposing prostitution, gambling, bookmaking, narcotics trafficking, liquor sales to minors, and extensive payoffs to city officials. During those hearings, Beaumont County Sheriff Charlie Meyer admitted to accepting more than $85,000 in "campaign contributions" in five years and lost his job as a result of the investigation.

Johnny remembers Meyer and Beaumont's red light district from his visits there in 1959 and 1960.

"There was a lot of prostitution and gambling in Beaumont—in the clubs, right in the open," he says. "Gambling, anything you wanted, cards and roulette. Ole Pa was too old to go with me but he paid for me to go to the whorehouse. They were on Crockett Street—the buildings were fairly run down. They didn't care how old you were. The men were all different ages. The women wore dresses and were fairly seedy. They were sitting around in front—you just picked your choice, paid five bucks, and went to a room upstairs.

"I knew Sheriff Charlie Meyer—the sheriff that let everything go on—he was a pretty good guy. Ole Pa told him to take care of me if I had any trouble. Ole Pa really took care of me. He died when I was still in high school—I hadn't made it yet. That was tough. They voted Charlie Meyer out about the time I started going out to the whorehouses. And soon as I got used to goin' to 'em, they closed them down. Tom James came down from Dallas and stopped everything; he screwed up our whole town. I don't know why he picked Beaumont to come down on, but he certainly did. He messed up a lot of stuff."

Sex, drugs, rock 'n' roll, and the groupies that accompany success as a musician hadn't yet transpired for the young teenager, but he was on his way. Once he tasted fame and the spotlight—even in a small way—his days of paying for sex at brothels would be a distant memory.

Winning the Johnny Melody Contest, having a record on the radio, and playing school functions changed the way Johnny was treated. He had found acceptance, but more importantly, he had broadened his circle of friends, and tasted the success that would inspire him to pursue a career in music.

"Johnny didn't have a lot of friends per se," said Drugan. "His friends were musicians. People at school said things that hurt his feelings. Being an albino, he felt that he wasn't accepted. But I didn't see anything different about him. I was very open to bringing him into my web of friends, bringing him to their houses. Johnny was very shy and I broke him out of his shell by introducing him to my friends. He opened up and started talking to people when he went into rock 'n' roll.

"His classmates didn't talk to him much until he played a school function. We were accepted after we played at the school, a sock hop, or talent contest in the auditorium. We played 'Johnny B. Goode' and they were floored completely."

"Being treated badly in school changed as I got older," says Johnny. "By the time I was in high school, things were different. I was playing in clubs and had a band. I wasn't old enough to be in clubs, but I was going to clubs and had a whole different lifestyle. The high-school kids weren't important to me anymore. Playing music was—playing gigs."

Music gave Johnny that aura of cool that had eluded him during his childhood. He and Drugan went to school dances with their hair slicked back in pompadours à la Elvis Presley, sporting the sunglasses they wore at their Beaumont Country Club gig. "We thought that was the cool thing to do—like we were the Blues Brothers," said Drugan with a laugh.

Determined to make his mark as a musician, Johnny promoted his new persona on band posters, calling himself Johnny "Cool Daddy" Winter. "As we grew older, he had this big pompadour, the sunglasses, the guitar, and the girls," said Edgar. "Johnny was living proof an albino could be cool."

One of Johnny's coolest gigs during that era was playing a drive-in theater in 1958 that featured the film *Go Johnny Go*. Large black letters on the drive-in marquee announced In Person, Johnny Winter along with the movie titles. It wasn't quite Woodstock, but it was his first outdoor concert.

"We played on top of the drive-in theater—above the concession stand—before the show started," said Drugan. "We had to push all our amplifiers up there. Johnny had a very heavy amp and I remember getting all the stuff up on a ladder to get on top of there. They had speakers set up so people could hear us, and everybody got out of their cars and came over to watch us play. It was a big thing—we got a lot of publicity."

As leader of Johnny and the Jammers, Johnny fronted the band on vocals and guitar, booked the band, and handled the finances. "If we were lucky, we got ten dollars a man—five pieces—fifty bucks," he said. "In 1959, that wasn't bad." It was a natural position for him and the other band members were comfortable with that arrangement.

"Johnny was a very dominant personality and a natural leader and was always the bandleader," said Edgar. "Johnny also had ambition. He dreamed of being famous from an early age. He always wanted to watch *American Bandstand* and I would want to watch *Frontier Theater* and cowboy movies."

Johnny had plans for his band and—even at fifteen—knew that stage presence and a flashy appearance would translate into more gigs. He held onto a portion of the band's income so they could dress like professional musicians.

"He'd just tell us how much we made," said Drugan. "I don't think anybody ever asked how much the whole job paid. At the end of the night, Johnny would always figure out how much money he had in the kitty. He'd say, 'You get two dollars.' I'd say, 'How much is left?' and he'd say, 'Don't worry about that—that's for our shirts,'" Drugan said with a laugh. "In those days you wore uniforms, the same colored shirts. We went to a place called 'The Crack in the Wall,' a store in Beaumont that was about ten or twelve feet wide. They had the best lively colored shirts in town. We got fire-engine red shirts and gold shirts; Johnny liked flashy stuff—the flashiest shirts he could find—with black dress pants. We were real class."

Inspired by photographs of Muddy Waters, B. B. King, and John Lee Hooker, Johnny and Drugan went down to Gordon's Jewelry in Beaumont to buy flashy jewelry to complete the look. Johnny made an initial fifteen-dollar down payment on a diamond ring he still wears nearly half a century later.

"I had to pay it off while I was wearing it." Johnny says. "It took me a long time; about a hundred years to pay it off," he adds with a laugh.

With the wardrobe and the bling, Johnny and the Jammers moved up from school functions to clubs and roadhouses. The band's first gigs for adult audiences were at a roadhouse in Beaumont known by two names—Lucille's and Tom's Fish Camp. The band played a ninety-minute set, followed by a twenty-minute break, and an hour-long closing set. Johnny knew how he wanted each song to sound and paid close attention to every note.

"If he didn't like the notes you played, he'd turn around and give you a dirty look," said Drugan. "He was pretty strict with his brother too. If he did something he didn't like, Johnny would give him a whack with his guitar. Edgar would say, 'I'm gonna tell Momma on you.' We did Ray Charles's 'What'd I Say,' which was very popular at the time. Edgar played a Wurlitzer keyboard and kept tuning it because Johnny would go crazy if something wasn't tuned right.

"We played Lucille's every Friday night. After a while we played every Friday and Saturday. We were underage, but it was a backwoods thing and people didn't care. We weren't allowed to drink but we played until about eleven o'clock."

Although patrons may have been skeptical when they noticed the age of the musicians, their skepticism dissolved once the Jammers began to play. Texans were used to hearing country music; the music Johnny played didn't fit into that mold. "They were amazed," said Drugan. "There were a lot of country and western bands, but as far as blues and rock 'n' roll, it was just getting started."

Johnny remembers Tom's Fish Camp as a rowdy roadhouse that served beer and all you can eat portions of fried catfish and frog legs. He was fifteen and Edgar was only twelve, so it took a little convincing to get their parents to allow them to play the club.

"Our drummer's daddy was a patron of Tom's Fish Camp," says Johnny. "That helped them let us play there. My parents didn't like it, but they finally let us play. Dave's daddy was supposed to be lookin' after us but he wasn't really. He was just drinkin'."

"Tom's Fish Camp was owned by an old couple, Tom and Tiny," said Edgar. "Tiny was a 250-pound lady. They had sawdust on the floor and people came in to drink and dance. We had four pieces—

guitar, piano, bass, and drums. Sometimes I played the tenor guitar and then we had two guitars, bass, and drum."

A raucous backwoods club located next to a swamp, Tom's Fish Camp attracted patrons that often drank to excess. Drugan remembers one night that had the band scrambling to get out as quickly as possible.

"There was a big fight, but we never told Johnny's parents because that would have been the last time we played there," he said. "One night a couple who had just gotten married came there for their wedding night. The bride was dancing with another guy and the husband was chasing him around with a baseball bat. Then everybody started fighting, and a girl started tearing the bride's wedding dress all up.

"Johnny was handing the instruments out the back window saying, 'Let's get out of here.' It was a swampy area so you couldn't run too far in the back without being eaten by alligators. Johnny's going, 'My amplifier is still in there—we have to get it out.' The bottles started flying out the windows, and I said, 'I'm not going in there.' It was a mess, but by the next week, it was cleaned up and we played again."

Even then, Johnny took his gigs very seriously. He was committed to playing both sets, no matter what condition his musicians were in.

"One time we were fooling around outside," said Drugan. "I was shooting off fireworks and one of 'em went off in my hand. I said, 'I don't know if I'm going to be able to play, Johnny. My hand is really smarting.' Johnny was so mad, he said, 'Oh yes, you are.' I wound up playing anyway."

Johnny was the only band member with a fake ID, but as long as the band drew a good crowd, it was never an issue. "They never questioned our age," said Drugan. "I can't ever remember police coming there or anybody checking people who went in there. It was a local sheriff and he probably looked the other way. I remember Tom and Tiny said, 'You boys really play good guitar—keep playing like that and you'll be here every week.' We played there for awhile."

Johnny and the Jammers had an extensive repertoire of songs, including blues, R&B, and rock 'n' roll. Ray Charles, a favorite of both Johnny and Edgar, was well represented, as were songs by Buddy Holly, as well as the Crickets, including "Peggy Sue," "That'll Be the Day," "Oh, Boy," and "Maybe Baby." They always played Chuck Berry's rock 'n' roll anthem, a song Johnny would call his own for nearly thirty years.

"'Johnny B. Goode' was always one of my favorite songs," says Johnny with a laugh. "I got a lot of leverage out of that song."

Although Johnny was the lead vocalist, Edgar would pitch in on vocals. "I would sing maybe three or four songs a night," said Edgar. "Johnny would sing the lead and I would find the harmony part; we would work up the songs and the arrangement that way."

Johnny's innate feel for music allowed the band to play the latest rock 'n' roll hits on the *Billboard* charts, as well as songs by classic blues artists.

"We had about fifty songs when we first started playing because of Johnny's ability to learn songs so fast," said Drugan. "He probably knew at least one hundred songs by the time he was nineteen. He was very good at remembering songs. If he didn't, he put his own lead or whatever he needed in there. We'd get calls for Elvis Presley songs—that was one of Johnny's favorites. We played 'Blue Suede Shoes' once because a guy gave us ten dollars to play it. Johnny saw the ten-dollar bill and said, 'We know that song.' It was amazing the amount of songs Johnny could come up with. When somebody wanted country and western songs I'd never heard of, Johnny could play them just from hearing them on the radio. He'd pick up the melody and that was that."

•◆•

Johnny initially achieved his dream of playing onstage with professional musicians at the Red Lion Club, where he went to hear Clarence Garlow. Johnny had grown up listening to Garlow's *Bon Ton Roulet Show* at KJET in the late 1950s and 1960s. Garlow promoted his own records on the show, as well as his upcoming club dates. A Louisiana Creole, he's been described as a pioneer zydeco artist, a rhythm and blues and jump blues artist heavily influenced by T-Bone Walker. Garlow enjoyed national recognition with sales of his single "Bon Ton Roula" and played clubs in Texas and Louisiana.

Enamored by the Creole bluesman, Johnny made a tape recording of one of Garlow's records, then called the radio station and played it to Garlow over the phone. KJET was close to Johnny's grandparents' house, so he often visited Garlow at the station and forged a friendship that inspired the budding musician. Johnny showed up at many of his gigs, and Garlow would call him up out of the audience and hand him his guitar.

"He'd bring me up and let me play," says Johnny. "I was fifteen or sixteen and had a fake ID I got from some kid. It was a selective service card with somebody else's name. They asked to see it once in a while; a lot of times they didn't care. I was about 5'10", my hair was white, and I looked older. Clarence liked it that some white kid was loving his music. He got off on it. We wouldn't play together; I'd usually have to use his guitar. He had drums, bass, guitar, piano, and two saxes. He had a special introduction: 'This is the boy that loves me.' He wanted to make sure everybody knew I was in love with his style.

"Clarence told me about using small-gauge strings and playing with unwound thirds, when the third string of the guitar doesn't have any winding on it. I found out it was easier to bend the string with an unwound third. It's just easier to play."

Prior to that, Johnny was using heavy-gauge strings that wouldn't stretch and made it impossible for him to bend notes. Just listening to records, he had no idea how to replicate the sound he was hearing. Garlow took the time to mentor the young guitarist and show him how to create the sound he was searching for. It left an indelible impression.

Deeming Garlow "the main Texas guitar player that influenced me," Johnny later paid his respects by covering Garlow's "Bon Ton Roulet" on *Raisin' Cain*, his 1980 Blue Sky LP, and "Route 90" and "Sound the Bell" on his 1985 Alligator Records release *Serious Business*. Johnny dedicated *Guitar Slinger*, his 1984 LP on Alligator Records, to Garlow.

Feeling Garlow never received the recognition he deserved, Johnny interviewed him in the 1980s for an article for *Living Blues*. The article was never published, an omission that still bothers him.

"I interviewed Clarence for a magazine but it never came out," says Johnny. "Nobody cared about it, I guess. Nobody asked me to do it—I did the interview on my own. I just had it recorded on tape. They said it was too much trouble to put it on paper."

B. B. King is another artist who influenced and encouraged Johnny as a teenager.

Jim Crow laws were very much in effect in Texas when Johnny met King in 1960, with Jefferson County segregated into black and white neighborhoods. But Johnny's love of the blues overcame the culture of racism and drew him to clubs on both sides of town.

"When I was sixteen, there were two or three white clubs the band could play," says Johnny. "The Black Cat Club and the Pleasure Pier Ballroom in Port Arthur, and the Red Lion Club in Beaumont. They were beer joints where they had fist fights and a few knives. They served Lone Star beer in longneck bottles. Later on, they passed laws where they could drink booze, but in those days, there wasn't anything but beer.

"At the white clubs, the jukeboxes had a lot of country and western. Growin' up in Texas, you had to play country and western music to get a job. I played whatever was popular on the radio at the time. I learned a few hillbilly songs—'Fraulein' was the big one that we played in white clubs.

"The Raven Club in Beaumont was a black club. Texas was definitely racist when I was growing up. Black clubs and white clubs were in separate parts of town and most people stayed in their own part of town. At the black clubs, the jukeboxes had Muddy Waters, Little Walter, Bobby Bland, Junior Parker—the same music I was buying in the record stores."

Determined to hear the music he loved, Johnny, Edgar, and his friends started frequenting the Raven Club, where they saw shows by Bobby "Blue" Bland, Little Junior Parker, Al "TNT" Braggs, and B. B. King. Decked out in jackets, ties, and dress pants, the teenagers appeared older than their years and demonstrated respect for the artists by emulating the attire of blues bands of that era.

"I was about fifteen or sixteen when I first went to the Raven Club," Johnny says. "I went with the guys in the band; we were the only white people there. We were a little bit scared, but we pretended not to be. I was sixteen the night I sat in with B. B.—that was a great night. I was there with Edgar, David Holiday, and probably Willard Chamberlain. It was a completely black audience. I wanted him to hear me—to let him know somebody else could play that music too. But he didn't want to let me sit in."

King had a strict policy of not allowing anyone to sit in unless he knew the musician and his level of expertise. But he was impressed that four white teenagers had ventured into the black part of town and had the chutzpah to ask. King thought about the dynamics of a white musician asking to sit in with a black band in a black club, and didn't want his refusal to be construed as racist. He decided to let Johnny sit in, but for only one song.

"He didn't know if I was any good or not, and didn't want to take a chance," says Johnny. "First he asked to see my union card. I showed it to him, and it surprised him that I had a union card. I said, 'Please, let me sit in, Mr. King; I know your songs,' and he finally let me play. I played his guitar Lucille. I played 'Goin' Down Slow,' just played the one song. He says he let me sit in for a few more songs, but he didn't. He just let me sit in for the one song and took his guitar back.

"It was fun. He had three horns, drums, bass, guitar, and organ; it was the first time I played with such a big band. I got a standing ovation, and that surprised him. He said, 'I'll be seeing you down the line; you were great.' That made me feel great. It meant so much to me to have a great bluesman, somebody who I always idolized, encourage me. I always knew I wanted to be famous and that was great—it made me feel like I can do this and have people like me.

"Later on, I heard B. B. was afraid we were from the IRS—that we were comin' down to the club for his taxes. We all had on black trench coats—it was cold and nasty out—and most white people didn't go to black clubs unless they had a reason to be there. I didn't know he felt that way until later on when I heard him talking about it on an interview.

"We were treated real well at the Raven Club, but that changed when young black people started getting down on the blues. They felt like blues was the sound of the suffering of the black people, the music of the depressed era. People who liked it kept buying the records anyway, but they listened to it in the basement instead of in the living room. The younger black kids didn't really like us coming to the black clubs. They'd say, 'Hey, whitey,' and things like that. I didn't stop going but they made it uncomfortable."

Johnny and Edgar also frequented the Tahiti Club, a black jazz club in Beaumont. Johnny wasn't a jazz aficionado like Edgar, but was impressed with the musicianship of black players. "There was one jazz band that played in the Tahiti a lot," says Johnny. "I'd go up all the time with Edgar and sit in. Not that jazz meant much to me, but I wanted to play with black musicians."

"The Tahiti was the only place I could go and hear real jazz," said Edgar. "It wasn't supper-club jazz; it was fully extended jazz, really nice all out playing. I played the Tahiti maybe one night or a couple of nights. Johnny sat in too; everybody loved blues, even jazz lovers."

Although Edgar loved jazz, Johnny preferred the primitive sounds of the blues and didn't want the more sophisticated arrangements of jazz to affect his style. But when he wanted to learn how to play songs by Bobby "Blue" Bland, he let Edgar show him a few jazz chords.

"There were certain songs that had more chords in them than the normal songs—not just major and minor chords, but diminished and augmented chords," said Edgar. "I showed him those chords and he learned them, just to be able to play those songs. As I got more and more interested in jazz, I tried to show him jazz chords. One time when I tried to show him a chord, he said, 'I don't want to learn that chord. If I learn it, I might start playing it.' He could have played any of that stuff. I have heard him sit in with jazz bands and play solos and really complex chords just playing by ear.

It's so perfectly like Johnny in wanting to keep his style pure. If he learned that chord, he might start to use it and it might affect his changes and feel of his playing."

A longtime admirer of Bland's music and his musicians, Johnny not only added Bland's songs to the band's repertoire, he traveled to see him and other blues artists that had made a strong impression on him.

"I saw Bobby Bland at a club in Levelland, Texas," he said. "I also went to the Pleasure Pier Ballroom in Port Arthur, which was right on the water, out on the pier on the Gulf of Mexico. I saw Lonnie Brooks, Lightnin' Slim, and Lazy Lester there. I liked Lonnie Brooks the best. Port Arthur was about twenty miles away, so Willard, our saxophone player, usually drove. I drove once in a while, but I wasn't supposed to because I couldn't see well enough to drive."

Drugan still has vivid memories of the day Chamberlain let Johnny drive. "He was driving down the street on the wrong side," said Drugan with a laugh. "He had to drive on the wrong side of the road so he could see the curb. Johnny says, 'Why can't I do this? There's no cars in the way. That's the only way I can drive 'cause I can see the curb over here.'" It was a little too much for Johnny's friends to handle, and it didn't take long for Chamberlain to take the steering wheel and relegate Johnny to the passenger's seat.

Johnny enjoyed playing gigs for live audiences, but knew he had to cut records to achieve success as a musician. Despite "School Day Blues" reaching number eight on the Beaumont charts, Hall was reluctant to record another single.

"I heard Bill didn't think I was gonna be any good because I was an albino," says Johnny. "That it was gonna stop my career from being really successful. I don't know if that's true but I heard that from one of his other artists. It really pissed me off. If you asked him, he would have denied it. Even if he said, 'Yes, because he's an albino,' I don't think anybody would do anything about it. That was a normal thing. I could understand it, but there wasn't anything I could do about it. All I could do was get mad."

Although Hall didn't want to record Johnny as an artist, he was savvy enough to use the young guitarist to back up other artists he produced. "I still played as a sideman for him on other people's records," says Johnny. "Rod Bernard and a lot of people—there were so many different ones, I don't remember who they were. We made $3.75 an hour. I knew it was because they didn't have to look at me. But I didn't say anything because he was the only act around."

Johnny still yearned for the spotlight and it didn't take long to find a producer with a record label willing to record him as a headlining artist. In 1960, he met Ken Ritter, nephew of Tex Ritter, the country and western singer and star of cowboy movies in the 1930s and 1940s. Ken Ritter owned the KRCO Record label and was eager to produce and record him. He became Johnny's manager (although Johnny insists he never signed a contract) and took him into Hall's studio to record a number of singles.

"I did several records for Ken Ritter," says Johnny. "The first three records or so I paid for and after that he started paying for 'em. 'Creepy' was on KRCO. It was a pretty good blues instrumental I wrote. I also wrote a ballad, 'Oh My Darling,' for the flip side. He charged me about $150 to press a couple hundred records. We used money from the gigs. It cost him the same amount that he charged me; he didn't make any money off it. We'd usually sell 200 to 300 copies a record. I didn't make any money on records back then and I never did make any money on records with Ken."

"Creepy"/"Oh My Darling" was released in 1960. Johnny also wrote two songs for his second single for KRCO Records, "Hey, Hey, Hey"/"One Night of Love," released later that year. Edgar played keyboards on "Hey, Hey, Hey," and most of Johnny's early singles.

In 1961, Johnny cut "Shed So Many Tears"/"That's What Love Does" for the Frolic label. It was recorded at the J. D. Miller Recording Studio in Crowley, Louisiana. Miller was a songwriter and producer with a studio known for Cajun and swamp pop releases, and records for the Excello label by Lightnin' Slim, Lazy Lester, Lonesome Sundown, and Slim Harpo, Lightnin' Slim's harp player.

"That was a better studio than the Bill Hall one," says Johnny. "We had Lazy Lester playing harp on 'That's What Love Does'—we had to bail him out of jail. He was in jail for drinkin', I think. J. D.

Miller knew where he was, so we bailed him out, took him to the studio, and he played just fine."

In 1962, Johnny returned to the studio to record his next single on Frolic Records, "Voodoo Twist"/"Ease My Pain." "'Voodoo Twist' was a twist song with a lot of horns," says Johnny. "'Ease My Pain' was a blues song I wrote and dubbed harmonica on. It was more bluesy than any other song I recorded back then. Slim Harpo had a hit with 'Rainin' in My Heart' so Ken wanted harp on one song. I also played a Marine Band harmonica on a song with Ronnie Bennett called 'Travelin' Mood' on Floyd Soileau's Jin label."

Influenced by the sound of Little Walter on his Muddy Waters's records, Johnny had taken up the harmonica in 1959. "I started playing harmonica when I was about fifteen," he says. "I liked the way it sounded. I loved Little Walter—he was my favorite; he was better than anybody else, way better. I could hear what he was doin' on the record and I just picked it up on my own. I eventually stopped playing because it was too hard to keep it up. You had to keep practicing or you'd lose your lip."

In 1962, Johnny met Albert Collins, the Texas bluesman dubbed "Master of the Telecaster," at the Gulf Coast Recording Studio. Although many of Collins's biographers place both Johnny and Janis Joplin at the studio that day, Johnny doesn't recall Joplin's presence.

"I was in Bill Hall's studio when Albert Collins recorded 'Frosty,'" says Johnny. "I didn't really know him except from his record 'Freeze.' He wasn't famous at the time; he just had one record out. He was a real good guitar player—he didn't sound like anybody else."

Despite his increasing forays into the music business, Johnny continued to attend Beaumont High School. His parents made it clear he couldn't allow music to interfere with his education, so he worked hard to keep up his grades, especially in math.

"The hardest thing was math," he says. "I hated math. I just couldn't get it. A girl in high school helped me with my math once a week. I'd go to her house, get her to help me with my math, and smoke cigarettes with her. I was taking college prep courses; I always knew I was goin' to college. I had two algebras [Algebra I and II] and a geometry class. I took Latin and was terrible at it. I didn't even make good Fs—I made zeros sometimes. I couldn't do it. Daddy used to do most of the homework help, though Momma was the smarter one of the two. He'd go over the homework with me—not every night, but anytime I needed help."

Johnny graduated from Beaumont High School in June 1962 and enrolled in Lamar State College the following fall. He majored in business, taking three business courses, including Business Administration and Business Orientation, as well as introductory courses in English and in math.

Despite his academic pursuits, Johnny still yearned to travel to Chicago, the home of Muddy Waters and so many of his blues idols. He called Drugan, who had moved there in 1960, and made plans to check out his band. Undaunted by the 1,200-mile, seventeen-hour drive each way, he and Chamberlain took a weekend road trip from Beaumont to the Windy City.

"We were very close, and kept in contact after I left Texas," said Drugan. "He came here in 1962 with Willard to see what Chicago was like. I was playing at the Last Resort at Fox Lake, a suburb about forty miles outside of Chicago, in a band called Jimmy and the Gents. The lineup included Terry Kath and Walter Parazaider, who later went on to form Chicago. Johnny just stayed that evening—that was a one-shot deal for the weekend. They drove all the way, stayed that night, and then drove back to Texas."

That trip changed Johnny's life and perspective; he decided to forgo his plans for higher education and move to Chicago the following summer. "I passed all my classes but only stayed one semester," he says. "I decided to leave college 'cause I had the deal going to move to Chicago. I wanted to play more music and I found out I couldn't do both well at the same time. So I quit school because college was getting in the way of my music."

While Johnny finished up his classes at Lamar State College, he played in a band called Diamond Jim and the Coastaleers for about a year. "Diamond Jim was the bass player and he also sang a little bit," says Johnny. "We played R&B and some blues ballads. We played a club called Yvonne's in Beaumont, and played at a club in Louisiana.

"In 1963, I recorded a single, 'Cryin' in My Heart,' under the name Texas Guitar Slim for Diamond Records, Diamond Jim's label. Guitar Slim was a pretty big name in the South and we figured we might get some sales for Texas Guitar Slim. Elton Anderson, a black man with a band in Louisiana, came up with the idea for me to try the Texas Guitar Slim thing. He played a lot of the same clubs we did and I sat in with him in Louisiana. That song was recorded on Diamond Records and then leased to Floyd Soileau's Jin label because it was bigger. It wasn't very big but it was bigger than Diamond. I never did make any money off those records either."

When Ritter discovered Johnny was recording under another name for a different label, he demanded the record be taken off the market. Johnny complied, even though he didn't find Ritter's demand reasonable. "It was really nothing [to him] because I didn't have a contract with him," he says.

"Roadrunner"/"The Guy You Left Behind," a single produced and recorded by Ritter, was Johnny's next release. "Ken leased that one to Todd Records, but it didn't sell many records," Johnny says. "I had a number ten on one of those early '60s records. The disc jockeys were pretty good with local guys. They'd put your record out in the Top Ten even if it wasn't sellin' many records. I still have all of my 45s."

Although Johnny's singles weren't the blues recordings he longed to make, and his band played rock and R&B, he found encouragement and inspiration in a white blues artist named Joey Longoria, who performed as Joey Long. Johnny met him in a club in Houston, and later saw him at the Sam Houston Coliseum when Long opened for Fats Domino.

Born in southern Louisiana in the early 1930s, Long, raised by parents who worked in the cotton fields, was captivated by the sound of acoustic blues coming from the home of a black family down the road. He began his musical career playing country and western music, but soon turned to the blues. Johnny was thrilled to hear a white man successfully playing the music he loved and was encouraged by the bluesman.

"I met Joey Longoria when I was about seventeen and had started playing clubs in Houston," says Johnny. "He was the first white person I met playin' blues. Joey was a blues guitar player in Houston. I loved it because he was a white guy makin' it playing black blues. I played with Joey a lot. He couldn't make as much money by playin' blues, but at least I knew you could make a living doin' it. He said, 'Keep on tryin', you can make it, just keep on pushin'.'"

With Long's words ringing in his ears and resonating in his soul, Johnny continued his musical journey.

# From the Windy City to the Deep South

Chicago was Johnny's next destination. Drugan lived there so he knew he would have a band to play with and a place to stay. He quit his gig with Diamond Jim and the Coastaleers, packed his bags, and booked a flight. Arriving in early summer 1963, Johnny stayed with Drugan for two weeks before renting a studio apartment with a fold-up bed in the beach area of Lake Michigan. His girlfriend then moved up from Texas and into the North Side apartment with him.

"We started playing as soon as Johnny got here," said Drugan. "I was playing up at Fox Lake where there were a lot of places to play. His first job was with Jimmy and the Gents at the Last Resort, an old resort with a big stage and a dance floor overlooking Fox Lake."

Formed in 1962, Jimmy and the Gents consisted of a guitarist, organist, saxophone player, bass player, drummer, and a vocalist named Jimmy Rice. Their set list included a wealth of Elvis Presley songs, so they had bookings at several Chicago area clubs.

To Johnny's chagrin, he soon discovered that although he was living in Chicago, he wouldn't be playing in a blues band, and he wouldn't be playing guitar. "They played twist music," says Johnny with a laugh. "I didn't know that before I left Texas. I got my first job playing drums. The drummer had his tonsils out and I played drums until he got well. I didn't really know how to play drums; I just kind of faked it."

Johnny's strength on guitar eventually led to the ouster of Jim Guercio, the band's guitarist. It was a fortuitous break for Guercio, who moved to L.A., where he eventually managed Chicago and took them from an obscure club band to stardom. He later produced records by Chicago, the Beach Boys, Blood, Sweat & Tears, and Frank Zappa, and built a state-of-the-art recording studio at his ranch in Boulder, Colorado, where Joe Walsh, inspired by the picturesque surroundings, recorded "Rocky Mountain Way."

With Johnny taking on the role as leader and guitar player, he remembers the band changing its name to Johnny and the Gents. Drugan remembers it simply as the Gents. Either way, the band was making fifty dollars a night per person, rather than the ten or fifteen dollars a night Johnny had made in Texas. Johnny didn't consider the musicians on the same par as the players in Johnny and the Jammers, but the money was great and they were playing a minimum of five nights a week.

After playing a number of Fox Lake resort gigs, the band set its sights on Chicago's Rush Street entertainment district. "It was the twist era and all the good money was on Rush Street," said Drugan. "Chubby Checker was coming out and clubs were dying for bands that could play the twist. Rush Street was where people would come into town to have a good time. They had go-go dancers in white boots on the side of the stages; they'd dance up front on the floor too. Drinks were six dollars, which was a lot of money back then. There were always lines of people waiting to get into those places."

"Rush Street was a seedy area with a lot of twist clubs and strip clubs too," says Johnny. "We started at the Tony Paris Show Lounge, and also played the Lemon Twist West. We wore sharp suits with velvet collars, tapered legs, and Beatle boots; and I had my hair combed back in a pompadour. One time we came in wearing matching shirts and the owner got pissed off. He said, 'You can't come in here wearing shirts—you have to wear suits or forget it.'"

"We were wearing Beatle-type jackets with cutaway collars like priest collars—with velvet collars and velvet pockets," said Drugan. "They were turquoise blue with black velvet. Johnny wore candy apple red shoes with metallic toes—he loved those shoes. We also had red suits with Beatle-type jackets with black velvet. We got 'em at Smoky Joe's in Chicago, which catered to musical groups."

"When the Beatles came out, we were already wearin' clothes just like what they were wearing," says Johnny. "Real nice iridescent gold clothes we bought in the South Side of Chicago."

To meet the demand for danceable songs, the band's set list consisted of rock 'n' roll, soul, and songs by Elvis Presley. "I couldn't work any blues into the sets at Tony Paris's Show Lounge," Johnny says. "It didn't have to be a twist song; but it had to be a twist beat, which gets pretty boring after a while. We played a lot of things like 'Midnight Hour.' I sang 'Midnight Hour,' but I can't remember most of the songs I sang because I didn't like them that much. We did some soul songs—"Out of Sight" and "Barefootin'."

Playing songs the club owners demanded gave the band steady work; they played Rush Street clubs six nights a week, at gigs that ran from 9 PM until 2:30 AM. When they got restless during the breaks, they did what they could to amuse themselves.

"Sometimes we'd go to a room upstairs," said Drugan. "Johnny liked to bring his glasses up there. When we finished, we would smash them on the wall. Johnny thought that was fun. The bouncer would come upstairs and say, 'I hear some noise up here.' His name was Rico; he was about seven feet tall and weighed 300 pounds. He parked the Cadillacs outside and he'd let us sit in them and listen to the radio. We were kinda bored after a while—we didn't know what to do in between sets."

That problem disappeared when the proprietors, who owned both the Tony Paris Show Lounge and the Scotch Mist, decided to have the band play their other club during their breaks.

"On some weekends, we never got a break—just long enough to go to the other club," said Drugan. "We played nonstop. They advertised continuous entertainment at the Tony Paris Show Lounge, so our band would play during the break time. The regular band was Bobby and the Troubadours (which featured keyboard player Barry Goldberg, who cofounded the Electric Flag with Mike Bloomfield in 1967 after Bloomfield left the Paul Butterfield Blues Band). When we finished playing at the Scotch Mist, we'd go down the street and play during the break for the other band. We did that for about a month or so. It was tough. One of the owners said, 'Anybody bothers you guys, you let me know about it.' He looked like one of the Sopranos. There were a lot of *Soprano*-type guys around those places. Everything was 'you guys better do it.'"

With the Rush Street gigs in such close proximity, it wasn't difficult to move the band's equipment from one club to another. One night things literally got out of hand.

"Johnny and I were rolling the amplifiers down the street from one club to another," said Drugan. "We lost balance and it fell over and broke my toes and Johnny's too. We hobbled down the street and played with broken toes."

Playing six nights a week didn't give Johnny much free time. He got home around 3 AM, listened to records to unwind, and slept until two or three in the afternoon. But he read about the Fickle Pickle, a coffeehouse on the North Side of Chicago managed by a nineteen-year-old blues fanatic and guitar player named Mike Bloomfield. Bloomfield would locate blues musicians from the '20s and '30s, book them at the coffeehouse, and introduce them to a new audience of mostly young, white hippies. Artists included guitarist Big Joe Williams, harp player Jazz Gillum, guitarist Walter Vincson, and bass player Ransom Knowling, who played on Arthur "Big Boy" Crudup's recording of "That's All Right." Hoping to hear and maybe jam with some blues legends, Johnny decided to check out the scene.

"I had heard Mike Bloomfield was a real good guitar player and had played with a lot of the black guys," says Johnny. "So when we weren't playin' out, we went to the Fickle Pickle."

Although disappointed most of the players were white on the night Johnny sat in and jammed with Bloomfield, Johnny was encouraged by Bloomfield's heartfelt, "You play good blues, man." That jam was a serendipitous stop on the road to Johnny's destiny. Five years later, Bloomfield, who had become well-known playing in the Paul Butterfield Blues Band and the Electric Flag, would rave about Johnny's guitar playing to a *Rolling Stone* reporter.

The artists Johnny really wanted to see—Muddy Waters and Otis Rush—played clubs in the South Side, but neither Johnny nor Drugan would venture into that side of town after dark. Drugan had a bad experience in that predominately black neighborhood when he first moved to Chicago.

"I went to the South Side to see Muddy Waters in 1960, and got beat up and robbed," he said. "I took a taxi cab down to Silvio's with a friend from Texas. They let us out of the taxi and said, 'Go right in that door.' We went in that door and got beat up. It was actually the alley of the club and we thought it was how you got in the club. It was a horrible experience. That was the last time I went down there to see if I could find somebody in a blues club."

Johnny and Drugan drove through the South Side during the day, checking out the posters outside the clubs—Pepper's Lounge, Theresa's Lounge, and the Blue Flame—as well as Silvio's on the West Side. "We went to the South Side in the daytime, but not at night because it was dangerous," says Johnny. "During the daytime, we looked to see if there was anybody good playin'—we saw Muddy was playin' at one club. We were the only white people there and it was a little scary, but we never had any trouble. We stayed in the car most of the time."

When summer turned into fall and Johnny still hadn't heard any of his favorite blues artists or had an opportunity to play blues, it was time to leave. "All the music I was hearing in Chicago was completely rock 'n' roll—that's why I didn't want to stay there too long," he says. "I stayed about four months. I was tired of the music we had to play. I missed Texas and missed playin' the songs we wanted to do."

"Johnny left Chicago in late October," said Drugan. "I drove him back, straight through from Chicago to Texas. He wanted me to stay so we could get a group together, but I liked Chicago. I just stayed there over the weekend and drove back."

After Johnny returned to Beaumont, he immediately immersed himself in the music scene. He recorded Johnny "Guitar" Watson's "Gangster of Love" and an original ballad entitled "Eternally" with Edgar on drums and horns. "Eternally" sold well locally on the Frolic Records label, so Atlantic Records picked it up for distribution. "That probably made it sell a little bit better," says Johnny. "I don't remember exactly how much it sold—it wasn't real big though. 'Eternally' got airplay all over Texas and was big on the jukebox in a pavilion at Garner State Park."

The 1964 release on Atlantic Records positioned "Eternally" on the A side and another Johnny original, "You'll Be the Death of Me," on the B side. "Eternally" began receiving airplay in Texas and Louisiana, and the band started getting opening act bookings at bigger venues. Billed simply as "Johnny Winter," they opened for Jerry Lee Lewis at the Beaumont Civic Center and for the Everly Brothers at the Sam Houston Coliseum. The shows featured as many as twenty opening acts, playing one or two songs. Johnny's band played "Eternally" and earned twenty-five dollars. The pay didn't matter; the experience and the exposure made the gig worthwhile.

Years later, when Johnny was a rising star and ran into Jerry Lee Lewis at the Scene, a happening nightclub in New York City, he walked up to the legend and asked if he remembered him from that gig in Beaumont. "He was a real asshole," says Johnny, laughing at the memory. "He said, 'Boy, What are you doing with hair like that? That hair looks pitiful, boy.' I said, 'Jerry Lee, your hair was as long as mine is now.' He said, 'No, man. I never had hair like that.' He liked me when I didn't have long hair, and he was pissed off at me when I did."

When Jerry Lee met Johnny in Beaumont, the Beatles hadn't landed on American shores and Johnny's slicked-back pompadour was still the rage. On August 3, 1963, the Beatles debuted on the U.S. *Billboard* charts with "From Me to You." On January 18, 1964, "I Want to Hold Your Hand" topped the charts; "She Loves You" hit number one the following week. Their three appearances on *The Ed Sullivan Show* in February 1964 changed the face (and the hairstyle) of American music.

Johnny remembers the first time he heard the Beatles on the radio. "I loved 'em as soon as I heard them," he said. "I saw 'em on Ed Sullivan too. I liked what they were doing and thought it was the kind of stuff I'd like to do. It really turned me on; it was great music with only two guitars. The Beatles were also the first group that wrote their own songs. That made me want to write and play more of my own songs."

Johnny also watched the Rolling Stones make their U.S. TV debut on *The Hollywood Palace* in June 1964 singing "I Just Want to Make Love to You," a song written by Muddy Waters and Willie Dixon. "I liked the Rolling Stones and I liked their image," he says. "When I saw them on TV, I couldn't see how they made it—they dressed so horrible. And they had girls—I thought that was pretty good. They played good blues. The style of blues they played was not as authentic as the blues I played, but I was glad they were doin' it."

Shortly after the Rolling Stones appeared on *The Hollywood Palace*, President Lyndon B. Johnson signed the Civil Rights Act into law, prohibiting discrimination against black men and women in public facilities, in government, and in employment. House and Senate votes were divided by region, not by party, with the majority of Southern Congressmen and Senators voting against the bill. Enforcement powers were initially weak and many Southern states simply refused to comply with the law.

"Back then, Beaumont was still segregated," says Johnny. "Schools weren't integrated yet. They had all-black and all-white water fountains. A lot of restaurants, too. Black people sat in the back of the bus. White people figured they were better than black people. It pissed me off. We had some black people at St. Mark's Episcopal Church. They went to the early service, but they still went to a white church. There weren't any black people at Momma's Baptist Church. I felt like black people were as good as white people and there shouldn't be any segregation anywhere. I wasn't inclined to be prejudiced. I figured black people were playing the best music, so I couldn't be prejudiced against them."

Johnny's parents never objected to him and Edgar frequenting black clubs. In fact, Johnny never got any flak from anyone for playing with black artists because race didn't seem to matter when it came to music. But socializing with black musicians outside of the clubs had its drawbacks.

"We had a black singer in a band for a while and we went out to eat at a drive-in restaurant, where you drive in front of the restaurant and carhops come out and take your order," says Johnny. "We were all kinda scared about it because we had a black person in a car with us. We were goin' to a white restaurant where we had been a lot of times before, but we knew people weren't gonna like it. So he got down in the backseat of the car so nobody would see him. It was embarrassing, I guess. That's the way it was back then."

•◆•

While Johnny was playing clubs in Chicago, Edgar, who was still in high school, continued to play gigs with the rest of the Jammers. Determined to expand his club circuit beyond Texas, Edgar took the band to Atlanta to audition for the Johnny O'Leary Booking Agency.

"After the audition, Johnny O'Leary agreed to put us on tour," said Edgar. "We were planning the tour when Johnny came back from Chicago and said, 'Hey, I want to do that.' I was relieved—'Thank God I don't have to be the frontman and sing the songs.'"

Stylistically, Johnny's music would be an easier sell because Edgar's original idea was to play jazz, which had a smaller market. "What people really wanted to hear was more exciting—R&B, rock, and blues, which was what Johnny was doing," Edgar said. "That band started as It and Them and later became the Black Plague."

Johnny remembers things differently. "When I was in Chicago, Johnny O'Leary's agency called Edgar and said if you ever get a real leader, we'd like to use you guys," says Johnny. "I was their leader, so when I came back, we all moved up to Atlanta and started working for that agency."

Although the band's name changed frequently, the lineup remained the same with Johnny on guitar and vocals, Edgar on keyboards and saxophone, Ikey (Isaac Payton) Sweat on bass, and Norman Samaha on drums. "We had different names for the bands," says Johnny. "We'd get tired of one name and call it something else. If we didn't have a big enough following on one name, we'd change names, try something different, and see if we could get a better following. Sometimes it helped. The Crystaliers was a name I thought up—that was after Johnny and the Jammers. It and Them was after I started playing Louisiana. We didn't know anything about Them, Van Morrison's band at the time. I was It and they were Them. Johnny Winter and the Black Plague was another one I made up. Called it the Black Plague because we all wore black—collarless coats and black turtlenecks."

"I was in my last year of high school when Johnny and I went on the road with It and Them," said Edgar. "Then it became the Black Plague and we played for the Southern club circuit doing the Whisky a Go Go in New Orleans. We were doing all the Whisky a Go Gos—Atlanta, New Orleans, Mississippi, Florida, all through the South."

From 1964 to 1966, the band toured the Deep South, playing upscale clubs that held 500 people in Shreveport, Bossier City, and New Orleans, Louisiana; Birmingham, Alabama; Savannah and Atlanta, Georgia; and Pensacola and upstate Florida. The agency provided steady work as soon as they moved to Atlanta.

"I would call up the agency and they'd tell us where we were going next or that we were going home," says Johnny with a laugh. "That was the worst possible thing to hear—'You don't have any jobs; go back home for a while.' Sets were forty-five minutes on, fifteen off—10 to 2 AM, and sometimes 9 to 3 AM. The band members made twenty-five bucks a night, and I made fifty dollars because I was the leader. The agency took twenty-five percent. We got paid once a week. We didn't make much money, but enough to get by. We were young and having a good time."

The band rented a U-Haul trailer for their equipment and hitched it to the back of Ikey's car. "We could've bought two or three real nice trailers for all of the rent we paid," says Johnny. "We really never got far enough ahead money-wise to buy the things most bands have. We had a homemade PA set, U-Haul trailers, and old cars."

Yet the excitement of being away from home for the first time, traveling to new cities, and playing clubs for appreciative audiences—especially women—was ample compensation for any sacrifices the band made.

"Down South we had a pretty big following," says Johnny. "We had groupies and I did as good as anybody. If you brought 'em back to the room, somebody would go in another room for a while. It wasn't an overnight thing."

Edgar was the first band member to start growing his hair long and combing it into bangs; Johnny and the rest of the band quickly followed suit. Unfortunately, it didn't bode well with Southern audiences and club owners. The band's set list remained the same—predominately soul and R&B, with songs by James Brown, Wilson Pickett, Otis Redding, and Bobby "Blue" Bland. But the long hair, black turtlenecks, iridescent bluish-gold collarless suits, and suede low-heeled boots caused them to lose a lot of gigs.

"None of the club owners were honest, really—just some of 'em were better than others," says Johnny. "I played one club for a week—five days straight—and didn't get paid. That's the only time that's ever happened. The only reason he didn't pay us was because we had long hair. The audience seemed to like us better when we had short hair combed back. He paid us when we had short hair, but said with long hair, 'It's not workin'—I'm not gonna pay you.'"

As songs by British artists started climbing the charts, the band incorporated them into their set list. "We played everything on the radio, and all of the British Invasion—Beatles, Rolling Stones, Herman's Hermits, Dave Clark Five," said Edgar. "We played everything out there. 'Midnight Hour,' 'Knock on Wood,' 'Hold On, I'm Coming,' were right up there.

"We used to do 'Honky Tonk,' a Bill Doggett sax song that was probably one of the biggest instrumentals ever in the South. Johnny did a killer version of 'Cryin'' by Roy Orbison. We did a lot of the Beatles songs too. We did Little Richard and Chuck Berry songs, James Brown's 'Out of Sight,' and 'Papa's Got a Brand New Bag.' We didn't do much blues, honestly. The only traditional blues song was 'Baby, What You Want Me to Do,' the old Jimmy Reed song," Edgar added.

"We played songs by the Rolling Stones—'Satisfaction,' '19th Nervous Breakdown,'" says Johnny. "I picked the songs by what was on the radio and what albums were good. I made all the decisions—I was the leader and that was just the way it was. A lot of our songs were R&B. I liked R&B but I wanted to be playin' blues—

real blues. Most white people didn't know what blues was, and if you didn't play music the people wanted to hear, you wouldn't keep the job very long."

It didn't take much to start a fight in a juke joint. Longhaired hippies and musicians were a prime target—especially musicians that wouldn't take requests to placate drunken patrons.

"I used my white Les Paul to hit people," says Johnny with a laugh. "I was lucky enough that it didn't happen a lot, but it happened in a club in Galveston in the beach area. This big guy—he was built like a football player—wanted the same song over and over again. I said, 'No,' and he said, 'Well, I'm gonna wipe out the bandstand.' I figured he could probably do it. He backed up and got ready to rush the stage and I wiped him out with my guitar before he could get the drums. He went down and didn't get up. After that, his friends took him out to the car. My guitar had a bent headstock but I could still play it.

"A typical redneck didn't like longhaired musicians. They were usually drunk—they drank a lot of beer down South. A lot of fistfights in the parking lots—mostly over girls. We got some of that—where they'd ask you to go out to the parking lot—but it usually started in the clubs."

In Southern juke joints, it wasn't unusual for unruly patrons to throw drinks at the stage. "A lot of guys didn't like musicians because musicians get all the girls," says Johnny. "I had people throw beers and drinks at me while I was playing. Throw it out of a glass, usually do it in a way that will juice it to you real good. We've played behind chicken wire like they did in *The Blues Brothers*. They do that all the time—mostly in Louisiana. They had chicken wire exactly like that to keep the bottles from comin' up onstage. It was 'play the song they want to hear, at the time they want to hear it, or they'd throw a bottle at you.' So the club owners put the stage wire up."

Art also imitated life during the scene when the Blues Brothers' bar tab exceeded the band's pay. "We did a good bit of drinkin'—there were times where we drank more money on the bar tab than what we'd made," says Johnny with a laugh. "That happened in Louisiana too. Instead of gettin' money, you'd end up payin' money.

I was probably the biggest drinker in the band. But that didn't happen very often 'cause I carried a bottle of Jack Daniels with me and used to buy Cokes."

It was during the Deep South touring years that Johnny had his first taste of marijuana.

"We started doin' grass when we were on the road in about 1965," says Johnny. "We got it from another band. I was so high I couldn't go out. I was wrecked; I had to lie down on the bed and listen to albums. I couldn't stop laughing. That was the first time I smoked grass. After that, the whole band smoked it regularly—we usually bought it when we were home. It was twenty dollars an ounce, and five dollars for a matchbox—a small wooden box that stick matches come in. They had Southern sheriffs but they didn't seem to bother anybody much. You'd smoke it in the back of the club or when you got home."

Although they still worked for the Atlanta agency, Johnny and the band moved to Houston. Several band members had settled down and gotten married, so Johnny figured he'd give it a try. On February 28, 1966, five days after he turned twenty-two, Johnny married Mary Jo Beck, also aged twenty-two, at St. Mark's Episcopal Church in Beaumont, Texas.

"I knew Mary Jo for about six months before we got married and then we were married for about six months," says Johnny. "Everybody I knew was gettin' married, so it felt like the thing to do. We had a small wedding at my dad's church. We lived with my folks when we were in Beaumont but we moved to Houston real quick. We had a second floor apartment with a bedroom, living room, and a small kitchen. She wasn't workin' but I made decent money with the band."

Throughout his life, Johnny has always lived with women; he very rarely, if at all, lived on his own. He also had a difficult time staying true to any one woman. Like many bluesmen before him, he always had at least one woman on the side. It didn't take long for the bloom to fade on his impetuous first marriage and the concept of monogamy.

"Married life was shitty," he says. "I was always bothered all the time about one thing or another. She was always sure I was gonna be goin' out with somebody else. I wasn't goin' out with anybody—not at first I wasn't. She was just crazy. I got tired of hearing it and started going out with other people. We had a big screamin' fight. She was tearin' up my stuff, wreckin' anything she could find, and I wasn't gonna have that. I had my folks take her to Galveston and put her in a mental hospital, where she stayed about three weeks. She was gonna kill herself; she was that crazy."

Before she was discharged, Johnny moved his clothes and records to a friend's apartment in the same building. "I knew she'd try to break up anything she could find of mine, so I took it all downstairs," he said. "When I got the divorce she didn't get anything because I didn't have anything. It's a good thing I got married before I made it. That was the only time I was married [prior to marrying his present wife Susan in 1992], but I lived with a lot of girls and always had girlfriends. I didn't figure on getting married again—I hated it. Not for me. I figured I'd just live with people. It was too big a deal to get a divorce. I felt like I was real lucky to get out of the marriage as easy as I did."

After his divorce, Johnny briefly lived at his parents' house during a break in the band's schedule. Restless when he wasn't touring, he found gigs for the band in his hometown. As soon as the agency called, they were back on the road, living the life they loved.

"You'd see different girls, different clubs, different towns; there was always something different about it to make it fun," says Johnny. "The band got along pretty good. Sometimes we'd get on each other nerves—have money arguments like, 'Why ain't we making more money?' I made a little bit more, but they knew I should be makin' more money because I was doin' everything. We all wanted to be makin' more money, but we were doin' as good as we could. I think we stayed together so long because we liked each other and we liked the music. I love playin'—nothing ever made me want to stop touring. It never seemed like a job—it always was fun to me."

Oscar Wilde said, "I can resist everything except temptation." Johnny had a lot of temptation on the road, and followed Wilde's philosophy. "I was just an asshole," Johnny says with a laugh. "I didn't want to resist."

Among the temptations was the lure of married women, and Johnny had more than his share. "With married women, you don't have as much to worry about," he says. "They're already married so they're not gonna pester you much. It gives you freedom."

But when the woman was married to a close friend and musician in his band, it had a chilling effect on their friendship. "I once went with Ikey's wife," says Johnny. "I wanted his wife—because it's really something to get somebody else's wife. Sometimes it's just that—wantin' to be with somebody else's wife. I still played in the band with him. One night we were out eatin', and he told me, 'I know you fucked my wife.' I said, 'Ikey, how do you know that?' He said, 'I just know.' I don't know how he knew; maybe she told him. I felt bad about it. But they had [been] broken up for a while; they weren't living together when I went to bed with her. They were broken up and got divorced after that."

Johnny carried a gun and a knife when he toured the Deep South. That and his penchant for messing around with married women led him down a dirt road that could have been his last.

"I never used my gun but came close to it once," he says. "I was about nineteen or twenty, in a car with some friends. I had a guy coming after me. I had gone to bed with his wife and he was following me down some back roads. We finally stopped—I had a .22 Derringer in my pocket and he had a gun too. I didn't know whether I should shoot. He had his gun out and every time I'd get my hand close to my pocket, he'd say, 'Keep your hand away from your pocket.' I couldn't have gotten to my gun quick enough, I don't think. He finally started crying and left."

•◆•

By 1966, all four band members had their fill of touring; some had wives and children and no longer wanted to live their life on the road. The band's car had broken down and they couldn't afford to buy a new one.

"We had done that circuit several times," said Edgar. "Everybody was pretty tired and exhausted and wanted to take a break and settle down for a while. We had a car, were pulling a U-Haul trailer, and loading and setting up all our gear. We were responsible for everything and it gets to be a pretty demanding pace, to be out there continually like that."

Settled in Houston, Johnny focused his energy on recording. He had never stopped making records. On a break that took him back to Beaumont in 1964, Johnny cut "Gone for Bad"/"I Won't Believe It," recorded on Frolic and leased to MGM. Johnny considered it his last stint as a studio musician and last recording for Ritter. A handshake agreement ended their four-year relationship, but Ritter wasn't about to go away. He would later resurface and lay claim to Johnny's music.

While living in Houston, Johnny met Roy Ames, a twenty-nine-year-old independent record producer who entered the record business in 1959. Ames started Aura Records (which evolved into Cascade Records) in the early 1960s, and was working as a record promoter/distributor for Don Robey's Duke/Peacock label when he met Johnny in 1966. Seeing potential in the young guitarist, Ames tried to lure him away from Ritter with the promise of a record deal with Duke Records.

"Duke was a black label out of Houston and Roy knew I liked working with black people," says Johnny. "He figured it would be a good way to talk me into signing with him. But Bill Hall tried to say I was signed with Dart Records. He said he bought my contract from Ken Ritter but he never did. He never took me to court but he tried to say I had not been fair to Ken Ritter. I didn't see how I could be unfair when I was supposed to get royalties and had never gotten a penny from anybody."

Hall's interference blocked Johnny's deal with Duke Records but that didn't deter Ames. He produced a single by Johnny and Edgar under the artist name of "Insight" for his Cascade Records label. Capitalizing on the holiday season and the Winter brothers' exquisite harmonies, Ames released "Please Come Home for Christmas" with their rendition of James Brown's "Out of Sight" on the flip side in 1966.

Johnny's only authorized project with Huey Meaux, another producer with a studio in Houston, was a single on Pacemaker

Records with "Birds Can't Row Boats" as the A side and "Leavin' Blues" on the flip side, recorded in 1966 and released in 1967.

"'Birds Can't Row Boats' was a song makin' fun of Bob Dylan," he says with a laugh. "'Leavin' Blues' was the first song I ever played slide on—it was pretty decent. I'd only been playin' a few months. It didn't sell great, but it sold as well as anything else I put out."

Johnny was living in Nacogdoches, a town 140 miles northeast of Houston, playing with a band called Amos Boynton and the ABCs. "I played with them when I first went to Houston," says Johnny. "They had a black singer named J. J. Johnson and played R&B, with Amos Boynton on drums, Charlie Wheeler on bass, and me on guitar and vocals. We changed the name to the Great Believers just for one record, "Coming Up Fast" on the Cascade label."

Although the stint in the band was short-lived, it introduced him to Carol Roma, a woman who would be his live-in partner for the next five years. "I met Carol when I was playing with Amos," says Johnny. "She was from Nacogdoches in East Texas. Carol had been goin' out with Amos for a year when I met her. He was married, but he went out with her. She was nineteen or so back then—I was in my early twenties.

"I wasn't married to Carol Roma, but we lived together a long time. We first got together when she moved to Houston, where she was a beautician. I liked smart girls and skinny girls and Carol was both. I took her out a couple of times and was living with her within a month. I went out with other girls too. I didn't want to be true to Carol; I felt like I needed to go out with other girls. It made it hard for the relationship.

"Carol went to my gigs pretty often at first—I was playing soul music at the Hit Factory club with Edgar, Ikey Sweat, and Norman Samaha on drums. When we first started living together, I was making real good money at the Act III, $150 to $175 a week. But when I started playing blues, my money was definitely not as great. For a while there I wasn't makin' anything. She didn't mind—she was supportive of my music."

Johnny's band played six nights a week at the Act III, a Houston club located at a major intersection. The band played in front of a large picture window, flanked by go-go girls in mini dresses and short white boots dancing in elevated cages behind them. Although the club pushed the mid-'60s envelope by flaunting go-go dancers in the window, management demanded songs that made the charts. The owner told Johnny what songs to play and which tunes he expected them to learn by the following week. Johnny learned most Top Forty songs by listening to the radio, and only occasionally had to buy the record.

In 1967, Johnny also performed briefly with the Traits, a Houston-based band, and played on "Tramp"/"Parchman Farm," a single with a pressing of 300 records on the Universal label. He joined the band after vocalist Roy Head left, which was shortly after the release of the band's hit single "Treat Her Right." A popular road band, the Traits played clubs throughout Texas and Louisiana.

Although Johnny couldn't play blues at the clubs, living in Houston allowed him to see and meet musicians that shared his passion. He heard his first live performance by Lightnin' Hopkins, a Texas country bluesman, in that city.

"I heard Lightnin' when I was still in Houston," says Johnny. "He made his living playin' on street corners in Houston—he played whorehouses too. They had a room downstairs where people would congregate and choose their girl and they had bars where you could drink and listen to music. Lightnin' also played on buses. He had a friend who was a bus driver, who would take him to the liquor store and buy him a bottle of booze. He'd stay on the line for a while and play for the people who got on the bus. He got tips. He was playin' at clubs at that time but he liked playin' in the street too."

Johnny also met Keith Ferguson, a musician who shared his love of the blues and later played bass in the Fabulous Thunderbirds. Johnny was playing in the Phil Seymour Band at an afterhours gig at a gay club when drummer Eddie Rodriguez introduced the two likeminded musicians.

"Eddie played that gig and he knew I loved blues and he knew Keith loved blues and he got us together," says Johnny. "We were about the same age and we both liked the same music. He had a big record collection, a lot of 78s that his Daddy gave to him and he was sellin'. He was the only white person I knew in Houston that was into blues."

Through Ferguson, Johnny was introduced to Cactus Records on Alabama Street, where Keith's father, John William Ferguson, worked as a classical music buyer. The elder Ferguson was also a musician; he had been a concert pianist with the Chicago Symphony.

"I bought a lot of records in Keith's father's store," says Johnny. "It had a better selection—a lot of the old reissues on albums, 45s made into albums. I had a Philco set with six- or eight-inch speakers. I listened to records all the time, straight blues and a few of the hippie records like Firesign Theatre and *Psychedelic Lollipop* by the Blues Magoos. I usually bought records I couldn't hear on the radio. I bought Hendrix—the first records—*Are You Experienced.* I bought Bob Dylan albums—electric and folk—I liked Dylan a lot."

Ferguson, like many of Johnny's close friends and fellow musicians, died young. He died of liver complications at age fifty on April 29, 1997, but talked about his initial meeting with Johnny in an interview the previous year.

"Since blues was all Johnny liked, these local musicians thought it would be hysterical if we got together: 'Let's put these two freaks, these two mutants, together,'" said Ferguson. "Johnny flipped out; he never saw that many 78s in his life. He had records too, but I had more." Ferguson recalled being dazzled by his new friend's virtuosity and said he had to remind himself not to stare when Johnny cranked out a scorching solo in the middle of a song.

It wouldn't be long before Johnny dazzled a much wider audience.

# The Legend Begins

The year 1968 was one of tremendous turmoil and change. Martin Luther King Jr. was assassinated; and within two hours, 125 cities across the U.S went up in flames. Dr. Benjamin Spock was convicted for counseling and aiding draft evaders, and the death toll in Vietnam skyrocketed to more than 30,000 young Americans. Presidential hopeful Senator Robert Kennedy was shot to death in California, and riots broke out during the Democratic National Convention in Chicago.

The winds of change also permeated America's airwaves, as progressive FM rock stations lured listeners away from Top Forty AM stations. The Supremes and the Beach Boys were losing their stronghold on the top of the charts, while the Doors, Janis Joplin, Jimi Hendrix, and Jefferson Airplane emerged as America's answer to the British Invasion. The Rolling Stones and Cream sold millions of records covering the songs of American blues artists, and Johnny knew it was time to return to the music he loved.

He was still playing soul music six nights a week at the Act III, when Uncle John "Red" Turner, a drummer from Port Arthur, Texas, approached him about forming a blues band.

"In Port Arthur, our background was blues," said Turner. "The jukebox at the hamburger juke joint where the juvenile delinquents hung out by my house had Muddy Waters, Little Walter—all those kinds of people. We didn't know much about the Beach Boys and Pat Boone, but we knew about Muddy Waters, Little Walter, Lazy Lester, and Jimmy Reed."

Turner started on guitar in 1957, switched to bass, and was playing drums in a band called the Nightlights when he first met Johnny. "I met him in 1960," said Turner. "We crossed paths when we were sixteen and our respective bands were playing at a kids' Christmas party put on by the OCAW [Oil, Chemical, and Atomic Workers] union."

By 1968, Turner had migrated to Houston, where Johnny hired him to replace a drummer who almost cost him his gig.

"Jimmy Gillan was perpetually late, and the club owner told Johnny, 'If you're late again, you'll have to fire the drummer or I'll fire you,'" said Turner. "Sure enough, Jimmy was late and I got the job."

Johnny had mixed feelings about playing soul music because his heart was in the blues. "That's when Uncle John talked to me," he said. "Nobody had before because they weren't willing to take that cut in pay. Uncle John said we might not make much money at first but he thought it would work out in the long run."

"Johnny wanted to play blues; he just had never been in a position to be able to," said Turner. "The people in his band expected to make a living. We were the first guys that would go out on a limb with him and gamble for the future. Before that we were doing songs like 'By the Time I Get to Phoenix,' 'Lady Madonna,' 'Holiday,' 'Shadow of Your Smile'—we were a cover band."

To complete the rhythm section, Johnny and Turner traveled to Dallas to recruit Tommy Shannon, who was playing bass in a soul band. Shannon grew up in Dumas, Texas, and had moved to Dallas after he graduated from high school.

"I knew Tommy would jump at the chance," said Turner. "We were close friends and I knew he had the same desire to play blues as I did."

"I met Johnny at the Fog, at the same club where I met Stevie," said Shannon, who later played with Stevie Ray Vaughan from 1981 to his tragic death in 1990. "I was playing eight hours a night in a band called the Young Lads, making really good money. Uncle John and Johnny came in one night and Johnny sat in. I had never seen an albino before. When he got up under the lights, with that long white hair he looked like some kind of god—I was mesmerized by him. I knew I was going to be starving my ass off but I had this feeling it was the right thing to do. I quit my band and joined up."

As a blues trio, their gigs were limited to weekend nights, and Johnny's income immediately plummeted from $150 to fifty dollars a week. The band still couldn't play all blues, but worked blues into their sets, which included Top Forty songs, as well as Jimi Hendrix's "Purple Haze," "Manic Depression," and "Fire."

"Even Muddy was restricted to the amount of blues he could play on his own jobs," said Turner. "People didn't like blues. So Muddy stood in the background and acted like he was playing the guitar, and the band played a bunch of soul songs. Then Muddy did about fifteen minutes of Muddy Waters songs at the very last part of their show."

Before they played their first gig, Johnny gave Shannon a crash course in the blues.

"I didn't know anything about blues when I first started with Johnny," said Shannon. "I would look at a Cream album and see Robert Johnson and thought he was a friend of theirs. Johnny sat down with me one night and spent hours taking me all the way through the blues, from field hollers to the present. He had a wall of records and took me through his whole collection, playing and explaining each one. After that night, I understood what I was doing."

"Sometimes Johnny went through whole songs and taught Tommy the notes he wanted," said Turner. "I knew everything Johnny did because I came from the same place, so it didn't take long for all of us to create a tight musical chemistry. We were already listening to Jimi Hendrix, so it was pretty easy for all of us."

Once they got the band together, they needed a name and a gig.

"At first, we tried to call it Winter: The Progressive Blues Experiment," said Turner. "We tried to pattern ourselves after the Electric Flag: An American Music Band, a band with a subtitle. It sounds funny now, and of course it didn't work. Johnny Winter was too powerful a star. It had to be just Johnny Winter. Jimi Hendrix had the Experience, but it was just Jimi Hendrix. He could play with anybody in his band."

The first gig the band played was at a club called the Plantation.

"It was a gay bar with all these guys dancing," said Shannon. "They hated us but they liked our roadie because he was good looking."

The band's club circuit consisted of weekend gigs playing the Vulcan Gas Company in Austin, the Act III or the Love Street Light Circus in Houston, and an occasional gig in Dallas. Turner drove and booked the motel rooms, so Shannon dubbed him "Uncle John." To haul their equipment, the band pooled their money and bought a mode of transportation that turned heads wherever they went.

"We used to travel around in an old Packard hearse," said Shannon. "It was weird, but we didn't think it was weird then. Johnny would sit in the side seat behind the front seat. People would pull up at a light, look over and see a hearse, and see Johnny with pink eyes and white hair looking out. People would freak out."

The band's attire added to their mystique.

"We were pretty vain back then," said Shannon. "We'd wear whatever we could find that was really cool. I had a purple velvet Nehru shirt."

"We were ridiculous copies of English guys," said Turner. "There was a pseudo hippie joint in Houston, where we'd buy striped pants and stuff like that. We were flamboyant. We had our own cross to bear and were kind of asking for it, asking to be picked on."

Their outlandish outfits, as well as their long hair, often got them into altercations when they played rednecks bars in Texas. But Johnny didn't mind a good fight if he was provoked.

"I knocked down a guy in Dallas," says Johnny. "I was playing with Tommy and Uncle John in a club called Phantasmagoria. He said he was an off-duty detective. He was comin' out with all this anti-longhair stuff and I hit him and knocked him down with my fist. When he finally got up, the guy behind the bar—he was a friend of ours—had a big stick. He said, 'You get out and don't come back.'"

That incident left a lasting impression on Ferguson. "We used to call him the Stork," Ferguson said during an interview for the

*Dallas Observer.* "Nobody messed with him. One night he knocked out an off-duty cop for callin' him a girl. I saw Johnny Winter fight many times; he was real strong and mean. He'd go until you quit breathing and couldn't hurt him anymore."

The Vulcan Gas Company and the Love Street Light Circus attracted a mellower clientele. The band members loved the laid-back atmosphere.

Johnny remembers the Vulcan as a "hippie club" that held about 300 people and didn't have a beer or liquor license. The club, which was at 316 Congress Avenue and Third Street, catered to a younger clientele in their late teens and twenties, sold juice and other soft drinks, and charged a cover at the door. Divided into two sections, the Vulcan was comprised of a smaller room with tables and chairs and a juice bar, and a large open room with a stage at one end, a large backstage area, and an open space where people stood to watch the bands.

"The Vulcan was the first place we started playing the blues," said Shannon. "The Vulcan was the coolest club I've ever played. It was more like a family thing than a club, because I slept there a lot after the gig. Sometimes Johnny and Uncle John would go back to Houston and I'd stay and sleep in the back on floors and pool tables, whatever. Or we would all stay in one room at the Austin Motel."

Opened in October 1967, the Vulcan Gas Company was the brainchild of Houston White, Gary Scanlon, Don Hyde, and several other artists and musicians, who originally called themselves "the Electric Grandmother." The majority of the posters and handbills for the club were created by Gilbert Shelton (who later created the *Fabulous Furry Freak Brothers* comics) and Jim Franklin, a friend of Johnny's who became the Vulcan's artist in residence. Franklin later gained notoriety for *Armadillo Comics* and his posters and murals for Armadillo World Headquarters, the psychedelic club that filled the void when the Vulcan closed in the mid-1970s. He stayed in touch with Johnny over the years, traveling to Johnny's New York apartment to paint his portrait, which hangs in the South Austin Museum of Popular Culture, along with a portrait of Johnny, Shannon, and Turner painted at the Vulcan in 1970.

The creativity and camaraderie of the crew at the Vulcan Gas Company, teamed with the easy access to pot and hallucinogenic drugs, made Austin the place to be in the late 1960s.

"Austin was a virtual paradise to us," said Turner. "Hippies everywhere smoking pot, in the open, out in their backyard."

"It was *literally* paradise," added Shannon. "Smoking pot was against the law but it never stopped anybody. That was one of the cool things about it; it wasn't repressive. In the back of the Vulcan, they had this hole in the floor, a concrete cistern. We'd take acid and climb down a ladder into the cistern. Jim Franklin had all these weird Eastern instruments, and we'd get down to the bottom of the cistern and start chanting and echo, reverberate our voices off the wall."

"I had conga drums, a sitar, and some flutes," said Franklin. "It was a marvelous chamber, because you could be sitting right next to someone, and if you hit the note, it would resound off the wall. You don't hear it coming from the person; you just hear it coming from the wall."

"The Vulcan was a hippie family, and the cistern was like a hippie tearoom," added Turner. "We had great experiences."

The first time the trio experimented with LSD together, they used Timothy Leary's guidebook, *Psychedelic Experience: A Manual Based on the Tibetan Book of the Dead,* which included "instructions for an actual psychedelic session, under adequate safeguards."

"The three of us took acid together in our hotel room in Dallas," said Turner. "It was the room we always got—it had three single beds. Tommy had Timothy Leary's book, a great book to guide you through a pleasant, rewarding experience."

Although the band was having the time of their lives, they didn't have much in the way of income. Shannon and Turner crashed from place to place; Johnny shared an apartment with Carol Roma.

"Red's mother owned a beauty shop and we would practice there on the nights we weren't playing," says Johnny. "Red and Tommy were sleeping on couches, floors, at the beauty shop, friends' houses—wherever they could. I did okay because I was living with Carol."

"I slept on floors, lived at Uncle John's mother's house in Houston," said Shannon. "We were so hungry we'd go down to the fried-chicken place and eat all the fried batter they threw out."

"We really didn't have any money," said Turner. "We got paid about sixty bucks a piece a night, and Johnny got eighty dollars. We played two nights a week. And that wasn't every week. I lived on about $300 a month. We played hippie joints where if people liked what you did, you could play anything. By then, our set was all blues and Jimi Hendrix. We played just about all of Jimi's songs."

Another counterculture club that allowed the band to play blues was the Love Street Light Circus and Feel Good Machine in Houston.

"Love Street Light Circus was similar to the Vulcan Gas Company—they didn't serve beer, we made about the same money, and it was about the same size," says Johnny. "You had to walk up some stairs to get to it—stairs on the outside of the building. They had go-go girls there too. We usually went on at nine and played two hour-and-a-half sets. There was always pot and chemicals, strobe lights and lightshows. It was great!"

"I remember the Love Street Light Circus," said Shannon. "I had this big bass amp and you had to carry your equipment up four flights of stairs—it was hell getting your equipment up there. I can't believe we actually hauled that gigantic bass amp up and down those stairs. We can't even get the one we use now into the car anymore. Now if I walked up to that, I'd go, 'Fuck it, I ain't playing.' We never really thought about it back then, we just did it. That was miserable, but the club itself was cool."

Although the club had seating to the left of the stage, the floor directly in front of the stage was lined with rows of pillows with wooden headrests so patrons could lie down and watch the show, which included psychedelic images projected onto the wall.

"The whole club was rows of pillows and pads with a backstop for a headrest," said Turner. "You laid down on the floor and watched the band play. They had go-go dancers too. Diana, one of the dancers, was Johnny's girlfriend. She danced behind the screen in the corner by the band, right behind him."

"Diana was cool, but a little wigged out," added Shannon. "He made her get tattooed. By the time he got through, she was tattooed all over."

"She got a bunch of tattoos—had 'em on her chest and groin," said Turner. "A whole lot of girls would have his autograph tattooed on their ass. Once they did that, the relationship was doomed. He had conquered the girl, and that was the vanquishing ritual. For them to get a tattoo of his signature that would be on their ass for the rest of their life signified they were weak."

Although Johnny loved women and psychedelics, his burning desire was a recording contract to extend his career far beyond the reaches of Texas nightclubs. Determined to have originals for a demo tape, Johnny started writing songs that would eventually end up on *Progressive Blues Experiment.*

"I wrote 'Tribute to Muddy' where I kind of linked songs Muddy did; I tried to take credit for it, but didn't get away with it," he says with a laugh. "I wrote 'Bad Luck and Trouble' and 'Mean Town Blues.' I didn't write about any particular experiences, just life in general. I wrote 'Black Cat Bone' for that record too—a black cat bone is supposed to be good luck."

*Progressive Blues Experiment,* one of Johnny's most powerful and critically acclaimed blues releases, was recorded at the Vulcan Gas Company. Along with Johnny's originals, the band played blistering versions of blues classics by his favorite artists: Muddy Waters's "Rollin' and Tumblin'," Slim Harpo's "Got Love If You Want It," Sonny Boy Williamson II/Willie Dixon's "Help Me," Blind Willie McTell's "Broke Down Engine," B. B. King's "It's My Own Fault," and Howlin' Wolf's "Forty-Four."

Although the club was closed, Franklin projected a lightshow to set the mood and the band put on a show worthy of a full house. Bill Josey, who owned Sonobeat Records, produced and recorded the tape. Josey had approached Johnny at a club about recording for Sonobeat and signed a contract with him for one album and one single. Josey promised to pay him twenty-five cents a record, but Johnny never earned a penny on anything he recorded for Josey, including *Progressive Blues Experiment.*

"We had been playing together about a year and wanted to put out a record," says Johnny. "It took two nights to record the album, about four hours a night. It was just the band, Bill Josey, and the people who lived near the Vulcan. We used a four-track reel-to-reel recorder—and just played. I played a Fender Mustang because it had a bigger sound. For slide, I played a Gibson twelve-string with six strings on it. I strung it that way because I liked the sound. I got my first National [Resonator] guitar when I was about twenty-five and played slide on it for that record too. I like the sound of a National—it's trebly and nasty-sounding—raw. The recording technology in those days wasn't as good as it is now, but in a lot of ways I liked it better. The sound wasn't as neat and clean—it was nice and funky.

"I played mandolin on 'Bad Luck and Trouble' because it was a real country-blues instrument. I never did play electric mandolin—it was always acoustic mandolin. I still play it once in a while."

"*Progressive Blues Experiment* is still my favorite record out of all of them," said Shannon. "We just set up at the Vulcan Gas Company. We didn't go through any mikes; we had one overhead mike for the whole band. We weren't on the stage. We just put our amps in a circle in the middle of the concrete floor and played a set of songs."

The Vulcan Gas Company wasn't a blues club, but the owners hired blues artists such as Jimmy Reed, Freddie King, and Muddy Waters along with their schedule of psychedelic bands. When the club's manager booked Waters for August 2 and 3, 1968, Johnny was the opening act.

Bill Bentley, who worked in promotion/publicity for record labels and artists throughout his career, remembers that fateful night.

"Muddy's band pulled up in front of the Vulcan in a station wagon with Illinois plates," said Bentley. "When they walked into the club, they were in shorts and high argyle socks. It's so hot in Texas in August—it's at least one hundred degrees every day, some days it's 105. When they came out, they were in slick pants and silk shirts—it was too hot for them to be in coats and ties."

Thrilled to finally meet his musical hero, Johnny brought a camera to the shows and set up a small reel-to-reel tape recorder on the stage to tape Muddy's performance.

"It was great to open for him—that was the first time I ever saw him live," says Johnny. "We played every other set. We went on, Muddy went on, we came back, and Muddy played the final set. We talked a little after the show and he said he liked my music. We mostly talked about music and he asked me about my National guitar 'cause he had played one too. We didn't play together that night. I felt honored just to meet him because he had been my idol since I was eleven or twelve years old."

"Johnny was like a kid in a candy store," said Shannon. "He was right in front of the stage and had his little tape recorder playing on the stage at Muddy's feet. He was like some groupie type guy you would see at any club, standing right there in the front."

Muddy and his band were backstage when Johnny and his band played, although a band member would occasionally come out to check out the show. Even Muddy—impressed by what he heard—went to the front of the club to watch Johnny play. Muddy recalled that evening in an interview with Tom Wheeler for *Guitar Player* shortly before his death in 1983: "I said, 'That guy up there onstage—I got to see him up *close*."

Hearing and seeing Johnny was a revelation for both Muddy and Paul Oscher, who played harp in Muddy's band. Johnny's pale complexion and white hair, as well as his playing, amazed the elder bluesman.

"Muddy didn't realize albinos were white as well as black," said Oscher. "He thought Johnny Winter was probably black. Muddy thought he was a good musician and was very impressed with his slide playing. Muddy said, 'That boy can play!' or something like that. Johnny could play in Spanish tuning. 'Kind Hearted Woman.' Very few people knew how to do that at the time, at least white musicians. I hadn't seen many white musicians play Muddy's style on slide, so I thought that was pretty impressive. Johnny may have played 'Rollin' and Tumblin'' that night. Something like Muddy because Muddy said that [his playing] was pretty close to him."

Johnny also didn't fit the image of blues musicians of that era, black or white.

"A lot of white blues musicians had a hipster image—with a goatee or greased hair—kind of a jazz image," said Oscher. "When I started with Muddy's band [February 1968], you had to wear a black suit with a crossover tie—one of those ties Frank Sinatra made famous. Later Muddy bought us red Nehru jackets and white turtleneck shirts with cufflinks that we wore with black pants."

With his white hair flowing down to his collar in a Beatle haircut, dressed in an orange shirt with blue polka dots and puffy sleeves, and bell-bottom jeans, Johnny looked more like a rock musician than a bluesman.

"I thought of him as a rock guy—blues-rock," said Oscher. "There were a lot of blues guys around at that time. Magic Sam was still alive, T-Bone Walker was alive, Junior Wells, Otis Rush. The white musicians who played the blues, you could count on one hand—Paul Butterfield, Charlie Musselwhite, myself, Johnny Winter, John Hammond Jr., Mike Bloomfield. It wasn't that recognizable to be a blues musician if you were white anyway."

Bentley attended Saturday night's performance, and remembers the buzz around Austin that Johnny's Friday night performance was better than Muddy's. "I heard that on Friday night, Johnny came out and was just blasting," he said. "And Muddy came out and didn't do much of a set; he didn't really pull out the stops."

Franklin, who did the poster for that show and was there both nights, agreed. "Muddy's band and Muddy... their attitude was, 'This is a Texas Podunk town, we're just gonna clean up and get to Houston or where ever the next big-city gig was,'" said Franklin. "He's doin' 'Got My Mojo Workin'' and he's looking at his watch. Right in the middle of the song, 'I got my Mojo workin', let's see how long this Mojo got to work tonight,'" Franklin said with a laugh. "They weren't even in the house when Johnny played the first set, so they came up and did a ho-hum, routine set. They caught Johnny's second set and realized they better get serious because this guy was all over the place. So the next night, Muddy had his hair done, and they were all dressed up. It was a serious evening. One of the key points in Austin blues history."

Oscher disagrees with that scenario. "That's ridiculous," he said. "There wasn't ever any kind of a competition. Johnny Winter cannot kick Muddy Waters's ass. Period. At any time. It could have been just a crowd reaction. The band was Otis Spann, Luther 'Georgia Boy/Creepin' Snake' Johnson, Pee Wee Madison, Sammy Lawhorn—those were pretty tough cats—great musicians."

Regardless of which band put on a better performance on Friday, Saturday night's sets by both artists were phenomenal.

"Johnny was great that night," said Bentley. "He came out and was devastating; he was so good it was unbelievable. I had never heard a guy—especially a white guy—like that. It was real loud guitar but it was blues, it wasn't rock. He was playing a lot of slide, and with just a trio, the guitar totally stood out. Johnny did most of the songs from Sonobeat's *Progressive Blues Experiment* because when the record came out, I remember thinking that's pretty much the set he played that night.

"Johnny was amazing. You could tell opening for Muddy was a big thing for him and he didn't hold back at all. From the very first song, he went for it. I think he scared Muddy a little bit so Muddy really bore down and played. You could tell with Muddy it was, 'Oh, yeah, you're real good, boy, but here's how a grown man does it.' That night by Muddy Waters was the best blues I ever heard in my life."

When Johnny opened for Freddie King at the Vulcan Gas Company, he was less intimidated, and jammed with that blues legend at the end of the first night.

"Freddie King was more equals meeting," said Turner. "Freddie was more rocked out. They had a great guitar battle that night. We all jammed that night too. That's one of the beautiful things about the experience of playing with Johnny Winter. You get to play with all these people."

Psychedelics curtailed any thoughts of jamming with King the following night.

"We had Freddie King booked for two nights; the first night he played for thirty people at the most," said Franklin. "Then Johnny came in and jammed with Freddie during the second set. It was sizzling. Word got out immediately. The next night the place was crammed with people. Johnny was there, but he had taken some mescaline. We'd been doing it for several years, but it was his first time, and he would never go onstage if he was not in control. Freddie didn't know what was going on and told the audience, 'Don't go away. I'll be back with my friend Johnny.' I had to go onstage and explain Johnny is not going to play, and please don't tear the place up."

Three months after the gigs with Waters and King, Johnny decided he had waited long enough; it was time to take destiny in his own hands. With a copy of the tape he had made at the Vulcan, and an acetate LP of early songs he had recorded for Ken Ritter, he flew to England with his friend Keith Ferguson to get a record deal.

"We had already gone all around the states and it seemed like there was a better deal in England for white blues artists," Johnny says. "We went to a lot of different record companies here, though we never did try Chess or those kinds of labels because they were black labels. They didn't care about white blues artists in the States, and they did in England. There weren't any other white blues artists in the States that I knew about at that time.

"Keith was a big blues freak—he knew a lot about the blues. Keith wanted to go to England, so we went together. I had a little money saved, and Carol gave me money to go. She didn't mind me going without her—it was something she knew I had to do. So we flew out of Houston to see what it was like."

"Keith Ferguson was one of the most unique people that any of us knew," said Turner. "When I first got with Johnny, there weren't a lot of blues collectors. Keith and Johnny had blues in common—they were islands in the stream with their blues collections. They could talk about Mississippi John Hurt or Fred McDowell. I never heard of any of those people until I met Johnny and Keith."

Johnny went to England with a list of contacts from Mike Leadbitter, coeditor of *Blues Unlimited* magazine. "It was a list of people from around London—some who played blues and Chris Wellard, a guy who owned a blues record shop," Johnny says. "They were the main contacts. I met Mike Leadbitter when he came to Houston to sign some local artists to London Records. We helped Mike find out where to go and who to see during his trip to Houston.

"He was interested in black artists—he didn't even hear us I don't think. He wasn't interested in white artists at all. He had bought some of my records and was upset when he met me and found out I wasn't black. He had bought 'Creepy' and 'Gangster of Love' and thought they were good until he found out I was white. Then he didn't care about having them at all. He told me to my face, he sure did. It made me feel shitty but there wasn't anything I could do about it. It wasn't just him. A lot of people thought the same way and would say it to your face. That kind of stuff always bothered me."

Johnny and Ferguson stayed in England for two weeks, sleeping on floors, chairs, wherever they could find a place to crash. Wellard welcomed them to hang out at his record shop during the day, use it as their home base, and sleep there at night. They also spent a couple of nights in London at the home of a clerk who worked at the shop.

"I remember it was November and starting to get cold," says Johnny. "The guy had a coal furnace. I didn't know how to work a coal furnace, but I was damned sure gonna try to keep it from being cold in there. We slept in chairs in front of the coal furnace, so I learned to shovel coal in it and light it."

Johnny accomplished his main goal—to find a record label willing to produce and release a white blues artist—when he met with Mike and Richard Vernon, owners of Blue Horizon Records. Formed in January 1965, Blue Horizon Records had proven to be a very successful British blues label; it released two Fleetwood Mac albums in 1968, and had a licensing deal with Epic, a subsidiary of Columbia Records, which released their records in the U.S. and Canada. During the late '60s and early '70s, the label released dozens of blues records including albums by Elmore James, Johnny Shines, Sunnyland Slim, Earl Hooker, Lightnin' Hopkins, B. B. King, and Otis Rush. The leading producer of British blues bands in the late 1960s, Mike Vernon produced the legendary *Bluesbreakers: John*

*Mayall with Eric Clapton* LP. He also produced the Bluesbreakers' only album with Peter Green, and records by Chicken Shack, Duster Bennett, Savoy Brown, and Ten Years After.

When Johnny and Ferguson met with the Vernons, Johnny played the Vulcan Gas Company tape. He also gave them an acetate demo LP containing songs he had recorded with Ken Ritter in the early 1960s. Ironically, it was Mike Leadbitter who introduced the Vernon Brothers to Johnny's music. Mike Vernon remembered it as "fantastic, great Texas blues with strong vocals and outstanding guitar work," and immediately knew Johnny would be a great fit for his label.

"We started Blue Horizon as a British white blues label to challenge Chess and Atlantic," he said. "The world needed a blues label for more than just U.S. black R&B products. Johnny Winter was exactly the kind of U.S. act we wanted to sign."

Richard Vernon remembered the day he first heard one of Johnny's recordings.

"I was in Bexhill-on-Sea one off-season weekend—God knows why—to see him [Leadbitter]. He always seemed to know about stuff before anyone else," said Richard Vernon. "He played me the Sonobeat single 'Mean Town Blues/Rollin' and Tumblin'' and said, 'This is somebody you should sign.'

"'Is he white?' I asked. Stupid question, I guess; and from here on it gets vaguer. I remember Johnny being in the U.K. and meeting with him to discuss a deal—I think we were going to license the Sonobeat album and sign him to a deal."

Mike Vernon had a clearer recollection of his initial meeting with Johnny.

"I met Johnny in November 1968 when he and Keith Ferguson came over to discuss the realities and possibilities of Johnny recording for Blue Horizon," he said. "We may have met over lunch or dinner or at our new but shabby office/record shop in Camden Town in London. Johnny was very affable—he knew what he wanted but seemed prepared to take chances when offered if it meant taking steps forward to better things. He wanted commitment and some front money—he really wanted the opportunity to have his music heard worldwide, not just locally. [We talked about] a lease deal for the Sonobeat album and then I would produce for future Blue Horizon Records. No decision was made at that time whether such sessions would take place in the U.K. or the U.S., probably the latter."

"I had a deal; I just hadn't signed anything yet," says Johnny. "I brought the tape back home with me and was supposed to go back and record with the Vernon Brothers. I think I was gonna use my own band—I wasn't exactly sure how things were supposed to go. But I didn't have to go back to England to record because we ended up getting a big deal with Columbia in the States."

•◆•

While Johnny was meeting with the Vernon Brothers in England, *Rolling Stone* was going to press with an article that would change his life. On December 7, 1968, the counterculture music magazine ran a cover story written by Larry Sepulvado and John Burks, who traveled to the Lone Star State to report on the music scene. The main illustration, a photograph of Johnny in a formal seated pose with the caption JOHNNY WINTER, ALBINO BLUESMAN, was spread over two pages and ran beneath the "Texas" headline. Although the article mistakenly called Edgar his "identical twin brother," it gave him instant credibility with Mike Bloomfield's acknowledgement that Johnny was the "best white blues guitarist he had ever heard" and Chet Helms's description of him as "incredible." A former Texas resident, Helms had talked Janis Joplin into leaving Austin and later convinced Big Brother and the Holding Company to hire her as their singer. With credentials like these, along with his famed "Family Dog" concert and light-show productions at the Fillmore and Avalon ballrooms, Helm's opinion carried weight.

"When I got back to Texas, *Rolling Stone* had this big article that said how great I was," says Johnny. "It was everywhere—everybody read *Rolling Stone*. It called me the hottest thing in Texas outside of Janis Joplin. The reporter saw me in the Love Street Light Circus but I never knew he was there. That article was excellent; I didn't know how much it would do, but I knew it was gonna be a big help to us. It helped us get more money at the club, and I was going to New York to talk to Steve Paul, who wanted to be my manager."

Steve Paul, a twenty-seven-year-old New York entrepreneur from the Bronx ("one of the best boroughs in town") owned the Scene, a trendy nightclub in Manhattan. A former restaurant publicist with numerous contacts in the music industry, Paul was fascinated by the nightclub scene and remembered "loving and sneaking into all sorts of New York nightlife at an early age.... My concept [for the Scene] was organic, eclectic, and open minded," he said. As owner of the hippest club in New York City at a time when the rock music scene was exploding, Paul enjoyed the music and company of a wide circle of rock stars and famous musicians.

"Everybody had an amazing time, including me," he said, as he tosses off names of notable artists who frequented and jammed at his club. "Johnny Winter, Jimi Hendrix, Janis Joplin, Jim Morrison, Eric Clapton, the McCoys, the Who, the Velvet Underground, among others," he said. "How can you not like all these people, especially when they come to your club? They're all great musicians and interesting characters." The Rolling Stones, Beatles, and Led Zeppelin also frequented the Scene, and Paul considered Johnny "equal to the best of them."

Before Johnny met with Paul, he and his band flew to San Francisco to talk to record executives at Mercury Records. Texas native Doug Sahm, founder of the Sir Douglas Quintet, whose single "She's About a Mover" on Mercury Records reached thirteen on the charts, set up the meeting.

"Doug Sahm got Mercury Records to pay our way to San Francisco," said Turner. "The *Rolling Stone* article came out at the same time. Record labels were calling our hotel room from the East Coast saying don't sign anything yet—give us a chance. I don't know how they knew we were in San Francisco. I guess the word got out."

Also in relentless pursuit, Paul who had talked to Johnny for hours on the payphone at the Vulcan Gas Company, left phone messages at Johnny's parents' house, and tracked him across the country. "I was really into blues and great players and Johnny seemed like an exciting and colorful musician, which indeed he is," said Paul.

"When I went to California, he called me at every place I was there," Johnny says. "I don't know how he got my number. He'd call me at restaurants, everywhere. I thought he was kind of an idiot. I wasn't sure if I believed him or not. Believed he really was who he said he was."

Johnny and company stayed on the West Coast for several weeks. Mercury Records arranged for them to play a Tuesday night audition at the Fillmore and a gig at the Matrix, a small, hip club near North Beach.

"The Matrix was owned by Grace Slick's husband," said Turner. "Jerry Garcia was there; he was part owner. It was a club like the Scene, although it was nowhere as big or as cool. But it was a cool place to play; there were a lot of record people there."

Although Mercury Records offered Johnny a lucrative deal, the label wanted artistic control, something Johnny was determined not to give up. He returned to Texas to see what Paul had to offer.

"Steve Paul looked up my number in the phone book and called me when he flew in to Houston," says Johnny. "He came to my house. I thought he was kinda crazy; he saw us but he never said he liked us or not. We couldn't figure out why he was so excited about signing us if he didn't have any feelings for us. It was very strange that he never said he liked us."

Paul may not have told Johnny he liked the band, but considered that meeting "exciting and enjoyable" and on a personal level, found Johnny to be "really smart, funny, and enjoyable to be with." Nevertheless, Johnny doesn't think that goodwill ever extended to the rest of the band.

"Later on I found out he didn't like Tommy or Uncle John at all," says Johnny. "He didn't think they were as good musically as they needed to be, but he didn't say anything about that for a good while. He waited. He never did have opinions of his own. He would ask his friends what their opinions were and he'd get enough opinions in one direction and that would be his decision. He was real strange about that."

Despite Paul's comments that he loved the blues and blues artists—Muddy Waters was the first recording artist he hired to play at the Scene—Johnny believes he only embraced the genre because it was trendy in the late '60s.

"Steve Paul wasn't into blues—not particularly. He just knew blues was very popular at the time. He was a New Yorker, a fast talker. He wasn't like anybody I ever knew. He never seemed to have a thing for girls—he never liked guys either. We couldn't figure out what he was, but he just didn't go for either sex. He didn't want us to know—I guess he felt we would be down on him if he told us he was gay, so he didn't tell us.

"He said, 'Let's go to New York and I'll show you what I can do.' And he did. I stayed at his house and he took me to the Fillmore to see Mike Bloomfield and Al Kooper. I sat in with them and played 'It's My Own Fault,' and blew everybody away. The crowd gave me a standing ovation. They just flipped out completely. They'd seen all the stuff in *Rolling Stone* and were waitin' to see what I was like. Everybody wanted to sign me up after that. Steve didn't make me sign until after he had gotten a deal with Columbia—I had already signed with Columbia when I signed a management deal with him. He had owned the Scene for several years when I met him. It was a big club on Forty-Sixth and Eighth Avenue, a basement club under a dirty bookstore. I played a lot at the Scene and played with a lot of people there including Jimi Hendrix."

"Steve Paul was a cool person," said Turner. "A brilliant, fast-thinking New Yorker, he hung with the Warhol crowd. Steve Paul delivered the $600,000 deal. He got the money and he also brought Johnny to New York to his club and got him to jam with Jimi Hendrix. In our mind, this guy was powerful."

"Being a hick from Texas, I didn't know what to think of Steve Paul," said Shannon. "I'd never seen a New York Jewish guy before. It was weird how it happened. One night, Uncle John and I were sleeping on the floor with our clothes in footlockers. The next day, we fly into the airport, where there were two beautiful girls waiting on us. We went from there to some mansions in upstate New York. We went from sleeping on the floor to living in mansions overnight."

Shannon also had another experience in New York he had never encountered in Texas.

"When we first moved to New York, there was a black guy named Jason who was supposed to be our valet," said Shannon. "He was gay and fell in love with me. I was so dumb, I had no idea. One night, we went out and ate with a big group of people. He came over and sat in my lap, and I still didn't get it. Everybody started laughing and I couldn't figure it out. Someone had to tell me he was gay. After that it was like, 'Get away from me, man!'"

Steve Paul enjoyed traveling with an entourage. Whether the initial destination was a restaurant, a concert, or a Broadway play, the group always ended up at his nightclub. He had opened the Scene just off of Manhattan's theatre district in 1964. The blue-canopied basement club quickly became the place to see and be seen. Tiny Tim of "Tip-Toe Thru the Tulips with Me" fame got his first break at the Scene in 1965 when Paul hired him, and he soon earned the title of House Freak. The Scene was also a spawning ground for up-and-coming musicians and the place where legendary players always stopped by for the good-looking groupies and impromptu jams.

"There was always a line outside the Scene and lots of celebrities," says Johnny. "Jimi Hendrix and all of the English bands who came to New York—once they left their gigs, they came to jam. It was a real well known place for rock 'n' roll people. There was everything in the Scene in 1968—heroin and cocaine, speed, ups, downs, grass. They pretty much did it in the open and nobody cared."

Turner and Shannon were also dazzled by the Scene and the musicians the club attracted.

"All the people at the Scene were famous," said Turner. "Rod Stewart, Joe Cocker. One of the first times we went there Jerry Lee Lewis played."

"The first time I went to the Scene I couldn't believe it," said Shannon. "Jimi Hendrix and Rod Stewart were there, as well as the most beautiful girls you can imagine. You have to remember, we were hicks from Texas. I couldn't believe Jimi Hendrix was sitting over there, Jerry Lee Lewis was there—any night of the week, you would go in and there'd be great musicians. I played with all the great guitar players just about . . . Eric Clapton, Jeff Beck, Muddy

Waters, and all the Kings [Albert, Freddie, B. B.], just about all the great guitar players except Jimi Hendrix."

Early in their careers, Jimi Hendrix, the Doors, the Rascals, Blood, Sweat & Tears, and the Chambers Brothers performed at the club, which was known for its horrible ventilation, deafening acoustics, and laissez-faire attitude. Raven, a Buffalo-based rock/blues/jazz band that relocated to New York City, played there regularly, and was the backdrop for Johnny to dazzle new audiences with his mastery of the guitar. Other house bands included the McCoys; Free Spirits, a jazz-rock band with Larry Coryell and Jim Pepper; and Players, which featured Dan Armstrong, the studio session guitarist and luthier who invented the clear Plexiglas guitar. Patrons witnessed musical history in the making at amazing jams by Janis Joplin and Eric Burdon; Tiny Tim and the Doors; Richie Havens and Joan Baez; Jimmy Page and Jeff Beck; Hendrix and B. B. King; the Monkees and Frank Zappa; Hendrix and Jim Morrison; and Hendrix and Johnny Winter.

•◆•

The excitement and success of that nightclub attracted more than just celebrities, musicians, and groupies. A local thug named Junior—purported to be a member of organized crime—demanded a cut of the club's income. When Paul and the club's manager Teddy Slatus, who later became Johnny's manager, refused, Junior retaliated with a show of force. In late August 1969, he planted a number of thugs in the club and staged a fight that started a brawl and injured a number of patrons. An off-duty detective celebrating his wedding anniversary used the office phone to call police. Police arrived and made several arrests, but not in time to save Slatus from a brutal beating. Slatus, who left the club alone when he locked up at 4 AM each morning, refused to testify against the wise guys. The club never reopened after that fateful night, but before it closed its doors forever, it played a pivotal role in Johnny's career.

After Johnny captivated New York by sitting in with Bloomfield and Kooper at the Fillmore East and jamming with Hendrix at the Scene, Paul announced that sealed bids would be accepted from four record companies: RCA Victor, Columbia, Elektra, and Atlantic. The competition flamed the fires of desire. Johnny continued to play his heart out and let Paul handle negotiations with record executives who flocked to the Scene to check out this amazing new talent. Columbia won the bidding war with what Columbia president Clive Davis called the "largest amount ever given to a new performer in Columbia's history."

"There was a bidding war between Jerry Wexler at Atlantic and Clive Davis before I signed with Columbia in February 1969," says Johnny. "They were the two big name bidders. The Columbia deal was $600,000 over a period of five years—I had to do two albums a year. They said it was the highest advance in history but I don't think it really was. We only got $50,000 at a time for each record we put out. We ended up not making two albums a year—we made one album a year. It came out to just about $600,000 over a long period—about ten years."

Danny Fields, who managed the MC5, the Stooges, the Ramones, Steve Forbert, and Jonathan Richman, was an influential figure on the New York and Detroit underground punk music scenes during the 1960s and 1970s. As a member of Warhol's social circle, he frequented the Scene and traveled in the same crowd as Paul. Fields offered insight into Paul during an interview with Paul Trynka for the biography *Iggy Pop: Open Up and Bleed.*

"Steve was very smart and very canny and had been in show business since he was fourteen," said Fielding. "He seemed to be in everything. He ran poker games at hotels. He was a publicist for the Peppermint Lounge and he was in the real early sixties Mister New York Highlife and the Scene was *the* scene. Jimi Hendrix was there every night. He's a character. Steve Paul could construct a visionary, a tableau of the timeline of the future and he was going to change Johnny and Edgar and do the first albino brother act in history and all this worked out. He didn't give any of the other supporting players [a chance] to express themselves or become themselves. He's got the scenario, and here's the script, and this is what will happen.

"That was the strategy with Johnny from the beginning. They thought they would get a buzz going and then he would get some figures tossed around. I think he wanted $600,000 for signing him, which in '69 was a lot of money for a blues guitar player. . . . Steve had such a hype going that it was dominated by the price; the amount of money had been broadcast in the industry. He broadcast the asking price for Johnny Winter as if that was evidence of his work. In other words, 'I won't start under $50,000 or $75,000 upon signing.' And everyone is supposed to go, 'Whoa! They must really be fabulous!'

"He suckered Clive into doing it because he's so persuasive and so eloquent, visionary and brilliant, and has incredible linguistic skills. That's why anyone calling him a fool is one. He may have done or be doing foolish things, but he ain't no fool. He's like a Jewish James Joyce when he gets on a roll. He's formidable and the domitability of him is that if you want to shut him up. 'Here's $600,000; I have someone else waiting to see me.' 'Thanks, Clive, you won't be sorry.'"

Paul invested "a fair amount" of time and money into building Johnny's career. The cost of limos, housing, hotels, food, and traveling with an entourage was substantial. Johnny's income was deposited into a corporate account. Paul paid expenses and the band drew a salary. Although Johnny initially earned up to $10,000 a performance, he and his band members received one hundred dollars a week.

"We just drew money off the corporation," said Turner. "I didn't think much about it. At the time, it was enough money to get along. They paid our room and board; everything was paid for. That one hundred dollars was spending money for drinks and clothes, and we spent plenty on both."

"We got nothing out of the advance," said Shannon. "We got one hundred dollars a week; it was like a salary. We did the same thing with Stevie [Ray Vaughan] except we were drawing $1,750 a month. Expenses were paid; we paid for clothes, amplifiers. A girl I met named Eleanor took me out and helped me buy all these cool clothes—velvet bellbottoms, really cool shirts, shades . . . she got me looking like a rock star."

"I always let Steve handle the business end because he knew more about it than I did," says Johnny. "It's not that I didn't care about money at all—it's something you have to be aware of—but it wasn't the main part of it. Music was the main thing. Having more money didn't affect me very much. I just got to get the things I wanted—it was nice in that way. I could buy all the records I wanted. But then you had to take care of your money—that was hard because you had to trust your accountant. Accountants you could trust were hard to find. In that way, it was hard to make it [be successful], keep the money coming in right, and have somebody to take care of it.

"When I got the deal, I moved to New York with Red and Tommy. We all lived in a house in Staatsburg, New York, close to Rhinebeck. Five minutes from Poughkeepsie, about a hundred miles out of New York City. It was a lot cheaper to live in Staatsburg than living in the city. When we stayed in the city, we stayed at the Chelsea Hotel."

Located at 222 West Twenty-Third Street and officially called "Hotel Chelsea," the Chelsea Hotel attracted writers, visual artists, musicians, actors, and film directors. Famous residents included Robert Mapplethorpe, Arthur Miller, Joni Mitchell (who wrote "Chelsea Morning" while staying there), Jimi Hendrix, Janis Joplin, Patti Smith, Leonard Cohen, Bob Dylan, Tom Wolfe, William Burroughs, Tennessee Williams, and members of Andy Warhol's circle, including model Edie Sedgwick, Ultra Violet, and Viva. *The Chelsea Girls*, Warhol's 1966 film about his Factory regulars and their lives at the hotel, was shot on location.

"I loved the Chelsea Hotel because when you walked in, there were girls sitting around and you'd say, 'Do you want to come up to my room?' and they would go up with you," said Shannon. "There were always bands rehearsing on one floor, and other bands on another floor. It wasn't a typical hotel; it was a real rock 'n' roll–type hotel. Whenever we came to New York City we would stay there. We stayed there two weeks one time... Uncle John and I shared a room."

"When we started going into New York City, we stayed here and there—nicer places," said Turner. "But pretty soon we learned that the Chelsea Hotel was the place for us to stay. It was run down but it was a musicians' paradise. I remember seeing Jefferson Airplane there. The people in the Chelsea Hotel catered to artists and musicians. The bellhop had everything you wanted. He'd take you up to your room and ask you if you needed anything. He meant pills, drugs, alcohol, and women."

Shortly after the move to New York, the band went into the studio to cut their first album. Before signing with Columbia, Johnny insisted on two prerequisites.

"I made sure the band went with me and I had total creative control," says Johnny. "That meant I could do anything I wanted to do with the record—pick the songs, do the recording, and the producing."

*Johnny Winter*, released on April 15, 1969, is a seminal blues recording with appearances by legendary bluesmen Willie Dixon on bass and Walter "Big Walter" Horton on harmonica, as well as Edgar on horns and piano.

"It took several months to do that record," Johnny says. "I picked Columbia's Nashville studio because it was more laid back than New York."

"We did it in Nashville because, according to Steve Paul, the New York scene had too many restrictions on working situations in the studio," said Turner. "The union was heavy in New York. They would only work a certain amount of hours or they got paid double time. Steve Paul always saw angles."

"I wanted to make an album that Johnny would believe in, and hopefully would introduce him for the fine musician and great artist he is," said Paul. "Nashville was free from New York distraction and we could concentrate totally on the recording and good chicken and biscuits. It's also a very musical town, which Johnny and I had respect for. Eddie Kramer [who was credited as production consultant] is a great engineer, producer, and photographer, and helped us make a good record."

The craft of songwriting doesn't come easy to Johnny, but Paul encouraged him to write several for *Johnny Winter*. "I usually can't write enough songs for a whole record—I usually write two or three songs," Johnny says. "I wrote 'I'm Yours and I'm Hers,' 'Back Door Friend,' 'Leland Mississippi Blues,' and I wrote 'Dallas' from my experiences there with Red and Tommy."

Johnny was referring to the gig at the Phantasmagoria in Dallas, but Turner remembered another incident that made Johnny reluctant to play that town.

"Our second job in the world was in Dallas," Turner said. "Me and Tommy had been playing at the club for a year or two before that. Our tradition was to go out and eat at the same restaurant after the gig, so we brought Johnny with us. It was his first time there. I remember coming back from the bathroom and seeing Johnny with his back up to the wall and his feet up, defending himself against two rednecks who decided to attack him. They were fighting but there wasn't a lot of leg room in the booth, so he was between the wall and the booth with his feet up kicking. For a long time Johnny just thought Dallas was a big redneck place."

Johnny played a Fender Mustang on *Johnny Winter*, and was thrilled to perform a song with Dixon and Horton on that recording. "Willie Dixon played acoustic bass on 'Mean Mistreater,'" says Johnny. "Big Walter Horton played on that song too. We had a hard time getting just one cut out of him. He was interested in playing with a water glass and I hated it. He'd move the glass around in front of the harmonica to make a vibrato. I had never seen anybody do that and I hope I never see anybody else do it either. It's terrible. He wouldn't let me record anything more than once, so we had to keep on coming up with different songs for him to play on. Finally he got tired of playing with a glass and we got through 'Mean Mistreater' with him playing okay. He laid down one real good track and we were happy to get one track out of him. Edgar played piano on one track and horns on another. *Johnny Winter* sold a couple of hundred thousand copies. For a first record, that was pretty good."

"Willie Dixon spent his time sort of hustling Johnny," said Turner. "He spent most of the time trying to sell Johnny some more of his songs. He had a whole briefcase full of songs, trying to get Johnny to do some of them. Walter 'Shakey' Horton was an ornery old dude; we finally had to do whatever he wanted to do. He wanted to use a glass like a wah-wah pedal on his harmonica. Of course, we didn't want that. We wanted him in his blues glory. Eventually we had to get him to start a song and play along with it."

Shannon missed a take at that session and Johnny's offhand remark about it became part of the album. "Right before 'Leland Mississippi Blues,' Johnny says to me, 'Don't mess up, Slut, and I won't either,'" said Shannon. "Slut was my nickname, and I screwed up the take before that, so he said, 'Don't mess up, 'Slut.'"

Steve Paul is credited on the liner notes of that album (and several others) as "Spiritual Producer." In a decade that extolled the virtues of peace, love, freedom, and happiness, Paul said it seemed appropriate at the time, but it never made sense to Johnny, who produced the LP.

"That was his thing," says Johnny. "He wanted to be a spiritual producer. He wasn't a spiritual person but he thought he was. I just wanted him to put manager because that's what he was; he wasn't a spiritual producer."

"Spiritual producer is the name he gave himself," added Shannon. "He was the furthest thing from spiritual I have ever seen."

Spirituality didn't appear to be a guiding force for *any* of Johnny's former managers and producers. After the glut of publicity that resulted from his deal with Columbia Records, his past came back to haunt him. Josey had kept a copy of the Vulcan Gas Company tapes, and had already pressed several hundred records on his own label. In fall 1968, he began selling *Progressive Blues Experiment* in a plain white jacket for six dollars a copy at Phil's Record Shop on West Twenty-Fourth Street in Austin. By the time the ink had dried on Johnny's Columbia contract, Josey sold the LP to United Artists, which released it on Imperial with the same title and a distinctive Burton Wilson cover shot of Johnny wearing a cream-colored satin Nehru shirt and love beads, staring at his reflection in the back of his National guitar.

According to Wilson, when Josey hired him, he specifically asked for a series of standard promotion shots against a seamless white paper with Johnny in "various hippie costumes" with his guitar. Johnny brought four or five outfits to the shoot and as many guitars. Wilson shot several rolls of film following Josey's directive, but when Johnny picked up his National guitar, he became creative.

"With only one exposure left in my camera, I decided to do my own thing," he said in *The Austin Music Scene Through the Lens of Burton Wilson*, an impressive book of music photography that spans three decades. "I asked him to hold it so his face reflected on the back of the guitar and I snapped the photo." Josey sold all of Wilson's photographs to United Artists; the label used four additional photos on the back cover.

The release of *Progressive Blues Experiment* came as a complete surprise to Johnny. "I didn't know the record was coming out and didn't have much say about it, but they left it pretty much the way I recorded it," he says. "I never made a penny off of it. How they got away with that, I don't know, but they did. Bill Josey had the tapes and he got the money. Even now when they sell that CD, I don't get any money. I was used to that. When I talked to a lawyer, he said it wouldn't be worth pursuing."

Prior to that, the band didn't have any reason to distrust Josey, so were taken aback by the release of the LP. "We broke down one time, and Bill Josey came sixty miles out of town to get us so we thought he was pretty nice," said Turner. "But he was not a nice guy—he stole money from us. As the publicity came out on the first Columbia record, he took advantage of that by releasing it to Imperial/United Artists. That hurt us because we had a record on the charts at number twenty-four and another record on the charts at number fifty-two—both at the same time. We felt that if Bill Josey hadn't done that, we would have busted the Top Ten on the *Johnny Winter* record. Bill Josey took advantage of us—he never paid us anything, and he put his record out and used the CBS/Columbia advertising campaign to his advantage. Today, I play that record and like it a lot, but was disappointed at the time at how he did it."

Josey was the least of Johnny's worries. Roy Ames—who managed him during his early years in Texas and haunted him throughout his career—sold his three-year-old recording contract with Johnny to Atlantic Records. Atlantic had lost in the bidding war, but now claimed it, and not Columbia, had Johnny under an exclusive and valid recording contract. According to reports never confirmed by Atlantic President Ahmet Ertegun and Vice President Jerry Wexler, the label paid $50,000 for the contract. Ames sweetened the pot by including enough old masters and tapes for two "vintage" Johnny Winter LPs.

"I worked with Roy Ames right before I went to New York," says Johnny. "He was my manager but he never got anything done as far as my career; he just got a percentage of the records. Roy was also a pornographic artist—he took pictures of little boys to sell to perverts. He did that all the time, even when he was doing records. I don't think he ever stopped taking pictures. We recorded some songs for Roy but never made a penny. He said he was putting too much money into promotion and wasn't recouping enough back. And he said he wasn't making any money off our royalties. I talked to a lawyer about him too, but he said you couldn't do anything about it."

Meanwhile, Ken Ritter, another one of Johnny's early managers, jumped on the bandwagon and tried to make money off of Johnny's newfound celebrity.

"When Johnny started making it big, Ken Ritter, who was the mayor of Beaumont, had his old contract, which was about four or five pages long and had Johnny's signature on the last page," said Turner. "He took the staples out of the contract, typed up a new contract, kept the back page, put the staples back in, and sued Johnny for breach of contract. Johnny talked to his New York lawyers about the possible potential of a lawsuit. They told him Ken was Tex Ritter's nephew, the mayor of Beaumont, and you're just a longhair hippie. You won't have a chance—don't even think about it—we're not interested. There wasn't anything he could do about it; if he tried, he would have lost. That's pretty high handed, though, to take the staples out and forge a contract. And the back page was decidedly more yellow than the ones on top of it."

As Johnny's star continued to rise, he discovered fame had many drawbacks. He soon found out friendship and a private life doesn't come easy to artists living in the spotlight. The more successful he became, the more people demanded and expected.

"People started to know who I was as soon as I came up to New York and started playing at the Scene regularly," he said. "We played a lot of festivals that summer, which helped to make me fairly big. Being a celebrity was real different. I guess I did like it because we had tried to make it for a long time. There were some things I didn't like about it, but I'd been trying to get there for so long, I wasn't gonna admit I didn't like it. For a while I did like it, but I ended up hatin' it. People liked you because you were famous and not because you were a nice guy or anything like that. You couldn't trust anybody. You didn't even have a chance to get to know anybody—everybody wanted something. I didn't feel like I had any friends anymore. It was no fun at all."

Johnny's celebrity and the ongoing publicity about his "record-breaking" advance affected the way critics and even some fans perceived him. Journalists called him the "Great White Hype" and enjoyed trashing the man who appeared to be an overnight success rolling in money.

"People like you on the way up and don't like you when you've made it—that's what it seemed like to me," says Johnny. "Once you make it, people expected more beyond what you could come across with. Getting good reviews was easy when I just started and it got harder. They expected more of me. I couldn't imagine having too much publicity because before I had none. But obviously it wasn't a good thing because it hurt us.

"I read the bad reviews but it didn't affect my playing. Then there were good reviews that only mentioned me and didn't say anything good about Red and Tommy. That made them feel bad because they were working as hard as they could and nobody was saying anything good about them."

•◆•

One of the perks of fame that Johnny loved was meeting and jamming with Jimi Hendrix, who he, Shannon, and Turner had seen in Houston and whose songs they had been playing in Texas bars not too long ago.

"We first saw Jimi Hendrix at the Music Hall—it was about a 2,500-seat auditorium in Houston," said Turner. "Then we saw him when he came back and played a bigger gig at the Houston Coliseum."

"I remember that concert," said Shannon. "I was so mesmerized. I couldn't take my eyes off Jimi—he was like a god. I remember Johnny sitting there saying, 'Nobody can be that good.' He kept saying that over and over—'Nobody can be that good.'"

Despite his initial reaction to Hendrix's virtuosity, when Johnny met him in New York, he knew he had to play with him.

"I don't remember when I first met Jimi, but I went up to him and asked if he wanted to jam," says Johnny. "We got together at the Scene and I remember being a little intimidated. I jammed with him at the Experience in L.A. one night too—we both happened to be there."

Hendrix's favorite after-hours spot for jamming was the Record Plant, a recording studio that opened in New York in 1968. Hendrix recorded *Electric Ladyland* at the studio's first session. A premiere studio with a living-room ambiance and what was then cutting-edge twelve-track equipment, the Record Plant's early client list also included Frank Zappa, Buddy Miles, Velvet Underground, Traffic, and Vanilla Fudge. Johnny and Jimi got together for a jam there one night. In 1990, more than two decades later, Reprise released *Lifelines*, a Hendrix box set that included "The Things That I Used to Do," a song they recorded during that late night jam.

"After he jammed at the Scene, he'd get a few people together to go over and record," recalls Johnny. "So I went with him to the Record Plant and played on some songs. He did it a lot. I think he had time booked late at night so if he wanted to play, he could. The Scene usually closed at four and the jams in the Record Plant would go to five or six in the morning.

"He wasn't messed up all the time, but he was high—he took acid and that affected his playing I'm sure. He'd tape everything and listen to it the next day. I usually gave him the reins pretty much—I mostly played rhythm. But on the song we recorded, 'The Things That I Used to Do,' we traded off—I played slide guitar and he played regular guitar. It came out real well. I believe that was the only song that was recorded. I played with him about ten times maybe and thought he was the best guitar player around. I didn't really know him as a person because he was high most of the time. He was hard to talk to; he didn't talk about a whole lot."

Dallas Taylor and Stephen Stills also played on "The Things That I Used to Do." Although Johnny knew the recording existed, he didn't know if and when it would ever be officially released.

"I was glad it came out because there was a record out that everybody said was us, but it wasn't," he said. "'I Woke Up This Morning and Found Myself Dead' was a jam recorded at the Scene [in March 1968] with Jimi and Jim Morrison and me supposedly—but it wasn't me. Jim was just screaming, "Oh yeah, oh yeah," and that was about it. He was drunk and it was a real mess. I didn't play with him; I never even met Jim Morrison. It really worried me that they had that record out and said I was on it when I wasn't. So I was glad to see something come out that was decent."

# The High Price of Celebrity

Johnny's success, which mirrored the rise of Hendrix's career, cast the band members, and especially Johnny, into a perpetual spotlight. Steve Paul generated phenomenal press coverage including cover or feature stories in *Rolling Stone, Look Magazine, Time, Circus, Downbeat, Hit Parader, Creem, Melody Maker, New Musical Express*, and the *New York Times*. Achieving celebrity status so quickly was a major adjustment.

"Becoming celebrities was a big deal to us," said Turner. "I adapted by being humble, learning, and listening. Steve Paul was hanging around with the Warhol crowd and was a guru to us and the New York City scene. He guided us by his own actions and gestures. After we grew our hair long, we started wearing pretty wild clothes, psychedelic stuff, striped pants, two-tone pants with two different colors, scarves around our necks, Beatle boots. We were discreetly following the Rolling Stones, Jimi Hendrix, and the Who. Then we slowly evolved into something reasonable."

"It was hard for me at first," said Shannon. "I still had that hick-from-Texas feeling and then started getting treated totally different, which I really liked. The first year in New York, I became a rock star and started getting respect from these other cool musicians. I felt lonely, oh sure. It's a nasty business, it really is. You do not know who you can trust. People come up to you as nice and helpful as possible and then turn around and screw you. You honestly do not know who to trust, except each other.

"Johnny took the overnight-celebrity thing real well; he knew what we had to do and he did it," added Shannon. "At the same time, it was difficult for him because he had never been through anything like that. All of sudden, being up there in front of thousands of people almost overnight; that's how fast Steve Paul was. So, he had difficulties. Johnny was self-conscious over being an albino. Growing up he caught so much shit over that—that was still with him when he got older."

"Johnny was already such an oddity and had been one all his life," said Turner. "Being applauded made it worse, because he was always standing outside of everything and looking in. Yet, he had the confidence of knowing he was that good, that he could go out there on any given night and create a lot of excitement."

Johnny's sudden celebrity status mirrored the dichotomy he had discovered during his childhood research on how albinos were treated in different cultures.

"I'd been born a reject and suddenly I was worshipped as a god," Johnny told a *Rock* magazine reporter in 1973. "If I wasn't worshipped, I was hated by jealous people. Both attitudes pissed me off. Either way, I felt left out, lonesome. I couldn't handle it."

As the star and more easily recognizable member of the band, Johnny was constantly followed by throngs of fans, which made it difficult to lead a normal life. He found that aspect of hero worship unnerving.

"It was very strange," says Johnny. "Wherever I went was a drag. Restaurants—you couldn't eat without somebody comin' over to you. I'd stay at the Chelsea Hotel and if I tried to walk down Twenty-Second Street, people would come up to me all the time. They'd follow me when I went shoppin' for clothes; they'd follow me everyplace. It made it harder to go to a concert or club. If I went out, there would be a whole bunch of people comin' over and tryin' to talk to you. Asking for guitar picks, autographs, whatever, a lock of your hair. It made it impossible for me to see a band. I'd try to talk to as many people as I could without it making me crazy.

I didn't feel comfortable telling them to leave—sometimes I did, but I never did feel comfortable doing it. Steve Paul never did anything about it; he was probably scared somebody would knock him in the head. After a while, I just quit going places. It was a drag but it was the only way I could deal with it.

"People would try to take my hats, grab picks off my hand—I got a lot of that when I was onstage. I'd reach out to hold somebody's hand and they'd try to grab my thumb pick. Girls came up with scissors to get a clip of my hair. It made it hard for me—I stayed home a lot. But I wanted to be famous and did everything I could to get there and had to put up with the shitty things about it. I didn't know it was gonna be as bad as it was, though."

Friendships are a rare commodity for celebrities, who are surrounded by sycophants and self-serving hangers-on with ulterior motives. Then there are the star struck fans that can't get past their celebrity status. Fans by their very nature have an idealized image of celebrities, and never view or relate to them as real people. It makes most encounters very one-sided.

"You didn't get a chance to know anybody because they wanted to know about you," says Johnny. "They wanted to just deal with me and what was going on with me at the time; you didn't really feel like you could be friends with anybody. They say, 'How long you been playing guitar?' 'How'd you like playin' here?' 'How'd you like playin' there?' Just bullshit. It's hard to have real friends when you're famous because people don't really get to know you. They think they know you real good, but they don't. It's hard to convince them that you're not what they think you are. Sometimes you don't care, but sometimes it's important."

For many fans, an opportunity to meet Johnny backstage after a concert was a memorable event, so they came bearing gifts.

"People gave me presents," says Johnny. "Oh, hell, all kind of presents—religious statues, guitar straps, tee shirts, flowers. I liked that. But if they met you at a festival when you met one hundred people, they'd think you should remember them the next time they see you. 'I'd say, 'I don't remember you.' 'Well, you met me down at this certain festival.' 'Well, I met one hundred people at that festival—I don't really remember you.' Sometimes it would bother them but I couldn't help it."

Johnny's celebrity attracted scores of women who wanted to bed a rock star, no matter who he was. The anonymous nature of those encounters didn't faze him.

"That didn't bother me," he says with a laugh. "I figured we were both gettin' what we wanted out of the deal. I got plenty of women wantin' to go to bed with me, and I liked that. It wasn't any big deal. I always liked a lot of girls. That probably had something to do with me getting into music; it made people like me. Most of the people I went with weren't groupies. I've been out with a few groupies, but not many. I was afraid of gettin' the clap. I had the clap so many times; I tried to stay away from people who were all over the place."

Johnny was living with Carol Roma while enjoying the sexual perks of stardom, but their relationship was never a deterrent. "I was lucky enough that I was living with people when I was goin' with groupies too," he says. "Carol knew I was goin' with other people and it was just one of those things. I told her I couldn't stand being married again. She had to put up with it or go away. I think she minded but there wasn't anything she could do about it. She could have done the same thing to me, but I would have broken up with her."

•◆•

Drugs have always been an integral part of the music scene, but in the '60s and '70s, marijuana and psychedelic drugs made their way into popular culture. Tim Leary told America to "Turn On, Tune In, and Drop Out"; and the rock musical *Hair* celebrated pot, hashish, opium, and LSD. Cheech and Chong built a career on drug humor, and head-shop owners made a fortune selling drug paraphernalia—from roach clips to bongs, hash pipes to flavored rolling papers—in cities across the country. Sharing drugs created instant camaraderie, even with strangers.

"Lots of people would offer me drugs, and I'd take them," says Johnny. "It was the only way they could show me they liked me.

Back in the '60s and early '70s, everybody was doin' drugs—psychedelics mostly. LSD and mescaline; I did everything. With acid, you never knew what it was and it got to be more speed than anything else. I hated speed. I liked mescaline and psilocybin mushrooms; they give you a nice high without makin' you nervous or jittery like speed did. Mescaline was more under control than acid, not as intense. Mushrooms were the smoothest. I did 'em a couple times a week. We would take mushrooms up at our house in Staatsburg with friends, at the clubs, and our shows. There were a lot of people around those places and they always had drugs."

At a press party in L.A., an anonymous stranger upped the ante by giving Johnny his first bag of heroin. It marked the beginning of a phase of escalating drug use that almost destroyed him and his career.

"Somebody out of the crowd asked me what drugs I liked and if I ever tried heroin," recalls Johnny. "I said, 'No,' and he said, 'Here's some if you ever feel like tryin' it.' I carried it around with me for several months before we did it. I waited because I wasn't sure about it—it wasn't something I wanted to do."

Johnny snorted his first hit of heroin before a gig in New Jersey. The band's equipment hadn't arrived and he was worried about not being able to play.

"Once I did it, I wasn't worried anymore and I felt good," Johnny says. "At first, I did it just to get high. I snorted it—maybe every week—for a long time. It cost ten or twenty bucks for a hit and you stayed high for a couple of hours. Sometimes you got sick and threw up afterward. I got it from a lot of different people. Some people gave it to me but not too many. They gave it to you free to get you hooked. After you got to where they knew you wanted it pretty bad, they upped the price on it. I snorted it for about a year before I started shooting it. I had no problem getting needles; you could buy needles in Texas at the drugstore. Red and Tommy started taking it same time I did. They pretty much did it whenever I did it. Both of them got to be addicts too."

Shannon says he never got deeply involved in heroin when Johnny did, but still has vivid memories of his first time. "I got real sick, threw up, and had to lie down on my bed," he said.

In a 1999 interview with the British edition of *GQ*, Keith Richards said he used heroin early in his career to isolate himself from the demands that came from being a celebrity. He compared it to a cocoon he could hide in, which provided a buffer from the outside world. Johnny felt the same way.

"Heroin definitely was something you could hide in," he says. "When you wanted to talk to somebody about drugs, they didn't care who you were, they just were sellin' heroin to another guy. Who you were wasn't important; you were just another addict. It made you forget everything—that's what was good about it. You're not nervous about anything; you're not bugged about things that normally bother you. You're off in your own little world. It's a lot better than downs. With downs, you might play real bad because you're wiped out. With heroin, unless you do too much of it, it makes you relaxed without being tired, without being downed out where you're gonna play bad.

"A lot of artists are high on heroin when they play. After a while, you developed a tolerance and didn't stay high as long. My fame didn't really make it okay, but it made heroin easier to get a hold of. I guess to some extent, I might have thought, 'I'm a rock star, and rock stars do heroin.' Having money helped. You wouldn't be able to buy it unless you had a pretty good paying gig."

Johnny's breakneck touring schedule and escalating fame that eventually led him to harder drug use included festivals across the country, and concerts at high profile venues such as the Fillmore, Fillmore East, Hollywood Bowl, and the Spectrum in Philadelphia. One of his warmest memories is playing the Fillmore East with B. B. King in January 1969.

"We opened for B. B.," says Johnny. "That was the first time I saw him since I played at the Raven Club. The Fillmore show was fun. He said he was really happy for me and was glad to see me making it. He said, 'I told you, you were gonna make it.'"

Johnny jammed with King for the first time at the Newport Jazz Festival that July.

"We played with jazz artists a good bit of the time at other festivals, so it was just another show," says Johnny. "I remember the fences coming down at Newport and the police tear gassing people. That was a real drag; I was backstage when that happened. I jammed with B. B. at the end—that was great."

In early August, Johnny played the Atlantic City Pop Festival.

"I remember the Atlantic City Pop Festival vaguely," says Johnny. "It's hard to remember any of those festivals because there were so many. The festivals were a big blur when you were taking drugs. Sometimes I was tripping. I think it made things worse, but a lot of times the audience couldn't tell."

"Nineteen sixty-nine has been called the greatest year in rock because they had pop festivals with audiences of 80,000 to 150,000 people in all the major cities," said Shannon. "Woodstock was half a million. I never dreamed there would be crowds like that. We played all of those festivals, Fillmore East and West, Royal Albert Hall. It was really a trip; I grew about ten years in that one year."

The band played every major festival that summer, but never had an opportunity to experience the "sex, drugs, and rock 'n' roll" ambiance that permeated the festival crowd.

"You can't see much from the stage—it's hard to tell what's going on," says Johnny. "You had to stick around the stage area because if you tried to go see people on the outside, they would mob you. That was frustrating. So we'd stay behind stage to see the other artists. That was great. I met Mick Jagger and Keith Richards at one show. I remember Mick saying, 'Mr. Winter, Mr. Winter, it's Mr. Jagger. Wait for me.' Mick Jagger was always pretty nice. Keith Richards said I played blues as good as any of the Chicago guys. That was so nice. I hung out with them, but never did get to play with them. Last time I saw Keith was at S.I.R. [Studio Instrument Rentals] in New York—he was practicing in a rehearsal room before a show.

"We never had a chance to meet other artists for any amount of time there because it was a 'do it and get out.' It was frustrating because you didn't get to hear the bands as much as you'd like to. I was supposed to play with Jeff Beck at one festival. I was talking to him before the show and he said his band didn't show up. I said, 'You can go on with my band' and he said, 'Sure, great.' We played, then announced him, and I saw him running out across the field in back of us. He just ran away—he wouldn't do the show. So I said, 'I guess Jeff Beck's not gonna play.'"

That incident was at the Laurel Pop Festival, held at a racetrack on July 11, featuring Led Zeppelin, Edwin Hawkins, Jethro Tull, Al Kooper, Buddy Guy, Jeff Beck, Ten Years After, and Vanilla Fudge. A driving rain almost cancelled that festival but Johnny's band refused to let their fans down.

"Everybody bailed out—most bands either didn't come or left," said Turner. "When we got there, the crowd was still there, standing in the rain. The other bands didn't want to wait around for it to stop raining. Our attitude was if those people are gonna stand out there in the rain waiting for music, we can sure sit here in this trailer waiting for it to stop raining. So we waited for it to stop raining, and played. Everybody thought we were heroes because everybody else gave up."

Playing festivals on massive stages was a far cry from playing small clubs and roadhouses in Texas, but Paul taught the band how to adapt to larger venues. "He helped us learn how to be rock musicians on a larger scale," said Turner. "He told us to increase our movements—throw our arms around, jump around, move around more."

The crowd loved Johnny's wild stage antics, which went a little too far at one gig.

"One of the early stages of moving around led to Johnny falling off the stage in Kansas City," said Turner. "Johnny started a song back by his amps and started dancing. He had his head toward the microphone in the front of the stage, then he turned back and was lookin' at me while swaying and moving toward the mike. He went past the mike and fell off the front of the stage. It was funny at the time, but he actually sprained his ankle and was limping around for two or three weeks."

Johnny still remembers that misstep in the Midwest.

"I fell off the stage," he says with a laugh. "I wasn't even high. It was a big hall with a raised stage. I was jumpin' up and down—I jumped up in the air and came down on the people in the front row. My leg landed on their seats and I broke a few cameras. It took me awhile to get up; I was hurt and my leg was sprained. But I got back up onstage and played sitting down for a while."

While Johnny was cavorting on massive stages across the country, his brother was playing clubs in Texas. So Johnny invited Edgar to New York to sit in with the band and showcase his musical talents.

"We had made the big time and Edgar was still playing nightclubs in the entertainment district in Houston," said Turner. "Of course, whenever we got a chance, we'd go back to Houston to show off," he added with a laugh. "We told Edgar, 'Why don't you come to New York and play with us, and try to get your own record deal? We'll play thirty minutes as a trio, and then we'll play thirty minutes with you, and you can show off what you can do.'"

With Johnny's goodwill and considerable clout behind him, Edgar moved to New York, joined his brother's band, and soon had his own management deal and recording contract.

"I played on *Johnny Winter* but didn't join that band until later," said Edgar. "I signed with Steve Paul when I signed my recording deal with Columbia Records. That was one of the inducements of signing with him. Obviously, he could see the potential for us as brothers. That was probably part of the reason Johnny was so adamant about not doing too much work together. He didn't want to see that exploited. As we grew older, Johnny was really adamant about not wanting to become known as the Winter Brothers. He wanted us to have separate identities and our music became very different."

Johnny made it clear to Steve Paul and to Columbia Records that they were and would remain separate musicians—not the Winter Brothers. But Paul's single-minded focus on the bottom line, as well as his concept of marketing them as albinos, had an adverse effect on their relationship.

"It's really hard to say what Steve Paul thought of me as a person," says Johnny. "I don't think he cared much about me as a person; it was just payin' the bills for him. I don't think it would have mattered who I was. He wasn't the kind of person you wanted to hang around with; we didn't hang around with him at all. He just thought of me as an artist and not as a person. He'd talk about me when I was in the room—that made me feel bad. When Edgar was just startin' to play with me, Steve said, 'If you can't make it with one albino, get two.' That pissed me off. I came real close to punchin' him when he'd say those things. I don't think he cared or realized what he was saying or thought it would hurt anybody. Nothing bothered him too much.

"At first I liked him, but I got tired of him real quick. He wanted us to do more rock 'n' roll than I wanted to do. He was too controlling. I didn't need or like control. He'd try to control me with the songs he wanted me to do, how much he wanted me to play, things like that."

Despite their tentative personal relationship, Paul's savvy as a manager continued to catapult Johnny into the spotlight with high profile gigs. After the blues-soaked Yardbirds disbanded, their guitarist Jimmy Page formed Led Zeppelin. When the Jeff Beck Group cancelled out of an American tour, Led Zeppelin's manager Peter Grant convinced the promoter to take a chance on this unknown group, and they opened for Johnny on a number of gigs. One show was at the Spectrum, an 18,000-capacity stadium in Philadelphia. It was a night (and a nightmare) the band will never forget.

"It was horrible," says Johnny. "The Spectrum had a revolving stage, and we were all trippin'. The stage turned around real fast—that terrified me. It was like being on a sonic merry-go-round. I'd walk away from the mike, not remember where it was, and couldn't find it. I wouldn't play any revolving stages after that."

"We played the Spectrum during our short-lived acid days," said Turner. "We had some LSD someone had given us. Based on our past experiences, we thought we could split a tablet and be able to play just like we had done before. But it turned out to be the strongest LSD we ever had. We realized we had gotten ourselves out on a limb, and walked in thinking, 'This is going to be tough.' Then we looked up and saw Led Zeppelin on the revolving stage. The stage felt like it was going around one hundred miles an hour, but it was barely moving. From the stage, you could see spotlights all the way around the room. We were revolving around, with all these colors changing, and became totally disoriented. We couldn't even tell if we were playing at all—we were in a trance."

When the show finally ended and the stage stopped, the band thought their nightmare was over. But just like *Alice's Adventures in Wonderland* by Lewis Carroll, things weren't always what they appeared to be.

"We had approached the stage from behind our amplifiers," said Turner. "When the stage stopped, it stopped in the opposite place from where it had started, with the back side of the stage facing the front row of the audience. But we were way too high to realize this. So Johnny thinks he is getting off the stage to go back to the dressing room and he jumped off the stage into the front row. The crowd just jumped on him. They were going to consume him, so the roadies grabbed him by the arms and pulled him back up on the stage."

Crowd control was an issue at the Denver Pop Festival, a three-day festival at Mile High Stadium. Johnny played on June 28; the Jimi Hendrix Experience closed the festival the following day. Although tickets were only six dollars a night or fifteen dollars for all three nights, about one hundred gatecrashers stormed a chain link fence the first night. The night Johnny played, a crowd of between 300 and 400 charged through the fence. Police hurled teargas canisters into the crowd, which tossed them back at police. Clouds of teargas choked thousands of fans; two people were rushed to the hospital.

"Someone said, 'Don't let a fence stop you,' and they tore down the fence," recalled Shannon. "I was running around trying to find a place to hide because people just came rushing over the fence. They finally got it under control."

Johnny also played the Memphis Country Blues Festival featuring many of the early acoustic artists he had heard on the radio in his bedroom. The lineup included Reverend Robert Wilkins, Walter "Furry" Lewis, Fred McDowell, and Sleepy John Estes. The program read: Johnny Winter, a down-and-out young Houston blues musician as recently as a year ago, is now one of the hottest properties in rock and a leading popularizer [sic] of traditional blues styles.

Johnny was thrilled for the opportunity to meet his idols. "Johnny was really wigged out that this old blues guy from Mississippi was playing," said Turner. "He was particularly excited about meeting Fred McDowell."

The Memphis Country Blues Festival attracted a more mellow audience than the Denver Pop Festival, but that didn't let Johnny off the hook. Like Bob Dylan at the 1965 Newport Folk Festival, the band caught flak for using amps at an acoustic festival.

"Most everybody was acoustic, both traditional black artists and the white bands that played the blues," says Johnny. "But the promoters wanted us, so we figured we'd give it a try. We played most of the blues songs on *Johnny Winter*. The audience seemed to like us pretty good. Johnny Woods—he played harp—came out and said, 'You Elmore James, you Elmore James.' But we got put down by the white bands that were playing old-style blues. I guess they'll always be blues purists who want everything to be old-style blues, and they got the right to like whatever they want."

Johnny's current philosophy about blues purists is a far cry from the mindset of his younger days when he told reporters that purists "wouldn't know blues if it climbed up their ass."

"Since I've gotten older, I've become more tolerant of people's ideas than I was," he says with a laugh. "It was just a matter of how I felt at the time. I've mellowed out a bit. I wasn't always mellow; I was pretty shitty back in the old days. I thought everybody should do things my way. Now I feel like everybody should have their own say and do what they want."

The First Atlanta International Pop Festival held on July 4 and July 5, 1969, was a festival Shannon and Turner will never forget. Performers included Janis Joplin, Chuck Berry, Blood, Sweat & Tears, Canned Heat, Joe Cocker, Al Kooper, and Led Zeppelin, but it wasn't the incredible lineup that stands out in their memories.

"Uncle John and I got busted after the Atlanta Pop Festival," said Shannon. "It was one hundred degrees when we got back to the hotel and got busted. Somebody snitched us out. I had a lot of dope and had a feeling something was wrong. I told everybody, 'I have a bad feeling—we better hide our dope.' I stuck the majority of mine under the Coke machine. I still had some downs and pot that I was going to use to get high, and that's what they caught me with. They took Uncle John and me to jail for possession. We were in jail overnight and Steve Paul paid $5,000 to get us off."

"I had thirteen tabs of mescaline and nine tabs of acid," said Turner. "The members of various bands stayed downstairs in the hotel because they were afraid they were gonna get busted. It seems like someone set us up. We paid the fine and were told to stay out of Georgia for six months."

The most well-known festival Johnny played in the summer of 1969 was held on Max Yasgur's dairy farm in Bethel, New York on August 15–17. The Woodstock Music and Art Fair drew nearly 450,000 people to a pasture soon transformed into the Woodstock Nation, a counterculture community. Naked bodies roamed the muddy campsites; stoned-out hippies made love in public. Dope dealers openly sold pot, LSD, mescaline, speed, Seconal, and hash without repercussion. LSD was the drug of choice for many concert-goers and performers, and Johnny was no exception.

"We were trippin' for Woodstock too," says Johnny. "I don't remember very much of Woodstock. I remember sleeping in a press trailer and then waking up and wandering up to the stage with the band to see what was going on. Nobody was there, so they stuck us on. We just happened to be there—we had the band together, so they put us on. We were supposed to go on sometime during the day but didn't go on till around midnight."

Johnny played a Fender Electric XII with only six strings. The set list included "Tell the Truth," "Johnny B. Goode," "Six Feet in the Ground," "Leland Mississippi Blues," "Mama, Talk to Your Daughter," and "Mean Mistreater." Edgar joined the band on "I Can't Stand It" and "Tobacco Road." Johnny played slide on "Mean Town Blues," their encore song.

Although Johnny wanted to stick around for Hendrix's show, logistics caused him to leave before that early morning performance.

"We wanted to be on the stage for Jimi Hendrix, but the helicopters weren't stopping very often, so we got out of there before he played," says Johnny. "We missed one and if we didn't take the next one, there was no promise we'd get another one. Everybody went in and out of the festivals on helicopters. Ridin' in them was alright; it was a way to get out. They took you back to the hotel in upstate New York where everybody was staying. From the helicopter, I remember seeing a sea of mud and people messin' around in the mud. It was something else. There was still a good crowd when I was leavin'.

"As far as eating and sleeping—we had a hard time. I don't remember eating at all. We were in a press trailer and I went to sleep on a bag of garbage. Everybody had to sleep in the mud, but we were in the press trailer so we were pretty safe. We had one of the best places going—at least it was dry. A lot of people never got paid for Woodstock, but we did—we got $3,750."

"Woodstock was a trip," said Shannon. "We rode bubble helicopters. You know where you get above the Earth and you can only see so far? That is how the people looked... it just went on and on from the air. It was like, 'Wow!' We didn't know it was going to be that big until we got there. You couldn't get there by car. We had heard it was a big deal, but I didn't think it was going to be anything like that. We went on about ten hours later than we were supposed to. We were late going on and then they came up and said, 'You got to go on, you got to go on.' We weren't even prepared—mentally or in terms of our equipment. First thing I said was, 'Where's my bass?'"

Psyched about playing for such a large crowd and the opportunity to hear so many phenomenal bands, Turner was determined not to miss a minute of the experience. Unlike Johnny, Edgar, and Shannon, who slept before the show, he took amphetamines to stay awake and still has vivid memories of Woodstock and the days leading up to that festival.

"We played in Chicago and Detroit the Friday and Saturday before Woodstock," said Turner. "We were scheduled to play on Sunday, so we were watching it on the news on TV. We got into New York City at about seven o'clock in the morning. We were scheduled to take a private plane up to the Woodstock airport at 11:30 AM, so we checked into a motel near the airport to try to get some sleep. The roadies overslept and didn't wake us up, and we missed our flight. Steve Paul had to run around and charter two small airplanes to get us to the Woodstock airport.

"When we got to the Woodstock airport, there was a blinding rainstorm. They had helicopters going back and forth. We started out toward the festival site in a little whirlybird helicopter with just a seat and a glass bubble, and a gigantic black cloud started coming toward us. So he turned around, went back to the airport and set the thing down. I arrived at Woodstock at three o'clock—that's the time we were supposed to play originally. Everything was so messed up by then, we ended up not playing till midnight. Played forty-five minutes or something like that. Because the thing was running so ridiculously late, they were cutting the times short.

"The first thing I saw backstage was a large tent for the staff and the performers. Then I saw Jerry Garcia and somebody else sitting on stools, singing through a small sound system in the tent. Then I saw Jimi Hendrix's manager carry Mitch Mitchell, Jimi's drummer, out of the mud so he wouldn't get his English boots muddy before the show.

"As soon as we found out we're not going on at three, I popped some more pills—diet pills to stay awake. I tried to see everybody. Johnny was smarter—he found the *Look Magazine* guy who had a trailer—Johnny stayed and slept in the trailer. I stayed up the whole time. I was exhausted by the time we played but I stayed up and saw Santana, Crosby, Stills, Nash & Young, several people.

"People brought their own rented trailers—there were 500 trailers in the backstage area and maybe 1,000 people. In back of the stage area was a freight elevator that moved all the people and the equipment up and down. So I'd see somebody playing, go back down for a while. Then when a band came back on, I'd go back up to the stage on the elevator and see somebody else playing. I watched everybody playing before us from the side of the stage.

"It was so exciting to see all those people playing. I stayed all night to see Jimi Hendrix. About eight o'clock Monday morning—Jimi Hendrix hadn't come on yet—I looked backstage and there was only one car left. Everybody was gone. The guy who was getting into that car had a crew shirt on. I thought if I don't catch this ride,

I don't have a ride back. I had no idea where I was, so I had to go back to the hotel in Woodstock with that last guy. I'm driving off the Woodstock grounds with my window open and I hear Jimi starting out. And I had stayed all night to see him."

Although Johnny played an incredible set at the festival, his performance never appeared in the *Woodstock* film or on the soundtrack album. Filmmaker Michael Wadleigh recorded his performance, but Johnny's manager refused to let them include it in the film.

"Steve Paul didn't want us to be in the movie because he thought we wouldn't make any money," says Johnny. "Woodstock had lost money up to that point and he thought it was gonna be a drag so he didn't want us to be on it. Of course it helped a lot of people's careers. I wish I could have been in it. Later on he admitted he fucked up. I heard the filmmaker said he thought the act was too strange. I don't know if that's true, but I heard that. The whole thing was full of strangeness—that's what Woodstock was all about—strange people."

The audio and video of Johnny's fiery slide playing on "Mean Town Blues" eventually hit the stores, but it took years to surface. In 1994, the audio and video was released as *Woodstock: Three Days of Peace and Music, 25th Anniversary*; *Woodstock Diary* was released as a CD. The fortieth anniversary in 2009 generated a glut of DVDs and CDs, including *Warner Home Video Woodstock: 3 Days of Peace & Music Director's Cut—40th Anniversary*; *The Woodstock Experience*, a ten-CD box set by Sony Legacy; and *Johnny Winter: The Woodstock Experience*, a two-CD set by Sony Legacy.

•◆•

Johnny spent Thanksgiving weekend 1969 playing the West Palm Beach Festival in Florida, a three-day festival featuring the Rolling Stones, Janis Joplin, the Chambers Brothers, Sly and the Family Stone, Jefferson Airplane, the Byrds, Steppenwolf, and others. It was his first meeting with Joplin and proved to be a concert and an evening neither one would forget.

"I met Janis at the Miami Pop Festival where I ended up jammin' with her and doin' vocals and drinkin' Southern Comfort," says

Johnny. "I had taken acid before and Janis and I were drinking Southern Comfort on the stage like it was Kool-Aid. Later on down, I got real sick. I threw up on her in the helicopter. We went back in the helicopter and I threw up all over her. It was terrible—it was a mess. She was alright with it; she called me up later on and asked me for another date."

Turner remembers that weekend in Miami. "Here were two misfits from Beaumont and Port Arthur on top of the world and they were determined to sample each other," he said. "They went about this odd courtship for a while. Janis was determined to hook up with Johnny that weekend. We played the first night and she played the first night. On the second night, Janis shows up with a quart of Southern Comfort and proceeds to get Johnny drunk. She got drunk too and they jammed with Vanilla Fudge. It was pretty funny—the whole affair. They got real drunk and rode back to the hotel in a helicopter. Johnny is so drunk, he keeps throwing up; and Janis has his head in her lap, saying, 'Oh my baby, my baby.' Roadies had to carry her from the helicopter to her room. Pitiful, but that's the way we lived."

Johnny saw Janis several times after that but it never evolved into a serious relationship.

"I didn't see her a lot, but from time to time I'd see her," Johnny says. "When we got together, she would usually call my agency and I would call her back. One time her office called my office and asked if I wanted to go to the premiere of *Myra Breckinridge* with Janis. It was Mae West's last movie. That was the first time I spent any real time with her. We went to the premiere in New York and it was a lot of fun. We were both dressed up. I was wearing a long velvet coat with bellbottom pants and a long scarf. Janis dressed in feathers and a big ole cape.

"Janis was a real sweetheart but she was drinking too much and taking too much dope—mostly drinking too much. We both felt comfortable being around each other because we were both born in Texas in towns close to each other. We didn't really have a relationship—I'd just see her once in a while and we'd go to bed together. We stayed on Fifth Avenue when she was in New York.

"She had talked to me about going to her high-school reunion; I guess it was because I was from around that time. I didn't think it would be the kind of thing I would like, so I didn't go. It sounded like it was pretty bad—they were screamin' at her, 'Remember me in the back of the car,' and stuff like that. I don't know why she wanted to go. I guess she wanted to prove she was cool. But those kinds of things never work.

"Me and Paul Butterfield jammed with her at Madison Square Garden that December. Janis asked me to play with her at that show. It was her last night with the Full Tilt Boogie Band; I never was crazy about that band. Janis was doing heroin at the time. She really didn't want me doin' it at the same time she was doin' it herself. She told me it was a bad thing. She tried to keep me from it—she didn't succeed, but she tried."

Johnny's fame allowed him to meet and hang out with famous musicians, but it was Steve Paul's reputation and nightclub that led to a meeting with noted artist Salvador Dali. "A lot of artists came to the Scene," explained Paul. "Great men fascinate each other and that's how Johnny got invited to his suite."

Johnny remembers meeting Dalí, accompanied by a small pedigree dog wearing diamonds, during one of the gatherings in the artist's suite at the St. Regis Hotel on East Fifty-Fifth Street.

"He thought I was a deity and wanted to meet me," says Johnny. "He asked me to come to his suite in the hotel where he always stayed when he was in New York. He thought it would be a good experience if we could get together. It was like he was holding court—he had people all around him. He gave somebody a chance to speak. Then he went to the next person and asked them what they wanted to say. I saw him once after that in the same hotel. He showed me a photograph of an albino rhinoceros fucking a girl. I guess that was supposed to mean I was a deity. He never showed me his paintings—just showed me the albino rhinoceros fucking a girl."

When Paul and Johnny were invited to Dali's suite for lunch, Paul broached the concept of him designing one of Johnny's album covers. Aggressive in his approach, he soon felt Dali's scorn.

Johnny's childhood home on 275 West Caldwood Drive in Beaumont, Texas. (Photo by Susan Winter)

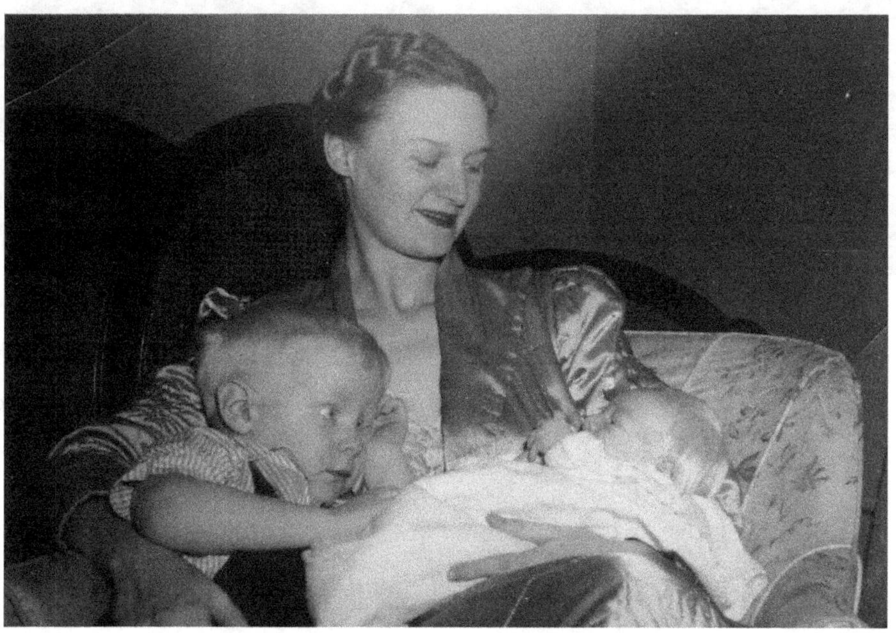

Edwina Winter with infant Edgar and little Johnny. "The boys were musical from birth." (Photo by John D. Winter Jr.; courtesy of Johnny Winter)

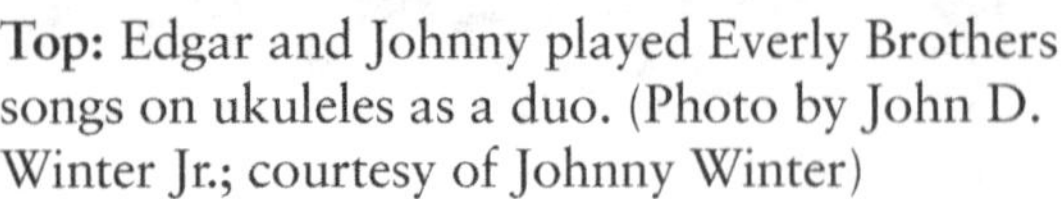

**Top:** Edgar and Johnny played Everly Brothers songs on ukuleles as a duo. (Photo by John D. Winter Jr.; courtesy of Johnny Winter)

**Right:** Edgar and Johnny outside Beaumont TV station KBMT, where they won their first talent contest in 1953. (Photo by John D. Winter Jr.; courtesy of Johnny Winter)

Marquee at the Beaumont Drive-In for Johnny's 1958 gig on top of the concession stand. (Photo courtesy of Dennis Drugan)

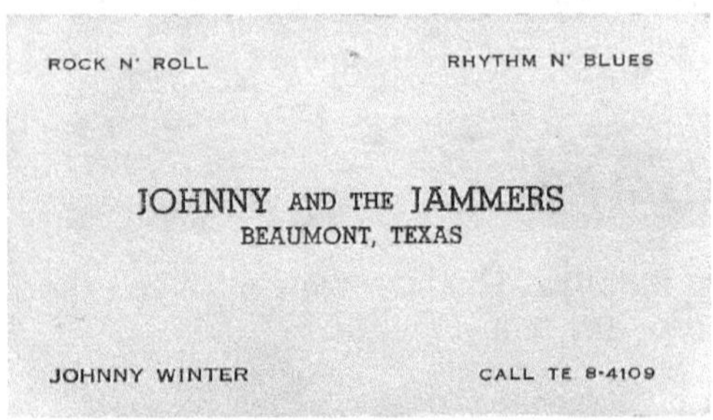

ROCK N' ROLL RHYTHM N' BLUES

JOHNNY AND THE JAMMERS
BEAUMONT, TEXAS

JOHNNY WINTER CALL TE 8-4109

Johnny's first business card. He used this at age fifteen. (Photo courtesy of Dennis Drugan)

Johnny and the Jammers (with Edgar on keyboards) at a school dance. (Photo courtesy of Dennis Drugan)

Johnny Winter's Orchestra with their trademark shades and Edgar on tenor guitar. (Photo courtesy of Dennis Drugan)

**Top:** Johnny with his first collection of guitars. L–R: early '60s Fender Precision Bass; late 1950s Les Paul Custom (Black Beauty); early '60s white Gibson Les Paul Custom, SG body style; 1960s Gibson acoustic J45. (Photo courtesy of Dennis Drugan)

**Right:** Johnny "Cool Daddy" Winter with his diamond ring and record collection—he still has all his 45s. (Photo courtesy of Dennis Drugan)

**Top:** Marquee featuring the Gents on Chicago's Rush Street in 1963. (Photo courtesy of Dennis Drugan)

**Left:** The Gents wore suits with velvet collars before the Beatles. (Photo courtesy of Dennis Drugan)

Tommy Shannon, Uncle John Turner, and Johnny in a shot that graced the back cover of *Progressive Blues Experiment*. (Photo by Burton Wilson)

Johnny, Shannon, and Turner with lightshow at the Vulcan Gas Company in 1968. (Photo by Burton Wilson; from the personal collection of Uncle John Turner)

**Left:** Johnny at Palmer Auditorium in Austin in November 1969. (Photo by Burton Wilson)

**Bottom left:** Acetate record Johnny used to shop for a record deal in England in 1968. (Courtesy of Mike Vernon)

**Bottom right:** Turner, Shannon, and Johnny at the Staatsburg, New York, house where they lived when they moved to New York. (Photo from the personal collection of Uncle John Turner)

Johnny in the rehearsal space in Staatsburg. (Photo from the personal collection of Uncle John Turner)

Both Johnny and Janis Joplin were featured in ads for Tijuana Smalls in 1969. (Photo by Susan Winter)

Jimi Hendrix jamming with Johnny at the Scene in 1969. Jimi is playing Tommy Shannon's 1962 Fender Jazz bass. (Photo by Charles Harbutt)

Promo shot for *Johnny Winter*. (Photo courtesy of Sony/Legacy)

Johnny and Janis shared a warm rapport—on- and offstage. (Photo by Steve Banks)

Johnny joined Janis Joplin at a December 1969 gig at Madison Square Garden. (Photo by Steve Banks)

Johnny with Jimi Hendrix engineer/producer Eddie Kramer during the *Johnny Winter* sessions in Nashville. (Photo from the personal collection of Uncle John Turner)

Triumphant return to the Vulcan Gas Company in Austin in March 1970. (Photo by Burton Wilson; from the personal collection of Uncle John Turner)

Johnny and Susan Winter, who has shared his life since 1972. (Photo by Bob Gruen)

Johnny Winter And: The band that earned Johnny's only gold record. (Photo courtesy of Bobby Caldwell)

**Left:** Johnny at the Auditorium Theatre in Chicago in 1975. (Photo by Jim Summaria; www.jimsummariaphoto.com)

**Bottom:** *Saints and Sinners* billboard for the Long Beach Arena show recorded for the *King Biscuit Flower Hour* in 1974. (Photo courtesy of Doug Brockie)

Edgar sits in with Johnny in 1976. (Photo by Bob Gruen)

Johnny with bassist and close friend Ikey Sweat during the *Nothin' But the Blues* tour. (Photo by Bob Gruen)

**Top:** Johnny and Muddy Waters at the Palladium during the *Hard Again* tour. (Photo by Steven Pearl)

**Left:** James Cotton blows his face out during the 1977 *Hard Again* tour. (Photo by Susan Winter)

Johnny with Clarence Garlow, his mentor and main Texas guitar influence. (Photo by Susan Winter)

Eric Clapton, Muddy Waters, and Johnny jam at Chicago Stadium in June 1979. (Photo by Paul Natkin)

**Left:** Johnny backstage with his trademark Gibson Firebird. (Photo by Susan Winter)

**Bottom:** Johnny's guitar collection in New York. Lying down L–R: mid-'60s non-reverse Gibson Firebird, and seven early '60s Gibson Reverse Firebirds. Standing L–R: early '60s Gibson Thunderbird bass, two Dobro resonator guitars. (Photo by Susan Winter)

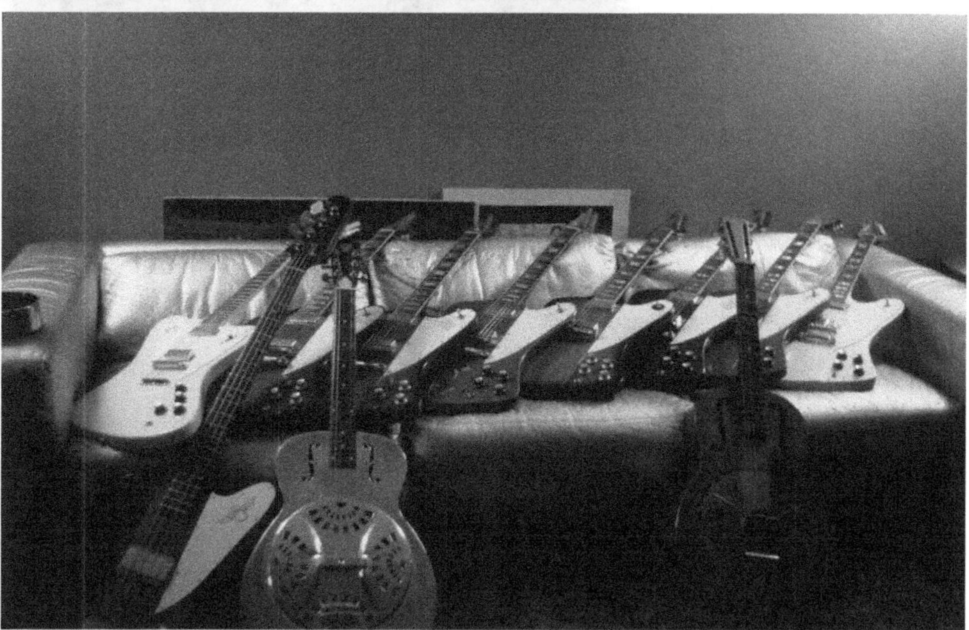

With his father and namesake, John Dawson Winter Jr. (Photo by Susan Winter)

Johnny and Susan Winter—the early years. (Photo by Susan Winter)

Soaking up the sunshine on his New York City balcony. (Photo by Susan Winter)

Johnny with the beginning of his extensive cane collection in a shot for *Raisin' Cain*. (Photo by Susan Winter)

Standing L–R: Styve Homnick, Johnny, Willie Dixon; seated: Sonny Terry. Cover shot for *Whoopin'*. (Photo by Susan Winter)

Johnny, wearing an Ikey Sweat tee shirt, shows Styve Homnick exactly how he wants him to play the drums on *Whoopin'*. (Photo courtesy of Styve Homnick)

Johnny played his 1920s National resonator during the *Third Degree* sessions. (Photo by Paul Natkin)

Albert Collins and Johnny at the Park West in Chicago in 1984. (Photo by Paul Natkin)

Johnny's rendition of "Mojo Boogie" at the Mohegan Sun Casino in 2008. (Photo by Charles Fitzsimmons)

Johnny proudly displays his "Screamin' Demon" tattoo and Lazer guitar. (Photo by Paul Natkin)

"'You are just business, business; we want to talk art,'" Dali told Paul, in an incident Johnny gleefully shared with his artist friend Jim Franklin. "Steve always wanted to be right in the middle and Johnny was so pleased that Dali put him in his place, which was across the room, where managers should be," remembered Franklin. But Johnny passed on Dali's suggestion that he put a microphone up his derriere so his inner body sounds could also be broadcast when he was performing.

•◆•

When they weren't on the road, Johnny and his band lived in a house Paul rented in Staatsburg, New York, a rural town in the Hudson Valley about ninety-five miles from New York City. The house was part of what they called the quadrangle, consisting of two houses and two renovated barns, not far from an estate owned by the Astor family.

"It was an old house on an estate that looked like a compound," said Turner. "A large brick three-story house with four bedrooms and a brick wall around it. Behind it were two barns. The newer barn was one big room with fourteen-foot ceilings for an artist studio and one bedroom. The other one had two bedrooms and a hayloft. Steve Paul eventually rented the main house too. Originally, it was occupied by a Shriver. He had used it as a getaway for several years and came up on weekends. Our all-night affairs, plus our goings-on in the large heated pool outside between the two houses, ran him off."

Shannon remembers one bizarre evening when the band dropped acid and headed into the cold winter's night for a swim in the heated pool. "Johnny decided Steve Paul was literally the devil," said Shannon. "We did a lot of drugs in Staatsburg—mushrooms, acid, pain pills. All of a sudden, all of that dope was free and we took advantage of it, tried stuff we never tried before. We were pretty high. When you reach a certain point of success, people start giving you drugs all the time."

It was at the quadrangle that Edgar wrote the riff to a song that eventually became "Frankenstein." That single reached the top of the *Billboard* charts in only eleven weeks, and boosted sales of Edgar's

1973 Columbia LP, *They Only Come Out at Night,* to more than 1.2 million copies.

Edgar has fond memories of living in Staatsburg with Johnny and his band. "Living at the quadrangle with Uncle John and Tommy, it really felt like a band, and was very reminiscent of the old days," said Edgar. "We had a great big rehearsal room in the back of our house. We could make as much noise as we wanted and play any time of the day or night. It was what we had always dreamed of when we were little kids, having our own place and having a band and being able to play music at whatever time we wanted. That was when I originally developed 'Frankenstein'—in that house with that band. We called it the 'Double Drum Song.' I played Hammond organ and sax and did a drum solo with Red. I wrote the basic riff specifically with Johnny in mind, thinking of his band, and an instrumental that would have a bluesy feel, and make sense in an instrumental show."

"We'd start the song with Edgar on the organ," said Turner. "Then we'd get to a point where the band would stop and I would start doing a short solo in time for Edgar to leave the organ and take a seat at my extra set of drums. As soon as Edgar would get seated, I'd do a special fill, and then Edgar would come in and take it for a little while. We had the tandem drumming thing worked out so we drummed together. Edgar is always a real joy to play with; he is such a great musician."

Edgar played with Johnny's band from time to time, and took on a bigger role in Johnny's second Columbia recording. Johnny returned to the studio in late 1969 to record *Second Winter,* which had a harder rock feel than the straight blues of *Johnny Winter,* and introduced Johnny's version of "Highway 61 Revisited." Although pegged as a blues-rock record, *Second Winter* marked the beginning of Johnny's move toward rock and away from the blues. The inclusion of songs by Chuck Berry, Little Richard, and Dylan wasn't lost on him, and he had serious misgivings about taking that musical direction.

"It was mostly Steve's idea," he says. "They were blues-rock songs—all bluesy but not straight blues. He convinced me I wouldn't be around for long if I didn't play more rock on my records. It seemed like the blues was so big in the late '60s, that by the early '70s, people were tired of the blues—they wanted more rock. I felt like I had to do 'em or I wasn't going to make it. And that would really hurt me if I had gone so far and then become a nobody. That scared me. By *Second Winter* I was doin' more rock 'n' roll, but I don't like it as much as I like blues.

"Blues purists didn't like that record. They said I sold out, and I guess I did.... It hurt me to hear that but you just had to deal with it. It's hard because people have strong opinions about what blues should be like. You miss a lot of good music by saying anything but straight blues is not blues and by not playing rock 'n' roll because there's a lot of good rock 'n' roll out there too. To say it's not blues unless it's acoustic blues—that's just crazy to me."

Jimi Hendrix producer/engineer Eddie Kramer, who is credited as producer consultant on *Johnny Winter*, was hired to help with production of *Second Winter*, but never made it to the end of the sessions. "He wasn't doing his job," says Johnny. "He was outside the studio recording rainstorm sound effects. So we fired him midstream leaving me and Edgar to finish the job of producing and recording the album."

"Eddie Kramer was uppity in the studio; that's why he got fired," said Turner. "As to recording the rain, I don't know if it was Eddie Kramer who instigated that or us. I thought it was at our instigation, our psychedelic nature, that we recorded the rain. Eddie was very good. On the *Johnny Winter* album, Eddie was the one that got in there, set up the mikes, did the sound. I didn't like the sound he was getting, but it turned out to be real good. But he was uppity about the way he approached things. We could have got a lot more from Eddie. We looked at him as the opposition. We had our own big egos. That's why we fired him on the second record. We thought we could do a better job and we couldn't," Turner adds with a laugh. "We fired him shortly into it. It was just a few days and we paid him off and sent him home. Eddie was a no-nonsense guy. I don't think Eddie wanted to record the rain; I think Johnny wanted to record the rain. We were all together on stuff like that—'Yeah, let's record a rainstorm, ha ha. Roll me another joint.'"

The hip counterculture scene pulsated with psychedelics, light-shows, and lava lamps; and famed photographer Richard Avedon had begun experimenting with the Sabatier Effect, a darkroom technique also called solarization, to create hallucinogenic images. By partially developing a negative or print and then overexposing it to light, he could make the whites silvery, eliminate detail, highlight or darken shadows, and get a distinct black line around the edges. In 1967, he created psychedelic posters of the Beatles, and a solarized photo of John Lennon for the cover of *Look Magazine*.

Avedon created a striking blue and purple cover for *Second Winter*; the front cover is a dramatic full-face headshot and a right profile of Johnny with his silky hair blowing in the wind. His hair from the cover shot flows onto the back of the album, where the tip of his nose is the only feature unobstructed by his tousled mane. Avedon captured the detail in his face and hair and used purple ink to fill in the shadows and create the solarized effect. The inside cover shot is a black-and-white group shot with all four musicians looking in different directions.

"The picture on the cover was my idea," says Johnny. "I liked the posters Richard Avedon had done of the Beatles; that's why I picked him. It was done in his studio and it didn't take long at all. We posed the way he told us to for the inside cover and he used a wind machine to get the effect with my hair."

*Second Winter* was a double album pressed on only three sides. Technology for recording on vinyl demanded wider grooves for louder volume; after about twenty-two minutes a side, squeezing more music onto a record could only be accomplished to a limited degree and at the expense of volume. The liner notes on that LP gave the following explanation:

> The original plan was to cut as much material as possible and pick the best of what was cut to make up a regular one-record album. After we finished, we found out that if all the songs were used we might lose some volume if only one record were used. Since it was very important to us that our album be as loud as is technically

> possible, we had a problem. We had to cut everything that we wanted to and everything we had planned on doing and we didn't have anything else that we really wanted to do. We also really liked everything we'd done and didn't want to leave any of the songs out. We couldn't honestly give you more, and we didn't want to give you less, so here is exactly what we did in Nashville—no more and no less.

"We didn't have enough music to make four sides and we had too much to just do two sides," says Johnny. "So we decided to make a three-sided record. I don't know why CBS let us do it, but they did."

Columbia released *Second Winter* in late 1969, and by then more of Winter's former managers had come out of the woodwork, trying to make a quick buck off of anything he had ever recorded, regardless of the sound quality. In August 1969, GRT Records released *The Johnny Winter Story*, an album of old material the label bought from Ken Ritter.

"The music wasn't all that great on that record," says Johnny. "I had recorded it years before, somewhere around 1961 to 1964. They had a guy playing horrible slide on it but it wasn't me because I didn't even play slide back then. They overdubbed a whole band on some of the cuts. In one place, you could hear two drummers, and one was hitting the beat at [a] different time. It was awful. They were dumbasses; they didn't know what they were doing.

"Ken was my manager in Texas when I was about seventeen. He put out several singles on different labels, KRCO, Frolic Records—we weren't on any major labels. We never did get any money; he said it wasn't selling enough. Columbia was really good about *The Johnny Winter Story* coming out. Their lawyers never went after anybody because they said it wouldn't be worth it."

GRT Corporation, which wholly owned GRT Records and fifty percent of Janus Records, also bought twenty sides of Johnny's old material from Roy Ames. Those cuts were released on *About Blues* on the Janus label in November. One month earlier, Buddah Records released *First Winter*, which contained four tracks from *About Blues*. Buddah president Neil Bogart said he bought his tapes from Huey Meaux, a Houston record producer. Johnny didn't know about any of the unauthorized albums until friends mentioned seeing them in record stores.

"*About Blues* was real old stuff recorded around 1961 to '63," says Johnny. "It was all kinds of different music—some Bob Dylan, some R&B songs, some rock 'n' roll tunes. I talked to Roy when it came out and he said it would help me in the long run. *First Winter* was tapes they bought from Huey Meaux, who got the tapes from Roy. Edgar was on some of them but the bands were made up of a lot of different people. The quality was not too good."

The influx of unauthorized Johnny Winter albums confused fans, who assumed they were buying his latest album. When an occasional fan told Johnny his latest LP wasn't as good as his earlier ones, he'd discover they had purchased a bootleg record. Material he had deemed not even good enough for local labels competed with his Columbia releases and threatened to tarnish his reputation.

"I felt very hurt when that happened," Johnny says. "I hated it because it wasn't nearly as good as the material I was comin' out with. It just wasn't the right thing at all—for that to happen to us. I didn't make any money, and career-wise, it definitely wasn't good. It was a real drag. There were so many coming out *Rolling Stone* gave me a chance to tell everybody they weren't very good and not to buy them." An April 16, 1979 article titled "Johnny Winter: It's Just Bad Music" addressed the four unauthorized releases and explained why Johnny was more concerned about the quality than the lost royalties. "I just don't want that bullshit out," Johnny told the reporter. "It's just bad music."

•◆•

In December 1969, after the release of *Second Winter*, Steve Paul rented the second house in the quadrangle, and moved the McCoys to Staatsburg. Paul had met the McCoys—a band that included Rick Derringer on guitar, Randy Jo Hobbs on bass, Bobby Peterson on organ, and Rick's brother Randy Zehringer on drums—when they wandered into the Scene and asked if they could play.

"I thought they were really talented players and individuals, and were incorrectly perceived by some as a teen pop band," said Paul. "People like Jimi Hendrix and Janis Joplin and Johnny Winter surely appreciated just how good they were."

A teenage band from Ohio, the McCoys experienced short-lived phenomenal success and opened for the Rolling Stones on their 1965 American tour. Signed with Bang Records, their first single, "Hang on Sloopy," hit number one on the *Billboard* charts. "Fever," their second release, peaked at number seven two months later.

Pigeonholed as a teenybopper band playing bubblegum music (their photograph appeared on the cover of *16 Magazine*), the McCoys struggled after leaving Bang Records and signing with Mercury, where they released two albums. Poor record sales and the reactions of audiences wanting to hear "Hang on Sloopy" left the band between a rock and a hard place. Paul signed on as their manager, negotiated their release from Mercury Records, and invited them to Staatsburg to regroup and write new songs.

The McCoys' house was about one hundred yards away from Johnny's band's house with the rehearsal room. When Johnny wasn't practicing with Shannon and Turner, Derringer practiced his new material with the McCoys. The proximity of the bands' houses naturally led to jams with both bands, as well as some really strange experiences for Johnny and his band members.

"I didn't know it, but Rick knew the whole band was crazy," says Johnny. "One time, I was walkin' on ice on the Hudson River in the middle of the winter. The river was partially frozen, and they were all walkin' on the ice, so I figured it was safe and walked out there too. I figured they all lived up north and should know what they were doin'. But they didn't—they were just crazy.

"I fell in but Bobby Peterson thought I was walking on the water. I fell in up to my neck and got out real quick. Me bein' as hot as I was and the water being cold, steam came up when I fell in. So Bobby thought I was God, and I walked on the water. He wasn't doin' much drugs; he was just crazy. After that he would follow me around the house, calling me God. He started watching me sleep. He would just sit there when I went to sleep. When I woke up, he'd still be sitting there. Having somebody like me is great, but watching me sleep is definitely too much. I thought it was crazy—I still think it's crazy."

Peterson's bizarre behavior continued to escalate, attracting the attention of the local sheriff and almost landing the band in the slammer.

"One night Bobby went out in the woods and tried to hang himself," said Turner. "It was a rainy evening, and when he came back, he had a broken rope around his neck. He found it in the garage, hooked it around his neck, jumped off, and broke the rope. He came in with that rope and a red mark around his neck and said, 'I hanged myself, Johnny.' We didn't know what to think about that—it threw us for a loop."

"Bobby Peterson hung himself on a tree in the backyard," says Johnny. "The rope broke and he said, 'See, the tree doesn't even like me—the tree threw me out.' We took him to the hospital and all they wanted to do was to call the cops and put him in jail. I was screamin' at 'em, 'He's not taking anything—he's just suicidal.' They thought he was on drugs and the poor guy was just fucked up."

"You know the song 'The Mighty Quinn (Quinn the Eskimo)' by Bob Dylan?'" asked Shannon. "He's an actual sheriff up there. He came to our house when Bobby Peterson tried to hang himself. Somebody freaked out and called the police. The sheriff came out to the house and we got worried he was going to bust us. To get out of that, we went over to one of the Vanderbilts' houses—she was living up there too, in the same part of the country. We played acoustic guitar, and sang all these sad songs like "By the Time I Get to Phoenix" on her front porch to get her to tell him to back off."

After that evening, Peterson's behavior continued to become more and more erratic.

"He started wearin' a rope around his neck," says Johnny. "He thought he was Judas Iscariot. He thought he wasn't a good person. He couldn't eat or dress. He was always a little bit off, but it was so much different from anything he had ever done before—just changing clothes was hard for him. It came out of nowhere and he wasn't doing any drugs."

That wasn't the only disturbing behavior band members witnessed. In January 1970, Johnny and Shannon attended Hendrix's Band of Gypsies concert at Madison Square Garden, and were devastated to see him in such a state.

"I was at the Band of Gypsies concert when Jimi walked off the stage," says Johnny. "I was backstage. It scared me to death that he would be fucked up enough to actually give up, to quit playing. It scared me to death. He just said, "I'm sorry—I can't go on.' I thought it was drugs but I didn't think they'd kill him. Things might have turned out different if he got a little help. He had played so many good shows. He had good and bad shows—most of 'em were good—but he had his share of bad shows too."

"I saw Jimi Hendrix about four times," said Shannon. "I remember going to the Electric Ladyland, Jimi Hendrix's studio—we hung out there for a while. I saw him that night at Madison Square Garden too. He came out and did about three songs and he just broke down and sat down on the front of the stage, put his head in his hands, and started crying. Then he got up and just walked offstage. I remember Buddy Miles saying, 'Jimi isn't feeling too good right now, we'll try to come back,' but they never did come back. It was the last time I saw him."

•◆•

In the winter and spring of 1970, Johnny continued to tour with Shannon and Turner. The band's itinerary included a European tour with appearances at the Bath Rock Festival and the Royal Albert Hall in England, the *Beat Club* TV show in Germany, the Isle of Wight Festival, and a benefit for Timothy Leary at the Village Gate in New York City.

"We did as much promotion and interviews as we possibly could for the European tour; there was a lot of interest," says Johnny. "Steve Paul went with us to check everything out before we did it. The clubs in Europe were good-sized—we played both indoor and outdoor places. The *Beat Club* TV show in Germany was a live-performance show. We played two songs ["Johnny B. Goode" and "Mean Town Blues"]; it wasn't a whole set. Our first headliner was the Royal Albert Hall. That was something else. It was a full house. Somebody yelled, 'Play the guitar, you faggot,' he said with a laugh. "I loved it. . . . That's the main thing I remember."

In March 1970, Johnny had a gig at the Olympic Auditorium in L.A. Jim Franklin was in town to join Robert Crumb and other *Zap Comix* artists—Gilbert Shelton, S. Clay Wilson, Spain Rodriguez, and Kim Deitch—to paint murals at the Whorehouse, a Santa Monica bar. They created quite a spectacle when Franklin brought the crew of underground artists to the Century Plaza Hotel, a nineteen-story luxury hotel, to meet Johnny and Edgar.

"We drove up a small hill to a horseshoe driveway by the front door, and pulled up under a canopy," said Franklin. "We were in this funky old car full of beer cans up to the door sill. So when the doorman, who is dressed in a Beefeater costume, opened the door, a cascade of beer cans comes out and rolls down the driveway—and all these gangly artists, hairy creatures get out. It was really a scene straight out of a Freak Brothers comic."

Johnny was taking a shower when they arrived, so they went to Edgar's room and partied until it was time to go to the gig. "Everyone dispersed after the gig and I felt bad because they never got to meet Johnny," said Franklin, who recalled another time when Johnny was literally hanging out in his hotel room, surrounded by guests.

"Johnny knew people were curious about if he has albino pubic hair, so he came out naked, and says, 'There it is; that's what it looks like,'" Franklin said with a laugh. "I could tell he was practiced at it."

Johnny also played at the May 1970 "Holding Together" benefit for Timothy Leary at the Village Gate. The benefit was to provide cash for Leary, who had escaped from a minimum security prison and was living on the lam in Algeria. Leary had been arrested for possession of two roaches of marijuana, which he claimed were planted by police, and sentenced to ten years in prison.

"I did the Village Gate benefit because Timothy Leary was a good guy to support," says Johnny. "He got put in jail for almost nothing, and people didn't think he deserved it. They threw him in jail just because he was a big guy in the drug scene and they didn't like that."

Despite the band's itinerary that included concerts at festivals and prestigious venues across the U.S. and Europe, they returned to Austin to play a benefit for the owners of the Vulcan Gas Company, which was in rough shape financially and about to go out of business.

Shannon said they were happy to help because the Vulcan was "our old stomping grounds," but Turner said their motivation to play the gig was not just based on purely altruistic reasons.

"We came back and played it to be triumphant," said Turner. "We wanted to show off and say, 'All you people who never came here to see us, you're all here now.'"

Although the band reminisced about their early struggles and the roots of their success when they played the Vulcan gig, changes were brewing that would quickly lead to the dissolution of that lineup. Johnny was becoming increasingly concerned about the impact of reviews trashing his rhythm section.

"Reviewers seemed to feel like I was better than the rest of the band," says Johnny. "Tommy and Red got a lot of that. I thought their playing was fine. The critics wanted fancier stuff. Tommy and Red were blues players and I think that hurt them. English critics were rougher on bands because they wanted a super group. We weren't a super group; we were a blues band."

"People misunderstood that whole band," Johnny told a *Creem* reporter after the band parted ways. "It was supposed to be just what it was, a country, raw type blues thing. It wasn't a Cream type thing where the drummer and bass player worked out; they were just there to play background, to play rhythm stuff."

Turner took the bad reviews in stride. "We quickly learned that the purpose is just to get your name out there," he said. "Just getting them to talk about us is the important part."

Reviews that trashed or ignored the rhythm section cut Shannon to the bone, but he feels that now, with the passing of time, people have come to respect and acknowledge the power and talent of that lineup.

"That hurt, that really hurt," said Shannon. "But once we got up there and saw how these great musicians did it, we started to step up to the plate. We were playing our ass off. I feel vindicated now because people look at that band as *the* combination, especially after listening to the live recording of the show at the Royal Albert Hall. That Sony Legacy remastered edition of *Second Winter* in October 2004 was great because it included the concert at the Royal Albert Hall. It's incredible; we were on fire."

"If it had been released in 1970, it would be revered today as one of the greatest live rock albums of all time, on a par with the Who's *Live at Leeds*, the Rolling Stones *Get Yer Ya-Ya's Out!*, and the Allman Brothers Band *Live at Fillmore East*," writes Andy Aledort in the liner notes. "The fact that Johnny's biggest-selling record is *Johnny Winter And Live* only serves to strengthen the case."

"*Live at Royal Albert Hall* is a magnificent release," agreed Turner. "We went into that European tour wanting to show our concept of the blues, as people who had grown up in an environment where blues is not a state of mind but a fact of life. The energy level is incredible; we are driving the music hard, right on the cutting edge."

Regardless of how well they played in retrospect, the blues wave that had started in the mid- to late '60s was starting to subside. Paul envisioned Johnny as a rock star and wanted powerful players who could back him up.

"Steve Paul was pushing me to make the break with Red and Tommy," says Johnny. "He convinced me I couldn't make it doing blues that I had to get into more rock 'n' roll, more rocking blues. Some record labels don't mind letting you have your way playing blues. But lots of 'em just want the records to be stone rock 'n' roll. They're not gonna stay with you if you don't do something that's gonna really make it. I think Columbia wanted me to go more rock 'n' roll."

Johnny reluctantly agreed to go into a more rock-oriented direction, and tried to bring Shannon and Turner along. He wrote new material in the rock 'n' roll vein and the trio practiced and recorded four songs. But it didn't come together the way Johnny had hoped it would.

"It was easy for me to cross from blues to rock 'cause I was used to playing both," Johnny says. "Red and Tommy were more used to playing blues than rock 'n' roll. I tried to use them in some rock 'n' roll stuff and they just didn't fit in quite right."

He wanted musicians who could write and sing and become a dynamic part of a band, rather than just being sidemen. It all went back to the critics demanding a supergroup. Paul's push to move Johnny in a new direction with a different band was upsetting to Turner and Shannon, but it didn't come as a surprise. Before they left for the April 1970 tour of Europe and England, that included that Royal Albert Hall show, Johnny told the band they would have to go their different ways.

"Steve Paul never really wanted me and Tommy; it wasn't like we were so stupid we couldn't see that," said Turner. "He always had it in his mind to get us out of the picture. He wanted to find new musicians for Johnny. He brought Rick Derringer and the McCoys up to his house to start jamming with Johnny. Steve Paul treated Johnny well but he always wanted to get rid of us, always. He was the kind of guy who always had a strategy, an underhanded strategy. He was a bit of an unsavory person."

"Steve was trying to get rid of us from the start," agreed Shannon. "I think a lot of it was that Johnny loved us and we loved Johnny, and he wanted Johnny to himself. He was feeling like if he could get Johnny alone, he could control him more because Uncle John and I would always give him [Johnny] an earful. He had big plans of making Johnny a rock star and talked him into branching out away from the blues. Johnny didn't feel real good about that, but he thought that would be the best thing for him because Steve Paul kept shoving it down his throat all the time. But Johnny loved blues and I think the whole thing with the new band was a little awkward for him at first."

Having to fire friends who had been with him from the beginning, and had lived like paupers so the band could fulfill its dream of playing blues, wasn't easy for Johnny.

"I had to tell them," says Johnny. "I told them I loved them and I hated to do it but I needed a band that could play more rock 'n' roll. I didn't want to be a nobody; to be a group that nobody cared about. I wanted to do something people would like. I didn't want to be another Ultimate Spinach because they were a perfect example of a band that made it, had one hit record, and nothing else after it.

"Steve Paul didn't want to be there when I told them. He didn't want to have to tell them. What made it so hard? I loved them. They had helped me make it, man. When we were really trying and nowhere, they were still there with me. I hated to have to see them go. I told them I was gonna try to do more rock 'n' roll and they said, 'Okay—we understand.' There were no hard feelings. I still loved them and they understood it completely. They formed a band called Krackerjack in California—a rock-blues band. Tommy finally ended up in Double Trouble with Stevie Ray Vaughan. When Tommy started playing with Double Trouble, Uncle John started playing with several different bands."

Getting fired by their old friend from a band they helped create and which, in retrospect, has been credited by some critics for creating Johnny's greatest recordings (*Progressive Blues Experiment*, *Johnny Winter*, and *Second Winter*) was rough on Shannon and Turner, emotionally and financially. The original plan was for Johnny to get fifty percent and Shannon and Turner twenty-five percent each, but when the break came, they only received a severance pay of $2,000 each, with the explanation that the band was still financially in the hole. Yet the love between the three musicians runs so deep, the breakup of the band never got in the way of their friendship.

"Johnny says, 'I'm going to do something new here, I'm going to try and play with this other band, the McCoys; I hate to let you all go but I'm going to have to,'" said Shannon. "We knew it was coming, we knew it when he first started going down there jamming with them. After he told us, we stayed there maybe another week and then we went back to Dallas.

"It was horrifying, you had built up this whole vision of yourself that is really cool, had all the cool girls, a lot of cool friends, popularity, and all of a sudden you're nobody. It was really painful. But

Johnny was still our friend. I loved Johnny, he was my friend, and we used to hang out all the time. He would fly me to New York and I would stay with him a couple of weeks, just hang out; and he would have me sit in. I love him; he is still my friend. Uncle John and I forgot about all of that."

•◆•

With Turner and Shannon back in Texas, Johnny and the McCoys started rehearsing full time. In May 1970, the new lineup, which included Derringer on second guitar, Hobbs on bass, and Zehringer (Randy Z) on drums, rehearsed for several weeks and went into Columbia's New York studio to record *Johnny Winter And*. Ironically, the McCoys weren't familiar with Johnny's music and Derringer told one reporter he was disappointed when he discovered Johnny wasn't another Jimi Hendrix or Eric Clapton. He also couldn't comprehend Johnny's widespread acclaim as a guitar player.

"The first time I heard Johnny play at the Fillmore East, I wasn't really impressed," Derringer told Tom Guerra during an interview for *Vintage Guitar*. "He had come on the scene with everybody telling me how great he was, and I didn't hear it. Johnny overplayed, and because of his eyesight problems, he would sometimes go to the wrong fret and hit the wrong note. I was a little kid from Ohio that was into perfection, and I just didn't get it! I was hearing a bunch of mistakes, when all of a sudden, he strapped on the slide guitar, and I said, 'Now I get it.' There was nobody at the time who was playing slide guitar like Johnny, and nobody, or no white guys at least, that was playing country blues like that on the acoustic guitar. And it was at that point that I realized what Johnny had to offer."

Derringer desperately needed credibility and respect; teaming up with Johnny offered both.

"The McCoys were in a bad situation," Derringer told Guerra. "Our music had become characterized as 'bubblegum,' and we didn't want to be seen like that. We wanted a way to gain some credibility since we thought we were pretty good players. Johnny came on the scene with real respect, so we looked at this as an opportunity to get what we were looking for, some respect ourselves."

Despite the McCoys' lightweight reputation and teenybopper following, both Paul and Johnny were impressed with their musicianship.

"I first heard 'em play across the street from me in their house," says Johnny. "I thought they were a good rock 'n' roll band—I knew they weren't a bubblegum band. 'Hang on Sloopy' was good for what it was, but it wasn't what I was tryin' to do.

"After I let my band go, I asked Steve if he thought the McCoys would be a good band to get with and he said, he thought so. They could play a lot of different kinds of music, and were looking for a leader. I took over but I didn't realize how nuts they were. At that time, I was smokin' [pot] and doin' smack with Randy Hobbs, and the rest of the band was just smokin' a little bit. I did the singing and Rick sang back up. I didn't want to call it Johnny Winter and the McCoys because they were known as a bubblegum band. So we just called it Johnny Winter And."

In spite of his initial misgivings that the McCoys would be too tight and clean for his musical tastes, and he'd lose his audience for straying from straight blues, Johnny enjoyed playing with the new lineup. "It didn't take long for the band to mesh; the band came together pretty quickly," Johnny says. "I felt more part of a whole in that band because we all played a part in it; before that it was more like my band. Steve Paul liked the new direction and Columbia seemed to like it too. Critics liked it and the audiences loved it."

Because Derringer had produced his own albums on Mercury, Johnny invited him to share producer credits on *Johnny Winter And*. But he was still hesitant about having another guitar player in his band.

"We did that album in August 1970," says Johnny. "It didn't take long. I played a solid body Epiphone guitar—Rick played a Les Paul and a Gibson 355. I thought I'd try working with another guitar player and see what happened. People liked it. I didn't like it though because I just wanted to play myself. I didn't need another guitar player. I used Rick as a coproducer because I thought he knew enough to help me in the producer role. He didn't know more than

I did but he did know a lot which is why I wanted him to play with me and help me produce it. I liked the results."

"I think he just figured I was a guy who would listen," Derringer told writer Dan Muise during an interview for *Gallagher, Marriott, Derringer & Trower: Their Lives and Music.* "I think just being a guitar player/musician in his band helped. He looked at producers and engineers as kind of executives from the record business. He looked at me as a rock 'n' roll guitar player. He saw me as a lot more on his wavelength.... I was inspired by Johnny. He had an idea of what direction we needed to go in. He knew that it didn't have to be a narrow kind of version of rock 'n' roll. It really could be something that we created."

The band rehearsed the songs prior to going into the studio, and the sessions were quick. Having a fellow musician who understood what he wanted in terms of production, allowed Johnny to have his input understood and implemented.

"We played all of the songs on the first *Johnny Winter And* [album] every day before we recorded them, so when we got in the studio, it was totally easy, as we knew exactly what we wanted to do," Derringer told Guerra. "My job at that time was to communicate Johnny's wishes to the engineers and to the people in New York. He felt that on his first projects with Eddie Kramer... his wishes weren't getting through. So as a guitar player and a guy who has some common sense and a friend of his, I was able to communicate his wishes to the hierarchy."

"On the *Johnny Winter And* record, we did a lot of songs Rick had already written and played with the McCoys, but hadn't recorded," says Johnny. "I wrote 'Guess I'll Go Away,' 'Nothing Left,' and 'Prodigal Son.' Rick wrote 'Rock and Roll, Hoochie Koo,' 'Look Up,' 'On a Limb,' 'Ain't That a Kindness,' and 'Funky Music.'"

Derringer's later version of "Rock and Roll, Hoochie Koo," recorded on his *All American Boy* LP in 1973, generated more airplay and sales than the single released by Johnny Winter And. But Derringer wrote it especially for Johnny.

"I specifically was there to bring more of a rock sound to Johnny," Derringer told Muise. "And Johnny would only allow it to go so far. . . . The first song I wrote for Johnny was 'Rock and Roll, Hoochie Koo.' 'Rock and roll' to satisfy the rock 'n' roll that I was supposed to be bringing into the picture, and 'Hoochie Koo' to satisfy the kind of blues sensibility that Johnny was supposed to maintain. And it worked out great."

Johnny wasn't as impressed with the record, which he said "sold worse than anything we had out."

"I didn't think *Johnny Winter And* was as great as everybody else thought it was, but I was glad they liked it," says Johnny. "I didn't know what people would think; I just hoped they would like it. The reviewers liked it. I didn't think 'Rock and Roll, Hoochie Koo' would do as well as it did 'cause it was a little corny. Rock and Roll, Hoochie Koo. You don't ever know. *Johnny Winter And* was more structured than most albums. Less jamming, because rock is more structured than blues."

By 1970, mono records had become obsolete, with stereo the new standard. *Johnny Winter And* was his first LP recorded in stereo, but Johnny found that approach "very clinical" and hated to move in that direction. He bought a Back To Mono tee shirt he saw advertised in *Rolling Stone* and wore it to express his disgust with the new format.

Zehringer played drums on *Johnny Winter And*, but his erratic behavior took a toll on the band. Although Johnny liked his drumming style, he only played two or three gigs with the band before Johnny had to let him go. Bobby Peterson hadn't been the only member of the McCoys with psychological and behavioral problems.

"One day we were all in the car goin' to look for amps," says Johnny. "Randy, Rick's little brother, said, 'Look at my shirt.' We said, 'What's wrong with your shirt?' He said, 'It just doesn't look right—I can't go down there looking like this.' And he jumped out of the car in the middle of the freeway and went home. Things like that. He wasn't doin' drugs—he was just messed up. I had to get rid of him because he wasn't in any shape at all to be playing in a band. He told Steve he couldn't play onstage because it made him cry and he didn't want to cry onstage. He was also afraid the band would make him drink water. I don't know why; it was just one of his crazy ideas. We knew we couldn't work with him. Rick had been puttin' up with it for years so letting him go didn't affect him.

"It was real strange being around that band. You know these guys aren't playing with a full deck. Randy Hobbs would call me at four o'clock in the morning to say, 'Weren't we supposed to practice at four?' 'Yeah, we were supposed to practice at four this afternoon.' They were nuts and I used them for a long time."

With a full tour planned, Johnny had to act fast to fill the drummer's position. Until he could find the right musician to take Zehringer's place, he called on his brother to help. One of the gigs Edgar filled in as drummer was the Second Atlanta International Pop Festival, where Johnny jammed with the Allman Brothers.

Held on July 3–5, 1970, the Second Atlanta International Pop Festival had an all-star lineup that also included B. B. King, the Chambers Brothers, Mountain, Jimi Hendrix, Jethro Tull, and Ten Years After. More than 200,000 fans—some of them naked—braved the unbearable heat that hovered at one hundred degrees at 10 AM and reached 105 degrees by the afternoon. Water trucks were eventually brought in for the crowds, and salt tablets were distributed through the audience.

"I remember it being real hot," says Johnny. "It was horrible playing in that heat. I played with the Allman Brothers. I met them at one of the festivals and we started playing together a lot. It was great music—great blues-rock. Duane was still with them. I liked him a lot—his slide playing—all of it. I liked Dickey's style too. That day, I jammed with Duane and Dickey Betts on 'Mountain Jam.' I never felt like it was a 'cuttin' contest' with Duane. Our styles went together pretty well and we took turns doin' leads. There wasn't any rivalry—it was just fun."

Edgar was having the time of his life playing drums in Johnny Winter And, but his enthusiasm took its toll on his hands. "Edgar was the only person who knew the songs, but Edgar's not a drummer," Johnny said during an interview with *Creem*. "He said he'd help us out though till we got somebody. By the time he was done his hands were all wrecked and bloodied, just a *mess*."

"Johnny asked me to fill in when Rick Derringer's brother left the band," said Edgar. "I played drums for a couple of weeks. After the Atlanta Pop Festival, it just got progressively worse and worse. When I was a kid, I played drums at the clubs, but I had never played drums in that kind of situation. On a concert stage, it's just massive levels. Johnny was using six Fender twins on each side. It was extremely loud and they didn't really have adequate monitors so you could hear everything the way they did in later years. So I was just banging as hard as physically possible to play and still couldn't hear what I was doing. I got to the point where I had tape and Band-Aids on my hands and had difficulty hanging onto the sticks because of it. I loved it though; it was great playing drums in a real rock band. Johnny was playing 'Rock and Roll, Hoochie Koo' and all of the songs from *Johnny Winter And*. It was very exciting."

"Edgar played loud no matter whether he could or not," adds Johnny. "His hands were actually bloody from playing so hard."

# Broke-Down Engine

Despite Edgar's heroic efforts, it was obvious Johnny had to find a new drummer fast. Johnny Winter And was gigging throughout Florida with Tin House, a Florida-based band that Steve Paul also managed, as the opening act. He discovered Tin House that April. In June, the band signed with Paul, who booked them as Johnny's opening band, got them a record deal with Epic Records, and moved them up to Staatsburg. Tin House guitarist Floyd Radford would later play in Edgar's White Trash, and join Johnny's band as second guitarist in 1974.

During that tour, Johnny kept hearing about a drummer named Bobby Caldwell. Radford suggested they audition him in Orlando.

"We set up these big amplifiers, P.A. system, drums, everything in my bass player's parents' living room, where we rehearsed," said Radford. "Bobby didn't know it was an audition; he thought we were just getting together to jam."

Caldwell, age eighteen, was playing in a Florida band called Noah's Ark, which had been signed to Decca Records and Liberty Records for several singles. Ironically, he almost didn't go to the audition.

"A friend called to ask if I would like to come down," said Caldwell. "I politely declined. He said, 'But it's Johnny and Edgar Winter.' I said, 'Okay, but I'm not really big on jammin' with people.' When you're playing drums, you're just providing a back drop for everybody to solo. It could go for hours and it's not challenging. I went and stood around for three hours. Hour after hour, these people are coming in and out and I'm thinking, 'C'mon! You want to play—let's play.' Finally they called me in and I started playing this MACH 3 type of drum patterns. They all joined in and we played for thirty-five to forty minutes. At the end, Johnny asked me if I could travel, and said he wanted me in his band."

Caldwell joined Johnny Winter And in July 1970 and moved up to Staatsburg. He had jammed with the Allman Brothers Band; that connection wasn't lost on Johnny. "Bobby Caldwell was a real aggressive drummer," says Johnny. "A real good rock drummer."

Caldwell felt alienated from the rest of the band, but pegged it to being the new kid on the block. "There was nobody in that band or organization you could talk to," he said. "It was very cold initially. Johnny seemed like a nice enough guy, but was a little bit standoffish in the beginning. If I had a problem, I'd go to Teddy Slatus, our tour manager, but he had to ask Johnny. It was frustrating. Initially it was very much a sideman situation, but it got to respecting how good it was, and we became more of a band and got very close."

With minimal rehearsals, the new lineup played their first gig in Florida, then flew to Europe and headlined a festival in Marseille, France. Johnny introduced a Rolling Stones song at that concert that would become one of his signature live numbers.

"When we finished at Marseille, we did 'Jumpin' Jack Flash' as an encore," said Caldwell. "We had jammed on it at the house in Staatsburg. We never intended on doing that. We were just screwing off and started playing that song. Johnny loved it 'cause he loved the Rolling Stones. Johnny would start it onstage and we'd all fall into it. Rick would look at me. I'd look at him, Hobbs would look over, we'd all look at Johnny, sort of straighten our tie a little bit—figuratively speaking—and play."

Before the official release of *Johnny Winter And* in August 1970, Paul delivered advance copies to progressive-rock radio stations in Detroit—WKNR-FM, WABX, and WXYZ-FM—to generate a buzz for the show at Detroit's Eastown Theater. Prior to that gig, Johnny attended the Ann Arbor Blues Festival—getting up at 9 AM (which was and still is an ungodly hour for him) to see his idols Howlin' Wolf, Albert King, Bobby "Blue" Bland, Otis Rush, and Son House, as well as Hound Dog Taylor, Johnny Shines, Roosevelt Sykes, and Robert Lockwood Jr. Throughout most of the three-day festival, Johnny remained a spectator, telling a *Creem* reporter, "They don't need any modern blues up here." But on Sunday, he joined Luther Allison for an inspired jam that spectators described as a "killer competition" with both guitarists playing at the peak of their powers.

Mark Erlewine, the luthier who owns Erlewine Guitars in Austin, and sold Johnny his first Lazer guitar in 1984, remembers that performance.

"Our family traditionally ran the backstage bar at the festival," Erlewine said. "When Johnny Winter came, I was worried about him thinking, 'He's a white kid, a great rocker—poseur as a blues player; I don't know if he should go onstage and play with Luther Allison.' But it was an incredible duel between the two of them—just grinnin' and having the best time. I was shocked how good it was."

Johnny Winter And played a date in London, then flew back to New York to perform at an antiwar rock festival held at New York's Shea Stadium on August 6, 1970. An estimated 20,000 people showed up at the Summer Festival for Peace to hear twelve hours of music by a lineup that included Jimi Hendrix, Janis Joplin, Paul Simon, Steppenwolf, Creedence Clearwater Revival, Al Kooper, Richie Havens, and Miles Davis.

"The twelve-hour festival at Shea Stadium was pretty radical," said Shannon. "There were a lot of speeches by Abbie Hoffman, a bunch of people like that. There wasn't violence but there was a feeling of violence behind it, like they came there for the rally instead of the music."

To be closer to the gig, the band stayed at the Chelsea Hotel, where Johnny and Caldwell had an unexpected visitor. "Janis Joplin came to the hotel room that afternoon," said Caldwell. "Janis came in and tackled Johnny right at the door. Started calling him affectionate names in a good-natured way. 'Honey.' 'You ole SOB!' Johnny was stone sober, but she wasn't of her right mind. She had been drinking excessively when she came down to Shea Stadium that night, and started an altercation with a bunch of photographers and reporters."

Johnny Winter And soon became known for its wild stage show, as well as the musicians' prowess. Johnny and Derringer played inspired guitar duels that pushed both musicians to greater heights.

"I remember it was really unbelievable, charismatic," Liz Derringer, Rick's wife during that timeframe, told Muise. "They used to get in such a frenzy and so crazy that Rick used to run between Johnny's legs and Johnny would jump over him. And they'd do a lot of battling dual-guitar stuff. It was pretty incredible."

Paul believed in the power of theatrics and encouraged the band to push the limits.

"One of the things Steve Paul liked to dwell on, as a manager, was, 'A good musician belongs in the pit,'" Derringer explained to Muise. "What that meant is you can go to any Broadway show and hear great musicians but you never see one. 'Cause those great musicians end up in the pit. So what makes the guy on the stage? He's more than a great musician. He is a great entertainer. So we were always schooled first and foremost in being entertainers."

"I dressed more rock 'n' roll in that band," says Johnny. "I had a sequined silver tee shirt that was tank top on one side and had a sleeve on the other. I wore suede vests with fringe and had a dark blue leather jacket with long fringe. We were doin' more showmanship than before 'cause we were doin' rock 'n' roll. Rick was down on the floor and I had my guitar pointed down at him. We played off of each other. We did a lot of jumpin' around too."

"Johnny and Rick were great onstage together," said Caldwell. "They played so opposite. Rick can't play like Johnny stylistically—he just doesn't hear music that way. Johnny couldn't play like Rick does if he had to. It's two different worlds because Johnny doesn't hear it that way either. Once we started coming together—it was a juggernaut—bigger than big. If Johnny started to play a song out of the blue, we jumped in. Everybody knew that anything could happen at any given time and not in a negative way. Rick didn't like the fact Johnny could not play something over and over the same way—in a structured way because Rick is such a polished person playing wise. But he would simply grin and bear it. He knew this was his shot at getting exposure."

Despite his misgivings about playing with another guitarist, Johnny enjoyed playing his Les Paul gold top with Derringer in the band. "I liked being a frontman, but with a second guitar, I was free to do more solos; I wasn't tied down so much because he played rhythm," says Johnny. "I liked him a lot as a guitar player. His style complemented my style really well. We planned out the parts ahead of time. Rick could tell what I was gonna play and fit himself into it. He was great to work with; there were no clashes at all. I always took the reins when we were playing; I was gonna make sure it was my band."

There was a great deal of camaraderie both on- and offstage in Johnny Winter And. "Rick and I were pretty good friends," says Johnny. "We'd smoke pot and talk about music. Randy Hobbs was one of the best bass players I ever heard; I probably got along with Randy the best."

But there was a black cloud on the horizon that hit on September 19, when the band played the Boston Tea Party, a psychedelic club in Bean Town. The somber announcement of Jimi Hendrix's death came over the club's sound system during that gig. Devastated by the loss of a musical icon and friend, the band worked through their grief by memorializing him in a song.

"That night we huddled together in somebody's room and threw together a tune called '21st Century Man' about Jimi Hendrix," said Caldwell. "It's a single we recorded in Columbia Studios two days after his death. It wasn't a tribute song, but it was inspired by Jimi's death. It's a pretty cool song and it still sounds great."

Never released on a Johnny Winter And LP, "21st Century Man" was put out by CBS as the B side of "Rock and Roll, Hoochie Koo." Derringer got songwriting credit; he and Johnny shared production credit. Those credits didn't seem fair to Caldwell. "It was collaborative," he said, "but at that time there was the caste system of India going on."

Hendrix died on September 18, 1970. His death certificate listed "inhalation of vomit, barbiturate intoxication, insufficient evidence of circumstances, open verdict" under cause of death. His family requested a private funeral for family and friends; the service was held at the Dunlop Baptist Church in Seattle on October 1, 1970. Invited guests included childhood friends as well as Hendrix's bass player Noel Redding, his drummer Mitch Mitchell, Miles Davis, John Hammond Jr., Buddy Miles, Johnny, and Steve Paul.

"I was on the road when Jimi died and it shocked me," says Johnny. "To be so bad where you just have to give up and die. I hadn't played with him recently when he died and it had been awhile since I had seen him. Janis Joplin and Al Wilson, the guitar player for Canned Heat, died around the same time period. It seemed like everybody was going. I was using heroin at the time but it [the deaths] didn't affect me at all. I figured it was a good thing to do—because it made things better. I didn't think it would ever kill me.

"I think a lot of it [his death] had to do with the pressures of being a star—the same reasons I was having troubles with were giving him trouble. Not having any real friends. I think he just kind of gave up on it. He wasn't making any money—I'm sure he wasn't making as much as he should have. Nobody made much money in those days—the record companies were making all the money. It seemed like he was getting worse but he never talked about it.

"I went to Jimi's funeral with Steve Paul—Jimi played at his club a lot. I went to the church. The preacher was very... it seemed like he thought he had all these sinners there and it was his chance to save everybody. He was saying stuff that sounded like he really didn't know too much about Jimi. He was saying things like, 'Jimi was great but the real great person is God.' A lot of stuff about 'Jimi is not important; the real important thing is God,' and nobody wanted to hear that. It seemed like the guy was insensitive.

"I don't think I went up to the coffin. There were some nice floral arrangements—floral guitars. I wondered what I was doin' there. I think Steve wanted to go, and talked me into going. I didn't feel like I was that good a friend of Jimi's to be at his funeral, but I guess there were a lot of people who weren't as good friends as I was. I'm just not comfortable going to funerals.

"We had a jam at the club at the Hilton Inn hotel where we stayed. Jimi may have paid for the party—I remember him saying he wanted to have a party instead of a funeral. I don't really know why he talked about that. I heard some of his band went out in the parking lot and cried—I don't know if that's true or not. Mitch Mitchell—I heard he was crying. But it was fairly happy—everybody was feeling like they were doing it because Jimi wanted them to party. So they were gonna try to do the best they could for him."

•◆•

Johnny flew back the next day to play a weekend of triple bills at the Fillmore East, with Tin House and Buddy Miles as opening acts.

"That was during Johnny's psychedelic phase," said Radford. "He was wearing blue jeans and an embroidered top with silver chains. Every time he would come on the stage, it was magical. He had an aura about him and everything he'd do. He's play a note on his guitar, or walk out onstage; and immediately, you felt it. When he played, his aura exploded."

Meanwhile, Caldwell was exploding over his sideman's pay, especially after seeing thousands of dollars counted out in hotel rooms after the gigs. He had been earning $150 to $200 a weekend playing in Noah's Ark, and wasn't doing much better in Johnny Winter And.

"I was making only a little better than that initially—which was an outrage," he said. "It wasn't a case of being paid what you were worth—it was a case of what you would tolerate. I remember sitting with Rick in Steve's hotel room in Miami. I said, 'I'm quitting the band. I don't give a damn. I don't care who it is. If I don't get paid more, I'm done.'"

Paul was envisioning a solo project for Derringer, and tried to smooth things over by telling Caldwell he could be part of that project.

"Steve Paul had an idea that someday he would like to manage Rick," said Caldwell. "He wanted me to be involved 'cause Rick and I play well together. Steve was only managing Edgar and Johnny at that time, and was directing Rick's affairs—whatever that meant. Steve said, 'Rick is going to be doing some things on his own in the near future—we'd like you to be a part of it and stick around.' I thought, that's fine—but we're still talking about money now. It was a pivotal moment because I didn't care. Things changed very quickly and he agreed to pay me what I was asking."

From Johnny's dramatic rise to fame in 1969 until the present, Johnny has always been the star with his musicians relegated to sideman status. Given that dynamic, Steve Paul felt that he and Johnny treated the band members responsibly. But Caldwell had concerns about the way the players were treated, especially Randy Hobbs.

"Randy was a very good bass player with a lot of experience, but he wasn't taken very seriously," said Caldwell. "He was a child star along with Rick in the McCoys, and he idolized Johnny. Randy was a sycophant and Johnny and Randy grew to be good friends. Everything was, 'Oh yes, Johnny, you're right, Johnny.'

"It was an ongoing joke. We'd all be sitting around, killing time on the road. We'd be reading *Rolling Stone* or *Creem* magazine and Randy would be reading *Guns & Ammo*. He was a redneck—I'm not saying that disparagingly. Nowadays, every country band member probably reads *Guns & Ammo*. But in those days, it was all about arts and music. Everybody was more into the yin, the feminine side of their energy, and Randy was firmly ensconced in the yang.

"When we were playing in Stockholm, we went to a club after the show. He'd just bought a new Stetson and some drunken girl kept hitting it. He was gone, but he had a tremendous reservoir of ability to hold it. You wouldn't know it—he could have drunk, done drugs, and still played and hardly made any mistakes. This woman kept hitting his hat, and all of a sudden it got pretty nasty. Randy slapped or hit her, and her blood went all over his new Stetson. Everybody stood up, and there was chaos. Another time, Randy had words with a union worker backstage. Randy had a pair of pliers in his guitar case and started chasing the guy with these pliers like he was gonna do some dental work or pull his nose off. That's the kind of things we dealt with—we'd laugh about it.

"Randy Hobbs was like a second-class citizen in that band. Everyone looked at Randy as someone to tolerate and politely put up with. He was a fine bass player but he was always high on something. Yet he could always get up there and play—every night. It was unbelievable."

•◆•

In early 1971, the band released *Johnny Winter And Live,* which made the *Billboard* charts that March, peaked at number forty and stayed on the charts for twenty-seven weeks. Johnny earned his first and only gold record in 1974 with *Johnny Winter And Live.*

"A live album seemed like the right thing to do at the time," Johnny says. "We recorded it at the Fillmore East and Pirates World in Florida [an eighty-seven-acre theme park in Dania with a large outdoor concert venue]. Our shows were ninety minutes, so we had three hours to pick from. The audiences seemed to like the new band pretty good, real good in fact. *Johnny Winter And* sold worse than anything we had out to that point, but the *Johnny Winter And Live* record sold more than any other record I ever had out."

A high-energy showcase that captures the intensity and excitement of that lineup, *Johnny Winter And Live* is the hardest-rocking recording that Johnny ever released, almost an anomaly in his catalogue. (*Captured Live!* comes close, but never reaches the intensity of *Johnny Winter And Live.*) The scorching guitars of Johnny and Derringer on "Good Morning Little School Girl" take the Sonny Boy Williamson blues standard into the outer stratosphere of rock, making the Yardbirds' version sound like Pat Boone. Many rock aficionados consider it one of the best rock 'n' roll records ever, and Caldwell explains why he thinks it earned that moniker.

"You can hear it's a real group—it's not a 'Johnny, you've got it all going, and I hope you can pull it off' like it usually is," he said. "Every night was a juggernaut. It was unstoppable; as big a stomping band as you've ever heard. It was like walking in the forest and there was King Kong standing there. You thought all the monkeys you had encountered on the path looked pretty big, and all of a sudden you see this thing that's one hundred feet tall. That's what comes across as a group on that record."

While Johnny toured with Johnny Winter And, Edgar put his own band together with a lineup of Louisiana and Texas musicians.

Edgar and his band lived at Hearthstone Farm in Clinton Corners, New York, not very far from Johnny's house in Staatsburg.

"When I was putting together White Trash, Johnny used to come out to the Hearthstone Farm and listen to the band play," Edgar said. "On occasion, he would sit in. He played slide on 'I've Got News for You' on the *White Trash* album. That song came out great. I loved the primitive authentic slide guitar in contrast to the Ray Charles R&B-style horn."

With their live recording on its way up the charts, Johnny Winter And began a tour to follow up the release. In January and February 1971, they played concerts in Denmark, Sweden, Germany, and England. During their off time in London, Johnny jammed with Traffic at a college gig. Two days later, Johnny celebrated his twenty-seventh birthday headlining the Royal Albert Hall.

"The Royal Albert Hall show was like Oscar night with the red carpet," said Caldwell. "Everybody who was in town came to see us that night: our competition, Johnny admirers, flaggers, whoever didn't like us. It was a great show."

The band returned to the States in March for a three-night gig at the Fillmore East with the Elvin Bishop Group and the Allman Brothers. *At Fillmore East*, the Allman Brothers Band's double album of that performance that earned a gold record and cemented that band's reputation, was recorded at those shows.

"The live *At Fillmore East* album gives you the impression they were headlining, but Johnny Winter And was the headliner," said Caldwell. "That was probably the biggest rock show there outside of Hendrix, the Rolling Stones, and the Beatles at Shea Stadium. Bill Graham did a tremendous job. Believe me, when it's time to go on, you better go on. It was run like a military operation."

Johnny's touring schedule continued to be exhausting. He'd been playing a breakneck schedule of gigs and festivals since he moved to New York. "The first three years were pretty chaotic," he says. "I was playing pretty much every night. We were busy all the time. We were always traveling—playing Europe and the States. Steve wanted us to work as much as possible and I wanted to play as much as I could."

Johnny needed drugs and alcohol to unwind and his drug use escalated with his fame.

"After the gigs, we had parties in my hotel room," he said. "We'd have psychedelic drugs and downs at the parties—usually Seconal—and I'd find a girl to go to bed with. The parties lasted three or four hours, just sittin' around getting' high, and talkin'. You'd be so keyed up from playing; it helped to take something to bring you down. You either drank or took a down. You get real anxious before you play, and it's hard to calm down when you know you're gonna be playin' for a whole bunch of people. Believe me, if there's not a bunch of people, I still get nervous. Even playin' in small places. I was probably drinkin' a fifth of Jack Daniels a night. When I did heroin, I wasn't drinkin' as much."

Caldwell remembers the tour schedule as grueling with added pressures hoisted on Johnny as the star.

"We were playing three or four nights a week," said Caldwell. "It was really grinding because we were traveling—going to the airports, then getting picked up, getting off the plane, getting into the cars, going to the hotels, from there getting to the gigs, doing sound check, coming back, meeting people. Johnny felt the pressure more. That's the hook about being famous; the more people know who you are, the more demanding they are. You're constantly being interviewed unless you're in the car with the rest of the band or you're home. I think Johnny felt that constant fishbowl thing in addition to traveling and playing."

With the continual touring and mounting pressure, Johnny viewed heroin as a harmless escape and made no bones about his drug use.

"I didn't hide it at all," Johnny says. "I didn't have any reason to hide it—I was real upfront about it. Everybody was pretty upfront about the drugs they did. They didn't talk about heroin as much as I did—but everything else. People admitted their drug use more than they do now. People would tell me sometimes, 'You shouldn't be so open about this,' and I'd say, 'Well, why not?' I didn't realize it was different from pot or LSD or magic mushrooms or whatever. Steve Paul hated it; he didn't want me to do it.

He told me how bad it was and I said, 'Yeah, maybe for some people but I'm smart enough to stay away [not get hooked] from it.'

"Teddy Slatus didn't like me doin' heroin either. Nobody around me liked it. Edgar knew I was doin' drugs—he did 'em with me but he stopped before it got too bad. When he knew I had a drug problem, he said he'd help in any way he could. I don't think I would have ever wanted to do heroin if it hadn't been for the fame. You just felt that lonely feeling; you couldn't get away from it. With heroin, you didn't feel bad about what was going on around you. Anybody that was trying to take advantage of you, you'd feel like you're gettin' what you wanted out of them. You didn't care about what people were doin' around you. You feel good within yourself and don't care about anything else. Drugs are amazing—they help a lot of stuff. They just don't keep lasting."

Heroin was considered to be just part of the scene. The band knew Johnny and Hobbs indulged, but had no idea of the extent of Johnny's growing addiction.

"It was common knowledge," said Caldwell. "He certainly wasn't trying to hide it from anyone in the band, and there was little made of it. No one had a problem; it was really a recreational drug, as dumb as that sounds. It was complete and total ignorance. I know Johnny didn't realize the ramifications of it."

In April, Johnny Winter And played the Fillmore West and the Fillmore East. In May, Johnny appeared at Liberty Hall in Houston with Willie Dixon and the Chicago All Stars, which included Willie Dixon on bass and vocals, Lee Jackson on guitar, Lafayette Leake on piano, Big Walter Horton on harmonica, and Clifton James on drums. Although he was probably delighted to play with those blues icons, he has no memory of that show.

•◆•

Johnny Winter And played the Spectrum with the Allman Brothers Band and the Detroit Rock Revival with them as well as Edgar Winter's White Trash, Bob Seger, and the J. Geils Band. They flew to London for another show at the Royal Albert Hall on June 22.

When the band played a show at the Fillmore East two days later, the musicians had no idea it would be their final gig.

"We were tearing it up—all the way to the point where he decided he had to go in to rehab," said Caldwell. "If he had been completely straight, he would have been playing one hundred times better—but nobody in any rock 'n' roll band was straight. I don't think Johnny was in that bad a shape—any better or any worse than most people—he was just a part of it."

Derringer was also taken by surprise when Johnny went into rehab. "We thought Johnny pretty much had it under control," he told Muise. "Obviously, he was dabbling with heroin. But that's all we thought it was. Just dabbling. We didn't see it excessively, hardly at all. It wasn't until he announced to us that he had a problem and he was going to stop the band and check himself into a hospital that we knew the problem was to that extent."

Johnny was in worse shape than he let on. Although he avoided overdosing by always letting somebody else shoot up first, within six months of mainlining every day, he had become a full-blown junkie.

"I tried to stop, but it was very hard—almost impossible," Johnny says. "I didn't think it would happen to me. I thought I was keepin' it under control. I didn't think I was doin' enough to get hooked. You started not being able to function correctly without doin' some heroin. If you didn't do it, you just didn't feel good at all—you'd feel real emotionally messed up. Physically it was even worse. I had the shakes. If you did more heroin, you'd just get normal but it didn't last very long. I was still playin' out and I remember goin' to California for the Fillmore West show and thinking, 'What am I gonna do here? I don't have any heroin and I gotta find somebody with some.' I felt terrible. Physically and mentally. You just felt bad, felt like nothing else would help to get you back on track but doin' some heroin. You hated yourself. As soon as that started to happen, I wanted to get away from it, but I couldn't get away from it on my own."

In early July, Johnny's management team told the band Johnny would be taking a break.

"When Johnny went into the hospital in the summer of 1971, Johnny Winter And broke up," said Caldwell. "There was talk of him taking a break or us taking a month off. It was rather sudden, but it wasn't like any major calamity or anything. The band was blazin'—we were having a good time but there was always some high drama. Everything is high drama with Johnny. It was like, 'If there wasn't a problem, let's create one.' That's how it was with Steve Paul and Teddy running the ship. Steve slave-driving Johnny for his own end, and Teddy seeing the same movie as Steve.

"This had been brewing for six weeks—we'd had a week or two off when they decided to pull the trigger. Teddy called and says Johnny's decided he's going to go in a hospital in New Orleans, we're gonna take a break, we're gonna send you a week or two weeks' pay; or some crap. The obvious question for everyone was, 'How long is he gonna be gone; how long is it gonna take?'

"Curiously, I had gotten a telegram from a couple of guys in Iron Butterfly who wanted to put a band together with me. The timing couldn't have been better. I went to L.A. and started Captain Beyond, a progressive-rock band, with the guys from Iron Butterfly [guitarist Rhino a.k.a. Larry Reinhardt and bassist Lee Dorman] and the original singer [Rod Evans] for Deep Purple. Rick moved over to play with Edgar and Randy just hung out and didn't know what to do—poor guy.

"Had Steve Paul and Teddy any brains and come to everybody and said, 'Johnny is gonna take six months off or nine months off. Do whatever you got to do—we'll put you on some kind of retainer so when Johnny's feeling better, we can reconvene and get back to it.' But because they were so opportunistic, greedy, and short-sighted—and so, 'I can fix, replace anybody, anytime,' they just missed the whole deal. Imagine if they had treated everybody right and that band had stayed together four or five years. It would have been a historical band; Johnny would have been worth a gazillion dollars and so would I. But they didn't have the foresight to see that would have been the smart way to do it."

Derringer has also expressed resentment about the way that band dissolved, as well as doubts about the extent of Johnny's addiction.

"I still don't think the problem was as drastic as he let on," he told Muise. "I believe that what happened... we were in England, touring. And he got a chance to see how they dealt with their drug addicts in England. They put them on a maintenance program. They allowed them to come and pick up their drugs, at cheap prices, from a pharmacy. Johnny returned from that trip to England and he said, many times, 'Man, that looks great. You never have to worry about dealing on the street with people. You can just go and the government's gonna give you the drugs for the rest of your life.' He said, 'Boy, that's what I would like.' So, in effect, I don't think he had as much of a problem as he let on at that time."

To deny the extent of Johnny's drug addiction or to believe he faked it to get on a methadone program demonstrates the bitterness some musicians still harbor against him for giving them a taste of success and then moving on without them. And also suggests just how close mouthed Johnny was with anyone who wasn't an old friend from Texas.

Despite the doubts of band members, Johnny was in rough shape, physically and mentally. Traveling with Roma, who was also frightened by his addiction, he went home to Texas to try to sort things out. Johnny saw what drugs had done to Janis Joplin and Jimi Hendrix and knew that he, too, had lost control of his life.

"You can't make a career out of drugs, and they tried to," Johnny says. "I did too. But I went for help because I didn't want to die. I don't think Jimi or Janis wanted to die, but I don't think they wanted to admit they needed help. They probably didn't think anybody could do them any good. You do have that feeling like the psychiatrists don't know what they're talking about. You're smarter than they are—a lot of people have that idea that it just wasn't gonna help. But I knew it was something I had to try before dying."

Johnny traveled to Beaumont to tell his mother he wanted to die and just couldn't handle his lifestyle anymore. His parents suggested therapy with Dr. Burns Belk, the psychiatrist who had conducted his IQ tests when he was a child. "I had great parents; they wanted to help me and did what they could," says Johnny. "They didn't know what to say, really—it was so far beyond anything they could imagine.

"Just trying therapy made things a little bit better. I went for sessions and talked to him but not for very long. It didn't take too long before they put me in the hospital—they could tell I was suicidal. I was thinkin' of how to do it. I thought I'd probably overdose on downs. I went through my first withdrawal right before I went in the hospital in Beaumont. They tried giving me tranquilizers, and I had sessions and group meetings. It helped, but not as much as I wanted it to—I still wanted drugs. They gave me antidepressants in the hospital and they just didn't do much good."

Johnny stayed at the Beaumont Neurological Center for six weeks, but it became obvious the center wasn't equipped to deal with heroin addicts. Dr. Belk researched other options and decided Johnny had a better chance at recovery as an inpatient at River Oaks Hospital in New Orleans.

Pat Rush, a guitarist Johnny met during his stay at the New Orleans hospital who later joined him for the *Nothin' But the Blues* tour and the recording sessions for *White, Hot & Blue*, remembers Johnny's state of mind when he decided he needed help.

"When Johnny was on the road with Derringer and those guys, they all were trying to see who could do the most dope and still play that night," said Rush. "But Johnny was really getting tired. He was calling Steve up and saying, 'I'm doing drugs to wake up, drugs to go to sleep, drugs to play, drugs for everything, I'm touring, and touring, and touring. I need time off.' Steve would say, 'Well, you're gonna be off the road for a month when you're in the studio.' Anybody in the business knows that off means off, not working in the studio. He finally got fed up, so he checked himself into River Oaks. I thought that was pretty amazing—that he did it himself."

Steve Paul remembers it differently. "I remember him expressing unhappiness, but don't recall him seriously speaking of suicide," Paul said. "At one point I called his parents and asked them to put him in rehab. I cancelled a virtually sold-out arena tour, and my only concern was that he get better."

Celebrities being treated for addiction and hospitals focused on addictive disorders were not an everyday occurrence in 1971. Many publications reporting Johnny's hiatus referred to River Oaks as a mental hospital; a 1972 *Rolling Stone* article described him as "Johnny Winter, frail Texas albino bluesman/turned/rock superstar/turned/ mental hospital inmate."

"River Oaks was completely drug free and I thought I'd give that a try," says Johnny. "They took in heroin addicts and a lot of different kinds of addicts—speed and everything else. I was in that hospital for nine months without doing anything at all. There were several floors and had eight people in a room. The people always changed—people got out and new ones came in. They had all kinds of manic depressives, people who had drug problems, any kind of mental problem you can imagine. It was all mental stuff. There were both girls and guys in the hospital—girls had their own rooms."

Withdrawal symptoms, which begin from six to forty-eight hours after stopping habitual heroin use and subside after a week, include dilated pupils, diarrhea, runny nose, goose bumps, abdominal pain, fever, physical and mental agitation, nausea, and vomiting. Kicking a long-term habit is also accompanied by a feeling of heaviness, cramps, cold sweats, chills, and severe muscle and bone aches. Quitting cold turkey causes muscle spasms in the legs and increases the intensity of withdrawal symptoms, including drug cravings, headaches, sleeplessness, confusion, depression, and anxiety.

According to the National Institute on Drug Abuse, heroin literally changes the brains and behavior of users because the body adapts to the presence of the drug. Heroin withdrawal can cause serious physical and emotional trauma, including stroke, heart attack, and even death. To avoid that risk, conventional treatment uses drugs such as methadone or valium to wean addicts off of heroin in a controlled environment. But the River Oaks Hospital staff decided Johnny could withstand withdrawal without medical intervention, and made him kick heroin cold turkey.

"They didn't give me any drugs for withdrawal; you just had to make it on your own," says Johnny. "I felt horrible for three months, mentally and physically. I thought I would die. Physical withdrawal lasted a couple of months—you can't sleep and you can't eat. I started to feel a little better after three months because I could finally sleep. But it went beyond physical addiction; it affected you long after the physical withdrawal. The mental part was the worst part; psychological addiction was the hardest part to get rid of. When you're tryin' to get off of heroin, it messes with your head. It's horrible, just horrible. There's no way to explain how bad it makes you feel. You just don't feel like you have any control over anything. Things you would normally love, you don't care about anymore. It's the worst feeling in the world and you can't make it go away. Except without doing more drugs."

Johnny couldn't have visitors for the first six months at River Oaks Hospital. He didn't mind the isolation; he was committed to cleaning up his act.

"At first I didn't like havin' people visit me," says Johnny. "I was trying to get rid of my drug problem—I didn't want to have people comin' in and tellin' me what they were doin'. I was in the hospital six months before Carol could come see me. That first visit was real nice. She'd come down every once in a while after that—some of my friends came to see me too. Uncle John and Keith Ferguson. Nobody from New York came to visit—not Steve Paul, Teddy, or Rick Derringer—just my friends from Texas. Steve and Teddy called so it didn't bother me they didn't visit."

Like most inpatient facilities, the days were structured between individual counseling sessions, group sessions, recreation, and personal down time.

"We had TVs and had a little time to watch them," says Johnny. "We could read—but for me, it depended upon how big the print is. I could read *Rolling Stone*; I got it at the hospital all the time. I don't read much now; my eyesight is worse than it was. I can see details if I'm close enough. Every day, you had an hour off to go outside and play basketball or whatever, and you had time off in the afternoon to take a nap if you wanted to.

"They had decent food at the hospital and you could wear regular clothes. We wore sandals, jeans, blue-jean shirts. I made some real good friendships. I got to be real good friends with one girl—I think

I was the first guy she went to bed with—she was about fifteen. We stayed in touch afterward—I've been friends with her for years."

Turner remembers Johnny talking about that friendship during one of their visits.

"Johnny told me he had a sexual experience with one of the girl patients," said Turner. "They had an encounter on the levee down by the river. Needless to say, it was against the rules, and he got in trouble for that."

Turner visited Johnny twice during his stay in River Oaks, and recalls Johnny being severely depressed.

"He was having trouble with his anxiety and from what he said to me, it was severe depression," said Turner. "River Oaks had people that were long term; one guy died in there shortly after Johnny left. That guy fascinated Johnny. He was a raving lunatic, completely mad. They would chain him to the bed; he would shit in his hands and throw it at the staff. I don't think Johnny got anything too special down there except a break. He just stayed awhile and when he felt better he left."

Although the hospital was considered drug free, alcohol wasn't considered to be a drug. "They didn't give out medication; you had to get an order from a doctor just to get an aspirin," says Johnny. "The hospital was real antidrug, but they had a happy hour where you could have one drink—one beer or one shot of Jack Daniels or whatever. You couldn't do that now—they think you'll just switch off to alcohol. They didn't have the twelve-step program there."

Johnny enjoyed individual sessions with his doctor; it helped him understand his behavior and learn ways to change it.

"My one-on-one therapy doctor was Bob Davis," says Johnny. "I liked him a lot. I talked about the things that were bothering me. He pretty much said I just had to put up with the things that were makin' me want to do heroin in the first place. Those one-on-one sessions definitely helped me to feel better. There was also group therapy—the counselors were real serious about that. There were about thirty people in group session; if you didn't want to talk you didn't have to. People would talk about any problems they had in the past or were having in the present."

His private sessions validated him as person, which was critical after being treated like a star and feeling he was little more than a meal ticket to his manager. But something was terribly askew at the group sessions, which heightened his feelings of not being accepted and brought back early memories of being shunned for being albino. During one session, the counselor insisted group members were more enamored by Johnny's celebrity than by who he was as a person. Johnny recalls members of the group countering that they liked him for who he was, but finally getting argued down by the counselor.

"That really pissed me off," says Johnny. "It seemed stupid to me. He finally got people to agree—it took him a long time, but he finally did. It really pissed me off. In an hour session, nobody would admit it to the very last. They figured it was just gonna go on forever if they didn't admit it. So people finally said, 'I guess we do think of him more as a star.' That really made me think I went there for nothin'. I didn't think it was right of them to say that, and it made me not want to quit."

Hurt and discouraged by the way he was treated, Johnny searched for solace and acceptance outside the walls of the hospital. Once again, he found comfort in fast friends who provided him with drugs to numb his pain.

"After a while, I could come and go as I pleased and I met people on the outside," he says. "I got drugs while I was in River Oaks. I'd go walkin' around and people would come up to me. There was a guy who lived right by the hospital who had drugs; I could go there and do anything I wanted. I got drugs on the outside, but I didn't take very many."

Johnny loved smoking pot and brought back a joint from one of his outside visits. With drug addiction rehabilitation still in its infancy, the staff of River Oaks had no clue that pot—compared to heroin or speed—was a relatively harmless drug. Trained to treat patients suffering from mental illness, who might become self-destructive during a psychotic episode, their response was harsh and punitive.

"I smoked a joint in the hospital," Johnny says. "They caught me and used arm and leg restraints to strap me into bed when I was sleepin'. I was strapped to a bed for twelve hours a day for a month.

The reasoning was that you might feel so guilty; you'd try to kill yourself. I didn't feel guilty at all—I felt like smokin' grass was fine. I thought that was pretty ridiculous. I wasn't suicidal."

Although he never played guitar *in* the hospital, music remained a strong force in Johnny's life. He used his time outside the hospital to work on his chops. "If you were good for a while, they let you go out on certain nights," says Johnny. "So I got to leave and play with Thunderhead at a club called the Nutcracker. I just walked in the club; they were all nice to me although they were kinda nervous. I didn't play with them the first night, but I did after that. I went to the band house too, where most of 'em lived. You needed a car to get there, but they didn't mind picking me up—I had a lot of fun with them."

"I met Johnny when he was in rehab and I was playing with Thunderhead," said Rush. "He knew Grego—Greg Howard, who owned the Nutcracker and was friends with the band. Everybody had their own place in New Orleans, but there was one apartment where we used to rehearse and hang out all the time. When Johnny started getting passes, he'd come and stay with us in our band house, and come out and play with us. We used to play at the Nutcracker a lot and we played with Johnny there. We also used to go to Thibodaux, an hour or so away, and play in big rock bars in Bayou country. During the first set, he hung out in the dressing room so nobody could see him. Then he'd come out in the last half of the second set and play a song or two with us. That would freak everybody out that Johnny Winter was onstage. He was doing it to work out his chops because, most of the time when he was in the hospital, he didn't play. Although I never went to the hospital to see him, I heard he had one of his Firebirds hanging off the bedpost. It was in there but he would never play it."

Thunderhead was a New Orleans–based band originally called Paper Steamboat. The lineup included Mike Dagger on vocals, Rush on lead and slide guitar, Ronnie Dobbs on lead and string guitar, and Othi T. Ware on bass. When drummer Bobby Torello (a.k.a. Bobby T.) joined the lineup, his nickname was Thunder, so they changed the band's name to Thunderhead.

Originally from West Haven, Connecticut, Torello moved to the Big Easy to fulfill a lifelong dream.

"My goal in life was to play with Johnny Winter, so I moved to New Orleans to find him," he said. "I heard he was there in the hospital, so I took a gig with a band in Mississippi. I played in Mississippi and hung out in New Orleans on my off nights. Johnny would jam with Paper Steamboat on weekends so I started jamming with them." Torello never met Johnny in New Orleans, but would meet him a year later through the Thunderhead connection.

Johnny had an opportunity to share a bigger spotlight when he joined his brother's band at a November 1971 show at New York's Academy of Music. That show was taped for *Roadwork*, a 1972 live double album by Edgar's Winter's White Trash that went gold.

"I played 'Rock and Roll, Hoochie Koo' with Edgar's band," says Johnny. "I was still in the hospital, but I went home for Christmas. It had been about six months since I played in front of an audience. It's hard to play after not playing out for a while, but I knew I wanted to do it. Playing with Edgar's band was a little different 'cause it's harder to play with musicians you haven't played with. My playing wasn't great; it could've been better."

"I was with Johnny at that show," said Jim Franklin, who traveled from Austin to see him. "Steve and Teddy always put me in touch with Johnny 'cause they knew I had a pacifying effect on him. He stayed in a hotel on Fifth Avenue right near Washington Square. I met up with him a few times that weekend, had lunch, and then went to the show. He seemed to be sharp because he wasn't stoned."

Johnny's appearance was unannounced until Edgar stepped up to the microphone, and said, "A lot of people keep asking me, 'Hey, where's your brother?'" as Johnny walked out onstage. "It was a great moment and somewhat of a historic moment with that introduction," said Edgar. "It was the first time he had ever sat in with one of my bands as opposed to me sitting in with one of his.

"I viewed it as a supportive thing to welcome him back, the perfect coming out experience for him. I really don't know if he did it as a favor to me or if he thought of it as something that was good for him. It certainly meant a lot to me personally; it is one of the most memorable moments of my entire career."

Six months after performing with Edgar's band, Johnny signed himself out of River Oaks Hospital. Feeling a bit shaken and disappointed by his experiences at the facility, he snorted heroin the day he was released.

"After nine months, the counselors kept saying, 'You don't really like Johnny because he's a good person, you like him because he's a rock 'n' roll star,'" Johnny explains. "I figured if they felt that way, I had no reason to stop. That was awful—thinkin' nobody liked me for myself. When I started again, I did a little bit of both—snorting it and shooting it. I got high when I got out but I just did it once in a while."

Then there was the unfortunate incident during a trip to Austin, where he ended up in a precarious situation that sabotaged his intentions to stay away from drugs.

"When he got out, Rocky Hill [Houston guitarist and brother of ZZ Top bassist Dusty Hill] and somebody else came to pick him up in a van," said Turner. "Rocky and everybody else was taking drugs back then. Rocky had a bunch of Quaaludes; more than one person could eat. The cops stopped them, so somebody quickly divided them up so nobody would die. Johnny didn't make it home before he was forced to take some drugs. Take drugs or go to jail—that was the choice in front of him. So it was sadly ironic that he didn't even make it home before he consumed a bunch of Quaaludes."

Between the Quaalude experience and his cravings for heroin, Johnny knew his stay at River Oaks had only provided a hiatus from drugs. He hadn't yet made a complete recovery.

"The first hospital withdrawal didn't do me much good," he says. "I put myself in different hospitals in New York several other times after that. I stayed at the Regents Hospital in New York for several months a little more than a year after I left River Oaks. When it finally worked, it was because I just got sick of it, sick of feeling that way. I was really tired of it. You have to be tired of it yourself and want to get off of it. I didn't go to a methadone clinic till after I got out of the hospital in New Orleans. I went to a clinic up in New York. I tried everything and I still wasn't happy, so I figured the methadone might do it for me and it did. I'm still doin' it. Makes me feel completely normal."

Long term use of heroin changes a person's biochemistry. Methadone, a synthetic substitute for morphine, helps former addicts function normally. Johnny's decision to treat his addiction in a long-term methadone maintenance program still draws criticism from people who perceive methadone as a way to substitute one drug for another, or view short-term treatment as the only acceptable use of the synthetic drug. Although it is not sedating or intoxicating, and blocks any euphoric or tranquilizing effects of opiate-class drugs, there is still a stigma attached to the use of methadone.

Derringer has been an outspoken critic of Johnny's participation in a methadone maintenance program, perceiving it as a substitute for heroin, with the same effects.

"I think it specifically was just something that he envisioned as a great lifestyle, strangely enough," Derringer told Muise. "And he used that opportunity to check himself into a hospital to put himself in some kind of situation where he could get stuff from legitimate sources rather than having to deal from the street. And that is basically what he still does today. It's sad to say... and he's been able to maintain that lifestyle of getting methadone from the state for twenty-five years."

Shannon, who still has a close relationship with Johnny, has a different understanding of the effects of methadone on Johnny's body.

"Taking methadone doesn't hurt you," Shannon said. "But if you quit after being on it for so many years, it will kill you. Because your body won't produce endorphins and enkephalins, which are natural painkillers. Johnny's body won't produce that anymore, so he has to stay on it."

The scenario of Johnny staying high on methadone and enjoying that lifestyle couldn't be farther from the truth. It wasn't until nearly two decades later that the interaction of prescription drugs with the methadone put him into a drug-induced state. That toxic combination almost destroyed his career and nearly cost him his life.

•◆•

Given Johnny's frame of mind, his use of heroin the day he was released from the hospital wasn't farfetched. Psychiatrists who work with heroin addicts have noted that many have self-esteem issues and suffer from repressed or buried feelings, such as grief or anger that they feel are too powerful to let out.

Rush wasn't surprised by Johnny's reaction to the patients' response to the facilitator at the River Oaks group sessions. Throughout the years Rush has known him, feelings of alienation were always lurking below the surface of Johnny's confident demeanor.

"Johnny always seemed to think the only reason anybody would associate with him was because he was this famous guy," said Rush. "I remember something he told me years later that always stuck in my mind. He said, 'You know Pat, with today's music, if I came out now, nobody would pay any attention to me. There are so many bands out there, KISS with the painted faces, Bowie with his thing, punk bands, guys with cockatoo haircuts, tattooed faces, masks, makeup. If I came out now, nobody would notice me. The only reason I made it, Janis made it, Jimi made it, was because at the time we were completely different from everybody else.' Especially him because of the way he looked. He has always had a bit of a complex about that. Because of the way he grew up and the hardships he went through, by the time he did make it, it was tattooed in his brain that the only reason people would want to have anything to do with him, was because all of a sudden, he is famous and cool."

Johnny's status of famous and cool continued to haunt him when he left River Oaks and traveled to Austin for some downtime with Franklin.

"When I went to Texas after rehab, I couldn't just go out and watch a band," says Johnny. "People would ask me to sit in, to give them a pick—give 'em something or do something for 'em, and I just wanted to be left alone. I wanted to be able to be just another guy—I didn't want to have to be a star all the time. It's really tiring. I felt like a jukebox 'cause that's what everybody expected from me—music. Put a quarter in and get their song. People don't relate to you as a person and there's not much they can do about it and not much you can do about it."

Johnny vented his frustration to *Rolling Stone* reporter Chet Flippo, who met him in Austin after he left the hospital. The interview took place in Franklin's studio above the Armadillo World Headquarters, a club in the National Guard Armory that became *the* place to hear music in Austin after the Vulcan Gas Company closed. In an article aptly titled "Just Act Like I'm A Person, Dammit!", Johnny openly discussed his addiction. The article ran with an unflattering photograph with a quote for a caption: "All I could think about was: You're a junkie, you're a junkie. I hated myself." "Smack just sneaks up on you, without you realizin' it," he told Flippo. "Pretty soon you just can't get up in the morning without it."

"I've never been very subtle about that kind of stuff so I pretty much answered his questions," Johnny explains. "I figured that maybe it could help other people that were goin' through the same thing."

Johnny felt grounded when he saw his friends from Texas; he knew them before he achieved fame and never had to question their motivation.

"I was honored that he decided to come here after he got out of rehab," said Franklin. "He seemed great. I was hoping it would last, but didn't really expect it to. I think just about every excuse is used by people that get out of rehab to do another hit. One time, we flew to New Orleans, where he ran into a musician that knew where to score. Johnny snorted it, and threw up right away. He offered me some but I don't have a predisposition for heroin. I wish I could transfer some of that gene to Johnny; he just has the addiction gene."

Although Johnny escaped a certain death by putting himself into rehab, he had another close call in Austin two years after he left the facility.

"In about '73, Johnny OD'ed in my apartment," said Turner. "Me and Jeanne Whittington, a friend of Johnny's, and my old lady Jill were there. He came into town and we got some heroin. He did the heroin and fell out—basically stopped breathing. We snatched him up, put him in a bathtub full of cold water, and I started slapping him like a rubber chicken, as hard as I could slap him, slappin' the shit out of him. God, I didn't want him to die in my apartment. We took his pants off, but I couldn't get his shirt off quick enough so I just threw him in. I was trying to get his shirt off, and time was of the essence. So I said, 'Throw him in the tub; fuck his shirt.' When he woke up, he was mad because I threw him in the tub with his purple velvet shirt on. He didn't realize what had happened, and when he came to, he said, 'God damn it—you fucked up my shirt.'"

That was a wakeup call for Johnny. No longer able to dismiss heroin as a recreational drug, he knew the repercussions could be fatal. That incident led him to the methadone clinic in New York and caused him to make serious changes in his life. He set down rules he says he has stuck to since 1973. He never works more than four or five nights a week, and never stays on the road for more than four or six weeks at a stretch. Avoiding junkies was another critical decision.

"I decided to not be around people who were doing drugs and not to be on the road all the time," he says. "With one-nighters, you gotta do so much travelin', flyin' from place to place. I just told Steve Paul how it had to be—whether he liked it or not, he had to do it."

Before Johnny formed another band, he spent time on the West Coast, regaining his confidence by performing for large audiences. During July and August 1972, Johnny sat in on a couple of shows at the Hollywood Bowl in L.A., jamming with friends eager to see him back in the spotlight. He sat in with Captain Beyond on July 23, when Caldwell's band opened for Alice Cooper's "School's Out" tour. Like his appearance with Edgar, the audience went wild when he walked out on the stage.

Johnny also sat in with the Allman Brothers at the Hollywood Bowl on August 6. He joined them for an encore, playing "Johnny

B. Goode" and jamming with the band on Robert Johnson's "Dust My Broom." He was back in the game and ready to take the world by storm. But first he had to take care of some personal business.

•◆•

When Johnny signed himself in to River Oaks Hospital, Carol Roma moved home to Nacogdoches and stayed with her mother. Johnny had kept his basement apartment in New York, but she didn't want to stay there alone, so far away from Johnny, her family, and her friends. After living with her mother for a while, she moved to Houston, got an apartment with a friend, and went back to working as a hairdresser.

His infidelity had always been a problem in their relationship, and the personality and lifestyle changes that accompany heroin addiction didn't help. As Johnny grew more and more dependent on heroin, drugs became the focal point of his life. He became isolated from Roma, as well as family and friends. He had to deal with the psychological stress of trying to rationalize and defend his drug use, and he experienced bouts of anger and depression as the heroin high became milder and more short-lived.

Johnny admits his addiction had an adverse affect on their relationship, but didn't foresee any problems by his drug use or his nine-month stay at the hospital.

"I couldn't put anything into the relationship because I was so unhappy about myself," he says. "When she found out I was doin' hard drugs, she didn't like it but there wasn't anything she could do about it. She did it a little bit too, but not near as much. She never got strung out."

With Johnny in the hospital, the possibility of a future together—at least to Roma—became nebulous. She turned to another man to meet her emotional needs.

"She didn't know if I was gonna get out of the hospital or not," says Johnny. "There wasn't much of an understanding. We hadn't really talked much about our relationship—I was too worried about myself. Everything was fine till I found out about the other guy. She had a thing goin' with a guy in Nacogdoches, and she didn't say anything when I was in hospital. I didn't know till I got out and went back down to Houston.

"As soon as I got out, I went to Houston to see her and to get back into playin'. I went to her apartment—her roommate Nancy was there but she wasn't home. I saw pictures of her and this other guy, and asked Nancy, 'Who's this?' She said, 'You don't know about whatever his name was,' and I said, 'No, you better tell me.' Carol came home when I was there and I tore up the place and broke up with her. She didn't tell me she was seein' anybody else; that's what made me mad. I wanted her to stay true and I got real mad when I found out she was goin' out with somebody else. I never told her to stay true—I just expected her to."

Devastated by Johnny's reaction, Carol tried to explain why she'd started seeing someone else, but it fell on deaf ears.

"I told her that was it," says Johnny. "She cried a lot. She said she didn't know if I was gonna stay alive or not—she was all by herself so she got involved with this other guy. That wasn't a good enough excuse for me. She went along with me seeing other people, but she finally went out with somebody else and that's what broke us up. I wasn't gonna put up with it. But I still didn't break up with her completely."

Johnny makes no bones about his double standard. "That's just the way it was," he says without apology. His fame and rock 'n' roll lifestyle attracted women who didn't mind being one of many and the women he lived with tolerated his infidelity.

With or without Carol in his life, Johnny never had a shortage of women eager to get to know him better. He met his next significant other as soon as he flew back to New York. Susan Warford, Paul's new driver, picked him up at the airport. Susan was living in Miami when she met Edgar's fiancée Barbara in Coconut Grove.

"I was a hippie," Susan said. "I didn't know what I wanted to do; I was just lying around doing whatever came along. When Barbara, who became Edgar's second wife, was down from New York, I met her in the park and we became friends. She said she was going to marry Edgar and she'd give me a call. About a year later, in 1969 or 1970, she called and said, "We're married, and he's going to do a show with Johnny in Miami."

Susan was nineteen when she met Johnny and Edgar in Coconut Grove, where they were staying at a friend's apartment. She thought he was "nice and sweet," and didn't become dazzled until she saw him at a large outdoor festival in Dania.

"I always tell people time stopped for a second—everything froze," she said. "There was some kind of connection there. I always remember that moment where time froze and Johnny came onstage."

Johnny doesn't remember much about their meeting in the apartment but has a vague memory of meeting her. "I remember thinking that Susan was kinda cute but I didn't really think a lot about it," he says.

Determined to see more of Barbara and Edgar and to work in the music business, Susan traveled to New York in 1972. "I came up to visit Barbara at her house in the country, and we drove into the city and had dinner with Steve, Rick and Liz Derringer, and Barbara and Edgar," she said. "Steve was looking for somebody to work for him, and they talked him into hiring me. I went back to Miami, got my stuff together, and two weeks later I was back working for Steve. I did everything—I was like a Girl Friday. I drove him everywhere, I made all his appointments, I picked up things for him—a little bit of everything.

"Steve was intimidating; he had a caustic mouth and I was always afraid he was going to turn on me. I lived in his house in Rye, New York. Living there was part of the job; otherwise I don't know what I would've done. I didn't have any money. I got stuck on the third floor in an attic room. I was working for Steve a couple of months before Johnny got out of the hospital and came up from Texas. When I picked him up at the airport in Steve's blue Lincoln, Johnny was very talkative; he was excited about starting new projects. He was crazy, but so was I, so we got along real good."

"I remembered Susan when she picked me up at the airport," says Johnny. "I thought it was a good thing she was Steve's driver—I'd probably put the make on her."

Getting a band together and recording a new album were Johnny's priorities, so he didn't stay in New York long. Derringer had joined Edgar's White Trash and Caldwell had Captain Beyond. Hobbs had just drifted, and met up with Johnny as soon as he got out. Despite Johnny's decision to steer clear of drug users, he quickly enlisted Hobbs for his new lineup.

"I stuck with Randy 'cause he was still my good friend," says Johnny. "He was takin' drugs, though. I wondered if it would affect me, but it didn't. But eventually he got so bad I had to let him go."

Johnny's contract with Columbia called for two albums a year, but his yearlong hiatus didn't jeopardize the agreement. Although it would have been quicker to cut a new album with studio musicians, Johnny didn't want the clean sound of seasoned professionals. He wanted a trio that would play with wild abandon, so he traveled to Boston, Houston, Los Angeles, and San Francisco to audition musicians. With Steve Paul giving him free rein over his choice of musicians, and cautioning him not to rush into anything, Johnny stayed at the Continental Hyatt House in L.A. for several months while he was auditioning players. He put up a notice at Musicians Equipment Rentals and held auditions at Studio Instrument Rentals.

"I always liked getting my own band," says Johnny. 'Studio musicians are too clean, and I wanted guys who can bash their instruments. I put advertisements in trade magazines and auditioned hundreds of people. It's hard to find people just out of nowhere. Sometimes they aren't any good; sometimes they're too good and don't fit in the way I want them to. I got a lot of crazy people and didn't find anybody I liked. They played pretty good but not what I wanted. They were more rock 'n' roll—I didn't get anybody who could play good blues."

Disappointed, but undaunted, Johnny returned to New York still searching for the perfect players to continue his musical journey.

# PART II

# Back with a Vengeance

While Johnny was in California, Derringer traveled to the Jersey shore to see Cobalt, a Johnny Winter cover band managed by his banker. "Our manager kept bugging Rick about jamming with us," said Doug Brockie, Cobalt's lead guitarist. "Rick finally gave in and came out and jammed."

When Derringer brought Johnny to see Cobalt at a dance in New Jersey, he was blown away. "It was amazing," Johnny said in an interview for *Play:Back*, published by Columbia Records. "Out of the fifty songs they knew, forty-five of them were mine. I just stood there with my mouth hanging open. . . . I grew up copying Ray Charles, and these guys were growing up doing me."

The minute Johnny heard Cobalt's drummer, his search was over. "Richard Hughes was a basher, a crasher, and could play anything I needed," he says. "He played real well, he played all my songs, and he was a good guy."

Formed by Brockie when he was sixteen, Cobalt was based in Point Pleasant, Mantoloking Bay Head on the Jersey shore. "I found Richard at a gig at my church, playing with Jim Bentley from the 1910 Fruitgum Company," said Brockie. "He didn't know any Johnny Winter material when I met him. I taught Richard all of the Johnny Winter material because I was a Johnny Winter freak. At fifteen and sixteen, Johnny was like my Robert Johnson."

As soon as he auditioned and hired Hughes, Johnny went into the Hit Factory in New York City to cut *Still Alive and Well*. After nine months in the hospital and even more time away from his music, Johnny was elated to be back in the studio cutting an album. "It felt great because it's something you love that you'd given up for a while," he says. "We cut seven songs in a row on the first take on the first night."

Released in 1973 on Columbia Records, *Still Alive and Well* was the perfect anthem for Johnny's triumphant comeback. Derringer wrote it as a member of Edgar Winter's White Trash, which released it on *Roadwork* the previous year.

"Everybody thought he wrote it for me, but that wasn't true," says Johnny. "Rick wrote it for himself—he was bragging he was still alive and well. I recorded it 'cause I thought it was a good song and I was 'still alive and well.' I wrote 'Rock & Roll' and 'Too Much Seconal' for that album."

Johnny wanted the sound of a power trio so most songs featured Hobbs and Hughes, with Johnny on vocals, guitar, slide guitar, and mandolin. But he also used several guest artists, including Derringer on slide guitar on "Silver Train," electric guitar on "Cheap Tequila," and pedal steel and click guitar on "Ain't Nothing to Me." Todd Rundgren played a Mellotron on "Cheap Tequila," Mark Klingman played piano on "Silver Train," and Jeremy Steig played flute on "Too Much Seconal." "I had heard his album, *Jeremy & the Satyrs* [a 1968 Reprise release]," says Johnny. "I liked Jeremy and liked the way he played. He was a famous jazz flute player who played real bluesy."

"Mick Jagger and Keith Richards gave me 'Silver Train,'" Johnny says. "They hadn't recorded it yet. I did 'Let It Bleed' on that album too—they'd already recorded that. I always liked the Stones' sound; they did a good job of writin' blues songs that were hits too."

Johnny was loose during those two-week-long sessions, tossing off asides that would amuse fans but make the FCC wince. At the end of "Let It Bleed," Johnny says, "God damn it. Did that get it or what?" and prefaces the intro to "Still Alive and Well" with "I'm hungry—let's do this fucker."

*Still Alive and Well* was rereleased on CD in 1994, and included the previously unreleased tracks "Lucille" and "From a Buick 6." Neither song had lead guitar tracks, so Johnny wasn't pleased when he discovered their inclusion. "They weren't ready to be added," he says. "They should have talked to me, but of course they didn't. Both of those songs were just rhythm tracks. They never told me they were gonna put them on the CD because I would have said something. I didn't want them on 'cause they weren't complete."

The inside sleeve of the album contains a black-and-white photo of Johnny with the words Thanks, Susan in the lower right-hand corner. That simple message reflected how quickly their relationship had evolved. "Living in the same house with Susan in Rye helped me to get to know her," says Johnny. "It made it a lot easier because she was always there. It was really pretty country and we did a lot of talking outside. I stayed up all night and she stayed up all night with me, so something was bound to happen."

When Johnny began seeing Susan, he was still involved with Carol Roma in Texas and had a few more women on the side. He still had feelings for Carol, who wanted to get back together. "It was still a big deal to break up with Carol, so I had her come up to New York to see how I felt about her, to see if we could get back together," he says. "When she came, Susan took off. I loved Carol in a way too. I didn't treat Carol very good but she really did love me. I just couldn't get close to her after she'd been out with somebody else. I didn't think I could ever live with her after that. Even though I was going out with other people, I wasn't going to put up with her going out on me. So I sent her back home and stayed with Susan. I still saw other people but Susan didn't."

Carol returned to Houston, and within a year or so, began dating Edgar, who was also living in that city. "Carol first met Edgar in Houston years ago when he was playing with me, and Edgar had been in love with her for the whole time," says Johnny. "He always liked her, but he said he didn't do anything about it because she was with me. When he first started seeing her, he told me he had been in love with her and hoped I didn't mind. I said, 'No, we broke up. You can do anything you want to.' They were goin' out awhile, but not too long, before they got married. I didn't go to his wedding. I'm not sure how long they were married. They broke up 'cause she was goin' out with other people and he found out about it. I never did think she loved Edgar—I thought she did it just to get back at me. She never did treat him right."

"Carol wasn't as loyal and dedicated to Johnny as other girls who were fixated on him," said Turner. "Her marriage to Edgar lasted a few years. It was fascinating to Johnny that his little brother had married his old lady. Like the rest of us, he thought it was really weird. He said she couldn't have him, so she took Edgar. It was the next closest thing."

After the final split with Carol, Johnny invited Susan to live with him in the basement apartment they had shared on Eighty-Fifth Street. She was still working for Steve Paul, but quit shortly after she moved into the City.

"We were living together real quick," says Johnny. "First at Steve's house, then in my apartment in New York. The more I lived with Susan and was around her, the more I got to where I really felt strong feelings for her. She was real sweet, not aggressive at all, and she didn't seem like she wanted anything from me. She seemed like she was being completely honest, and really true to me. A real, real person."

Within two or three months Johnny knew he was in love, but he waited to express his feelings. "I knew Susan probably six months when I told her I loved her," he says. "We were walkin' down the street, going to one of our favorite Italian restaurants and I told her I loved her. She said, 'I love you too.' It was pretty unbelievable that it happened that quick."

Although Johnny was busy with rehearsals and recording sessions, they savored their time together to enjoy their budding romance. "We went to plays, restaurants, movies, clubs," he remembers. "It's nice when you're first getting to know somebody. We'd go see plays on Broadway—going to the theater was Steve's idea. We saw *Grease*; we saw *Equus* with Richard Burton. I loved that; it was great. Steve always traveled in an entourage—he always wanted to have a lot of people around. Steve went with whatever friend he was courting at the time. Buster Poindexter would go sometimes. We'd go to Max's Kansas City, where Steve had his own table. He liked being a big shot and wanted everything his own way. He'd send back food if it wasn't to his specifications. I didn't like him—it was uncomfortable when he was like that."

Once Johnny and Susan became an item, they traveled south to meet his and her parents. "We went down to Cutler Ridge in Florida to meet Susan's folks and they treated me real nice," says Johnny. "Her father had been in the FBI—I thought it was pretty strange. He seemed like a cop a little bit; he had that feel about him. But he didn't have a problem with me. I smoked grass over there too. I waited until they went to sleep and me and Susan would go out on the front porch and smoke grass. My parents were cool when they met her; she made me happy and they were not going to tell me what to do. But my other girlfriends didn't like it very much."

To the chagrin of those girlfriends, Johnny invited Susan to join the band for the initial leg of the Still Alive and Well tour. "That was kinda silly," he says with a laugh. "I don't know why I wanted to do it, it was worse than Paul McCartney and Linda McCartney. It's ridiculous how people can get that way. I thought it would be fun. She played tambourine and she played a beer can one night. The first night Susan played tambourine with the band, she was scared to death. She was supposed to just stand there and beat the tambourine. She finally realized she was gonna have to drink to do it. Susan played a few gigs with us. She played *Midnight Special* too. She wasn't in the band very long. Two or three months, maybe."

Following the release of *Still Alive and Well*, Paul booked a coliseum tour of dates from March to June, with Foghat opening in April and May. That tour culminated at the June 16 show at Madison Square Garden. To create a look for that tour, Paul hired Bill Witten, a theatrical costume designer, whose musical clients included Earth, Wind & Fire, the Commodores, and the Jackson Five. During their initial meeting, Johnny demonstrated his own sense of style.

"I'll never forget the first time we went to meet Bill Witten," said Susan. "We were meeting him and Steve at the 21 Club or Sardi's. Johnny decided to wear a wraparound skirt I had made out of Indian material a couple of years before. I let Johnny walk ahead of me. I was so embarrassed; I had to walk about four feet behind him."

"I took the train from Connecticut to New York wearing that skirt and people laughed and said, 'What are you advertising? What are you sellin'?'" Johnny recalls. "I had my fingernails painted different colors, and I was wearing cowboy boots, a cowboy hat, a cowboy shirt, and a cloth skirt with a lot of different colors that hung down halfway between my knees and ankles. We took a cab from Grand Central to the restaurant. The driver didn't say anything—as long as he got paid, he could care less. Bill Witten thought I was funny. He liked my outfit, but Steve just went crazy. He scrunched down in the seat as much as possible like he didn't want to know me. I just wanted to freak everybody out, and it worked."

Witten designed costumes for Johnny's touring band, which included Susan, Hobbs, Hughes, and Jimmy Gillan, his old drummer from the Act III, as a second drummer. "Jimmy was a friend and he needed a gig real bad at the time," says Johnny. "So I used two drummers for that whole tour. He was a pretty good beater, but much too jazzy."

Johnny wore a black velvet cape with a red satin lining over a white spandex jumpsuit with silver-studded bellbottoms, suspenders, and a studded collar. His costume included an amethyst medallion that he wore on his bare chest and studded armbands adorned with silver streamers that draped down toward the floor. All band members wore a different colored spandex costume—Susan's was pale blue and cut low in the front, Gillan's was red and orange, Hobbs wore blue, and Hughes's costume was green.

"My jumpsuit was real stretchy, so it was pretty comfortable," says Johnny. "We wore those outfits for about six or eight months. After I stopped wearing it, I gave it to the Museum of the Gulf Coast in Port Arthur."

During that tour, Johnny was the consummate showman, playing on his knees, with his guitar held over his head, and behind his back. "Never learned how to play with my teeth though," he says, and cites Mick Jagger as his main influence for showmanship. Although his stage antics were a guaranteed crowd pleaser, he admits to having mixed feelings about combining theatrics with his music.

"Showmanship was a big part of it, but I didn't want it to be a main thing," he says. "Because I couldn't play guitar as well when I was doin' all that fancy stuff. It's fun to do it once, but if you have to keep doing it over again, it quits bein' fun. People expect it of you."

In 1973, late night TV shows featuring live rock 'n' roll performances debuted on two networks. Paul used his contacts in the industry—Don Kirshner and people involved with *The Midnight Special*—to hook Johnny up with what would be the precursors of MTV.

On July 6, 1973, Johnny appeared on *The Midnight Special*, a weekly late night rock 'n' roll show that debuted that February. Catering to hip, young audiences, the show aired on NBC at 1 AM on Saturday mornings. Guest host Jose Feliciano performed a few songs, and introduced artists Savoy Brown, the Staple Singers, Stories, and Tower of Power. Johnny headlined that show performing "Jumpin' Jack Flash," "Johnny B. Goode," and "Rock & Roll."

Despite his mesmerizing performance, Johnny had been reluctant to perform that night because of technical problems at rehearsals earlier that day. "The rehearsal before the show was so terrible, I felt like walking out," he says. "It's hard to play on a soundstage with cameras and they just didn't know what to do with us. They tried to get us to play quieter and we couldn't play quieter. *Midnight Special* was a rock 'n' roll show—you thought they'd know what they were doing. But they didn't know how to record people—how to get the sound right when you're playing loud."

Johnny also appeared on *Don Kirshner's Rock Concert*, a TV show that aired at 1 AM on Sunday mornings. Kirshner filmed Johnny's appearance at New York's Palace Theatre. That late night show included footage of rousing versions of "Rock and Roll, Hoochie Koo," "Jumpin' Jack Flash," "Silver Train," and his trademark "Johnny B. Goode."

Although Johnny enjoyed having Susan on the road with him, there were obvious drawbacks to having his girlfriend in the band. "I couldn't go out with other girls, and I couldn't get any groupies," he says. Eventually his touring schedule, with its late nights, and four weeks on the road for every week off, became too grueling. After six months on the road, Susan decided to stay in New York when Johnny was touring. Although they enjoyed their private time together, having Johnny leave to go back on the road bothered Susan a lot more than it bothered him.

"I didn't mind goin' on the road 'cause I got to be with somebody else," he says. "Usually I was with other people because I wasn't used to being true to one person. It was something I knew I couldn't do and I told her that. She put up with it for a long time."

Yet living with Johnny was not without its advantages. To escape the stifling temperatures of New York City summers, he always rented a big summer house with a pool in Westport, Connecticut for vacations and rehearsals.

"We needed a place to practice and I thought it'd be a nice idea to get a band house, where the band could come up and stay and practice. They wouldn't have to go back home every night," he says. "It's tough to stay in New York during the summer 'cause it's so hot."

Johnny still has vivid memories of the night one of the Westport houses caught fire.

"God, that was terrible. We had the fireplace lit, stayed up all night talking, went to sleep, and didn't wake up till about three in the afternoon. Susan saw smoke and I threw a glass of water on it but the fire was huge. Flames were up into the framing, into the roof of the house. The fire department came in and said, 'Get out of here, get the fuck out of here.' We wanted to get our stuff but they said, 'Get out of here now, don't get anything, just get out of here.' They stole some grass we had too, those mother fuckers. Stole my grass. Course they didn't want us to take anything out of there—bastards."

That fall, after a successful Still Alive and Well tour that proved his hiatus hadn't hurt his career, Johnny embarked on two projects, dividing his time between the Big Easy and the Big Apple. He produced and played on an album with Thunderhead and began work on *Saints and Sinners*, his last album on the Columbia label. He had agreed to help Thunderhead with its first LP, so when the band was ready to record, their manager Bill Evans sent Johnny a demo tape. Johnny liked what he heard, and two weeks later, Evans and Torello flew to New York to discuss the project. It was the first time Torello met his hero, and his eyes still light up when he talks about it.

"When I first heard Johnny play, I knew I'm made to play with this guy," said Torello, who later played on *White, Hot & Blue* and *Raisin' Cain* and toured with him for many years. "When I first met him, he was like my long lost brother. Me and him clicked like I never clicked with anybody before. We're still that tight. I liked everything he did, the way he went about things, his attitude, everything—even the male chauvinistic part of him. I liked it all.

"When we were doing the Thunderhead record, we'd stay up, hang out, talk, and party all night long. We were out on this farm with nothing to do. We had a bow and arrow and Johnny says, 'What am I going to shoot at?' So I started running around, being a target, letting him shoot at me. We had some really good times."

The Thunderhead sessions were held in Evan's studio in Bogalusa, an hour away from New Orleans. Johnny played guitar and produced the sessions; Edgar played piano and sang background harmonies. Although the entire band was thrilled with the sessions Johnny produced, politics came into play, and those sessions never made it onto the final record.

"It was a typical industry scam," said Rush. "We had a lawyer in California who represented artists. He began shopping the finished LP in L.A. and got ABC Records interested. He also represented a producer who produced the Osmonds and Cher. So he finagled a deal where he got us a record deal with ABC Records and brought in this other guy to produce the LP. They treated the album we had recorded as a demo, so we went back into the studio and rerecorded the entire LP."

Redoing the album without Johnny and Edgar and with a different producer resulted in a recording that didn't capture the band's sound, and created bad feelings all around. "When we had to do it over, we couldn't get Johnny back down again and Edgar was busy touring," said Rush. "The first LP was all original tunes we had written together; they had us do some cover tunes on the second album.

If you listen to the first non-album, it's pretty big sounding, real rock sounding, typical of the band. You listen to the ABC-produced LP and the guy buried everything in reverb. It sounded like he was doing another Cher or Osmond Brothers album."

Torello blames the band's naiveté for ending up with a record and a deal that didn't include Johnny in the producer's role or any of the sessions with Johnny and Edgar.

"Johnny played on the Thunderhead demo; he was totally instrumental in getting our deal and they screwed him out of that," said Torello. "Thunderhead signed the wrong damn contract and Johnny ended up not being the producer. He got knocked out by the money people and he was doing it all for nothing. He didn't even charge us because he was good friends with us. It was a hell of a time. We didn't talk for a while because they screwed him. Later we got back together and talked about everything and he realized it wasn't our fault; we were just stupid idiots and signed the wrong deal."

In the winter of 1973–1974, Johnny returned to the Hit Factory to cut *Saints and Sinners*, which was recorded quickly and released by Columbia in February 1974. Derringer produced the album ("I thought he was a good guy to produce it because he knew what I wanted"), which included Johnny on guitar and vocals; Derringer on guitar; Dan Hartman on piano, bass, and guitar; Edgar on keyboards and sax; Bobby Caldwell and Richard Hughes on drums; Randy Brecker, Alan Rubin, and Lew Del Gatto on trumpet; and Jeremy Steig on flute.

The album included two of Johnny's originals ("Bad Luck Situation" and "Hurtin' So Bad"), and veered away from blues with songs by Chuck Berry, the Stones, Van Morrison, Leiber and Stoller, and Alan Toussaint. "That album had more of a soulful direction because I wanted to try something a little different," says Johnny. "It didn't get a great response."

Before Johnny embarked on a coliseum tour to promote *Saints and Sinners* in late 1974, he recruited a second guitarist.

"Johnny auditioned seven guys," said Brockie. "After the last one, he turned to Richard and said, 'Should we audition Dougie?' I had an old Les Paul, with those old soap-bar pickups—the Gibson

P-90 pickups that were predecessors to the PAF humbuckers. I knew all the material and Rick had shown me many tricks when he jammed with me in Cobalt. I got the job 'cause I played 'I Love Everybody' at the audition. Johnny had forgotten the tune, and said to me, 'What's that song?' I said, 'It's yours.'"

When Johnny hired Brockie, he had an unusual way of letting him know. "What did he say when he hired me?" said Brockie with laugh. "He said, 'Fuck you, Dougie.' That's what he always used to say. He was a really funny guy. He'd be leaving the room, and he'd turn and give you the finger, and say, 'Hey Dougie, fuck you.' He was twenty-nine, and I was nineteen. We were both really young guys."

Brockie moved into the Westport, Connecticut mansion Paul had rented for the band. "We rehearsed in the mansion in October, November, and December 1973," said Brockie. "Living in that house was amazing. Some days, Johnny and me would be in the living room, taking solos in our underwear, jumping from couch to couch. It was the greatest; we had so much fun together. It was a family type thing; hangin' out and playin' at the house in Connecticut."

The *Saints and Sinners* tour ran from February through June 1974, and included sold-out coliseum shows in major cities in the United States and Canada. It was a big adjustment for a nineteen-year-old to go from small clubs and school dances to sold-out coliseums.

"The night before my first coliseum gig with Johnny, we did a huge club in Jacksonville just to loosen up," Brockie said. "To go from a club to a 30,000-seater is pretty scary. They had to give me a sedative so I wouldn't jump out of my skin. It was funny, because Johnny was as calm as could be. It was nothing to him; he was never nervous. Never. He wasn't doing much in the way of drugs at that point. Johnny drank a lot of booze and smoked a lot of weed but that was about it. Man, he could put down booze. He could put down a fifth a night before hitting the stage and play perfect."

Johnny's resolve to stay away from hard drugs led to an increase in his drinking, so there are some events where he has very little recollection. One was the February 12, 1974 grand opening of the Bottom Line in Greenwich Village, which celebrated its debut with a jam that included Johnny, Dr. John, and Stevie Wonder.

"I don't remember much about the grand opening—I was drinkin' a lot back then," he says. "I drank a lot of different things. Gin, peppermint schnapps, scotch. Scotch is nasty tasting—I drank a lot of nasty tasting things because I figured I wouldn't drink as much. I drank bourbon and grapefruit juice. That must have been the worst possible combination of anything, and I still drank a lot of it."

Rush remembers a wild night in New Orleans when he and Johnny attempted to sit in with a band at the Ivanhoe at the corner of Toulouse and Bourbon Street.

"We'd been out partying and had drank quite a bit of Chivas before we went to the bar," Rush said. "We sat at a table and Johnny leaned over and said, 'Pat, no matter what, don't let me get up and play. I'm too drunk—I can't stand up.' We're there five minutes, and the band sees Johnny and calls him up to play a song. Johnny stands up, 'Yeah!' I pull him back in the chair and say, 'Johnny, no. You're too drunk; don't do it.' He said, 'Come on, Pat, just one song. I'll sit on a stool and sing, and you play guitar.' So we got up and he sat on a stool. He had his top hat on and his fringed jacket. He leaned back to hit a note, the stool fell backward, and he fell into the drums and knocked the drums over on top of the drummer. I had to pick him up off the floor and take him out of the place—it was hilarious. We had some pretty amazing adventures in New Orleans."

•◆•

Johnny had grown up watching *Superman* on TV, so when the plane from that series became available, he couldn't resist.

"We had a small plane, and then we got a big plane," said Brockie. "The engine caught on fire on the little plane. The pilot's name was Johnny Walker. Johnny couldn't see, so I told him, 'You better tell Walker to keep the plane on the runway 'cause the engine's on fire.' Johnny says, 'Ah, shit!' and we didn't take off. Then we got the old plane from the original George Reeves *Superman* TV series. Grand Funk had owned it and then Steve Paul leased it. We could run laps in that plane. Sometimes we didn't know if we'd get off the runway."

Hughes recorded the shows every night during that tour. The band listened to the tapes on the plane on the way to the next gig, and Johnny didn't always like what he heard.

"As soon as my solo came up, Johnny would come down to where I was sitting, jumping up and down, going, 'You're fired!' said Brockie with a laugh. "I played my ass off and he fired me every night and hired me the next day. It was constantly a terrifying, scary experience. He had a great sense of humor but he was being serious too. He let you know when you're doing too much. He went through that with Rick too. He would jump up and read you the riot act and let you know: this is the Johnny Winter band and you can get yourself in trouble. Rick and I were on-fire type guys. You're only as good as the players you're with. If you had great guys around you, it makes you play better."

A highlight of that tour was Johnny's second sold-out appearance at Madison Square Garden. "Hearing all those people screaming was amazing," said Brockie. "Johnny was wearing that silver shirt with one sleeve over the shoulder, a scarf, and big high-heeled boots. We all wore scarves on our belts. I had on a rainbow-checkered shirt with leather pants. I remember Jon Lord from Deep Purple coming backstage. He had his dB-level recorder with him and came back and said, 'Johnny Winter's band is now officially the loudest band on Earth.' Richard recorded it, but unfortunately he left the cassette backstage."

During that tour, two shows were recorded for the *King Biscuit Flower Hour*, a nationally syndicated radio program of live concert performances that debuted the previous year. The shows included a gig at Toad's Place in New Haven, Connecticut, and a gig at the Long Beach Arena in California. Johnny didn't like the New Haven performance because the band was too conscious of being recorded, but they tore it up at the Long Beach show.

"At the Long Beach gig, we just let loose and did our normal thing and it came out amazing," said Brockie. "Johnny played me rough mixes around 2004. It's better than Johnny Winter And. He's singing at the peak of his power, playing the greatest guitar of his life, and he's got the greatest band he ever had behind him. You've got three feisty guys—Randy Jo, Richard, and myself—and we were breathing flames up his rear end. We sound like a buffalo herd locked underneath Johnny. The gig starts out real clean, like white fire noise. But when the booze kicked in, it got to be scorching and burning, UFOs hitting atmospheres. That tape sounds like Johnny has something on the level of Cream on the rhythm section. 'Be Careful with a Fool' on the *King Biscuit Flower Hour* is probably the greatest live rock-blues recording I've ever heard."

Johnny and Brockie are the only living members of that lineup. Hughes committed suicide at the age of thirty-five; Hobbs died of an overdose at forty-five. Having lost so many friends and members of his bands to an early death is quite unsettling to Johnny. The loss of life that accompanies a rock 'n' roll lifestyle also played a role in Brockie's change of musical direction.

"After the show, we went to parties and blew out big time," Brockie said. "That's the only problem with rock 'n' roll and fame. A lot of guys die; they lose their minds in it and they can't maintain it. Richard was one of my best friends and one of the greatest drummers I ever played with. He was never boring; he played like a wildcat out of the jungle. He had a great feel on the drums and was capable of doing just about anything, probably one of the best American drummers. When he died, he was one of those unsung heroes. Richard recorded everything at the board on a cassette deck. I remember hearing shows that were unbelievable. Unfortunately, when Richard died, all those recordings disappeared."

By the middle of the tour, Brockie grew bored with playing rock 'n' roll and wanted to venture into jazz. He left when the tour ended, but still has enormous love and admiration for the man who jumpstarted his career.

"Looking back on it, I regret we didn't stay together because we could have done so much," said Brockie. "Bands are all chemistry, magic. You change one member and you lose that magic. Being onstage with Johnny was insane. To this day, it's like yesterday—the excitement. He was like a spiritual master to me. It was like meeting a guru, because he had that effect on my life, along with the Beatles, Hendrix, and Cream. Johnny was right there at the biggest part, saying, 'Really go for it!' Not just in terms of playing; he's a huge influence on me in all ways. Johnny is my brother. I owe him so much, and I love him to death. Johnny is a major part of where I am and everything I'm doing in music to this day."

After the tour concluded, a new public television performance series called *PBS Soundstage* debuted with *Muddy Waters & Friends: Blues Summit in Chicago*, which aired over PBS affiliates in October and December 1974. Filmed in WTTW Studios in Chicago on July 18, 1974, the show featured Waters, Mike Bloomfield, Junior Wells, Willie Dixon, Koko Taylor, Dr. John, Buddy Miles, Nick Gravenites, Phil Guy, Paul Oscher, Pinetop Perkins—and Johnny Winter. It would be only the first time he would play with Muddy Waters, his childhood idol.

•◆•

By the time Johnny was ready to cut his next LP, Steve Paul, who was also managing Edgar, Derringer, and Dan Hartman, had formed his own label. Blue Sky Records was an apropos name for a man known to have a fetish for the color blue. Johnny was still signed to Columbia; Edgar and Derringer were signed to Epic; so CBS, the parent company for Columbia and Epic Records, distributed and promoted Blue Sky Records.

With the leverage of his own label and a stable of popular acts, Paul immediately negotiated a better deal for his artists. "It wasn't easy, but at that time Columbia wanted to develop my relationship with them," Paul said. "The first criterion I set forth was to raise the royalty rate for the artists I was managing."

Paul set up and oversaw two businesses in the same suite of offices: Blue Sky Records and Organic Management. He hired Rick Dobbis as executive vice president and general manager of the Blue Sky Records and Teddy Slatus took care of the day-to-day operation of Organic Management, Paul's artist management company. Slatus's role involved planning tours, working with Premier Talent Agency (the booking agent) and promoters, going on the road as tour manager, and taking care of publishing.

Dobbis was a record product manager at Epic assigned to the Edgar Winter Group when he first met Paul. "When Steve was forming

Blue Sky, he asked me to come and work directly for him and have responsibility for all the artists that were going to be on the label," said Dobbis, who went on to become President of Sony Music International, and currently runs his own Global Business Management Company. "That was great; it was entrepreneurial. Working at Epic was a great way to learn the business, a great place to go to college—it was my record business education. Working for Steve was graduate work because Steve was so inclusive."

Dobbis worked with Steve Paul and his artists from the conceptualization to the release of the records, and acted as liaison to CBS Records. "I worked very closely with the CBS Records people on the planning and execution of the release, the packaging, the marketing plan, the coordination of their sales and distribution network," said Dobbis. "I represented Blue Sky and the artists' interests with CBS, and saw that the vision we had for the project would be followed through, and the appropriate amount of attention required for it to meet its maximum audience be attained by the machine."

Creating his own record label was a savvy business decision because it gave Paul more control over how CBS handled the records. "There were three reasons to bring Blue Sky into existence," explained Dobbis. "One was to be able to sign and bring more artists into it; another was to control the product; the third was to make more money."

Edgar Winter, however, had concerns on how the Blue Sky label impacted CBS's commitment to the artists. "It seemed to me Steve was using his leverage as a manager to create what he felt was a better deal for the artist, but it wasn't a real label, it was a custom label," Edgar said. "He was able to obtain a higher royalty rate, but the money that would have gone back to CBS—had it not been a custom label—would have indirectly benefited the people out in the field, the promotional people, the radio people, the rack jobbers, the independent promoters, people who push radio airplay—all of the CBS machine. Instead of going back into CBS, that money was going to this entity called Blue Sky, which was just an office with a secretary with no promotional people, no nothing.

"My feeling was that although it was being distributed by CBS, it wasn't really a CBS label, so why would they have the same enthusiasm about working that record? Steve assured me it was going to have no effect, that it was a great deal, and we should trust him as a manager to make such decisions. But I noticed ever since that happened, there wasn't the same feeling, the same closeness between us and the record label as there once had been. I felt that was very damaging and the company wasn't putting the same energy into promoting and was just waiting for our contract to expire."

Neither Paul nor Dobbis agreed. Paul's take was that the CBS publicity effort varied according to the product. Dobbis thought the Blue Sky structure kept more pressure on Columbia to work harder and to spend appropriately.

Johnny's first release on Blue Sky Records, *John Dawson Winter III*, had a formal seated portrait of Johnny in a black tuxedo with wide brown velvet lapels and an oversized brown velvet bowtie. "It was hard comin' up with different names so I just used my real name," says Johnny. "I liked dressin' up for the cover. I have a tux of my own now but at the time, I had to lease it."

*John Dawson Winter III* took four months to record at the Record Plant; the late summer/early fall sessions were interspersed with Johnny's trips to New Orleans to write songs and to produce the Thunderhead LP. A departure for Johnny stylistically, *John Dawson Winter III* is a mixture of blues, rock, country blues, ballads, and country and western. Although Johnny played primarily with Hobbs and Hughes, producer Shelly Yakus added lavish production, with strings, synthesizer, keyboards, horns, and background vocalists on several of the songs. "You can't really categorize that record because it was pretty different from anything before," says Johnny. "It was important to me to let people know I could do something different."

With New Orleans as a getaway from New York, Johnny wrote five songs, more than he has ever written for any recording. He wrote "Stranger" ("a pretty ballad—one of my favorite songs that I've ever written"), "Self-Destructive Blues," "Pick Up on My Mojo," "Sweet Papa John" (a country blues song with lascivious lyrics), and "Love

Song to Me," a country and western song with lyrics reflecting his tongue-in-cheek sense of humor.

"That was about how much I loved myself," he says with a laugh. "I was just having fun. 'Sweet Papa John' was a blues tune about me too—about how cool I was. I used a solitary bass drum on 'Sweet Papa John' 'cause all the old blues groups did; it was something I had gotten used to hearing on Muddy's records. It was a dirty song," says Johnny laughing as he sings a bar. "'They call me Sweet Papa, 'cause my candy is the best. You know I melt right in your mouth, sure don't leave no mess.'"

"Rock 'n' Roll People," the opening track, was penned by John Lennon. Yakus solicited that song while working on Lennon's *Walls and Bridges* album. "I don't know why John didn't do it himself, but I liked it and was glad to have a John Lennon song," says Johnny. "It's hard to get songs from people you respect. You've got to find somebody who you like who's got enough material where they don't need to use it all for themselves.

"I met John just in passing at the Record Plant; we were both workin' in the same studio. He came in with May Pang. We mostly talked about music. That was the only time I saw him. I loved his song writing. He wasn't much of a guitar player but he was real good at writing and singing."

For the other five songs, Dobbis contacted songwriters, including John Fogerty, Cat Stevens, Van Morrison, Billy Joel, Alan Toussaint, and James Taylor. "We picked those artists because they're good writers," says Johnny. "We were lookin' for something bluesy that had potential to get on Top Forty radio. We'd usually have forty or fifty songs to choose from."

After listening to shopping bags full of tapes and acetate demo records, Dobbis selected fifty songs, and brought them to Steve Paul's house, where he, Paul, Johnny, and Yakus listened and made lists. Once they agreed upon the songs, Johnny went back into the studio.

Engineer Dennis Ferrante, who worked with Yakus on several John Lennon albums, remembers those sessions.

"We'd start at seven o'clock at night and go to one o'clock in the morning," Ferrante said. "In those days there was no clock; it was rock 'n' roll. Your session started at seven, and you'd stop when the artist was falling down, or you were tired. Those sessions were loose, very relaxed; there was no pressure."

Dobbis noted the differences between those sessions and contemporary ones, where time is of the essence. "Those sessions were long, intense, and experimental from the standpoint that there was a lot of openness to try something else, let's try it again this way, let's try it again that way," said Dobbis. "Johnny's style of playing uses a lot of improvisation, and studio albums were more structured. That is always a challenge for somebody that really lets loose live."

Ferrante, who worked with both Johnny and Edgar, noticed a distinct difference in their approach in the studio. "It was more feel for Johnny, it was rock 'n' roll," said Ferrante. "In the words of Rick Derringer, 'Edgar makes masters; Johnny makes demos.' It wasn't a bad inference. Johnny lets a lot of things slide, and Edgar is a perfectionist on everything he does. Edgar would spend a half hour on getting one note in a sequence, and Johnny would do a whole song. Just whatever happened, happened.

"You know how he always yells 'yeah' when he plays? It sounds very rock 'n' roll, but actually what it is, is he screwed up. That's how together he is with his playing. Not something noticeable, but with his ears—he had perfect pitch—he heard a bum note. He knows at the moment he made a mistake, he has to cover it up by yelling. He said, 'When I do that, I screwed up.' I said, 'You must've screwed up a lot.' He said, 'No, if I do it once, then I do it later on, because it sounds like it's planned.'

"Johnny and John Lennon were very similar in the studio. They didn't want to make everything too slick. John Lennon knew exactly what he wanted; the concept was in his head; we just had to execute it. With Winter, it was basically the same way. He came in, he had the songs written, he knew what he was gonna do."

Johnny used a MXR Phase 90 on several songs, a monumental departure for a man who always said he hated effects. He discovered it at Thunderhead's Bogalusa ranch house.

"Johnny was writing songs for *John Dawson Winter III* when he was staying with us, playing on and producing our record," said

Rush. "He wrote 'Stranger' in our living room. When we rehearsed, he played through my amp. I had this MXR Phase 90 phase shifter lying on the floor in a large box. He said, 'What is that?' 'A phase shifter.' He said, 'What does that do?' 'Well, step on it.' So he stepped on it and he heard that phase-shifter sound and it became part of his sound. The only effect he ever really liked; there were some years where he had it on all the time."

Another discovery he made during that period was Vandermint Dutch Chocolate Liqueur, which satiated both his love for chocolate and yen for alcohol. He drank a 750-milliliter white ceramic bottle by himself at each of the sessions.

"It was like drinking Bosco, but it was potent," said Ferrante. "He always came in with the same stuff and got so smashed on it. One night we were just kibitzing around, and Shelly called him a bleach-bottle blonde. Johnny says, 'No, this is my hair,' and Shelly said, 'I don't believe you.' So he drops his drawers in front of me and Shelly to show us that he is blonde everywhere. He was like a twig; he looked like a piece of birch bark. There was no color, no pigment anywhere. We were laughing, he started chasing Shelly around the console, and I ran out of the room. Later, he came walking out into the hallway. By this time he had his pants on. He was three sheets to the wind but he was holding up pretty good until we started talking. He was talking to me, leaning against the wall, and all of a sudden—like in slow motion—he went down very slowly and finally hit the floor. He just started laughing; he was so tipsy at that point, he didn't know what was going on. It was one of the most hilarious nights we ever had with him."

With the completion of his latest LP, Johnny was ready to go back out on tour. Despite his reluctance to use yet another second guitar player, Hobbs convinced him he needed a rhythm guitarist to fill out the sound and add to their live performances. Johnny hired Floyd Radford in June 1974. "Floyd's a real good guitar player," says Johnny. "He played whatever I wanted, whatever I needed—he was real good at it."

Radford had played on *Edgar Winter's White Trash*, released in 1971, and toured with Edgar's band. He played with both White

Trash and Tin House until June 1971, when Johnny went into rehab. "That's when everything around Johnny fell apart, including Tin House," said Radford. "I left Edgar and White Trash, and went back to Orlando with Tin House to regroup."

Paul thought Tin House needed a fourth player, but when they returned to New York as four pieces, Paul passed on managing them. In June 1974, when Radford was literally a starving musician in L.A., he looked up Paul at a music convention, hoping to sell him some equipment.

"I was real poor, so when I found out Steve Paul was going to the Columbia Records convention, I went there to try to sell him some guitar speakers," said Radford. "Steve said no, but Johnny needs a guitar player, so put a tape together and send it to me."

With no equipment except a tape recorder, Radford put a rough tape together, and Johnny called and invited him to New York for an audition. "I had a Gibson ES 355 and one Marshall at the audition," said Radford. "Randy Jo was on acoustic, Richard was on drums, and Johnny was playin' the Firebird. We jammed for about an hour and a half, one song after another, and Richard recorded it on Johnny's cassette player. I kept up pretty good. I had practiced songs on Johnny's albums with Randy and Richard, especially *John Dawson Winter III*.

"After the audition, Johnny says, 'We're gonna go in the other room and talk—you stay here.' I stayed in the practice room, biting my nails, wondering if I got the job. When they all came back in, Johnny says, 'We like your playing; you're in. We're going to tell that other guy not even to come.'"

Like Brockie before him, Radford moved into a communal house in Connecticut, and rehearsed with the band for a week before embarking upon a European tour. He also experienced a sense of closeness and family he didn't feel when he knew Johnny only as a member of his opening act.

"Johnny was very personable," said Radford. "It was like talking to your brother or your best friend. We got really close. After Johnny put down his guitar, we'd talk about things. Johnny would go on and on about not wanting to be commercial, wanting to play blues."

Although Johnny still longed to return to the music of his idols, he played predominately rock 'n' roll during that phase of his career, with a live set list that included "Jumpin' Jack Flash," "Johnny B. Goode," "Boney Moronie," "Rock 'n' Roll People," and "It's All Over Now."

"Johnny had a love-hate relationship with rock 'n' roll," said Radford. "Johnny is a blues guitar player and he was made to play rock 'n' roll. Everybody was trying to get Johnny to be a little more commercial, but I don't think his heart was in it fully."

Radford played a straight-ahead rock style of guitar and needed a bit of coaching to develop a rock 'n' roll style. "I grew up playing a lot of British-style rock: Eric Clapton and Jeff Beck; I was definitely a rock player," said Radford. "Rock is pretty solid and straightforward. Guitar players play it very straight, down the middle, down the line. The roll part of rock 'n' roll is little to the left or the right. Randy was a very strong rock 'n' roller and helped me develop that rock 'n' roll style."

Live performances ran from ninety minutes to two hours; their blistering rendition of "Jumpin' Jack Flash" was one of the biggest crowd pleasers. Hobbs and Radford clicked musically, and it's evident in videos of those performances, where they're jumping in unison and playing off of each other like musical bookends. Radford also fit in well with Johnny, and unlike Brockie, respected his position as second guitarist.

"Johnny was the leader and I'm good about following," said Radford. "We worked out solos and changes. He was very generous. He'd take the first solo and I'd take the second one, or Johnny would play a slide guitar solo, then I'd get a solo. I was very honored and excited that Johnny allowed me to play solos."

The fall 1974 European tour opened in London with a live studio performance for the *Old Grey Whistle Test* on BBC 2, Britain's premiere television music show. Radford had only rehearsed with the band three or four times, so he was understandably nervous. Johnny alleviated his fears with a lesson that had a strong impact on Radford's style.

"Johnny says, 'Don't worry about it; play how you feel,'" said Radford. "'Play how you feel' is one of the things I learned from

Johnny. We played 'Jumpin' Jack Flash' and a lot of songs on the *John Dawson Winter III* album. Johnny was never concerned about playing things the same way. Sometimes he'd come out and change things around, which made me a little nervous at times. But it was exciting to follow him."

That three-week European tour included sold-out performances in London, Paris, Munich, Frankfurt, Copenhagen, and Stockholm, and a TV show in Bremen, Germany. "European audiences weren't much different than the ones in the States," said Radford. "Johnny Winter fans are all very loud."

Johnny loved traveling on his own plane during the *Saints and Sinners* tour. When he heard the jet from the Led Zeppelin tour was available, he leased and customized that aircraft.

"The jet was one step bigger than a Learjet," said Radford. "He painted John Dawson Winter on the nose. When we landed in private airports, we'd be greeted by two limousines. The band would climb into one limousine; they put the luggage in the other one."

As Johnny's fame escalated, so did the size of the venues. During the '74–'75 U.S. tour, he played stadiums that held 50,000 to 75,000 people. Although he had vowed to slow down after his stint in rehab, that twelve-week tour only gave him a week off once a month. "We would go for nights in a row; that was the hardest thing," said Radford. "Flying to the next city, sound check, playing the show and party in the room afterward, get very little sleep that night, go to the next city, do another sound check, and do it all over again. There was little time for anything else."

A private person, Johnny kept to himself on the road, but occasionally he'd meet Hobbs and Radford at a restaurant for dinner. Although he was the star and the biggest moneymaker, they always had a hard time getting him to pick up the check. "When we ended up at a restaurant with Johnny after a show, we'd always look at him, but Johnny never paid," said Radford with a laugh. "He'd say, 'I ain't got no money.' That was Johnny—'I ain't got no money.' He finally did pay, after we made him."

Johnny hired Peter Frampton, an up-and-coming artist, as his opening act. With a mobile recording unit set up by the stage every night, Frampton recorded all of his shows. His performances at four venues during that tour appeared on *Frampton Comes Alive*, a double album released on A&M Records in January 1976. "After that record hit the charts, the tables turned," said Radford. "He'd be selling out 100,000-seat stadiums, so we'd have to open for him."

In fall 1975, Johnny joined forces with the Edgar Winter Group (with Rick Derringer) to play a series of dates recorded for two live albums: *Captured Live!* (with Johnny's band) and *Together* (with both bands). Edgar, who was still riding the wave of the success of "Frankenstein" and "Free Ride," both hits from his *They Only Come Out at Night* LP, headlined the shows, which consisted of a set by Johnny's band, a set by the Edgar Winter Group, and all the musicians onstage for the finale. Although both bands rehearsed together before the tour, having three guitar players onstage created intense competition. "Playing with three guitars was hard," admitted Johnny.

Radford described the vibe between Johnny and Derringer during that tour as "love/hate." "Guitar players are very egotistical," said Radford. "We love each other and we hate each other. So, there was a lot of competition and fighting. I loved it, even though it was very, very competitive. I was eighteen years old and trying to keep up with those guys. Occasionally I'd throw out a lick that they didn't do. I'd come back the next show and sure enough they'd be playing it. I did the same thing—I listened to their licks and said, 'Okay, you steal my licks, I'll steal yours.' It was an honor to have somebody play one of your licks, even though they won't admit it."

Radford also noticed a touch of sibling rivalry when Johnny and Edgar shared the stage. "Johnny and Edgar are brothers and act like brothers," he said. "They love each other, but they fight with each other. They both want to get their way. They're different in terms of how they express themselves. Johnny plays from the heart. He's not concerned with technicality or how things are arranged or how every riff is going to sound. Edgar also plays from the heart, but he's a little more of a mindset that it has to be technically correct. Johnny is fun-loving; he enjoys the music and wants to have some fun. Edgar does too, but he's very, very intelligent—keeps up with what's going on in the world, is technical about a lot of things. Even though they're brothers, Johnny and Edgar are almost opposites."

*Johnny Winter And Live* had been his biggest-selling LP, so Johnny decided to release a live recording that captured the energy and excitement of his latest band, as well as a live album of both bands with songs he and Edgar had played in the Southern bar circuit ten years earlier. Those albums were recorded at shows at three California venues—the Swing Auditorium in San Bernardino, San Diego Sports Arena, and the Oakland Coliseum Stadium—with the bands playing the same set all three nights.

No expense was spared in packaging the live albums. For *Captured Live!*, Mick Rock shot the cover photo of Johnny jamming on his Firebird, his head flung back, his hair flying. Jim Marshall shot the back cover photo from behind the stage, capturing the band in action dwarfed by the massive audience at the Oakland Coliseum Stadium. Richard Avedon shot a striking profile of Johnny and Edgar for the front cover of *Together* and an artistic shot that highlighted their white hair, eyebrows, and eyelashes for the back cover. One inside sleeve showcased a collage of childhood photos from their mother's attic; the other sleeve included photos of Johnny, Edgar, David Holiday, and Willard Chamberlain (of Johnny and the Jammers) with B. B. King at the Raven Club in 1960, and Johnny and the Jammers playing a New Year's Eve gig in 1964.

Blue Sky Records released both albums in 1976. *Captured Live!* featured Johnny on guitar and vocals, Radford on guitar, Hobbs on bass, and Hughes on drums. *Together* featured Johnny on guitar and lead vocals; Edgar on saxophone and lead vocals; Derringer on guitar and background vocals; Radford on guitar; Hobbs on bass; Dan Hartman (Edgar's bass player) on piano and background vocals; and Hughes and Chuck Ruff on drums. Johnny and Edgar worked out the songs with a minimum of solos and no jamming to keep the emphasis on the vocals.

"Randy and Floyd had both played in White Trash so they knew all of Johnny's songs and my songs too," said Edgar. "It was really great. It turned into an entirely new band with a different feel; it was very powerful. I loved the way the music felt with two drummers."

"It was kind of a nostalgia trip," said Johnny in an interview coinciding with the release. "The tunes were soul and rock 'n' roll. It had been quite awhile since I'd played live with Edgar. It felt really good. We sang harmony on 'Soul Man' by Sam and Dave—we did a lot of harmony that night. We sang harmony on 'You Lost That Lovin' Feeling,' Edgar sang the higher falsetto part. We also sang harmony on 'Mercy, Mercy' [and] 'Baby, Whatcha Want Me to Do.'"

"It was really fun to do the old songs we did in bands together," said Edgar. "That was the concept—to go back and do harmony songs like 'Lovin' Feeling' by the Righteous Brothers—songs that could lend themselves to a duet thing that he and I had done together. Almost every one of those songs was a song we would play in various bands when we were kids. It was very emotional for me, and lots of fun."

An interview with Johnny and Edgar was released on an album entitled *Johnny and Edgar Winter Discuss Together: Johnny and Edgar Winter*. Although the album was distributed to radio stations across the U.S. prior to the record's release, it didn't help sales. "That album sold mediocre," says Johnny.

But rockers still loved Johnny's band, which was at the peak of its power when the tour ended in late September. Many fans and critics called *Captured Live!* one of the best live albums of the decade. "When we were touring with Johnny, the band was getting better and better," said Radford. "The promoters were coming up to me to get to Johnny, saying we want Johnny to come back, we'll pay you double. We were already making a lot of money, but the shows were just getting better and stronger, and the promoters were willing to pay."

But Johnny had played rock long enough. When he got the call to produce Muddy Waters, nothing could have held him back. His musicians, like the lineup in Johnny Winter And, were completely surprised when he called a rehearsal and told them he had decided to call it quits.

"After we rehearsed, Johnny says, 'I'm going into the studio for nine months with Muddy Waters,'" remembered Radford. "And that was it. It was over. It was very quick. I don't understand why Johnny did it that way, but I think the decision came from Johnny's heart. On *Captured Live!* we played a lot of blues, but it was still rock 'n' roll. Johnny had a fair amount of fortune and fame by expressing himself through rock 'n' roll. But for him to go with Muddy Waters was the greatest dream of a lifetime."

# A Dream Come True

When Waters left the Chess label in November 1975, his manager Scott Cameron scheduled meetings with several labels. Ron Luxembourg, who headed Epic Records, came up with the concept of Waters working with Johnny. Cameron negotiated a record contract with Blue Sky, with the stipulation Johnny play on and produce the records. Paul was happy to sign Waters.

"Muddy Waters was the first recording artist I ever hired to play at the Scene," said Paul. "I loved him then and when I had a chance to sign him as a Blue Sky recording artist, I couldn't have been more thrilled."

Waters had been impressed with Johnny's talent and love of the blues when he met him in Austin and knew he was making the right move. "Muddy spotted Johnny's ability the very first time Johnny opened for him down in Texas, before Johnny had a record deal," said Cameron. "He knew his sincerity and [that Johnny] knew Muddy's music—he wasn't going to come in and try to change Muddy. He was just going to enhance it."

Having an opportunity to play with and produce his idol meant the world to Johnny. "I always loved Muddy—it was like a dream come true to be able to work with him on a record," he says. "I tried to do everything I could for him. The record company itself was behind him—they had a big picture of him up on one of the floors of CBS."

Johnny loved Waters's early Chess Records and wanted to produce records in the same vein. He felt the attempts by Chess to repackage

Muddy to suit the latest musical trends didn't do justice to the blues legend.

"I thought Chess had messed him up pretty good," says Johnny. "They had a Muddy Waters *Folk Singer* album. The *Brass and the Blues* record wasn't bad but it wasn't really Muddy. I hated *Electric Mud*. It just wasn't Muddy Waters at all. It wasn't Muddy's band; it was a psychedelic band playing the blues. The publicity shot—Muddy in a robe with his hair up—was pretty terrible. I don't think he had that good a relationship with Leonard and Marshall Chess. He said Chess wasn't doin' a lot to promote his albums, and he didn't make much money from his old records. He wasn't getting the proper control and respect."

Johnny respected the stylistic difference between his music and Waters's blues, which like the music of John Lee Hooker, didn't always stick to time signatures. Waters would throw in odd measures and make changes at unexpected times, which affected the meter. "Some of the old blues songs that Muddy played didn't change at the right times," says Johnny. "'Rollin' and Tumblin'' and 'I Can't Be Satisfied' are hard songs to follow because they don't change when you think they're going to—they change at a different point."

Guitarist Bob Margolin, who joined Waters's band in 1973, agreed that his style could be challenging to follow. "Muddy's blues in general had a behind-the-beat feel called delay time," said Margolin. "The note would come a little later than you would expect it to. A lot of bluesmen had it. I certainly didn't have it naturally when I got in the band—I really had to work on playing that way. Johnny was able to get with that too."

Waters used heavy strings with high action on his 1957 or 1958 Telecaster, compared to Johnny's thin-gauge strings, and his playing style was sparser than Johnny's, who said it felt natural to play more notes. Rather than using a guitar with open tuning for slide and a second guitar, Waters now used a capo on a single guitar with standard tuning.

Waters had set the stage for instrumentation with two guitars, bass, piano, drums, and harp; his sound, which combined blues from the Mississippi Delta and the South Side of Chicago, was like no other. "Muddy's sound was so distinctive that if he stopped playing, the whole feeling would change," says Johnny. "His slide was shorter and smaller than most slides. He'd only get two or three strings at a time, where most guys could get six strings. He never told me why he did that."

Waters's traditional method of making a slide never worked for Johnny, who tried it once or twice in his early twenties. "Muddy said he'd make a slide by wrappin' string around the neck of a soda bottle, soak it in kerosene, light it, let it burn until it went out, and then break it," says Johnny. "I never got that down. The bottle would break off in the wrong places."

Despite their stylistic differences, Johnny's knowledge of Waters's music and his love for the bluesman made their collaboration joyful. "Making *Hard Again* was fun," says Johnny. "You could tell it was fun by just listenin' to the record."

"Muddy loved working with Johnny," said Cameron. "He was very sincere with Muddy and he had a lot a respect for Muddy and treated him that way. What was important to me was that he brought the best out in Muddy."

"I think Johnny knows more about my music than I do," Waters said in an interview in the August 1983 *Guitar Player*. "When we went to do *Hard Again*, he was bringing up things I had forgot all about, and he was playing them just like they're supposed to be played. . . . He wanted to go back to the old sound, but I didn't know he went so far back."

Johnny laughs at the memory. "That's nice," he says. "Muddy probably meant I knew all the parts he was doin' in the songs more than he remembered in some cases. It made the Blue Sky records easier to do—that I knew so much about Muddy—his tunings, phrasing, slide, picks, everything involved in the old sound."

Johnny chose The Schoolhouse studio in Westport, Connecticut for the *Hard Again* sessions, which ran from October 4 to 10, 1976. Set in a one-room schoolhouse built in 1760, The Schoolhouse included fifteen additional rooms, and had a live-in maid and cook. The studio was owned by Dan Hartman, a multi-instrumentalist who had played in Edgar's band and on six of his albums, as well as on several of Johnny's LPs. Hartman, who was also a songwriter, producer, and engineer, released his own records on the Blue Sky label in the late 1970s and early '80s, including the gold disco single "Instant Replay." A $300,000, twenty-four-track studio, The Schoolhouse was the perfect setting because Johnny could record all the musicians in the same room.

"The Schoolhouse was a real relaxed studio that was close and sounded real good," says Johnny. "Dan Hartman put the studio in himself for his own recording. He didn't rent it out very often. The studio had a great big room—we set up everybody in that room. The control room was upstairs and the playing room was downstairs. I was playing and doing the producing too, so I'd run downstairs and play; and after we played a tune, I'd have to run up and listen to it. It made it a little crazy."

The Schoolhouse setup had two microphones near the ceiling, which created a room echo and captured the raw sounds of Waters's early blues recordings. "With overhead microphones, you get the sound of a whole band instead of separate instruments," says Johnny. "Everything fed through everybody else's mike. Regular miking ruined the sound of real raw blues. Studios did the same thing to early, nasty rock 'n' roll—made it too clean. Overdubs ruin the sound of raw blues, and we had enough musicians so we could get it without overdubbing anything, except for the vocals."

Johnny also used close miking—placing microphones close to the amplifiers for separation and a cleaner sound. "Johnny put mikes on each instrument and the drum set, and had two microphones near the ceiling, capturing the ambience in the room," said Margolin.

To ensure that engineer Dave Still knew the sound he wanted, Johnny gave him a crash course in Muddy Waters. "I played him a bunch of Muddy's records at my house," says Johnny. "I played him the good records and told him why they were good, and played the bad ones and told him why they were bad. He knew what I was trying to get before we went in the studio 'cause I had gone over all that stuff with him so particularly."

Johnny took a low-key approach to producing Waters, which mirrored the way he produced his own albums. "If the players are doin' something I like, I tell them; if they're doin' something I don't like, I tell 'em," says Johnny. "With Muddy's band, I didn't have to tell them much. They'd just count it off and play. Muddy already had the idea of what he wanted to do before we started."

"As a producer, Johnny was very concerned about capturing the essence of Muddy Waters and I think he did that," said Cameron. "He was not overbearing, nor did he give in. He wanted the quality of excellence out of Muddy. He knew Muddy could deliver and they worked to get that. They had an ability to communicate musically extremely well and their personalities seemed to get along extremely well. Muddy had a lot of respect for Johnny's ability at the board, in addition to as a player. Johnny's respect for Muddy was unquestioned."

"I've seen all kinds of producers," said Margolin. "Some take everything apart and take the joy out of it; some just try to help you be the best you can in a very nonintrusive way. Johnny didn't take things apart; it was just, 'We know how to play this stuff. Let's get the arrangement and cut the tune.' He had boundless energy and a lot of enthusiasm. He loved that old blues so much and was thrilled to be working with Muddy. It was just the way it sounded on the *Hard Again* album; it was friendly and fun, just a happy, good time. They were having a good time together and Muddy felt that too."

Waters had told Margolin he played harp as a boy, so Margolin thought it might be fun for him to play harp on that record. "I told him I'd buy him a harp, if he played it on the album," said Margolin. "He said okay. And I said, 'If you don't do it, I'm going to keep the damn thing' and I ended up keeping it."

"Bob was always trying to get Muddy to do off-the-wall things," says Johnny. "But Muddy was hard to talk into doing anything off-the-wall."

Cameron credits Johnny for getting Muddy's band to push him during those sessions, but Johnny knew he couldn't push Muddy to do anything he didn't want to do. "Muddy had his own ideas," says Johnny. "He was stubborn—he knew what he wanted. He was definitely more open to have somebody else try something, than to have him try it because he was used to having things the way he wanted them."

Johnny played all the slide parts and most of the solos; Margolin played the background parts and occasionally took a solo. Even though Waters's Telecaster was set up right next to him, Johnny couldn't get him to play guitar on the first Blue Sky album. "He didn't play at all on *Hard Again,*" says Johnny. "He didn't pick up his guitar. He did that back in the old days too—he didn't play the guitar very much at all. I think he considered himself a singer—mostly. I was disappointed that I didn't play with Muddy on *Hard Again.* But we did play together on some of the other Blue Sky records and we both played on the live album."

Although Waters never played guitar on that record, several reviewers—including one in the March 24, 1977 *Rolling Stone*—commented on his slide playing. "I guess the slide on 'Deep Down in Florida' sounded like Muddy a little bit," says Johnny. "I'd played like Muddy for a long time. The people just figured that on a Muddy Waters album, he'd be playin' a song."

"I remember seeing reviews that said, 'Muddy Waters's slide sounds very exciting and vital,'" said Margolin. "But it wasn't Muddy playing; it wasn't listed as such in the credits. Maybe they can't hear and they can't read."

Waters chose the lineup for *Hard Again,* which included his own vocals, Johnny on vocals and guitar, James Cotton on harmonica, Margolin on guitar, Pinetop Perkins on piano, Charles Calmese on bass, and Willie "Big Eyes" Smith on drums. Cotton and Calmese came from Cotton's band; Margolin, Perkins, and Smith hailed from Waters's band. Harp player Jerry Portnoy and bassist Calvin Jones from Waters's band were kept on retainer with financial help from Johnny.

"Muddy didn't want to get too many people from one band," explains Johnny. "He didn't want it to sound like somebody else's band so he was very adamant about using different people from different bands. James Cotton fit real well—he played real good harp and was used to playin' with Muddy. They had a pretty good relationship, but Muddy was the leader. Sometimes they'd argue about stuff but Muddy always got his way.

"Pinetop Perkins was a little primitive as a piano player, but good. He played certain things differently than I would have played them. He played kinda out of key. I don't think he did it on purpose; I think he thought it was right. He wasn't Otis Spann but he was one of the well known piano players around Chicago and there just wasn't anything better. He didn't play like anybody else; he has his own unique style.

"Willie 'Big Eyes' Smith was a real good guy and a good drummer. He wasn't fancy and he didn't rush things—he was behind the beat. Willie's drums were recorded up front; it was as loud as anything on the mix. I liked it 'cause it had a good backbeat on it and it made it [the sound] real. Charles was a great bass player. He was a little more complicated than a typical blues player. He used to do a poppin' thing with James's band. He didn't do it too much on Muddy's stuff. He may have overplayed a little bit, but he tried to accommodate Muddy."

Although Margolin was accustomed to playing with Jones, he enjoyed working with Calmese. "Charles was a little more modern player, certainly a little more versatile and energetic," said Margolin. "We had our first rehearsal the first night of the *Hard Again* tour, at the Capitol Theater the afternoon before we played. As we were setting up the instruments, Charles was getting the sound on his bass. He started playing some modern, popping stuff, which was very new back then. Muddy came out of the dressing room and put his nose right up to Charles's nose. 'I hate that shit.' Charles made sure he played as straight as he could behind Muddy. And he did a good job of it. Charles was a good guy—always great and friendly—we had a lot of fun."

Margolin met Johnny for the first time at the *Hard Again* sessions, and they immediately hit it off. "I really didn't know what to expect, but he presented himself as just another blues lover musician," said Margolin. "I really enjoyed the times I hung out with him socially as well as on the bandstand."

For Johnny, the feeling was mutual. "I liked playin' with Bob Margolin," he says. "He was a good guitar player to be with Muddy Waters. The other guitar players I'd played with played rock 'n' roll and a lot of different things. Bob was just a blues guitar player and he was better on blues than they were."

Muddy garnered respect from his musicians, and that translated into the way they performed, both in the studio and onstage. "Muddy ran a tight ship and told everybody what to do," says Johnny. "Anybody get out of control, Muddy would push them back into line. Everybody liked Muddy because he was the Father of the Blues. He liked to have good musicians and would give them a chance to shine. He didn't keep anybody in the background."

During his years at Chess, Waters learned to cut a record without wasting any time, and he recorded *Hard Again* in less than a week. "Muddy started out in the era of direct to disk," said Cameron. "The idea of overdub, and multi-tracking, didn't capture the essence of Muddy. Muddy like to record a performance versus perform a recording."

"We'd get in about noon and work till 5 or 6 [PM]," says Johnny. "In the studio, Muddy was straight-ahead work. Muddy didn't fuck around between cuts. He knew what he wanted to do and did it. Sessions with Muddy were quicker than other sessions I'd been to. He wanted everybody to play it right the first time, and everybody did. He picked the right musicians, so he didn't have to tell them much. The band didn't rehearse; they knew the songs. He just said what to play and we'd play it. You didn't want to do a song too many times to really be straight blues. I always felt like it should be spontaneous—that a few mistakes don't hurt. Muddy wouldn't do a song more than twice. If something didn't come out right, he expected me to fix it. And I usually could.

"I played slide on 'I Can't Be Satisfied' and the solo on 'Deep Down in Florida' because Muddy didn't want to play. I was hopin' he'd be happy with the way things were goin' and he was. Muddy was real good when I made suggestions. We wanted him to record acoustic songs, and he didn't really want to, but he did it for me. He said, 'I did that a long time ago.' I guess he got tired of it. Me and Bob Margolin played on the acoustic songs. We did it a little sloppy and we wanted to do it again, but Muddy wouldn't do it more than once. The second one, 'Feel Like Goin' Home,' ended up on the *King Bee* album."

Working with Johnny was life-affirming for Waters. Not only was he working with a producer who understood and loved his music; he had backing from his label, and control over his music and his image as a gentleman, both of which had been lost in the making of *Electric Mud,* a recording he referred to as "dog shit" in a *Guitar Player* interview with Tom Wheeler.

"Muddy said, 'This music makes my pee pee hard again, so I'll name it *Hard Again,*'" says Johnny with a laugh. "The Richard Avedon cover shot was Steve's idea; we wanted everything to be classy. Muddy looks like he's in control of everything and looks happy in that picture. They used the clothes he had on and shot it real quick, the same way he recorded it. Blue Sky did pretty well promoting Muddy. There was an ad in *Rolling Stone* and a lot of blues papers for the record. He wasn't used to having any promotion at all."

The *Hard Again* tour in early 1977 was a far cry from Johnny's previous tour, when he played stadiums and coliseums that held up to 50,000 people. He was performing at clubs that held 500 to 600 people, but that didn't faze him in the least. He was playing the music he loved, with a man he loved, and that was all that mattered.

"The *Hard Again* tour with Muddy was a lot of fun," says Johnny. "I liked playing in Muddy's band 'cause I could do what Muddy wanted and he liked pretty much the same thing that I liked. It was real nice with Muddy. During that tour, he didn't come on for a while because he liked to have the band play before him, then bring on the star."

"That was a tradition of Muddy's," said Margolin. "Let the band do as much as they can, and then come out as a feature and tear it up. He did play on those tours. He had his guitar out there and would play a slide solo. He had his Telecaster in his hand the whole time except when he was doing 'Mojo' or 'Mannish Boy.'"

Having three guitar players never created any problems because the players worked around each other without competing. "Muddy and I just listened to each other," says Johnny, who played a Firebird on that tour. "He'd play guitar on at least two or three songs.

It was exciting working with him and he seemed happy to be working with me. You could tell how he felt just by looking at him, by listening to him too."

"The band got along great on that tour," said Margolin. "Cotton and Charles Calmese and Johnny were all nice folks who got along. All the guys in Muddy's band were really special in getting along with each other and everybody else. If they had a problem, they talk about it, deal with it, and then let it go."

•◆•

When *Hard Again* won the *Rolling Stone* Critics Award and the Grammy for Best Ethnic or Traditional Recording, Johnny had finally earned recognition as a blues player—something he had yearned for throughout his career.

"A lot of critics, especially European critics, felt that white people shouldn't be playing blues," he says. "Black musicians I had worked with never did anything except help me and encourage me. Most of 'em figured it didn't make any difference what color you were. I always wanted to be respected as a blues player. I felt I'd made it as a rock 'n' roller but not as a blues musician until *Hard Again*. I just wanted to do a good record, but I was hopin' we would get a Grammy. I didn't know if people were gonna like it or hate it. I thought they might hate it, think it was too rock 'n' roll just because I was on it. After we won the Grammy, I felt that I could relax a little—at least I'd done what I started out to do."

Johnny was named Blues Player of the Year by *Guitar Player* magazine in 1977, 1978, and 1979. Although some of the Grammy-winning records he made with Waters didn't sell as well as his rock-oriented releases, it didn't matter. "Those records made me feel like I was supposed to be doin' more blues," he says. "Blues is my favorite; it's something I love to play."

While those records earned Johnny recognition as a blues artist, they also revived Waters career. "Those records made Muddy's career happen again," says Johnny. "Bein' affiliated with Columbia and Blue Sky helped—'cause he made the money he was supposed to make—instead of not getting the money like in the Chess days."

"Working with Johnny brought Muddy's career back to life," agreed Cameron. "It brought it to a much, much wider audience; and the reviews of *Hard Again* were phenomenal. It put a new spark in Muddy's career."

Johnny's collaboration with Waters created a renaissance for the blues, exposing the genre to a broader audience, like the Paul Butterfield Blues Band and John Mayall & the Bluesbreakers did in the mid-1960s.

"Nobody had put out a good blues album in a long time, and it was time for one," says Johnny. "People liked me and gave Muddy a chance because I liked him so much. Muddy definitely reached a different market. A lot of people told me they didn't know who Muddy Waters was before he started playing with me. They bought his record because I was on it, and got to know him through me."

Their musical collaboration also gave Johnny an opportunity to learn from and develop a personal relationship with his idol.

"Workin' with him made me get to know him a lot better," says Johnny. "You got to see what he was doin'—what he was all about. I could see what his ideas were about music. I learned a lot about being a leader from workin' with Muddy. Don't be scared to say what you feel. When he said something, his band did what Muddy wanted. To figure out what you're gonna do before you went in, to get ready for the session before you go in and do it. I got to know him on a more personal level too. He was a little bit nicer than I thought he might be—he wasn't conceited at all."

Johnny visited Waters several times at his home in Chicago, where he was treated to one of his hero's culinary specialties.

"Muddy was a great host. and his cookin' was the best part of it," says Johnny. "We ate in the kitchen, sitting by the stove. His chili was strong, really hot. I had a big bowl and I was sweatin', really big drops of sweat. You needed water 'cause it was so hot," he says, laughing at the memory. "It was gumbo, but Muddy called it chili. He put okra in it, and other vegetables, too. Muddy liked to cook and liked having people over. Another time we went to a birthday party for Koko Taylor at Muddy's house."

In the *Guitar Player* interview with Wheeler that ran after Waters's death, he whispered "that's my son" when Johnny left the room to get his guitar. It was the ultimate compliment, one Johnny never heard from Waters's lips.

"That made me feel great," Johnny says. "Muddy wasn't an emotional kind of guy. I think it was always in interviews where he said it about me to somebody else. Muddy and I had a strong bond because I worked with him—I helped his career a lot. I don't want to sound conceited, but I did. Muddy's acknowledgement made me feel like it was something I should be doin'. Made me feel like I could play better than most people doin' blues."

"Muddy loved Johnny," said Cameron. "I don't know that Muddy was an unemotional guy from my relationship with him. He was highly emotional; he just hid them very well. I think he had a lot of that old-school macho in him, which kept him from outwardly displaying certain types of emotions. He thought the world of Johnny and credited Johnny with helping him in numerous interviews."

•◆•

A week after the *Hard Again* tour ended, Johnny returned to The Schoolhouse and produced his own blues record on the Blue Sky label. "*Nothin' But the Blues* was the first time I got to do all blues since my first CBS record," he said. "Steve Paul didn't particularly like me doin' that but I had the power to do what I wanted. I used Muddy's band 'cause I had been workin' with them and they were a great blues band. Better than a British blues band 'cause the British stuff wasn't real."

Johnny paid all the musicians scale except for Cotton.

"James argued about how much money he was supposed to get," says Johnny. "He thought he deserved more because he was the frontman. I ended up payin' more than I was supposed to because he said he wasn't gonna come unless I gave him extra money. He won that one."

With the exception of "Walkin' Through the Park," Johnny wrote all the songs on that album. The sessions took several weeks, with Johnny miking the room like he did for *Hard Again*. But unlike the earlier recording session for Waters's first album, the band had played together before going into the studio and that affected the chemistry. "We'd been on the stage together as a band for a number of shows just recently, so we were a lot tighter and a lot more together than for *Hard Again*," said Margolin.

Johnny did the vocals, and played electric guitar, National acoustic guitar, bass, and drums. "I had two different Nationals, a single cone and a tri-cone," says Johnny. "I used the single cone for the slide. The single cone had a brittle, more trebly, more clear sound than the tri-cone, which is a little bassier. Charles Calmese was the bass player on that record, but I played bass and drums too because it was something I wanted to do."

Margolin's guitar style meshed well with Johnny's; they had the same influences and he never stepped on Johnny's toes. He'd play background to Johnny's leads, and when he did get a solo—which wasn't often—he'd give it all he had.

"Whatever Johnny played, I would find a part that would go well with it," said Margolin. "I was playing a little more straight Chicago blues, but when we did 'Tired of Tryin',' I did a long solo that was more of a modern style. Johnny's really got his own distinctive sound; he doesn't sound like anybody else. My guitar playing is a combination of my influences too, but it certainly isn't as recognizable as Johnny's."

*Nothin' But the Blues* was lauded by the critics; a reviewer in *Rolling Stone* wrote: "There's no shortage of hair-raising picking, for Winter simply has never recorded in as vital a blues context.... Winter has effectively bridged the gap between hard rock and the blues in a way that only great stylists like Jimi Hendrix and Eric Clapton have been able to, thus proving himself as one of our greatest musical resources."

Johnny needed a band to tour in support of *Nothin' But the Blues* and remembered the musicians who had befriended him in New Orleans. Torello was playing in Black Oak Arkansas, but had kept in close contact. When Black Oak Arkansas offered Torello a seven-year contract, Johnny paid his own attorney to review the paperwork, and Torello was advised not to sign.

"Johnny says it's time for you to play with me," said Torello. "Then he says, 'Okay, Bobby, you're in the band, pal, but you don't know how to play blues. All you know is the Allman Brothers; you don't know anything about blues.' So I sat in his apartment for two months listening. I learned quite a bit. Every night we'd sit and listen to all these old classic blues records, stuff you wouldn't even believe timing wise. It's called 'Follow the Leader' and that's all you had to do. Of course, I played it a younger, more powerful style, but it worked out well."

Johnny's original lineup for that tour included Rush and Hobbs, but Hobbs was replaced by Ikey Sweat when he passed out at a rehearsal and was taken away by ambulance. "I thought he got electrocuted," said Torello. "It looked like he was having an epileptic seizure. So Johnny flew Ikey Sweat in to play bass for that tour. Ikey was one of the nicest people I ever met in my life, a country guy straight out of Texas."

Rush, who was living in New Haven, Connecticut and had played with Torello in one of Michael Bolton's early bands, remembers Hobbs's sudden departure. "We rehearsed for the tour at S.I.R. for a few weeks with Randy Jo, then rented the Calderone, a concert hall in Long Island, for two afternoons and nights in their off times," said Rush. "We set the whole stage up so we could see how everybody wanted their gear set up. Randy put his bass on, turned around, started adjusting his amplifier; and all of a sudden, he fell over in the drums and passed out cold. We called the emergency guys and they came and took him away. We didn't see him again until he came out again to see us at a gig. Ikey flew in the next day; he had big enough ears that he could jump in and play."

The *Nothin' But the Blues* tour covered the U.S.; the band played four or five gigs a week for eleven weeks. One of Johnny's last U.S. tours at large venues and coliseums; they performed for 10,000 to 15,000 people each night, headlining over 38 Special and the Climax Blues Band. Gone were the wild outfits; Johnny dressed to suit himself, in a flat brimmed leather hat, blue-jean shirt, and old ripped up jeans with patches. Like the *Hard Again* tour, Johnny kept to himself, but traveled with one of his on-the-road female companions.

One of the more memorable gigs on that tour was one that didn't happen. After playing the Fox Theater in Atlanta on August 15, the band was scheduled to play Memphis the following night. The crew, with the tractor trailer carrying the gear, left early that morning but couldn't get into Memphis. Elvis Presley had died, traffic had stopped, and the interstate had turned into a parking lot.

"Johnny wanted to play and do a tribute to Elvis, but there was no way for us to get into Memphis," said Rush. "The crew couldn't get anywhere near the Coliseum. Even if they did get in and set up, we were flying in. The only way to get from the Memphis airport to downtown would have been by helicopter and there was no place to land. We're talking 1977—logistically, it couldn't happen. So we ended up having a night off in Atlanta. I don't think Johnny knew Elvis but everybody was pretty upset about his death."

Like the Johnny Winter And band that never knew what song Johnny might play, the *Nothin' But the Blues* band had to stay on its toes. "Johnny would pull out different songs from one night to the next during the entire tour," said Rush. "One night we did 'Honky Tonk Women'—he just pulled it out of his hat. We all went, 'Okay, one, two, three,' and played it."

•◆•

On October 11, 1977, the Hard Again band appeared on *The Mike Douglas Show*, where Johnny and Waters joined Douglas for a lengthy interview. Johnny was quite talkative; Waters didn't a get a word in edgewise unless Douglas asked him a specific question. "Muddy wasn't a good talker when it came to interviews," says Johnny. "I think he was nervous; he had a hard time comin' up with things to say."

Although the tour was billed as "An Evening with Muddy Waters, Johnny Winter, and James Cotton," only Johnny and Waters were invited to chat, much to Cotton's dismay. "James got out of joint that he wasn't gonna get to talk," says Johnny. "He said he deserved to talk, but there just wasn't room for him. Muddy took him back and talked to him but he was still pissed off about it. James thought he was always in Muddy's shadow. On the road, James always felt like he was gettin' taken advantage of. He thought he deserved more than he was getting—more respect, more money. I thought he was gettin' plenty."

Johnny regaled Douglas with stories of Texas clubs where "I never went to a gig without a gun in one boot and a knife in the other" and how he learned table throwing and to wipe out rednecks with his solid body guitar. Despite his obvious discomfort (Johnny put his head down and said he didn't like to talk about it), Douglas relentlessly grilled him about his drug use. "Did you go all the way? Acid, heroin?" Douglas asked. Johnny's amusing tale about losing his hair from doing acid and quitting because "I wouldn't be very cute bald," didn't deter him. "Then what? From acid to . . . ?" responded Douglas.

The show was taped in Philadelphia in the morning and aired in the afternoon, so not all of Johnny's responses made it to the national broadcast. When Douglas asked him, "Do you have anything to tell the youth of America about drugs? Like, don't do them!' Johnny didn't take the bait. "He just looked at him seriously and thought about it for a second," recalled Margolin. "Then Johnny says, 'Well, I've always thought anything that doesn't kill you makes you stronger.' That never got into the actual TV show."

During the musical segment, the band played "The Blues Had a Baby and They Named It Rock 'n' Roll," "Love Me with a Feeling," and closed the show with "Got My Mojo Workin'." Unfortunately, Waters exuberant dancing on "Mojo" was overshadowed by the ending credits.

Less than three weeks later, Waters and Johnny returned to The Schoolhouse to record *I'm Ready*. More polished than *Hard Again*, Waters's second LP on Blue Sky featured Jimmy Rogers, his guitar player from 1947 to 1955, and "Big Walter" Horton, a former harp player. Margolin suggested using Rogers and Horton and both Johnny and Waters loved the idea.

"Muddy played slide on '33 Years,' 'Mamie,' and 'Screamin' and Cryin'," says Johnny. "He played more 'cause I asked him to. I had more control of him and he was ready to play guitar—that's why he called the record *I'm Ready*. I didn't play on as many songs because we had Jimmy Rogers playing too. That was the first time I'd seen Jimmy Rogers; I played open tuning slide on 'Who Do You Trust' and he played the other guitar part. Me and Jimmy and Walter traded solos. He played a hollow-body Gibson and was playin' a little more distorted than I was used to, but it worked out fine."

"Muddy used my Music Man amp and Jimmy used Muddy's amp," said Margolin. "I set them up to have pretty heavy distorted guitar sounds. Muddy and Jimmy liked that—it was the way they sounded in the '50s when they played together. Johnny was up in the control room, and said, "Are you sure you want those amps that dirty?' They said, 'Yeah, we like that.'"

Before they began recording, Johnny asked Waters and Rogers if one of them wanted to play the top part and the other play the bottom. "They said, 'We don't care about that; we just play what we want to play,'" says Johnny. "I guess they were so used to playin' and not worrying about talkin' about it, they thought I was crazy for even mentioning it. They made me feel like an idiot, to tell you the truth," he adds with a laugh.

Both Johnny and Waters had misgivings about Horton, so they asked guitar player Johnny Nicholas to accompany him to the studio and make sure he didn't drink.

"Muddy worried that Big Walter might screw up in the studio because he's a screw-up," says Johnny still laughing. "He was an excellent harp player but he drank too much.

"Big Walter gave me a lot of trouble playin' through a glass at Columbia [the *Johnny Winter* LP], so I wasn't sure if it would work or not. But Muddy is a good leader. Big Walter was easygoing when it came to Muddy 'cause Muddy was the boss. He was anxious to play with Muddy and do a good job. We brought in Jerry Portnoy just in case. Jerry was a good harp player—he was fairly young and Muddy had used him before for several years. We worked both of 'em in. We didn't really need two harp players. We could have left Jerry out, but we figured we'd go ahead and use him."

Margolin credits Horton's respect for Waters for his good behavior. "I remember Muddy giving Walter some instructions and Walter's eyes got real big, 'Okay, Muddy. Anything you say, boss,'" said Margolin. "Walter's nickname was 'the Old Goat' because he could be cantankerous. He was a little lamb that day and played pretty well."

Portnoy had a close relationship with Horton and was thrilled to work with him on that record. "I love Big Walter," Portnoy said. "I used to go to his house and drink and exhort him to play for me. I just soaked it up. He had the greatest pure sound ever to come out of a harmonica. Walter certainly was a very eccentric fellow. A lot of those old-timers were, in one way or another. Sometimes you have to step around their idiosyncrasies to get what you want. I learned a lot just hanging around with him in Chicago, trying to imprint his sound on my head. I love his sound, and I dug him as a person too. He had a very crusty exterior, but he was a goodhearted guy inside."

Both Portnoy and Horton played harp on "I'm Ready" and "Hoochie Coochie Man." Portnoy played chromatic to Horton's diatonic on "I'm Ready." Both played diatonic—the standard blues harp—on "Hoochie Coochie Man."

Margolin had filled in on bass for Clarence "Gatemouth" Brown at a European gig in 1976, so when he eliminated his spot as a guitar player by suggesting Rogers, Waters asked him to play bass. "Bob Margolin played bass on everything," says Johnny. "He played bass real well. Charles was a better bass player but Bob played simpler."

Johnny didn't join Waters for the *I'm Ready* tour because it didn't make sense financially. He had helped Waters pay Portnoy and Jones during the *Hard Again* tour, and now had his own band to think about. "It cost so much to go on the first tour and I couldn't manage goin' in the hole again," he says. "It just about cost me more than I made 'cause we had different bands to contend with. I earned more money with my own band, so I just came around when he had something goin' on and I had the time to do it."

Johnny shared the stage with Waters at a "Foghat Blues Tribute" at the New York Palladium in 1978. The show, released on video in 1979, included Foghat, John Lee Hooker, Paul Butterfield, Otis Blackwell, Dave "Honeyboy" Edwards, and Eddie Kirkland. Margolin remembers the grand finale. "All the bands were jamming onstage," he said. "Johnny turned around to me and said, 'I can't see too well.

How many people are onstage right now?' I looked around, counted, and said seventeen. He said, 'Man, this is gonna set the blues back thirty years!'"

Johnny also joined Waters's band for occasional gigs in Europe, including a blues festival in France the following year. Johnny traveled with one of his girlfriends, who made quite an impression on Portnoy. "She had some kind of bustier, something low cut," Portnoy said. "Across the rise of her left breast was Johnny's signature tattooed into it. When he came out to join us onstage, the first song he did was "I Got My Brand on You." I got a tremendous kick out of that; I thought it was pretty hilarious."

•◆•

Johnny frequented clubs in Manhattan, and on an evening that would prove to be serendipitous, he stopped by the Bottom Line in February 1977 to catch Son Seals, who was opening for Mose Allison. He met Bruce Iglauer, the president and founder of Alligator Records, when he went backstage. "Johnny just showed up," said Iglauer. "He was very approachable, very friendly, not pretentious. He was like, 'Hey, I'm a blues fan, you're a blues fan; here we are.' There wasn't any sense of 'I'm a cool guy' at all."

They met again the following year when Johnny sat in with Seals at the Bottom Line in January. "He came in with the *I'm Ready* record and asked me what I thought of the cover," said Iglauer. "I actually didn't like it so I was beating around the bush, trying to tell him I wasn't crazy about it. He said, 'I hate it.' We liked each other right away and stayed in touch."

A week later, Johnny traveled to Chicago and stayed at Iglauer's house. "I had a lot of Alligator Records," says Johnny. "They had the best people around—they were a real good label. I thought it would be nice to get to know Bruce better and be friends with him. Bruce had a lot of good records, so when he went to sleep, I stayed up and played his records. He had one Junior Wells record I never had heard before."

Iglauer was delighted to have Johnny as a guest. "He just hung out with me and stayed in my spare bedroom," said Iglauer. "He was a wonderful houseguest, which sort of surprised me. He always made the bed. We went out to clubs every night—the Wise Fools, the Kingston Mines—and I asked Dick Shurman to take him out one night when I couldn't go. They got along right away too. After we got back from gigs, Johnny would want to sit up and listen to my record collection. As soon as he detected I was tired, he'd get on headphones so he wouldn't disturb me. He smoked pot and knew I was a little phobic about that. So he would very carefully clean up after himself and take his pot back to his room when he went to bed."

Iglauer invited Johnny back to play on a live Son Seals record being recorded at the Wise Fools Pub. He stayed at Iglauer's house; and once again, they had a great time talking about and listening to music. "Johnny had this huge vocabulary of blues knowledge and we talked music all the time," said Iglauer. "He was excited, fun, and funny, always very wired, twitching with the enjoyment of being in Chicago."

Although Johnny played several songs with Seals, none appear on *Live and Burning*, the album recorded at that gig. "It wasn't very good because they were too nice to each other," explained Iglauer. "I was trying to get them to go head-to-head, to have a little guitar battle, and everybody was holding back. It was, 'After you,' 'No, after you,' and they both played very conservatively."

During his time in Chicago, Johnny began a friendship with Shurman, who would produce several of his subsequent albums. "We got along 'cause he knew a lot about blues and he liked to talk about blues and I did too," says Johnny. "He was a good guy to hang out with. I remember him asking me a question to see if I knew what I was talkin' about. He asked me who's the girl in the song that—oh hell, a particular blues player that I can't remember the name of right now—but he asked me what the girl's name was on the record. I said, 'Lily,' and I was right. I don't know what he would have done if I had said the wrong name," he added with a laugh. "But I knew it was pretty off-the-wall and he was doing it to test me."

Despite a raging snowstorm that almost shut down the city, Shurman took Johnny to Biddy Mulligan's to hear Lonnie Brooks, who Johnny had seen in Texas in the early '60s. "Me and Dick had to push a car out of a snowdrift to get a parking space," says Johnny, chuckling at the memory. "I jammed with Lonnie that night. There weren't many people there but I liked it pretty well."

During Johnny's jaunts to Manhattan nightclubs, he also forged a friendship with John Belushi, who asked his advice about his Blues Brothers project with Dan Aykroyd. "I had seen John Belushi at several different clubs and got to be friends with him," says Johnny. "He called one night and wanted to know what I thought about him doin' the Blues Brothers thing. I told him nobody would take him seriously; they would just think it was funny. He didn't say anything back—I don't know if that's what he was lookin' for or not."

Luckily, Belushi didn't take his advice. In April 1978, he and Aykroyd made their Blues Brothers debut on *Saturday Night Live*, with Belushi as lead vocalist "Joliet" Jake Blues and Aykroyd as harpist/vocalist Elwood Blues, fronting a band of well-respected musicians. Their live album, *Briefcase of Blues*, released later that year, reached number one on the *Billboard* charts and went double platinum. The 1980 *The Blues Brothers* movie is still considered a classic.

•◆•

In late spring/early summer 1978, Johnny returned to The Schoolhouse studio to make *White, Hot & Blue*. Johnny produced that album, which includes three of his originals—"One Step at a Time," "Slidin' In," and "Nickel Blues"—as well as "just good ole blues songs I liked," he says.

Unlike *Nothin' But the Blues*, Johnny used his own band so it would be viewed as his own album. "I used Pat Rush, Bobby T., and Ikey," Johnny says. "Edgar played keyboards. I also used Pat Ramsey, a real good harp player."

Ramsey landing a spot on that album was a stroke of fate; he had played backstage for Derringer in Colorado, and been encouraged to send Johnny a tape. "Johnny had drawers full of tapes that people gave him in his music room in the penthouse," said Rush. "When I was living with him, I'd go through them, throw them in, and listen to them. One night, I listened to a tape by Pat Ramsey and played it for Johnny. He went, 'Wow! That guy is unbelievable. Let's call him up.'"

Johnny called and invited him to fly to Chicago to jam the same day, and then gave Ramsey a plane ticket to Connecticut to record *White, Hot & Blue* that weekend. "We didn't have any rehearsals—just went into the studio," says Johnny. "I liked him because he was a real fancy player. Pat Ramsey fit into the band real well, but I had to be careful because he was a pretty busy harp player in those days."

Unlike Johnny's previous recordings in The Schoolhouse, *White, Hot & Blue* had all the instruments—rhythm guitar, bass, and drums—miked separately on separate tracks. The majority of the vocals were overdubbed as were Ramsey's harp parts and Rush's slide guitar. Although Rush had been playing the harmonica parts of "Walkin' by Myself" on slide guitar during the *Nothin' But the Blues* tour, he didn't expect to play slide on the album. "I figured he would have Pat Ramsey do the harp on it, but was pleasantly surprised," Rush said. "As far as I know, I'm the only slide player playing on a Johnny Winter album except for Johnny. That's pretty cool."

Torello had a surprise in the studio as well, when Johnny asked him to play while listening to a click track, a recorded synchronization tool similar to a metronome. "That was kind of weird," said Torello. "Blues varies but Johnny says you got to play good here and I want you to play to a click track, so that's what I did. *White, Hot & Blue* came out pretty good."

Johnny, however, wasn't especially pleased with that album, which he felt took too long to finish. "*White, Hot & Blue* is okay; it's not real great," says Johnny. "It took longer than it should have. Ikey was not used to playing bass on blues, and the other guys were new too; that made a difference. But it sold pretty well. Blue Sky had ads in all the major magazines and did a good job promoting my records."

Unlike Caldwell, who felt underpaid, Rush and Torello thought Johnny treated them well. "We got session pay in the studio, and got paid by the week for the tour, plus all your expenses and per diem," said Rush. "For the time in musical history, the pay was quite good. We weren't on equal terms with Johnny, but we got paid twice as much as most people were making for tours at that time. He took really good care of us."

After the *White, Hot & Blue* sessions, Rush and Ramsey went their separate ways, and Sweat returned to Texas. "Ikey left because he was gettin' crazy," says Johnny. "He was going nuts because he had too many fans bothering him. The fans bothered everybody. We'd all stay at one hotel and sometimes he would stay somewhere else so they didn't know where he was. He had a hard time dealing with it. So he left and started doing country back in Houston."

Johnny wanted to tour without a bass player, but Torello convinced him it wasn't a good idea. "It was just me and Johnny," said Torello. "We're getting ready to go on tour and he says, 'Ah, we sound good with two pieces—all I need is a beat. All they care about is seein' me play guitar.' I said, 'Come on, Johnny, we got to have a bass player.'"

Johnny checked out his favorite haunts in New York and discovered guitarist Jon Paris. "Johnny calls me up and says I found my bass player," said Torello. "I said, 'How does he play?' He said, 'I didn't hear him play bass but he plays great harmonica.' I was laughing, oh man, what's this gonna be like? He says, 'Come in next week and we'll go see him play.' So we went in and Jon Paris was a blessing—the guy was great. He was so perfect in the band. He plays harmonica when he plays bass, he plays guitar, he knew all the blues stuff, he knew rock stuff. He was the greatest addition. We went on like that for about the next six years."

•◆•

In 1979, Johnny produced *Muddy "Mississippi" Waters Live,* his third Grammy-winning album with Waters. The shows were recorded at Detroit's Masonic Temple and at Harry Hope's in Cary, Illinois, about forty-five miles west of Chicago.

"It seemed like the right time to do a live album, which can be more exciting," says Johnny. "You hear the people screamin' in the background. But we had one guy who was whistling and that was a drag. He whistled all through the record—the real loud kind that pierces your ears."

The Masonic Temple gig was part of the Hard Again tour, which featured Johnny and Cotton. They played on "Mannish Boy," "Howlin' Wolf," and "Deep Down in Florida." Portnoy, who played harp on the 1978 tour, remembered the raucous audience at the Harry Hope gig. "We played the room on the second floor, and the audience stomped a hole right through the floor on 'Mannish Boy,'" he said.

When that album was released, Waters was doing a forty-seven-city North America tour as the opening act for Eric Clapton, who followed Johnny's lead in exposing the elder bluesman to new audiences.

"I think Muddy liked opening for Eric Clapton, but he probably didn't know who he was before that time," says Johnny. "Eric Clapton is a good guitar player. I first heard him on the John Mayall & the Bluesbreakers record."

Waters invited Johnny as a surprise guest to his June 12 gig at Chicago Stadium. Johnny joined Waters on "Mannish Boy" during his set and was called back onstage—along with Clapton and Willie Dixon—to play "Got My Mojo Working" during the encore. A headliner coming out to jam with the opening act attested to Clapton's respect for Waters. "He did it 'cause he loved Muddy," says Johnny. "And at the end of Eric's show, me and Muddy joined him on 'Kansas City' and 'Long Distance Call.' That was a nice jam. I think Muddy liked having the two of us out there together."

The Rolling Stones, who took their name from one of Waters's songs, were also big fans. So when Mick Jagger and Keith Richards, whose rehearsal space was adjacent to Johnny's at S.I.R., saw him at the studio, they asked him about the Blue Sky projects. "I talked to Mick about producing Muddy," says Johnny with a laugh. "I got real drunk and obnoxious and was slapping him on the back and being a real asshole. I was hittin' Mick on the back just for fun and almost knocked him over. I was terrible—really obnoxious. He took it pretty good."

Susan remembers that evening. "I met Mick and Keith that night," she said. "Johnny got very drunk and I couldn't get him out of the bathroom. So I knocked on their [rehearsal space] door and said,

'Can you help me get Johnny out of the bathroom?' They carried him out and helped me get him into a cab. They were very sweet."

By the time Johnny returned to The Schoolhouse to produce Waters's fourth album in May 1980, the goodwill that encompassed the earlier sessions was gone. The tension in the studio was palpable and it affected the album.

"It was only a month before Muddy's whole band split," said Margolin. "There had been a lot of tension for almost a year over money. It was mostly a conflict with Muddy's manager that went too far. During that time, Muddy and his manager and the band were all separate. There was a lot of tension in the studio and the music didn't come out very good."

*King Bee* took less than a week to record, with a lineup including Waters on slide guitar and vocals, Johnny on guitar and slide guitar, Margolin on guitar, Luther "Guitar Junior" Johnson on guitar, Calvin Jones on bass, Pinetop Perkins on piano, and Willie "Big Eyes" Smith on drums. Johnny played on every song except "Champagne and Reefer"; only he and Waters played guitar on "Mean Old Frisco Blues."

"I don't know why we had four; that was too many guitar players," says Johnny. "It could have been because of the friction in his band, but Muddy never said anything. Luther played on everything. I think Bob played on everything too. If I thought I could fit in some place, I'd play. If there was already enough going on, I wouldn't play. Playin' with three guitars was fun. Muddy would give us leads and tell us when to play. Nobody played real rhythm; everybody was playing leads.

"When we recorded *King Bee,* I don't think Muddy was in quite as good spirits. He wasn't willing to try as much and it wasn't as good an album as the other three. During the sessions, everything was just a little bit harder. Muddy always wanted to be quick, but this time he did it too quick and it really made a difference. I'd tell him, 'You need to do it again,' and he wouldn't do it again."

Cameron remembers Waters feeling a bit rushed going into those sessions. "I don't think he was as prepared as he would have liked to have been," he said.

*King Bee* was recorded in 1980, but wasn't released until the following year. "It took that long to get it done," explains Johnny. "I had to go through it and make it sound as good as I could. Muddy just didn't take enough time to get the songs right—he expected me to be able to fix everything and I couldn't in every case. There were some songs I couldn't make right. When I asked him to do it one more time or play something over, he just said, 'It's good enough.' We had to use outtakes from the *Hard Again* sessions—'(My Eyes) Keep Me in Trouble' and 'I Feel Like Going Home.' They weren't great, but they were decent. It didn't win a Grammy 'cause it wasn't as good an album as we had been puttin' out."

Regardless of how *King Bee* turned out, Johnny's recordings with Waters, including *Breakin' It Up & Breakin' It Down*, the 2007 Sony release of previously unreleased live performances from the *Hard Again* tour, had a strong impact on the elder bluesman's career, as well as his legacy.

"When I started working with Muddy back in 1971, he was not in much demand for anything, and his engagements were very, very few," said Cameron. "Prior to the time of his death, he was in great demand. Without Johnny Winter, I don't think there would have been a *Hard Again*, which was the rebirth of Muddy's career. His relationship with Johnny, the release of *Hard Again*, and all of the marketing and promotional efforts they made to get him in front of a wider rock 'n' roll audience made a tremendous difference, both before and after his death. The income for his family, the estate that I oversee, is still quite healthy."

# 10

# One Step Forward (Two Steps Back)

When Johnny wasn't touring or recording, he enjoyed living in his New York penthouse apartment on East Eighty-Seventh Street, decorated in his own inimitable style. The bedroom décor included black walls, a black ceiling, black curtains, and a black carpet. Purple and silver was the color scheme in his living room, with a purple carpet, purple walls, silver blinds, a silver couch, and silver accessories. A tall wooden cabinet custom built for his extensive record collection dominated his music room.

"We were on the twenty-second floor with a beautiful view," says Johnny. "You could see the East River and the Triborough Bridge. You could see the river, the ocean, ships coming in—you couldn't ask for a better view. The balcony wrapped around two different sides of the apartment. We'd use it for barbequing, and Susan had a garden."

Johnny didn't let his limited vision affect his fun. When mopeds became popular in the mid- to late '70s, he bought a pair for him and Susan. "I liked it in the nighttime mostly, but I went out in the daytime too," he says. "It was easier to see at nighttime, and the roads didn't have too much traffic on them. I'd drive on the regular roads and around Central Park. I was okay as long as I was careful and wasn't around too many cars at once. I drove it for a couple of years—till they passed a law that you had to have a license. It wasn't worth it to me to get in trouble, so I sold them."

On *Raisin' Cain*, his last record on the Blue Sky label, Johnny returned to the trio format and The Schoolhouse studio. "I was tired of two guitar players, so I just used Bobby and Jon Paris," says Johnny. "Jon was a pretty good harp player. I liked that he could play bass and harmonica at the same time. Bobby wasn't really a good blues drummer but I liked him a lot. He's a good guy but he played too much. Double bass drums were just too much. But I had him for a long time; his style and Jon's went together pretty good."

Produced by Johnny and recorded quickly, *Raisin' Cain* featured a mixture of musical styles. Although dominated by seven blues tracks, the album also featured early rock 'n' roll, R&B, a Dylan cover, and a slow ballad. "*Raisin' Cain* was alright—it didn't sell good at all though," says Johnny. "I think it was my worst-selling record."

Despite poor sales, Johnny's star as a guitarist continued to rise. His wild performances and touring schedule kept him in the spotlight. When *Guitar World*, a magazine that still covers his career, debuted in July 1980, Johnny's photograph graced the front cover.

"After we did *Raisin' Cain*, we went out and kept playin' and playin'," said Torello. "We played gigs throughout the U.S. and Europe—Paris, Spain, Sweden, Norway, England. We did Lorelei, an outdoor concert in Germany for about 30,000 to 40,000. We played in Cologne for 10,000 people; it was filmed for the *Rockpalast* show [a German rock music TV show that broadcasts live] and went out to 30 million people. Everybody in Europe saw the show. They put my name on the screen and every time I got out of a car in any country, I heard 'Bubby!' and it was usually women. I loved it!"

Punk rocker Patti Smith, who had been Steve Paul's driver before she began her musical career, was the opening act for that tour. Uninvited, she made her way onstage during Johnny's televised performance of "Johnny B. Goode," dancing around and joining in on vocals, and walked onto stage playing a clarinet during Torello's extended, energetic solo. Both were livid. Johnny blasted her in the tour bus after the show, causing her to break down in tears.

The band returned to Germany several times, and played large venues to appreciative audiences. "We did a heavy metal show there in 1981—we headlined over Ted Nugent, Molly Hatchet, Judas Priest," said Torello. "Ted Nugent was originally the headliner and he came in the dressing room and said, 'I'm not headlining over you; you're gonna go on last.' Johnny says, 'Bobby, you're gonna get your dream tonight. We're gonna play mostly rock 'n' roll.' That was a good night—we played for 50,000 people."

When Stevie Ray Vaughan and Double Trouble was a local blues band, they opened for Johnny whenever he played Texas. Tommy Shannon joined Double Trouble in 1980, so a gig at the Austin Opry House in September 1981 gave Johnny a chance to catch up with his old friend and see the guitarist he had first heard in Shannon's living room so many years before. "I liked his playing but I didn't think he was a real blues guy," says Johnny. "I thought he was a flashy player who played pretty much the same style—you didn't notice him taking any chances."

Torello left the band shortly after that gig to play on Grace Slick's third solo album, *Welcome to the Wrecking Ball*, and her 1982 European tour. He enjoyed playing with Johnny but Paul's attitude and Teddy Slatus's growing role in Johnny's management had a chilling effect on his income.

"When Steve Paul talked to you, he wouldn't even look you in the eye," said Torello. "He was like any manager; they only care about the artist because that's who's making the money. We were just hired guns. He told us right out, 'You want more money? We'll hire younger guys.' We never bothered Johnny about the money; I was getting a better deal than anyone else so I just kept my mouth shut.

"Teddy was a fantastic road manager; he took care of everything. He didn't drink, he didn't smoke—all he did was make the money and take care of everybody. He was the babysitter for all us babies. But when Teddy took over [more responsibilities], things progressively got worse. Our pay immediately got cut down. The venues were getting smaller due to playing blues. No more bus, now it's a Winnebago. Everything got scaled down, and we started working six months out of the year. I couldn't live in Manhattan on six months work. So when the Grace Slick thing came along, I took it."

When Torello left, Johnny brought back Richard Hughes. When Slick cancelled her tour to rejoin Jefferson Starship, Torello was out of luck. But he rejoined Johnny in 1982, and enjoyed being part of Johnny's flamboyant lifestyle on the road.

"What was Johnny like on the road?" he said with a laugh. "He's a maniac. He's crazy. Sometimes it got hairy when he got a little out of hand; he's a pretty eccentric guy. But for the most part, it was total fun. All you had to do was show up and play the gig. Very rarely would we do sound checks because we had a real tight knit band. We stayed at the best places, had twenty-four-hour room service all the time. Johnny usually had a girlfriend on the road with him. I had a different one in every time zone; he could afford to take one with him all the time. Every musician in the world would come to see us—the respect he has from musicians is incredible. The Rolling Stones in the audience, Van Halen waiting in the dressing room, all kinds of people.

In a move he soon regretted, Torello left Johnny in April 1983 to play with Michael Bolton, who was embarking on a career as a rock artist. He played on the *Michael Bolton* LP on Columbia, the MTV video for the single "Fool's Game," and the consequent tour.

"I thought it would be the next Bon Jovi," said Torello. "Johnny always told me: If you can find a better job, take it because it doesn't matter. I'll always play and we'll always be friends. I took it and it was the wrong move. The Michael Bolton organization . . . they didn't even call me and tell me I wasn't working anymore. Let's leave it at that. I tried to get back in Johnny's band. But by then, they said, 'Bobby's just gonna quit again because he keeps jumping ship,' and that was the end of it."

•◆•

*Raisin' Cain* fulfilled Johnny's original Columbia contract, and signaled the end of the Blue Sky label. "Blue Sky dissolved because Steve Paul lost interest in it," says Johnny. "'Cause there wasn't any big money in it. He was making good money off of all of us but he wanted big money. He wanted somebody huge. Selling almost a million copies, like the Beatles or the Rolling Stones."

With no record label and a burning desire to play blues, Johnny started checking out blues labels. "I just wanted to play on other people's records," he says. "We went to Malaco Records, but they didn't know what to do with me and they weren't gonna give me enough money. The record companies never wanted to pay blues artists—that's why so many couldn't make a living. Labels figured they could make more money on something commercial."

After gaining acclaim for reviving Waters's career, Johnny thought about producing other older bluesmen, including Memphis Slim and Otis Rush. He talked to Rush about a project, but didn't like his attitude.

"Me and Dick saw Otis Rush in Chicago," says Johnny. "I liked him a whole lot as a guitar player and he sang real well too. I asked him if he was willing to have me produce him or if he needed/wanted to get a record deal—he wasn't interested. He said he didn't care about the way it was produced or who produced him. He said the money's the only thing that made any difference to him. After hearing that, I didn't care about working with him anymore."

Determined to produce an older bluesman, Johnny approached several blues labels, but none were interested. "I didn't want any money; I just wanted a chance to do it," he says. "I don't know why they said no—maybe they didn't want any fresh ideas or different ideas from what they're doin'. There were great musicians who deserved recognition and needed help. Old musicians who were well-known but didn't have any money comin' in—who hadn't had anything goin' for them for a while. I felt like I was in a position where I could help people like that."

Johnny still kept in contact with Waters, frequenting his gigs whenever his idol was in town. When Waters played the Beacon Theatre in New York in March 1981, both Johnny and Cotton were guest stars. Johnny saw Waters at the Savoy two months later; Sonny Terry and Brownie McGhee opened the show. Johnny's wish came true when drummer Styve Homnick, who had played with the duo since 1978, approached him about producing Terry's next album. A country blues harmonica master, Terry was best known for acoustic albums with McGhee, his longtime partner.

"I walked up to Johnny, who was at a table with Edgar, and said, 'Sonny would like to do a record with you. Will you play guitar and produce it?'" remembered Homnick. "Johnny says, 'Damn right. I'd love to do that.' He gave me his phone number, and two days later, we were up in Johnny's penthouse with his manager, working out the details."

"I didn't know Sonny very well when I decided to produce him," says Johnny. "I think he saw what I did for Muddy and was hoping I could do the same thing for him. We got together at my house in New York and I got to know him pretty well. I loved him; he was a great guy. We talked a lot. He'd been on a bunch of different labels. He was well known for the folk music thing, but I don't think he made any money."

"Sonny and I were real close and he trusted me," said Homnick. "I said, 'Sonny, you haven't done any decent albums in a long time. You're getting old. It's time you did an album that's out of this world. Why don't you let me throw together the right crew?' He said, 'You put it together, whatever you want to do.'"

Aware of the impact Johnny had on Muddy's career, Homnick wanted him to produce Terry's last album.

"Sonny was getting to that point where he was about to stop playing; his arthritis and gout were killing him," said Homnick "I thought, it's gotta end with a bang. Who would be better than Willie Dixon on standup bass and Johnny Winter on guitar and producing?"

"Sonny had never done an album with an electric guitar player," says Johnny. "I always wanted to make a record with Sonny because I thought he needed a more Mississippi-style guitar player. Like me. I played a lot of slide on that record because it fit with his voice and his harp. Sonny was great at those sessions. He had a real unique style; he didn't sound like anybody else. He did the whoopin' thing, played great harp and sang great too. Sonny had a raspy voice—a Mississippi Delta sound. He could keep the rhythm going on his harp while he was singing. He was seventy when we did that record. He had bad arthritis and was having a hard time getting around. He was in pain all the time but he still played great."

Johnny wanted to work with Dave Still, who engineered all his records at The Schoolhouse studio, but Still had moved to Pennsylvania. So Johnny et al drove to Mechanicsburg for the July Fourth weekend to record at Baldwin Sound Productions, Inc., where Still worked.

"We picked up Willie at the airport with his standup bass, traveled down together, and had a hell of a time," said Homnick. "Sonny's wife Emma was in the studio the whole time. Sonny and Johnny got along famously. They got a kick out of each other. Johnny loved Emma, and Susan, what a girl! Everybody got along great. We all thought we were making history."

The Baldwin Sound Productions studio, a large square room with high ceilings, was an ideal location for Johnny to set up the mikes and the musicians to capture the ambient sound of early blues recordings.

"We set up in a circle," said Homnick. "Willie was on my left, Sonny was on my right, and I was facing Johnny. Like a baseball diamond. Johnny threw most of the mikes in the middle of the room, with a few mikes near my drum set, and mikes near everybody. It was incredible. Sonny and Emma picked the songs. Willie brought in a song he wrote that was never recorded—'I Think I Got the Blues.' He sat right there in the studio, sang it a cappella, and coached Sonny on how to do it the way he envisioned it. Ten or fifteen minutes down the line, Sonny got it the way Willie wanted it, and we recorded it spontaneously, just from Willie humming it."

The band had never played together, so they spent the first day in the studio just jamming. Like the sessions with Waters, the players followed the leader.

"Sonny did what he wanted to do and I fit my style into it," says Johnny. "You gotta follow Sonny 'cause all his songs weren't strictly by the book—they changed when he wanted to change."

"We all followed Sonny because Sonny really doesn't know twelve-bar blues," said Homnick. "He's just in another world. He'll turn around before the twelfth bar, or he'll go thirteen bars. Or he'll go to the eleventh bar and go one or two beats after the eleventh bar, go right around, and go back to the beginning. You don't know when he's going to do that, so if you don't follow him, you screw up the whole song. There is one song [on *Whoopin'*] where it is completely noticeable. You'll be tapping your foot and all of a sudden, it ain't workin'."

Just as Johnny couldn't get Waters to play guitar on *Hard Again*, he couldn't convince Terry to play electric harp to get the distorted raw sound of Chicago blues.

"We tried using the mike, but Sonny wasn't used to it—he wasn't comfortable doing it," says Johnny. "He played straight into the studio mike, which made his harp playing a little cleaner. I played piano on that record 'cause I thought it needed a piano. I liked that record a lot."

"Sonny could play electric harp; it's just not his thing," said Homnick. "He made a living as an acoustic Georgia boy harmonica player and he wanted to do what worked for him. I was disappointed because it would have made things completely amazing. Believe me, being with Sonny nine months a year, I heard him do things that nobody's heard. He could play Chicago blues like Little Walter. He could do it, but nobody can get him to play through an amp and get that sound. I know I tried."

Johnny's energy and enthusiasm sparked the players, who finished the album in record time. The band spent only three days in the studio (including the first day's jam), with all but one song recorded on the first take.

"We did the whole thing in pretty much one session," said Homnick. "We just played a live show. We didn't know until later that they recorded the jam session. The first thing we did spontaneously, 'Sonny's Whoopin' the Doop,' became one of the songs on the album. That's why Johnny called it *Whoopin'*. I've recorded and worked with a lot of different blues guys, but I never worked with anybody like Johnny Winter. He had an energy in the studio that overwhelmed everybody. He'd be jumping around yellin' 'Yeah!' and making everybody enthusiastic. Every tune was wonderful; there's only one song where we did a second take. He didn't want me to play drums on one song, and decided later that he wanted them. So I had to play the drums listening to the headphones."

Johnny was thrilled to be working with Dixon again, and found the sessions more enjoyable than the sessions for *Johnny Winter*. "Willie Dixon picked up things real quick," says Johnny. "He played standup bass, which I like better than electric bass. Big Walter was such a pain in the ass, it wasn't much fun working with Willie on *Johnny Winter*. This time it went a lot smoother."

Although Johnny was pleased with Dixon's performance, Homnick was critical of the bass, as well as the drums.

"Willie's bass didn't come out that strong in the recording," he said. "Willie hadn't played bass in a long time; I don't think his fingers were as dexterous. He was getting on in age; he wasn't at his peak at that session. I was very disappointed with my drumming because Johnny steered me to using the brushes the whole time. I use brushes on every darn song and I wanted to use sticks. The album could've been bumped up five notches if I was lightly slamming the sticks."

Homnick may have been disappointed, but Johnny wasn't fazed a bit. "Johnny thought, 'Oh man; this will get a Grammy award!'" said Homnick. "He was Mr. Grammy at that point; he had gotten a bunch of Grammys. He thought this is something different; everybody's gonna freak out. He was so nuts. I love that guy. He's one of the *nicest* people I've ever met. He'd get pissed off at me when I gave him a hard time but he was easy to work with. When it was time to perform, it was like seeing somebody from another planet. He brought everybody up."

Johnny released *Whoopin'* on Mad Albino Records, a label he formed specifically for that record. *Whoopin'* was pressed on red vinyl with a line drawing of Johnny's face as the logo. "I came up with the concept for the logo and asked a friend of mine to draw it," he says. "Susan took the picture for the cover."

Susan's photograph depicted all four musicians, whose names were also on the cover. "I almost fainted when the album came out and Johnny put my name in script, along with Sonny, Johnny, and Willie's name," said Homnick. "It was a real honor, another thing that showed me he was a true democrat. He said, 'You played drums, you brought us all together; I'm going to give credit where credit's due.' That's Johnny Winter for you, an amazing guy. A lot of love."

Running a label would have taken more energy than Johnny wanted to invest, so he pressed 300 copies through Baldwin Productions with the idea of using those records as demos to get it released on an established label.

"I didn't want to do the whole record company thing," says Johnny. "Starting your own label is more bullshit than I would like to worry about. Paperwork and everything else. I don't remember all that I had to do, but it was a pain in the ass, I remember that. I didn't do much with Mad Albino really—I just used it as a way of getting Sonny's record out."

When Johnny played the Dr. Pepper Festival at Pier 84 in New York that August, he billed Terry as a special guest. Much to the delight of the audience, Terry, Dixon, and Homnick joined him for five or six songs. "I figured it would help him some," says Johnny. "The audience seemed to like him real good."

*Whoopin'* eventually got international distribution when it was rereleased on Alligator Records in 1984.

"I told Bruce Iglauer, I'd go with him if he'd put a record out with me and release my Sonny Terry record on Alligator," says Johnny. "That was one of the prerequisites of me goin' with him. I knew Alligator would be better able to promote it and market it than me because I didn't know what I was doing. *Whoopin'* did pretty good. Bruce was really surprised he sold as many records as he did."

Iglauer was happy with the sales but doesn't remember it a part of the deal. "It was on top of the deal with Johnny," he said. "We released *Whoopin'* and *Guitar Slinger* as a double release at the same time."

Terry was thrilled with the distribution and sales. "Sonny was happy too; I don't think he had ever sold that many before," says Johnny. "It was Sonny's first electric album, and he said it was his favorite record. That made me feel great."

"Sonny played it on the cassette player till we finally got a CD," said Homnick. "'That's the best record I ever did'—he'd say that all the time. He loved the way he had a group behind him, and everybody followed him. He loved his singing, the way it was recorded, the tone, the arrangements. He loved everything about that album; he was tickled pink."

•◆•

Working with Terry reminded Johnny of the good times with Waters, so he made a surprise appearance during Waters's performance at the first Chicago Blues Festival in May 1981. During a September break in his schedule, he followed Waters's tour, traveling to shows at the Paul Masson Mountain Winery in California; the Delta Blues Festival in Mississippi; and clubs in New Orleans, Austin, Houston, and Dallas.

"I had been workin' with Muddy for a while and I decided I wanted to spend more time with him," says Johnny. "We stayed in little cabins in California wine country and had lunch and dinner with him. Muddy's whole band was there. It wasn't that good a band; they were pretty rotten. His band had given him notice they wanted more money, and Muddy gave them notice they were all fired. So he had to get another band together real quick. We flew to Mississippi and I played with him at the Delta Blues Festival. We drove to Texas to see Muddy too."

When Johnny and Edgar went to see Waters at the Savoy in October 1981, Memphis Slim and John Belushi were in the audience. Johnny didn't talk to Slim ("he seemed very standoffish—not like the kind of guy you could get close to real easy"), but had a few unkind words for his buddy Belushi.

"John Belushi was pretty big," says Johnny. "I was drunk and called him a fat pig. He just laughed. He didn't take me seriously. I'm glad he didn't. I shouldn't have said nothing."

Susan remembers that night and a later phone conversation with the comedian. "I was so mad at Johnny," she said. "Johnny sometimes speaks without thinking, but John forgave him.... I'll never forget the night John Belushi called. He was ranting and raving for about two hours. He told me to call him the next day and when I did, he didn't remember talking to me at all—he was so out of it when he called."

Belushi continued his downward spiral. Less than five months later, he died from an overdose on a speedball—a mixture of cocaine and heroin.

Waters's health was also on the decline. That January, he was diagnosed with lung cancer, had part of his lung removed, and began radiation. Waters wanted to keep his condition quiet, and his manager Scott Cameron respected his wishes. By late spring, his cancer was in remission, and he booked a new tour. But the cancer returned and he wasn't strong enough to undergo another operation. He died on April 30, 1983, without Johnny ever knowing the extent of his illness.

"He didn't want to be around his friends too much then, so I had no idea he was sick," says Johnny. "I never saw him after he got sick."

When Waters died of a heart attack, Johnny attended the services, even though funerals made him uncomfortable. "I went to Muddy's funeral; I just felt like I should," he says. "B. B. King was there; there were a lot of people there. It was a hard thing for me to go through. I was crying. I was trying to talk to B. B. King and I couldn't even talk to him I was crying so much. It hit me hard. I missed all the times we had recording together and getting to know him. All the good times we had together that we weren't going to have anymore. It was a hard thing for me to deal with. Seeing someone in a coffin is scary to me. You know you're not gonna ever see that person again."

At the beginning of the service, Waters's slide and vocals came alive over the sound system with "They Call Me Muddy Waters," "Hoochie Coochie Man," and "Got My Mojo Workin'." The sermon unnerved Johnny as well.

"Hearing Muddy's music was strange," he says. "It was so final. You know you're not ever gonna hear him playing again. The sermon was pretty lame. The preacher didn't talk about how Muddy got to be the person that he was. I don't think he even knew him."

Johnny traveled to the cemetery for the burial, devastated by the loss of his friend and mentor. That feeling stayed with him for quite a while. "Muddy's death affected Johnny a lot," said Susan. "They were close; he was very upset. He really loved Muddy after working with him. Spend a little time with him and you can't help but love the man. He was just a wonderful person."

Johnny eased his pain through music, appearing on *Tribute to Muddy* on MTV and playing several tribute shows, including a Lone Star gig with John Mayall and Canned Heat.

1982 was hard on the blues and on Johnny. Earlier that year, he lost another hero when Lightnin' Hopkins died at the age of sixty-nine. "Nobody sounds like Lightnin'," says Johnny. "He really had a unique style. Lightnin' didn't like me too much. I did 'That Girlfriend' and he thought I was stealing his songs. That's just the way he was—he was a character. So I didn't ever really get close to Lightnin' but I still respected him a whole lot.

"When the older guys are gone, it makes it harder on the blues. So many of the good players have died. I don't think people are as good today. Blues is a little more planned, not as spontaneous as it used to be. Not as real, not as much from the heart. It's the way people go about makin' their records; they're more concerned with sales. If the blues is gonna live on, there has to be new people coming on. Like Derek Trucks—I played with him and I like him a lot; he's real good."

Although Paul still wasn't having much luck getting Johnny signed to a major label, he arranged Johnny's appearance on MTV's *Tribute to Muddy, Late Night with David Letterman*, and *Nightline* (with B. B. King), in the spring and summer 1983. Paul's strategy was to showcase Johnny to wider audiences. "TV appearances are always good and those were good TV shows," said Paul.

"Steve wanted to get me as much TV coverage as possible," says Johnny. "I thought it was good but to actually perform on a show is hard. You have to know how to talk to a host. I was expecting Dave Letterman to be real shitty, but he was real polite, nicer than I thought he would be. He wasn't trying to make jokes about me or anything. I played 'Johnny B. Goode' with Paul Shafer and the band. Paul was always a real nice guy and his band was easy to play with because they were good musicians. *Nightline* was on a strange time at night, so you had a lot of night people on it and watchin' it too. Me and B. B. played little parts together and talked about what it was like to play the blues. It was just the two of us—I played one of my songs; he'd play one of his. I don't think TV appearances helped my career much. I still wanted to change managers 'cause Steve wasn't gettin' any record deals."

After Johnny fulfilled his Columbia contract, Steve Paul remained convinced that Johnny needed to play rock 'n' roll to get another record deal. Johnny reluctantly recorded five rock songs for a demo, which Paul shopped to various labels with no luck. "It's not always easy getting a record deal," Paul said. "Alligator Records is a great record label, but I still hoped we would get a deal with a major label."

"Steve wanted me to do more rock 'n' roll again but I didn't want to," says Johnny. "Nobody would let me do a straight-ahead blues album. Everybody wanted some kind of a modern, new improved Johnny Winter and that's not what I wanted. I felt like I should be able to make it as a blues artist. Steve didn't want to go to a blues label—he was waitin' to get something better."

After Blue Sky dissolved, Steve Paul still managed several other artists and started producing off-Broadway plays. Johnny felt he was spreading himself too thin. "He had too many people and didn't do enough work for his individual clients," says Johnny. "It was just time for us to part. Steve didn't really want to have another blues act; he wanted it to be bigger than that."

According to Steve Paul, "the relationship was no longer working," and he stopped managing Johnny for "various" reasons. Yet the obvious (and unspoken) one was Johnny's switch to blues, which would never give him the fame or income he made as a rock star. But Johnny didn't care about playing coliseums or the money those gigs generated. He had loved the blues for nearly thirty years and it was time—once again—to follow his heart.

Unhappy with Paul, Johnny asked Teddy Slatus, his road manager and Paul's right-hand man, to manage his career. "I got real upset with Steve Paul because he wasn't doin' anything," says Johnny. "I'd been trying to get Teddy to be my manager for a long time and he couldn't break off from Steve. He felt like he owed a lot to Steve Paul, but finally he realized Steve was holding him back and wasn't doin' anything for me. He saw Steve pretending he wasn't there every time I came to the office. Steve knew what I wanted and he didn't want the same thing, so he'd hide. Steve was trying to make me a big star; he wanted me to be the American Rolling Stones. I didn't want that—I wanted to be a great bluesman. So Teddy quit workin' for Steve and started working for me. Teddy made my career as a bluesman, instead of a rock 'n' roller."

Although Slatus was reluctant to leave Paul, who had taught him everything he knew, he too wasn't happy with the situation. "Steve somehow screwed over Teddy and they were both mad at him," said Susan.

Working out of a phone booth for the first few months, Slatus allowed Johnny to call the shots. "Teddy worked real hard but he was scared of doing everything on his own," says Johnny. "He never had been a manager before, but he'd been around Steve a lot so he picked it up pretty quick. I had a better personal relationship with Teddy because he cared. He really tried to make things work for me. Steve didn't."

The timing couldn't have been better. In 1983, Stevie Ray Vaughan crossed over to the rock charts with "Pride and Joy," a Top Twenty hit from *Texas Flood*. Vaughan's success with that debut record ignited a blues revival and made Johnny more determined than ever to make another blues record.

"Stevie was like a one-man blues revival," said Iglauer. "Between the era of Butterfield and Mayall and Johnny, there was nobody new who was bringing blues and blues-based music to a rock 'n' roll audience. There was this huge gap of time—literally ten, fifteen years—when blues was totally on the back burner in the rock 'n' roll world. When Stevie emerged, it was a huge breath of fresh air."

"Stevie's success showed there was still a market for blues," says Johnny. "Stevie being relatively young helped introduce younger people to the blues because they could identify with him. I'd been thinking about signing with Alligator for a while because they were the best blues label around. Finally I told Steve if he didn't call Alligator, I'd do it myself. The last thing Steve did was negotiate my Alligator contract."

# 11

# The Illustrated Man and the Alligator

Once Paul made the initial contact with Iglauer, Slatus became the point person and demonstrated his reputation as "the crusher" when he negotiated Johnny's record deal.

"The meeting in New York with Steve was sort of odd," said Iglauer. "He was arrogant and pushy, very full of himself. I negotiated the deal with Teddy. I was very nervous; I knew this could be a big deal for me. The only other white guy I ever recorded was Johnny Otis. I bent over backward to make sure it was gonna happen and I should've fought a little harder. If I realized how eager Johnny was to do it, I wouldn't have been so flexible."

Iglauer described Slatus as an insecure man with "artificial friendliness" that catered to Johnny. "He would always ask me how my mother was," Iglauer said. "You could tell right away he didn't give a shit. Teddy always asked me how he looked. 'Do I look okay?' I've never seen a guy so insecure in my life."

While Slatus was working on his record deal, Johnny began his lifelong love affair with tattoos. With his opaque, translucent skin, Johnny was a tattoo artist's dream. He became intrigued when he watched Keith Ferguson get inked by Spider Webb. When Webb told him his tattoos would be more vibrant because it would be like drawing on white paper instead of brown, he was hooked.

"I was about to turn forty and wanted to do something different that wouldn't be destructive and tattoos seemed like the best thing.

I figured I was old enough—it wouldn't be like getting one 'cause you're young and stupid—it would be more like old and stupid," he says with a laugh.

Johnny asked Webb to do a few lines without ink to see how it felt. When "it didn't really hurt much," he had several stars and starbursts tattooed on his right arm. The most painful was the multicolored dragon—the "Screamin' Demon"—covering his chest. He found inker Kevin Brady at Sunset Strip Tattoo, across the street from the Continental Hyatt House on Sunset Boulevard. A favorite haunt of rock stars, the hotel became known as the Riot House after Led Zeppelin rode Harleys down the hallway, tossed TVs out the windows, and hosted orgies with drugged-out groupies.

"It *was* a Riot House," says Johnny with a laugh. "A lot of artists stayed there. Girls and guys coming around all hours of the night, dope dealers, throwing TVs out the window. I just happened to see Sunset Strip Tattoo when I was staying there. I'd heard of Kevin Brady before and seen his work in tattoo magazines. He designed it for me; I thought it was cool lookin'. It took two days—one day to do the outline and the next day to fill it in. About five hours each day—with breaks. You had to take breaks in between 'cause it hurts like hell. I drank vodka and smoked when I was gettin' it—that helped."

Johnny's recollections in an interview for the Summer 1989 issue of *Easy Riders: Tattoo Magazine of Skin Art* are more vivid. "Man, it really fuckin' hurt," he said. "The second day it did. I was so drunk the first day I didn't know what it was. He put on Vaseline and all this shit, put the bandage on, and I woke up and didn't know what the fuck it was. . . . What the fuck did I get? Am I gonna like this?"

Although his signature has been tattooed on the breast and/or groin of several girlfriends through the years, he never had a woman's name tattooed on his body. His reasons for getting new tattoos are based on his mood and location. He started with six in 1984; his latest tattoo makes a total of nineteen.

"I kept getting them 'cause it reminds you of where you were at the time and it's fun getting 'em," he says. "You feel like you've done something when you go through the pain. I got tattoos in Australia, Sweden, Germany. New Jersey, San Francisco. I've gotten 'em all over. I got the state of Texas with the yellow rose of Texas tattoo in Austin. The one I got in Sweden is an off-the-wall tattoo. The tattoo guy designed it; it took about four hours. It's my guitar cord and a bunch of different things and the end of it is a dick," he says, proudly displaying the artwork on his arms.

Most tattoos hurt for several days after the inking. "The one on my chest hurt the most though because it was right there on the bone," he adds. "Getting tattoos is kind of a macho trip; I've always wanted to do it just to see if it would hurt."

His parents took his newfound hobby in stride. "Momma thought it was pretty strange but she knew I was strange all the way around so it didn't surprise her too much," says Johnny. "Same thing with Daddy. I think they both wondered why I wanted to do it but they didn't ask."

In 1985 *Guitar World* ran a photo essay of Johnny, Dickey Betts, and Brian Setzer displaying their tattoos. Johnny's photo also graced the cover of *Easy Riders: Tattoo Magazine of Skin Art* in 1989. Getting tattooed exposed Johnny's skin, and his music, to a new audience.

"A lot of bikers like my music now that didn't before I got tattooed," he says. "More bikers bought my records because they identified with me."

A line drawing of Johnny's Lazer guitar, a streamlined instrument that resembles a Steinberger bass, accompanied the 1989 interview "Rockin' Tattoo Blues." He bought it from luthier Mark Erlewine in the early 1980s, but didn't start playing it until 1984, when he broke a string on his Firebird.

Erlewine, who made the Automatic guitar for Johnny's friend Billy Gibbons in ZZ Top (as well as Don Felder of the Eagles and Mark Knopfler from Dire Straits), brought a Chiquita, a guitar about a foot shorter than a Stratocaster, to Johnny's gig at the Austin Opry House. Johnny liked the Chiquita. The following year, Erlewine showed him a Lazer, a lightweight full-scale guitar, and Johnny bought a black model.

"I remember trying it and liking it," says Johnny. "It feels real good and it s pretty lightweight. The Lazer is a little bit easier to play than the Firebird. The action is as high, but the strings pull easier. It sounds close to a Fender. It's a better sounding guitar than the Firebird; it's more biting and has more of a treble sound. But I still use the Firebird on slide songs; the slide still sounds better on the Firebird."

An instrument Johnny refers to as "the closest thing I've found to sounding like a Strat and feeling like a Gibson," the Lazer is thirty-one inches long and weighs only five-and-a-half pounds. A headless guitar, it has a single-coil pickup, a humbucker, and neck-through-body construction. With twenty-four frets, compared to the Firebird's twenty-two, the Lazer's design extends the range from a D to an E, and makes it easier to play the high notes.

Some of Johnny's fans aren't too thrilled with his switch to the Lazer, and believe it can't compare with the sound of a Firebird. Johnny takes it in stride. "People have gotten used to the Firebird and want it. I've had people that are really angry that I started playing a different guitar. People see something up there onstage, and it's like a member of the band. 'Don't use a different guitar,'" he mimics in an affected voice. 'We know that one, we've seen it before.'"

•◆•

Johnny was excited about working with Iglauer and recording on Alligator, but was adamant about retaining creative control. "I was surprised because Bruce tried to get me to do more commercial stuff, more rock blues actually," he says. "I think he figured if I did something more like 'Highway 61' it would sell better. I had to tell him it wasn't what I wanted to do; I went to Alligator so I could do blues."

Johnny flew into Chicago before the sessions, and met Iglauer at Shurman's house to discuss the songs and musicians for the first record. "Johnny wanted to make a real blues album with real blues players and not with rock players playing blues," said Iglauer. "We sat and discussed songs at length, throwing around ideas, and we all came up with songs. It was a great learning experience in terms of learning what Johnny knew. I wasn't used to somebody knowing songs I didn't know, much less Dick didn't know. He's a real encyclopedia."

Iglauer chose Albert Collins's rhythm section—Johnny B. Gayden on bass and Casey Jones on drums—as the core of Johnny's studio band. After two rehearsals at the Dress Rehearsal in Chicago, they went into the studio. Iglauer also brought in Ken Saydak on keyboards; Gene Barge, a former studio musician at Chess Records, on tenor sax; the Mellow Fellow Horns; and harp players James Cotton and Billy Branch.

Branch played harmonica on "Iodine in My Coffee" but Cotton's performance never made any of the early Alligator recordings. He played harp on "Murdering Blues," but it was remixed for *Serious Business*, with Paris redoing the harmonica part. Cotton also played on "Nothing But the Devil," on *Deluxe Edition*, a compilation CD released by Alligator in 2001.

Johnny's touring band, consisting of Paris and Tom Compton on drums, took a break while Johnny made his Alligator recordings. Johnny hired Compton when Torello left. Despite the band's great chemistry, Johnny was happy to use studio musicians on his Alligator recordings. "I thought those guys were probably better for a blues feel," says Johnny. "I'd heard the Ice Breakers play with Albert and I'd seen Ken Saydak playing with Lonnie Brooks. I liked Ken Saydak. He wasn't more powerful than Dr. John but he was good. We used horns for songs that needed a Gulf Coast sound. It was hard to find players that could play blues with power without gettin' in the way, but Bruce did it. That record went pretty quick because the group was so good."

Johnny's first Alligator sessions were held at Red Label Recording Studio in the mansion of Dick Meyer, a Jovan CEO who lived in a North Shore suburb of Chicago. Iglauer didn't like the physical limitations of the basement studio but booked it to work with Fred Breitberg, the house engineer who had designed the studio. Iglauer and Shurman had worked with Breitberg before and he knew how to get the sound they wanted. Unfortunately, booking a studio in someone's home would prove to be damaging to Johnny and Iglauer's budding relationship.

"Bruce got us kicked out the second night," says Johnny. "Dick Meyer didn't want us there anymore. He had brought us some champagne he wanted everybody to share, and Bruce said, 'This isn't a party—it's a recording session.' Bruce didn't want us to stop. He felt like it was his money and his time. He was being a real asshole about it. I can see where he wanted to get things going, but it wouldn't hurt to take fifteen minutes off and drink champagne with the guy. The next day, Bruce told me we were kicked out of the studio. It was my first session with Alligator and I was kinda pissed off. We were gettin' used to the place and he gets us kicked out."

Iglauer remembers the situation differently. "We didn't get kicked out—I left," he said. "I got in an argument and stormed out. It was at least the third night. Normally, you book the studio, and essentially you own your section of the studio. It's your time, it's your space.

"The owner came down in the middle of our struggling to get a Magic Sam song that wasn't coming off right. He didn't buzz down and say, 'When you're taking a break, I'd like to come down and have champagne.' He just appeared. I was really tense because the song wasn't happening and he was a convenient target because he was walking into my space. So I exploded at him and it escalated from there."

Meyer and Iglauer talked the next day, with neither one willing to budge in terms of access to the studio during the sessions. So Iglauer picked up cassette rough mixes of the sessions and began looking for another engineer who could capture the sound he wanted. He took them to Chicago Recording Company (CRC), but their best engineer couldn't duplicate the sound. Reluctantly, he took the tapes to Streeterville Studios, where he was introduced to a young engineer named Justin Niebank, who quickly duplicated and improved the sound Iglauer had in mind.

While Iglauer searched for a studio, Johnny scouted Chicago record stores or hung out in his hotel room, listening to records with Shurman, who empathized with his situation.

"Johnny had been trying for three years to get on this label," said Shurman. "He said he literally put his hands on Teddy's throat and said, 'I asked you to get me a deal with Alligator for three years.

If you don't do it, I'll just call myself.' He was really up for it and he comes in, and here's this guy who is so egotistical and into himself that he's gonna torch the whole project. Poor Johnny is sitting in his hotel room, not knowing what the hell to think or what's going to happen to the project now that he got kicked out of the studio."

Johnny's angst had turned to anger by the first session at Streeterville Studios.

"Johnny was drinking vodka real steadily and smoking pot," said Iglauer. "We were in a small room used as an overdubbing, soloing space. Johnny was really drunk and he kept saying I'm going to kill somebody. I'm going to kill somebody. And I was the somebody, of course. It was both scary and hilarious at the same time because I wasn't sure if he was going to kill somebody."

Johnny remembers that evening well. "I told Dick I was gonna show Bruce what it's like to be a jerk. I walked around all night saying, 'I'm gonna kill somebody, I'm gonna kill somebody.' I felt like murdering somebody—I was really that mad. It'd take a lot for me to murder somebody, more than just a fucked-up record, but I would if I got mad enough. I think it scared Bruce a little 'cause he was hidin'. I've got a reputation for not taking any shit."

The combination of alcohol and anger took its toll on Johnny's output during that session. The only useable take was the solo on "Lights Out." "We recorded some other things and they were useless," said Iglauer. "He was either fumbling or too drunk. First he was just too angry, then there was a moment of being able to play, and then he was just too drunk."

The first night at Streeterville Studios with the entire band started out just as badly, but Johnny surprised them when they realized the method behind his madness.

"Johnny was really rude to the band," said Iglauer. "He spent the whole night just changing strings, tuning, screwing around, and ignoring them completely. They didn't know what to do with that—they were pretty pissed. We cut 'My Soul' that night. Johnny asked for some very heavy strings because he wanted to play the solo on bass strings for a different kind of sound. It was about eleven o'clock at night and I was phoning around the city, trying to find a musician who had a big E string—it was like a .60. I didn't know what was going on until I heard the final song. I was baffled. I think Dick was baffled too. We cut the track and the band was just playing parts; they had no idea what song we were doing. They were playing patterns, and Johnny eventually built the song from the basic rhythm track."

Johnny didn't like too much structure in the studio; he wanted to be able to create the sound he heard in his head and change it until it felt just right. "My records tend to be spontaneous—not planned out," Johnny says. "You can change a song in a lot of different ways. Sometimes I play a song two or three different ways before deciding which version I like best."

Iglauer was accustomed to working with artists like Albert Collins, who would lay down tracks for six or seven hours and finish an album in two nights.

"I'm used to people coming in and saying, 'Okay, let's make a record, here's a song list, does everybody know the arrangement?'" said Iglauer. "With Johnny, you had to create the atmosphere to get him to record. Johnny also had his body-clock schedule where we couldn't start before a certain hour. We usually went to the studio around eight thirty. The first hour to hour and a half was often a big waste. He'd be getting his momentum up. Then there would be peaks of creativity, and he'd have a two-hour block of being extremely productive, doing songs quickly, leading the band, and showing them what he wanted them to play. He'd be really energized. He'd knock out three or four final takes in a row. When the energy started dropping, you'd usually get nothing after that."

In an interview published in *Jazz News*, Iglauer was less generous. "Johnny is a very high-strung and nervous guy, and it's hard for him to get focused in the studio," he said. "He works in 'streaks,' so that in five hours he may have thirty minutes of greatness, but that thirty minutes is truly great."

Johnny agrees with the first statement, but dismisses the notion that he was only on for such a short period of time. "I don't agree with that," he says laughing. "I think he got more than that. But maybe he felt that way."

Shurman felt that Johnny's energy level during a session depended upon his alcohol intake. "It wasn't temperament; it was how much he ingested and how long ago," Shurman said. "He liked to record his guitar sober, because he thought he played sloppy when he was drunk. But he liked to sing when he was a little bit drunk. Not over the edge, but just more relaxed. We'd have him do his guitar part in the earlier part of the evening. When he felt relaxed enough to start singing, he would sing until he got beyond the point where he was going to do anything productive. You could tell. He's start grumbling about small things, getting a little more scattershot in his approach and comments. It was obvious when it was time to stop for the night."

Johnny's first priority in the studio was laying down guitar tracks because he found it more difficult than the vocals. Although two of his solos were overdubs, he recorded the majority of his leads with the band.

"It's the hardest part for me, and it makes it easier to do it with the band playing," he says. "I do the leads first because they are harder to do and then do the rhythm parts. I do the vocals later because they're easier. I usually drink when I'm doing my vocals. It helps me to relax a little bit and do the songs better. I don't drink when I play the guitar—not as much," he adds with a laugh.

"Johnny never liked to do his final singing and playing at the same time," said Shurman. "The way he plays guitar is more or less steady through the whole song—compared to a lot of other blues artists. There is a little less call-and-response in his guitar patterns. So when he's tracking with the band, he wants to be able to concentrate on his guitar playing. He'll do enough of a vocal just to give the band an idea. The hope is he'll get his lead guitar track with the rest of the band because the band is playing with him when they do their track."

Iglauer also observed a nuance of Johnny's guitar style that set him apart from other blues guitarists. "Johnny tends to solo in four-bar segments," said Iglauer. "A lot of blues artists do but because he knows so many licks, his four-bar segments will sometimes be somewhat disconnected from one another. Like a four-bar Slim

Harpo, followed by four bars of Gatemouth, not imitation, but clearly inspired by. And he finds ways of stringing them together. His mind would swing from place to place to place very quickly; he was playing them that way, too. Not just because he's playing fast; the synapses work very quickly with his fingers."

On the third night in the studio, Johnny placed his guitar on a stool, and when Gayden walked by, he stepped on the cord, which wrecked havoc on the input jack. "It was my Lazer," says Johnny. "He broke the guitar; yanked the guts out of the inside where the cords connected to the guitar. I flipped out. I said, 'Oh no, man, how could you do that?' He said, 'I'm sorry, I'm sorry.' He didn't mean to do it, and I knew it wasn't his fault."

"Poor Johnny Gayden was waiting to see which one of us was going to kill him first, but fortunately Johnny was in a good mellow mood about it," said Shurman. "I think that helped with all of them. They saw Johnny was just a guy like them—he wasn't going to put some kind of attitude down because Johnny Gayden accidentally damaged his guitar."

Johnny's mellow demeanor also made an impression on Branch, who didn't quite know what to expect. "You get this image of this wild man with long white hair and tattoos, but he was cool, real mellow, and laid-back," said Branch. "He'd greet me very warmly; he was always pleasant and easy to work with. You got a good vibe. He wasn't like some people that you get a vibe, 'Okay, I got you guys working here, let's get this over, I'm a big star, the hell with you guys.' It wasn't that at all. He didn't talk a lot but you still got a warm feeling from him."

Johnny's initial Alligator recordings had three producers, which is atypical, but Iglauer and Shurman had worked together before with Albert Collins (and after with Roy Buchanan), and had their roles worked out.

"Bruce makes it happen, I help it happen," said Shurman. "Bruce would organize everything, do the business, and book the studio. We'd have a preproduction meeting at my house and go through the material, and Bruce would run the rehearsal. Bruce's nervousness drove a lot of artists nuts, so I would be on the floor with the band, to give them cues and take them through the performance. He would be in the control room with the engineer making sure it was coming out well on tape. It was a good complementary situation."

•◆•

MTV debuted in 1981 with the ambitious goal of playing music videos 24/7. A shortage of material in those early years allowed bands with professional videos to get airtime. So Iglauer decided to film a video for Johnny's "Don't Take Advantage of Me."

"It was very early in MTV's history," said Iglauer. "They would play all videos and there weren't that many videos. The video got on regular rotation on MTV—what they call lunar rotation, which meant very often. It was on in the middle of the night, but it was there. It was a big turning point for Alligator because that was the first time we were perceived as being something more than a blues specialist label."

Johnny's video is filmed in color in a Western bar; it changes to sepia tones when the scene flashes back to the Old West. Barechested with his multicolor "Screamin' Demon" tattoo and his trademark cowboy hat, Johnny sends cowboys flying into the wall with killer guitar riffs and brands barmaids with a touch of his hand.

Iglauer solicited friends and actors from ImprovOlympic for his cast. "One of the bar girls was Nora Dunn, who was later on *Saturday Night Live* [a regular cast member from 1985 to 1990] and plays a reporter in the *Three Kings* movie," said Iglauer. "The famous acting coach Del Close played the drunk, and the bartender was one of the ImprovOlympic guys."

"The video for MTV was something else," says Johnny. "I didn't know what I was doin'—I didn't have any confidence at all. I didn't know about making videos, so I went along with what Bruce had to say. You usually don't make videos for blues, so I was glad to be doing one. They shot it in Deadwood Dave's, a biker bar outside of Chicago. Bruce came up with the script. The video was a little corny but it wasn't bad. They had us walkin' around doin' dumb things. Spinning around onstage, ripping off my shirt."

By the end of the video and the recording of *Guitar Slinger*, Johnny and Iglauer had resolved their differences. But Johnny's reluctance to promote the record, teamed with Slatus's unwillingness to take a stand with his client, hurt their rapport. Slatus had been a gofer for Johnny when he worked for Steve Paul, and still played a subservient role.

"It was frustrating working with Johnny and Teddy on the promotion of the record, because Johnny would make commitments to do interviews—either live or on the phone—and break them," said Iglauer. "Teddy, rather than confronting Johnny and saying, 'You can't do this to the media, it's insulting,' would just make excuses. So we got tired of asking. There was so much more we could have done to advance Johnny's career if Teddy had been willing to act as an authoritative manager. But Teddy absolutely would not confront Johnny about anything. He would apologize for Johnny over and over again. Teddy was Mr. Apology.

"We had a big interview for Johnny in the Japanese *Guitar Player*; the guy was calling from Japan to do a phoner with Johnny. Johnny was home and the guy in Japan had screwed up on the time change and called at the end of the two-hour block of time. Teddy told me Johnny sat and listened to the guy on his answering machine but didn't pick up the phone because he wasn't calling at the right time. He never did the interview. Johnny is a kid; he has never grown up. In some ways, he's very spoiled."

Unlike major record labels, Alligator has a limited number of releases, and works their records to radio and the press for a considerable time. Even when the records are no longer getting airplay, Alligator promotes its artist's gigs to generate coverage on radio and in the print media. "We commit to working with an artist's career, not just the record," said Iglauer. "Johnny was an absolute priority for us. He was our bestselling artist at the time and I was proud of the records. But Johnny was problematic. At a gig in Chicago, he wouldn't do any interviews before the show because he was getting ready for the show. After the show, he wouldn't do any interviews until after eight. We wanted him to greet some store people, and by the time he was ready to greet, everybody had left. That was real typical. People would want to meet him, even if it was only a minute, and he was resistant to that. So we had a real hard time getting media things going."

Despite Johnny's reluctance to do interviews, *Guitar Slinger* earned a Grammy nomination and made the *Billboard* and *Cashbox* charts. It reached #183 in *Billboard* in August 1984 and was on the charts for four weeks. "It sold about 100,000 copies," says Johnny. "It did better than *Raisin' Cain*."

•◆•

In June 1984, Johnny played with Waters's Legendary Blues Band at the first Chicago Blues Festival, which was established to honor the memory of Muddy Waters. It wasn't a pleasant experience. Although Iglauer sent the band a tape of *Guitar Slinger* specifying the songs Johnny would play, they never bothered to learn them.

"I remember the band not being very good because they didn't know my songs at all," Johnny says. "They thought they were too good to have to learn anything; figured it was all blues and they could do it. I didn't want to use them. I wanted to use my own band, but they wanted me to use the Legendary Blues Band."

Understandably miffed, Johnny initially refused to go onstage. "Johnny was very angry and basically barricaded himself in the dressing room," said Iglauer. "The Legendary Blues Band did its own set; maybe thirty minutes before Johnny came out. The stage manager comes out to get Johnny, and Teddy is standing by the door. 'Johnny's not coming out.' Maybe Teddy groveled, or I groveled, or we all groveled, and he eventually came out. Johnny was rightfully pissed because when he tried to do 'Mad Dog'—with totally regular changes—they screwed it up. It was very disrespectful."

Once Johnny got onstage, drummer Willie "Big Eyes" Smith played off of the beat and ignored Johnny's tendency to push the front of the beat and his signals to pick up the tempo. "Johnny kept looking around at us, giving us the body language to urge Willie, to push him," said Jerry Portnoy with a laugh. "I looked around and saw Willie—he knew what was going on—he had his head up, his eyes forward, and he wouldn't look at Johnny. Willie

Smith is probably *the* most obstinate man on the face of the Earth. Once he makes up his mind, there's just no moving him."

Disgusted with the way he was treated, Johnny left immediately after his set. "I was too pissed off to ask them why they didn't listen to the record," he says. "I didn't want to scream at 'em, so I got out of there."

In 1985, Johnny went into the studio to record *Serious Business* with Gayden, Jones, Saydak, and Paris on harmonica. "Murdering Blues" and "Unseen Eye" had been recorded during the *Guitar Slinger* sessions; Paris's harmonica parts were dubbed onto the existing tracks.

Johnny had written five songs for *Serious Business*, but only "Good Time Woman" and "Serious as a Heart Attack" made it onto the album. "I wrote those two in my hotel room in Chicago," says Johnny. "It didn't take too long to write those songs. Sometimes if you're in the right frame of mind, they just come out. I wrote the music in my room and wrote the words after the band recorded the song. It was easier to write that way.

"Bruce didn't like any of my songs. He didn't want to use 'Serious as a Heart Attack' because of the line, 'I'm gonna make your blue eyes black.' He didn't like it because it was an anti-woman, anti-female song. I worried a little that it might be perceived as violent, but I wrote a lot of violent songs," he says with a laugh. "On that song, I was goofin' on the 'Don't It Make My Brown Eyes Blue' song."

Iglauer understood the humor, but felt the song also had a darker side. With "Murdering Blues" already slated for that LP, he was concerned about adding another song about violence toward women.

"Bruce didn't mind saying what he felt," says Johnny. "I didn't like it but I felt I had to give him some leeway because he owned the label."

"It was on *Serious Business* that we really fell out," said Iglauer. "He discovered I'm hardheaded and strongly opinionated. I like things my way and he does too. I'm not a flexible guy, and in those days, I used to have a really bad temper, and was much worse. Part of it was I used to drink a lot of coffee, and late at night I drank alcohol. I never drank in the studio because it would affect my judgment, but I drank afterward. So I was always going up or going down."

"I didn't have as much creative control at Alligator as I wanted to have," explains Johnny. "Bruce was very critical—that was his style. He didn't seem to like anything I did. It's always been hard for me to take orders from other people. He knew I had been a producer of all my records before that but he thought he knew more than I did."

Johnny also dubbed it as a personality conflict escalated by what he perceived as Iglauer's constant criticism. "I'm fairly easygoing but I sure wasn't with him. Bruce's criticism made it harder to play. I would talk to Dick and say, 'Bruce probably wouldn't like this.' I would get down on him before I even knew whether he would like it or not. I expected him not to like stuff. That can happen when somebody's always putting you down."

"I'm very controlling, and it was hard for him to share control," said Iglauer. "Johnny was used to being in charge of his own records. Most of the artists on my label had not worked with real producers, or were fine because they knew me better, or just thought, 'It's his record company; he's the producer." Most would have said, 'This is a break for me; I'm stepping up in the world.' Johnny was slumming; he was coming down in the world. Although we sold more records than his last few Columbia records, I didn't have the kind of experience he did."

As bad feelings intensified, it didn't take much to start a conflict. "We had gotten to the point where we were looking for excuses to argue," said Iglauer.

While dubbing the vocals for "Route 90," they argued about the way Johnny pronounced El Paso (he put the enunciation on the third syllable rather than the second). During most of the disagreements, Shurman took Johnny's side.

"I loved working with Dick because he knew how I wanted things to sound and always agreed with me," says Johnny. "I think Dick understood my music more than Bruce. Dick said, 'Johnny's from Texas, he says it the way somebody from Texas would say El

Paso, so why ya bitchin' about the way he's saying it?' Bruce finally gave up but he didn't like the way I was saying El Paso."

Iglauer became the scapegoat no matter how hard he tried to put Johnny at ease, even when he wasn't the guilty party. "We're doing a tune, and the vodka is just starting to kick in, and Johnny says, 'Bruce, which way do you want me to do this one?'" recalled Shurman. "Bruce says, 'I just want you to feel comfortable with it.' Johnny goes into a big rant about comfortable: 'Look who we got here. Bruce Freud, comfortable.' We actually had to stop for a while because Johnny was so pissed off."

During preproduction, Shurman made a tape of Johnny "Guitar" Watson's version of "Broke and Lonely," rather than the one Johnny recorded in 1963 as Texas Guitar Slim. That sent Johnny into a rage against Iglauer. "But it was me who had done it, not Bruce, and it wasn't an insult," said Shurman. "But Johnny would stew about stuff all the time because he thought Bruce was too critical and it made him doubt himself. Johnny thought Bruce didn't like anything he did and Bruce didn't intend to convey that. Their musical values were very close, but they just didn't connect."

Despite the tension, it took only five days to record *Serious Business*, and ten days to mix it. The final nail in the coffin came during the mixing stage, when Johnny and Iglauer battled over bass and snare drum sounds. "Bruce wanted a lower drum sound and I wanted a higher one," says Johnny. "We didn't agree on how we wanted the instruments to sound. We ended up giving in just enough where neither one of us was happy with any of it. It sounded harsh—real trebly—it didn't have enough bass to it. I didn't like the way it sounded and was determined not to work with Bruce anymore,"

"Johnny and I were hearing the record differently," said Iglauer. "My perception was he won those arguments; the record didn't come out sounding like I wanted it to sound. I always thought *Serious Business* sounded thin. It was a very odd little rollercoaster. Some of it was my fault; some of it was his fault."

The battle continued over the photograph for the album, when Johnny, who had photo approval, wouldn't let Iglauer use the photo he wanted. "The cover shot I wanted is an inside shot in the

*Deluxe Edition* package," said Iglauer. "Johnny hatless with his knee cocked, very cool shot. We designed the album cover around it and he said, 'Why would you pick a picture without my hat?' And I thought, if you wanted a picture with your hat, why did you sit for fifty pictures without your hat? We would have sold more of *Serious Business* with a better cover."

Despite the battles, Johnny still wanted to record on Alligator and Iglauer picked up his option for a third album. But Johnny refused to let Iglauer coproduce.

"I wanted to stay with Alligator because they kept their records out there," says Johnny. "But Bruce wanted to control everything, so I told him I didn't want to use him anymore. It shook him up a little bit, but he said ok."

"I was upset about it but we had so much tension, I didn't want to re-create that experience," said Iglauer. "I didn't maintain approval over the song choices. I approved the mixes, but I wasn't there for any mixes. I kept a very low profile, which is terribly hard for me. It was definitely a significant change for me, and very hard for my ego."

Despite their falling out in the studio, Johnny and Iglauer still like each other and feel badly about their battles. "I still say hi to Bruce him every time I see him and am still good friends with him," says Johnny. "I wish we could have gotten along better in the studio."

"Johnny's a sweet guy," said Iglauer. "He can be childish and petulant but only to a somewhat greater degree than I can be. He can be very charming, and he's an intelligent guy. Has real good taste in music. He's got a level of self-awareness and a real good sense of humor. We never argued about whether we liked or disliked each other. It was always about what a record or performance should sound like. I have nothing but affection for Johnny. We're probably just people who shouldn't work together."

•◆•

Without the tension between Iglauer and Johnny, the sessions for *Third Degree* went off without a hitch. "*Third Degree* was the best record we did," says Johnny. "Bruce didn't come out and it worked great."

Johnny played a scorching version of J. B. Lenoir's "Mojo Boogie," which is still one of his trademark tunes. "I changed the words around and my version was a little bit rockier. The words were perfect—'Got that Mojo Boogie, gonna slide on down'—so it was perfect for slide. Mac [Dr. John] turned me onto 'Love, Life and Money.' 'Bad Girl Blues' by Memphis Willie B. was a funny song really—it was about women liking women."

Johnny used Gayden, Jones, and Saydak as the core lineup, and invited his old friends Tommy Shannon, Uncle John "Red" Turner, and Mac "Dr. John" Rebennack as guest artists. Dr. John played on "Tin Pan Alley" and "Life, Love and Money."

"I've known Mac for years," says Johnny. "I love his playing. I think he's the best piano player in the world. He's got a great feeling for the blues. I met him in New Orleans in the early '60s, when I was with Edgar and Ikey and we were playing the Whisky a Go Go. He was playing at a club right across the street from us. We'd go over and listen to them and they'd come over and hear us during their breaks. Our musical roots are similar because we've heard a lot of the same songs."

The next two nights, Shannon and Turner stopped by the studio and recorded "See See Baby," "Shake Your Moneymaker," and "Broke and Lonely." Johnny got the idea to record with his old rhythm section at the Chicago Blues Festival the previous year. Stevie Ray Vaughan headlined the opening night, and Johnny went backstage to catch up with Shannon.

"Tommy, especially, really wanted to play on a blues album with me because he was making it with Stevie but they weren't really doing straight blues," says Johnny. "Red was playing blues with a real good Texas guitar player named Alan Haynes."

"Working with Johnny on *Third Degree* was a lot of fun," said Shannon. "We put down some real good tracks. It was healing being back together after all those years, very healing to play together again as the old trio like we did when we started out. The session was easy and we got to hang out a lot and talk, like the old days."

When Shurman called in Gayden and Casey to record "I'm Good" while Shannon and Turner were still in the studio, Shannon pegged it to reverse racism. "We only did three songs because Alligator didn't want anybody who wasn't black," he said. "Johnny was the only white musician on the label and they wanted Johnny to use black musicians."

But Johnny and Shurman thought the Icebreakers were better suited for that particular song. "I thought they'd be better at it because they were real good at straight blues," says Johnny. "It's hard to compare the four of them but they just had an easier time doing the blues stuff than Tommy and Red did."

But the studio players didn't have the longtime friendship and deep-seated love Johnny, Shannon, and Turner had for each other. "It felt great to work with Tommy and Red," says Johnny. "It makes a big difference when you love the guys you're playing with—the caring comes through in the music."

Johnny wasn't as comfortable when Shurman brought in legendary harp player Junior Wells to play on several tunes. Although they cut five or six songs, none came out good enough to make the album.

"Johnny was nervous about playing with him and got a little tipsy—as did Junior—in anticipation," said Shurman. "The music was sloppy and didn't jell."

"Junior Wells was a real good harp player and I got intimidated by him," says Johnny. "He was a pretty straight-ahead guy and knew what he was doing better than I did. I don't think we got a good take out of Junior because I was worried about him, scared of him really."

Early blues artists, like Robert Johnson, Muddy Waters, as well as Johnny's other heroes, had all played acoustic guitar. Johnny felt that to be an authentic bluesman, he needed to master the acoustic guitar, which he found harder to play because the action is higher. He practiced on his Nationals for a month before the sessions, and included two acoustic songs—"Evil on My Mind" and "Bad Girl Blues"—on *Third Degree*. "I played slide on the single cone," Johnny says. "It was an old National that sounded really raw and nasty, like a garbage can with strings on it."

Iglauer was producing Lonnie Brooks's *Wound Up Tight* album in another studio at Streeterville Studios while Johnny recorded *Third Degree,* so when Johnny's album was in the mixing stage, Iglauer invited him to play on Brooks's album. "I played 'Got Lucky Last Night' and 'Wound Up Tight,'" says Johnny. "He was easy to work with in the studio. We had already planned it out. He just said, 'Play here' and I played there."

Although Iglauer and Johnny were cordial during those sessions, *Third Degree* signaled the end of Johnny's relationship with Alligator. "We figured it was time to try something else," Johnny says. But his problems in the studio with Iglauer would pale by comparison to the experiences he would have cutting his next record.

There were other changes brewing as well. Susan had become a born again Christian and began questioning their living arrangement. She started pressuring Johnny to get married but he wasn't willing to make that commitment. "I didn't want to get married because I was still goin' out with other people and didn't want to stop," he says.

# Not Bad for a White Boy

In 1988, Johnny became the first white performer inducted in the Blues Foundation Hall of Fame. Founded in 1980, the Blues Foundation is a nonprofit organization based in Memphis, Tennessee. Johnny was thrilled to be recognized as a bluesman in a Hall of Fame that had honored so many of his heroes: Willie Dixon, John Lee Hooker, Lightnin' Hopkins, Howlin' Wolf, Elmore James, Robert Johnson, B. B. King, Little Walter, Muddy Waters, Jimmy Reed, and T-Bone Walker. He had officially earned equal status as a bluesman.

Although determined not to stray too far from traditional blues, Johnny was ready to claim his place among contemporary blues artists topping the charts with crossover hits. Stevie Ray Vaughan enjoyed widespread success, and George Thorogood and the Destroyers spent a year on the charts with *Bad to the Bone*. Billy Gibbons, another Texas buddy and ZZ Top guitarist, hit the charts with "Sharp Dressed Man" and "Legs" from the *Eliminator* LP. The Fabulous Thunderbirds, with guitarist Jimmy Vaughan, crossed over with "Tuff Enuff" and "Wrap It Up." It was time to cash in on the growing trend.

"I think Johnny looked around and saw people he had looked at as either protégés or disciples—the young bucks compared to him—on top of the heap," said Shurman. "He wanted to show these guys he could still be—if not the boss—up there with them if he chose to take that approach."

Slatus had been shopping for a major label, and negotiated a one record deal with MCA Records in 1988. He needed a producer with a proven track record for blues-rock hits; Terry Manning had the credentials. He began his career as an engineer at Stax Records and later became producer/engineer of Ardent Studio in Memphis. Manning had produced all of Thorogood's LPs, including *Bad to the Bone*, produced *Powerful Stuff* by the Fabulous Thunderbirds, had engineered seven ZZ Top albums, including *Eliminator*, and was engineer on *Led Zeppelin III*.

"Ted [Slatus] wanted something a little more melodic and commercial than just straight twelve-bar blues," said Manning. "He was looking for something that would push Johnny into radio, more into the rock scene. He was insistent on finding melodic songs with hooks people could remember, but not go too pop or ultra-commercial. I saw it as walking quite a fine line with going more toward radio and pop music without losing the core or essence of Johnny, which is based in the blues he loves so much."

Although Manning says Johnny was fully aware of the type of recording he was hired to produce, Johnny's recollections of what Manning said he planned to do and what he actually did are a bit different. "I was looking for a good record, one that was fun and blues but would have a chance at crossover," says Johnny. "Terry was looking for something crossover and nothing else. We had meetings before we went into the studio. I told him what I wanted and he said. 'Great, that's what I want too.' He just lied. I told him what I wanted but he didn't give it to me."

Johnny left Alligator specifically to cut a less traditional blues album, but wasn't willing to give Manning the leeway he needed to produce a hit. "We were willing to change but I didn't want as big a change as he wanted," Johnny says. "I didn't expect it to be that much rock; I wasn't trying to be commercial."

Manning pegs it to the difference between what Slatus and the label wanted, and what Johnny wanted. "You have to make a record they will accept because they have the right to refuse a record," he said. "It was more commercial than most of his albums, but it was something that was expected of me."

MCA released *The Winter of '88* in late September; musicians included Tom Compton and Jon Paris, with keyboards on several cuts by Lester Snell and Manning, and background vocals by William Brown. Both Snell and Brown were Stax session players. With no preproduction or rehearsals, *Winter of '88* took three weeks to record at Ardent Studio. "We had twelve songs and it took more than a day a song to rehearse it, learn it, get it down, overdub it, and get it finished," said Manning.

Manning taking full rein as a producer without consulting Johnny about what he was doing ruined any chances of a cordial relationship and eventually disrupted the sessions. It wasn't long before Johnny and Manning were at odds in the studio. "They weren't communicating; sometimes they weren't even talking to each other," said Shurman. "Terry Manning had Johnny play all these parts, so he could go back and forth, and pick and choose. Johnny didn't understand his method, and was pissed because Terry wouldn't explain what he was trying to do."

Incidents with Johnny's amp and Compton's drum sounds added fuel to the fire. "I was playing through my Music Man and he had my guitar miked to a Marshall in the back room," says Johnny. "He didn't tell me—I found out when I heard the amp echoing in the background. He had it hooked up to both amps but was just recording the Marshall sound. That's pretty bad. When I found out about that, it really pissed me off.

"He told Tom he was a real good drummer, too bad nobody will hear your drums on the record. He didn't say it in front of me, but when I found out I got pissed off. He had Tom play 'cause I wanted to use my own people. Terry Manning used Tom's drum sounds as a trigger. His real sound was the drum machine, which would hear what Tom played and play the same thing back. That just sounds stupid. He's doing it and sounding good, why bother to get something else? I talked to him about it and he said, 'I'm the producer and I'm gonna do it the way I want to.'"

Manning doesn't remember recording Johnny through a Marshall but admits it might have happened. He said he used Compton's drum sounds and only used a drum machine for the snare drum. "I probably did augment the snare, but nothing else," Manning said. "Not the bass drum, not the tom, not the cymbals. It would have been only one snare sound triggered from his snare exactly—it would not have replaced his snare, it would have only added to it. I never used the trigger sound louder than the normal snare sound, which makes it more like an effect, a reverb type thing. It makes the snare pop a little more, and that's what people want on the radio. Today it's the norm; at the time it was still somewhat of a new effect."

Nearly twenty years later, Johnny still harbors resentment about Manning. "Terry Manning was the worst—I never had a producer as bad as him," says Johnny. "He knew exactly what I wanted but he didn't want to do it. He was so bad; I almost got into a fistfight with him."

Manning initially denied any problems in the studio, but when pressed about Johnny's reference to a fistfight, he sighed and reluctantly shared his memories. "The fight was actually about pizza," said Manning. "Johnny says he was so hungry he had to stop. I said, 'No problem, what would you like?' He said, 'Pizza.' We ordered pizza delivery, and I told him the pizza would be here in thirty minutes or it would be free. He said, 'Great.' About two minutes later, he stopped the next take of the song and said, 'I'm hungry; I've got to eat.' I told him, 'I just said, we ordered pizza.' He said, 'No, you didn't say anything about pizza.' We calmed him down and told him pizza was on the way. We started doing another practice of the song, and he stopped again and said, 'I'm hungry. We're going to have to get some food. I can't play another note.'

"We all tried to say, 'No problem, the pizza is on its way, it'll be here in a minute.' He just went into a rage about being hungry and started grabbing instruments and throwing them around, and jumping at people and screaming horrible obscenities. Almost tore the studio up and made a big mess of the session. At that point, I came up to him and put my hand on his shoulder, and said. 'The pizza is on the way. Take it easy, we will eat in a minute. Whatever it is, we'll get through this.' Then he started pushing and swinging. I don't want to go too far with this. . . .

"I firmly grabbed him under the collar, by the shirt, and held him up against the wall and said, 'I don't want any problems here. The pizza is on the way.' He was shaking like a wild man and would not calm down. Everybody was trying to calm him down, and it wasn't possible. So I said, 'Session's over. I'm done with this project. I can't do this. This is not professional.' I left and sent him back to the hotel."

Manning waited it out at Ardent Studio, while Johnny tried to get out of the contract. The realization that Slatus had signed him to a record deal that wasn't blues-oriented eroded Johnny's trust in his manager.

"I wasn't sure Teddy still wanted what I wanted, which was to be a blues artist," says Johnny. "The record people convinced him he had to talk me into being more radio, become more of a Top Forty musician. I was willing to try it and he was sorry for that. I went up there in the middle of the night screamin', saying I can't stand this anymore. I ain't gonna put up with this shit anymore. Teddy tried to get me out of it, but we made a deal so we had to perform."

Three days later, Johnny called and apologized, ready to finish the album. "It may not have been the album Johnny wanted, but it was certainly the album his management wanted," said Manning. "Ted brought in a list of pop songs and said, 'We want the blues flavor in it, but we want pop songs.' I had just done a total makeover of ZZ Top. The album before had sold 700,000 or 800,000 copies. After the full makeover, going harmonies, pop hooks, no real drums at all, *Eliminator* sold 15 million copies. I'm sure that was highly seductive to a manager who had an artist with a blues background. But all elements have to click and Johnny wasn't prepared to quote—fully sell out. Not that he would or should, but I'm sure in his mind, it would be selling out to go to those lengths."

•◆•

After playing with Johnny for eleven years, Jon Paris left the band in 1989. According to Paris, it was to "concentrate on working with my own blues-rock group . . . singing, songwriting, and playing guitar and harmonica." Johnny remembers it differently. "We were having trouble that he played too loud," he says. "We figured it would be best if we'd part company or things would have gotten worse. He's still a good friend. I see him when I go into the city and he always comes out when I play."

Jeff Ganz replaced Paris, playing his first gig in May 1989 after three weeks of rehearsals. Both Johnny and Slatus were familiar with Ganz's chops, so he didn't have to audition. Slatus had managed Roy Buchanan up to his death in August 1988, and Ganz had played in Buchanan's band. A studio musician with a Broadway and jazz background, Ganz played fretless and fretted basses, including a six-string electric and an upright. He also sang a number of tunes on the road, including "Turn on Your Love Light," "Can't Judge a Book by Its Cover," "Politician," and "Born Under a Bad Sign."

Throughout the late '80s and early '90s, Johnny played clubs in the U.S. and Canada, with occasional dates in Spain, Denmark, Germany, and London. He would tour for three weeks, take off for two or three weeks, and go back on the road for another three weeks. The band rehearsed when they weren't touring.

"We traveled in a rock 'n' roll bus, but there wasn't any ridiculous legendary stuff going on," said Ganz. "We were just out there playing. Working with Tom Compton was great. Tom and Johnny were really locked in because they had already forged the dynamic of what they were doing in 1985. It took me a few minutes to figure out how I was supposed to play. I said to Johnny, 'This section here feels like it's rushing a little bit.' He turned to me and said, 'Well, I rush. If you'd be happier somewhere else . . . ' and I realized all bets are off. Just shut up and play; that's why you're here."

Ganz's collection of fretted and fretless basses was the perfect fit for Johnny's system of tuning down a whole step from normal guitar tuning. "Instead of tuning to E, he would tune down to D," Ganz said. "I had several Fender and Ibanez basses set up to that tuning. Johnny was intrigued with the eight-string bass, and loved the upright because it was closer to the roots thing."

Johnny still got hassled by fans, so he didn't go to clubs very often. But on July 13, 1990, he and Ganz stopped by Tramps to see Danny Gatton, a guitarist Johnny admired. Johnny met Gatton that night when he handed him his Telecaster and invited him to take the stage. "Johnny got up onstage and the audience went berserk," Ganz said. "Danny is a master musician, but not an entertainer. Johnny was not as technically proficient, but he was the whole entertainment package."

Johnny played B. B. King's "You Done Lost Your Good Thing Now" to the delight of the audience. When Gatton returned to the stage, he said, "Now, ladies and gentlemen, *that's* the blues." The respect was mutual. "Danny Gatton was great," says Johnny. "He played every style of music, a little bit of everything. He could play blues too. He played it pretty fancy, but he played everything."

•◆•

Johnny ran into Stevie Ray Vaughan on the road, and one night they got together to compare their versions of "Boot Hill." Vaughan recorded "Boot Hill" several times but never included it on his albums; he recorded it again in 1989 during the sessions for *In Step*, but again, it didn't appear on that recording. Although unreleased until the posthumous *The Sky Is Crying* in 1991, Vaughan told Johnny about the recordings. Eager to compare it to his *Guitar Slinger* version, Johnny invited him to his hotel room.

"I wanted to show him mine was better," says Johnny with a laugh. "He played me his version and I thought it was not as good as mine. When I played him the final version from my record, he said, 'That's real nice, man,' but he didn't admit it was better."

"Stevie and Johnny met up several times," remembered Shannon. "Johnny listened to the killer version we did on *In Step*, and they were both kind of battlin' there."

Their rivalry tended to be playful, so Johnny was crushed when he heard Vaughan deny knowing him. Artist Jim Franklin, who was in New York to paint Johnny's portrait, remembers his reaction vividly. "I think this was the same year Stevie Ray died," said Franklin. "Johnny was listening to him on a blues show in New York City, and the guy asked Stevie Ray about the influence Johnny had on him. Stevie Ray said he didn't know who Johnny Winter was. That tore Johnny up; he was hurt. I could see Johnny was shaken by that when he was telling me about it. Tommy was in

Stevie's band, he's got a trio playing power blues just like Johnny, and Johnny was well established when Stevie started coming to Austin. Johnny couldn't understand why he would not own up to knowing him. This was a real blow."

In late June 1990, Johnny suffered another emotional blow. Ikey Sweat was found dead in his own garage in Fort Bend, Texas with a gunshot wound through his left temple. Sweat, who was forty-five, had been Johnny's bass player from his early years in Texas, and one of the true friendships—like that of Turner, Shannon, and Franklin—that helped Johnny stay grounded.

The initial ruling of suicide didn't fit the evidence. Sweat was right-handed and police found his .25-caliber automatic, keys, and sunglasses by his left hand. An autopsy showed no evidence of gunpowder residue on either hand. Although Sweat had always talked about committing suicide, his wife Sharon Sweat was indicted and arrested on a murder charge.

"I took his death real hard," says Johnny. "I loved Ikey. He was one of my best friends. He was there from the beginning. I went down to see him in Texas pretty regularly. He used to threaten to kill himself all the time so nobody believed him too much. He said, 'I think I'm gonna have to kill myself—I can't stand this any longer.' He had a nonspecific urethra infection—now it's called Chlamydia. But in those days they called it NSU because they didn't know what it was. He got where he couldn't get hard anymore unless he did cocaine. With cocaine, he could get a hard-on. He left a note that blamed his doctor for not knowing what the hell he had—for not being able to get rid of it."

Johnny went to Texas for Sweat's funeral services, but did what he called a "deposition" over the phone from his attorney's office in New York City. "My lawyer listened to the conversation to make sure I wasn't incriminating myself in any way," says Johnny. "They asked me if he had ever talked about killing himself, and I said, 'Yeah, all the time.' I heard him talk about killing himself a lot, so I just don't know."

In March 1992, prosecutors dismissed the murder charges for lack of evidence. "The investigators ended up letting her go—which I hated—because everybody down there thought his wife had killed him," says Johnny.

The circumstances surrounding Sweat's death were custom made for tabloid television. Sweat had filed for divorce shortly before he died and had a long-term affair with a younger woman. According to his wife, his oldest bass guitar, which he wanted Johnny to have, disappeared from a shed outside his home around the time of his funeral. Sweat's son contested a 1989 will leaving everything to his stepmother, calling it a forgery. The courts issued a temporary restraining order and froze the estate. Six months later, a fire nearly destroyed Sweat's home.

"It was on *Entertainment Tonight* or *Access Hollywood*," says Johnny. "You know how those shows are—anything they can get that's crazy and fucked up, they'll jump on it. He'd tried pills and they didn't work, so he used something he knew would work. A gun is messy but it works."

Despite his loss, Johnny buried his feelings and carried on. "Johnny wasn't a screamer and a crier but it was obvious it affected him very deeply," said Ganz. "As close and as friendly as we were, he could still be a fairly stoic guy."

Meanwhile, Slatus had begun negotiations with Pointblank, a blues-oriented subsidiary label of the then-London-based Virgin Records Ltd. Started by John Wooler in 1989, Pointblank was working on a deal with John Lee Hooker. After the fiasco at MCA, Johnny was reluctant to sign with another label, but Wooler, who had always been a fan, convinced him he would have total control.

"We had a respect for each other," said Wooler. "He appreciated me letting him do the record he wanted to do. He said, 'MCA wanted me to be like Robert Cray, and I'm not like Robert Cray.' I said no, you're Johnny Winter, and you've made a lot more records than most people. I am not going to tell you how to make a blues record. I'm going to give you creative freedom, because I'm confident you know what you're doing."

"I wasn't in a hurry to sign with anybody else unless it was a real good deal," says Johnny. "Pointblank was willing to give us pretty good money and said they'd promote us real well. That was important. MCA didn't promote my record—they didn't do much of anything for it."

With Wooler and the label behind him one hundred percent, Johnny was ready to return to the blues and to working with Shurman, who understood what he wanted to do and did what he wanted. "After Terry Manning, I'd had enough of that shit," he says. "I went back to blues because that's what I always wanted to record. I went back to using Dick as producer because I like him a lot and enjoy working with him. I trusted Dick. It took a record or two [to build the trust] but he convinced me he knew what he was doing. I'm perfectly willing to, not perfectly willing, but I'll do a song over if he thinks it needs it. I may not like it, but I'll do it because I figure Dick knows and he's not gonna tell me something wrong. He's got a pickier ear."

Wooler gave Johnny free rein, as well as the money he needed to make the record he wanted. "John didn't confine us musically, and the budgets were good," said Shurman. "Tom Compton had a pretty big drum kit for a blues drummer; he had five toms and a lot of cymbals. Jeff Ganz wanted to bring about six basses. I was able to have one of the road guys rent a van and drive the equipment to Chicago. It was the best of both worlds. You had the resources and muscle of a major label, but you weren't swallowed up in this huge corporate structure."

Like the records on Alligator, the Pointblank albums were cut at Streeterville Studios, and took two to three weeks. Musicians included Johnny on vocals, electric, and acoustic guitar; Ganz on electric, fretless, and upright bass; Compton on drums; Dr. John and Ken Saydak on piano; and Billy Branch on harmonica. Dennis Drugan, his wife Margaret, and sons Johnny and Brian had stopped by the studio so they joined Shurman and others on the chorus of "Hey You."

"The *Let Me In* sessions were very smooth," said Ganz. "We rehearsed a few days but we didn't have hardcore arrangements; that didn't happen until we got in the studio. There weren't a lot of takes; by the third one, that was pretty much it. If Johnny felt good about his performance, that was the barometer."

"The chemistry was great—both Tom and Jeff are wonderful guys," said Shurman. "They're really respectful of Johnny and vice versa."

Ganz agreed. "If you listen to recordings of that era, Johnny started to really trust Tom and I," he said. "The band was playing with a lot of dynamics. Usually Johnny Winter songs went a million miles an hour from the beginning of the song to the end of the song. But we had some really nice contrast going on. I would deliberately play less, place stop time, play whole notes for two bars. More like a jazz concept."

Johnny played National guitar on T-Bone Walker's "Blue Mood," accompanied by Ganz on upright bass. Johnny added National slide licks to Robert Parker's "Barefootin'" and J. B. Lenoir's "Mojo Boogie," a crowd pleaser that he still plays as an encore. He wrote "If You Got a Good Woman" and "Let Me In" in his hotel room, getting his inspiration listening to WNIB-FM's late night blues shows hosted by "Mr. A, Your Entertainer" and Big Bill Collins, who spoke with thick Southern accents.

"They were Southern Negroes—I could understand them easy but a lot of people couldn't," says Johnny. "They were great. *Let Me In* was my favorite project with Dick. It had everything going for it. I was really happy with how it sounded. I hate to name just one project but if I had to, that'd be it."

*Let Me In*, unlike previous recordings, generated airplay on both blues and rock radio stations. "Illustrated Man" received the most airplay and also provided the soundtrack for a JBL TV commercial with the tagline "Concert Sound for Your Car."

"Johnny still had fans on rock radio, and we got a lot of airplay for that record," said Wooler. "He was considered a rock artist as well as a blues artist, and we got play on a lot of stations because it had more of a mainstream feel. We did over 100,000 in sales in America."

In October 1990, Johnny played a John Lee Hooker Tribute Concert at Madison Square Garden. Although a review by Jon Pareles in the *New York Times* called him one of the "concert's better performers," Johnny was beginning to have anxiety attacks that would plague him throughout the next decade.

"I wanted to die when that show was happening," says Johnny. "I don't know why I was anxiety-ridden—I couldn't figure it out. I was just feelin' terrible. It was real important to me to do the show with John Lee Hooker, so I just downed a lot of vodka and made it through. I played toward the end. I was so worried about myself, I'm not sure who was on when I played. I don't remember what song we played but I was real happy with the way it sounded."

Shortly after that concert, Hooker invited him as one of the guest artists on *Mr. Lucky* which also included Robert Cray, Albert Collins, John Hammond, Van Morrison, Keith Richards, Carlos Santana, and Ry Cooder.

"I liked playin' with John Lee on that record—I had a ball doin' it," says Johnny. "We didn't rehearse. You just had to get it when he was ready 'cause you weren't gonna get a second chance. I liked John Lee a lot. He was a real good guy. You better watch your woman though—he'll take a chick away from you in a second. He had a lot of charisma. There's not too many John Lee Hookers around. His playing was real Mississippi-ish—real bluesy. He was hard to play with because he did all his changes the way he wanted to—not the way they were supposed to be. You really had to work hard to play with John Lee."

•◆•

By the mid-1980s, Susan was in her mid-thirties and wanted to start a family. Johnny didn't want the responsibilities of fatherhood. "She started talking about it way back in our relationship," says Johnny. "I said, 'No, forget it.' I just didn't want kids. I was still enough of a kid myself—I didn't think I could be a father. She didn't bring it up a whole lot, but more than I liked. I was always on the road—gone all the time; and I didn't feel like it was something that I could handle."

The question of children came up often during Johnny's interviews; his standard answer was the lifestyle of the music business—constantly being on the road—would make it too difficult. Yet when he was interviewed by film director Lois Siegel for *Strangers in Town*, a tasteful and poignant documentary released in 1988 about the medical and social aspects of albinism, he delved much deeper into his feelings about being a father. He addressed the aspects of having both an albino child and a "normal" child.

"It [having an albino child] would be much easier for me and for the child, than if an albino child was born to parents who were totally normal—having a father you could relate to," said Johnny. "I think I'd like a little girl though. If I had a normal little guy, it would bother me a little bit that I couldn't go out and play baseball and football with the kid and do the things fathers normally do. That would bother me. But with a girl I wouldn't feel that pressure I know I would feel with a boy [now his voice takes on an inflection] be a man and do those manly things, play football, baseball, hockey, and everything we just can't really do. I did them anyway and it was really embarrassing to go through PE—physical education—and play baseball when you really can't see the ball but about half the time."

Susan reluctantly gave up her dreams of starting a family, but gave Johnny an ultimatum about marriage. "I told him, 'Either we get married or we break up; I believe in God and this isn't right,'" said Susan. "I let him go way past the ultimatum because I had invested my life in him and didn't want it to end."

Johnny never questioned the idea of spending the rest of his life with Susan until a woman from his past showed up at a gig. "I've known Diana [Williams] since she was a go-go girl at Love Street Light Circus and Feel Good Machine—she danced there every night we played," says Johnny. "I had had a thing for her since the old days. We had a real past. She remembered me from the good ole days, and I went to bed with her a couple of times back when I first knew her. I didn't see her for a while—until she came out to see me when I was playin' in Houston in the '80s. I had a hard-on, and asked her if she wanted to go on the road for a while. She went on the road with me for a month. She wasn't workin'—she was livin' with a guy who worked. After that, we started seeing each other every time I went out on the road and I was playin' pretty regular. I'd call her from practice and tell her when I was goin' on the road and she'd fly out."

Within several years, Johnny put Williams up in a high-rise apartment in Houston, where he stayed with her when he was in town. By then, he had become her sole source of support. "She was livin' by herself and I was sendin' her money," says Johnny. "We were together maybe two or three years steady. A lot of people thought she was my wife."

Williams knew Johnny was living with Susan but never pressured him about it. Unlike Susan, she didn't want children and never talked about marriage. "She didn't look that forward in the future—she was just glad to be with me at the time," says Johnny. "She was true to me all those years because she didn't want anybody else—she was in love with me. She may have been hopin' I'd leave Susan and come down there and live with her, but she never said that to me.

"I'd see her when I was on the road and see Susan when I was back at home. I'd been going with both of them for three years or so. Susan hated me seeing her too and finally told me, 'You have to marry me and have a normal relationship or I'm gonna leave.' She really put it to me good—'What do you want to do? Who do you love? You can't go with both of us anymore.' That convinced me Susan was the one I loved the most and I had to break up with Diana. I'm sorry it took so long but it was a hard decision to make."

Having to finally choose between two women, after spending his life with a woman at home and various girlfriends on the road, was emotionally devastating to Johnny. He had always insisted on free rein when he was on the road; now that door would be closed forever. "It was hard," he says. "That's one of the things that made me crazy, made me completely fucked up. I couldn't figure out which one I wanted. I really loved Diana too and it was hard for me to break it off with her. That's why it took awhile. I didn't want to get married 'cause I didn't want to commit myself to one person. I never thought I could do that. I don't know why Susan went along with that for so long. I'm glad she did though. Susan knew I loved her and I needed to take some time to work it out. She was real understanding."

Susan and Johnny separated in late December 1991, and he spent Christmas in Houston with Williams. When he returned, he agreed to get married. "It just seemed to be the right thing to do," he says. "I know how much she loved me and how much she'd given up for me and I felt like it was time to pay her back for all she'd had to go through. We'd been livin' together for twenty years when we got married."

In February 1992, they were married in a quiet ceremony in the Carlyle Hotel in New York. Susan's best friend stood up for her; a longtime friend and roadie stood up for Johnny. "I wanted Teddy to stand up for him, but we hadn't planned ahead of time," said Susan. "We had the room for the night, and had a bunch of food there, but everybody left, so we just went home. I was disappointed. I wish his parents and my parents were there. But after this long, I think they were just happy we made it official."

"We didn't have time to invite my parents and Susan's parents," adds Johnny. "We just wanted to do it in a hurry. Susan knew it was hard for me and I just wanted to get it over with. I wanted to have as little commotion as possible 'cause I didn't take it too seriously. She thought I wouldn't cheat if I was married, but I probably did in the very beginning. I'm true to her now. I've been married for sixteen years now and have been true to her."

Although Williams was given $12,000 as "severance" so she wouldn't be left high and dry without any income, she was devastated by the ending of their relationship. "Diana took it pretty bad," says Johnny. "Sometimes she tried to call me but she knew it was my decision. She knew it wasn't going to do any good to try to get me back. I saw her when I was down in Houston—when I play there she comes out and sees me. Diana said she still loved me. I told her I couldn't be married to Susan and see her too. We still talk to each other every once in a while."

•◆•

In May 1992, Johnny returned to the studio to cut *"Hey, Where's Your Brother?"*, which like *Let Me In* was recorded at Streeterville Studios with the same band members, producer, and crew. "There was no conscious distinction between the two CDs musically," said Shurman. "Johnny had his compass by the time he was pushing fifty. He wasn't going to tear down what he was and be something different."

Before they started that project, Edgar contacted Slatus and suggested using the HEY, WHERE'S YOUR BROTHER? slogan on a tee shirt with one Winter brother's photo on the front and the other's on the back. More than likely, Slatus pilfered that name for the album.

"I don't know if he got it from that or had been thinking about it on his own," said Edgar. "It is something that has been around in the collective consciousness of Winter fans ever since I said it on the *Roadwork* album. I connected it [with that album] because I just asked him about the tee shirt, but it may not have anything to do with it."

The musicians included Johnny on vocals and electric and acoustic guitars; Ganz on electric bass, fretless bass, eight-string bass, and upright bass; Compton on drums and percussion; Edgar on vocals, organ, and saxophones; and Billy Branch on harmonica. Johnny enjoyed working with Branch and the feeling was mutual. "I like Billy Branch," says Johnny. "He played like one of those old guys [Little Walter, Howlin' Wolf, Sonny Boy Williamson] except he was a little bit fancier."

"Billy liked to record with Johnny," said Shurman. "He told Johnny, 'You play more blues than any Chicago guys because they want to play crossover. You just want to play the blues.'"

Edgar sang harmony vocals and played alto sax and organ on "Please Come Home for Christmas," a song they recorded in 1966; he played organ on "You Keep Sayin' That You're Leavin'," and tenor and baritone sax on "Sick and Tired."

"Edgar was pretty good on that record, but sometimes he could get too particular," says Johnny. "He'll stay in the studio for days trying to get something better and if I don't get it in the first couple of times, I'll give up on it."

Although Edgar was featured on three songs and in the title, his photo wasn't included on the cover. "Johnny made it clear, this is not a Johnny and Edgar Winter album," said Shurman. "It's a Johnny Winter album and Edgar is going to be a guest on some of it. It wasn't a peer thing; it was a leader and subordinate."

The cover photo depicts Johnny with his band; he's playing a late 1938 Gibson Super 400 natural, which he used on "Blues This Bad." "I got it from my friend Ed Seelig, who sold me a bunch of guitars in the past and let me borrow it for the session," says Johnny. "It had a real blues acoustic sound."

Johnny wrote three songs for that recording, "White Line Blues," "You Keep Sayin' That You're Leavin'," and "Treat Me Like You Wanta," under deadline pressure in his hotel room. "That definitely makes a difference," he says. "When you have no time to do it in, you go ahead and do it."

Both *Let Me In* and *"Hey, Where's Your Brother?"* were nominated for Grammy Awards for Best Contemporary Blues Album in 1991 and 1992, respectively. Johnny attended the 1991 awards ceremony. "I went to the Grammys when Buddy Guy won for *Damn Right, I've Got the Blues* because I remember saying hello to him there," says Johnny. "I never went every time I was nominated—I got tired of losing. I'm glad to get the nominations though."

"Both Pointblank albums were a lot of fun," said Shurman. "*Let Me In* was just a little bit easier, because Johnny was in a real peak state when he did it. On *"Hey, Where's Your Brother?"*, he was still in a good state but I could sense the first slight ripples of what later developed into his big emotional/chemical crisis in the mid-'90s. He was starting to get a little shaky around the edges—in terms of his confidence and happiness."

In October 1992, Johnny was invited to perform at Bob Dylan's sold-out "30th Anniversary Concert Celebration" at Madison Square Garden. A four-hour concert commemorating Dylan's first album on Columbia Records, the lineup included Johnny Cash, Tom Petty, Willie Nelson, Ron Wood, George Harrison, the Band, Eric Clapton, Neil Young, John Mellencamp, Richie Havens, Lou Reed, Stevie Wonder, and Pearl Jam's Eddie Vedder.

Even among that impressive lineup, Johnny dazzled the audience with an incendiary performance of "Highway 61 Revisited" with a band that included Steve Cropper and G. E. Smith on guitar, Booker T. Jones on organ, Donald "Duck" Dunn on bass, and Anton Fig and Jim Keltner on drums. His long, agile fingers furiously flew up and down the frets of his Firebird to the delight of the crowd. When he drove the music higher and higher until it erupted in a feverish crescendo, there was no doubt in anyone's mind. Johnny Winter was the king of the slide guitar.

Although Johnny was thrilled to be on the same show with Johnny Cash, he is characteristically playful when asked which performers impressed him that night. "I just impressed myself—I thought I was great," he says. "I had a hard time too because when I first started, I couldn't hear myself at all. That was hard as hell to play without being able to hear myself. They finally got it turned up so I could hear myself and 'Highway 61' got a great response from the audience."

The music critics agreed. David Wild, who penned the liner notes to the CD released the following August, wrote "A monumental display of blues power came from veteran Texan guitar hero Johnny Winter, who threw down a furious deep blues take on 'Highway 61 Revisited.'"

That amazing performance, which continues to generate five-star reviews on YouTube, was his last blaze of glory before anxiety attacks, depression, overmedication, and his manager's out-of-control alcoholism turned the man and his music into a shadow of his former self.

# PART

# III

# Bad Luck and Trouble

After Johnny played the Dylan tribute, *Saturday Night Live* bandleader G. E. Smith invited him to play with his band on the show. It wasn't a pleasant experience.

"The band was pretty good except the fuckin' drummer was an asshole," Johnny says. "He fucked up. I told G. E. the song was too damn slow and he said, 'Play the song at the speed you want; the band will play with you.' I started it off and the drummer didn't go with me at all. He dragged it back down and it really pissed me off. The drummer can mess up anything."

Somewhere along that timeframe, Slatus, who had been a straight arrow, began to show signs of heavy drinking. Johnny was deeply disturbed by Slatus's behavior and knew the repercussions to his career would be damaging and widespread.

Between 1993 and 1997, Johnny didn't make any recordings and his touring schedule was sporadic. "I had a problem with being depressed and I didn't play as much," says Johnny. "I don't know what I was depressed about."

Already stressed out by having to give up Diana Williams, Johnny was devastated when, once again, death moved in on his circle of friends. In August 1993, Randy Jo Hobbs died in a motel room in Dayton, Ohio from a drug overdose. "Randy did a lot of drugs—we used to do heroin together," says Johnny. "I finally had to let him go because he was fucking up too much—he was too messed up. After I fired him, he just stayed around home. We were coming to his town in Indiana and I asked him to play with us. He went to

Ohio to jam so he'd be ready to play. He died of an overdose of cocaine. Snortin' it. He was forty-five. It was bad—it really hurt me."

Seven months later, Dan Hartman died of brain cancer after being diagnosed as HIV positive. "Dan Hartman was a sweetheart, a real nice guy," says Johnny. "He died of AIDS. I didn't know he was gay."

Ganz remembers Johnny's anxiety attacks starting around 1993, but says they never affected Johnny's performances. "Musically, he was always very focused; the shows were never a problem," he said.

Johnny was hospitalized in 1993 and 1994. His first stay was in Regent Hospital, a psychiatric facility on East Sixty-First Street, where he was given counseling and antidepressants. The 1994 hospitalization was at New York-Presbyterian Hospital/Columbia University Medical Center on West 168th Street. He wasn't playing out the first time he was hospitalized, but cancelled a tour to be admitted to New York-Presbyterian Hospital.

When asked about the diagnosis, Johnny, with his usual self-effacing sense of humor and a laugh, quips, "Just bein' crazy," before seriously answering the question.

"I felt like I was gonna die," says Johnny. "I really felt bad, like maybe there was no need to stay alive anymore. It was anxiety. The same kind of anxiety I've had in my life a few times—it's really no fun. They couldn't figure out what was causing it. The first time, I was in because I didn't know what to do about being with Susan or Diana. I couldn't figure out what to do because I loved both of them. I was worrying about it for a couple of years. I was in the hospital for a couple months, and saw the doctor every day. The second time, I was in the hospital for about a month. They tried different medications and gave me Klonopin—an antidepressant. It worked real good. Teddy helped me all the way through that."

Although the requirements for hospital visitors were stringent, Ganz was cleared and visited Johnny a number of times. "They were giving him some kind of drug therapy, but it didn't seem to be helping," said Ganz. "Because he couldn't get his hands on booze, I would say he was pretty sharp."

Johnny didn't stay sharp long. He was on prescriptions for Klonopin and Risperdal, taking his daily dose of methadone, and drinking Absolut vodka on the rocks. Both psychologically and physically addictive, Klonopin's side effects include drowsiness, impairment of cognition and judgment, memory loss, psychomotor agitation, lack of motivation, dizziness, and impaired coordination and balance.

Although often prescribed for anxiety disorders, Risperdal has anxiety as a side effect, as well as tremors, which is why Johnny's hands were always shaking when he performed. His penchant for vodka led people to assume he had the shakes from drinking.

Although Johnny was unaware that his medication interacted with his methadone, he was embarking on a deadly path. For more than ten years, he was taking the same combination of drugs that led to the death of Daniel Smith, the twenty-year-old son of Anna Nicole Smith.

With Johnny's health on the decline, Slatus desperately needed new artists to stay afloat financially. In 1993, he began managing Rick Derringer, who moved to Connecticut the following year. Slatus's association with Derringer would eventually lead both Slatus and Johnny to rural Connecticut.

After Johnny was hospitalized in 1994, he took a hiatus from gigging, but continued to jam/rehearse at S.I.R. in New York. Ganz left the band in July 1995. "He wasn't in the best shape, and I had done everything I could do there," said Ganz. "It was just time to go."

Ganz told bassist Mark Epstein about his departure and Epstein immediately contacted Slatus for an audition. "I met Johnny at S.I.R.," said Epstein. "He would have different guys come and play the whole night with him. I went two or three times, and got the gig. With Johnny, you never really rehearsed, you just played. We got together once a week in S.I.R. and later at his home in Connecticut. The set list was pretty consistent. Once he gets into a groove, he doesn't like to change anything. We played a mixed bag of big clubs, some festivals, and halls. We did Europe two or three times—Germany, Sweden, Denmark, Norway, and Luxembourg."

Johnny loved the sound of Epstein's Sadowsky five-string bass, and gave him free rein. "He just said play," added Epstein. "He told me, 'If there's something you need to know, I'll tell you.' He allowed me complete freedom."

•◆•

In March 1996, Johnny and Edgar filed a lawsuit in Los Angeles Superior Court against D.C. Comics for defamation and misappropriation of likeness for commercial gain. The lawsuit was in response to three issues of a five-part comic book miniseries, *Jonah Hex: Riders of the Worm and Such,* where Hex battled Johnny and Edgar Autumn, half-worm and half-human villains with albino features and long white hair. The spawn of a subterranean worm that raped their mother, the Autumn brothers ripped heads off of livestock, and devoured the brains of pigs after fornicating with them. Johnny Autumn wore a stovepipe hat like Johnny did when he played with Muddy Waters. According to an article in *Intellectual Property Litigation Reporter,* the D. C. Comics advertising campaign suggested people buy the comics to find out "exactly how rockers Johnny and Edgar Winter sort of turn up."

The lawsuit wended its way through the court system for seven years before reaching a final decision. Superior Court rejected their suit, stating the comics were protected from any right-of-publicity claim because the Autumn brothers were a "parody of some sort" of the Winters' persona. The appeals court affirmed that decision. When the case was appealed to the California Supreme court, it dismissed the appeals court decision and ordered it to reconsider. The appeals court reversed its decision, and the case ended back in California's Supreme Court, which ruled against the Winters, stating the comics contained "significant expressive content other than the plaintiff's mere likenesses."

Johnny, who didn't follow the case and was unaware of the legal costs, was philosophical about the verdict. "It was Teddy's idea to sue them," he says. "I thought it was too bad but I can understand why we lost. It's all part of being a public figure."

Justice wasn't served in terms of bootlegs either. Roy Ames, Johnny's unscrupulous manager and producer from his early years in Texas, continued to sell unlicensed tracks to various labels, filling the market with bootleg recordings of music dating back to 1966 and keeping all of the profits. Ames's bootlegs contained the same songs in varying order on more than a dozen labels, repackaged with different titles with different artwork. A 2003 search on amazon.com for Johnny's music yielded 117 results; a 2008 search generated 330 recordings. Less than fifteen percent of those recordings are legitimate.

"I love my fans and I feel sorry for them getting screwed on bootleg recordings," Johnny says. "I hate those damn bootleg records because it hurts your reputation. I don't know how these people get the material. It's stealing. It's just not right. Fans that sell pictures of me, sell my autographs, bootleg videos. That's a drag too. It's the same thing, it's stealing from me."

When Ames died in August 2003, I read him the obituary from the *Houston Press*, entitled Good Riddance to Bad Rubbish—Roy Ames, child pornographer and record producer, dies at 66.

"He died unhappy—at least that's good,' Johnny said. "He died out of jail, though, that's amazing. It's funny he didn't die of AIDS, as promiscuous as he was. He *was* promiscuous. One night, when I was eighteen or nineteen, he was taking me to a gig. He went to get gas, tried to put the make on the gas attendant, and the guy beat him up. I was in the car with him and I hated that. When there is this guy putting the make on you, you wonder about the guy who's sittin' in his car."

In the closing line of that article, John Nova Lomax wrote, "If Roy Ames somehow weaseled out of his ticket to hell, he's no doubt up there in blues heaven bootlegging the celestial jam."

"I'm not worried about that—he definitely went to hell," said Johnny. "I'm glad he's gone. I couldn't do nothing about Roy—he was just an asshole. A professional asshole."

•◆•

Fans catching Johnny's shows during the mid- to late 1990s were shocked and saddened by the changes in their hero. He moved slower and looked thirty years older than he did when he played Dylan's anniversary concert. His growl had disappeared and his once guttural vocals sounded weak and strained. Johnny often missed or hit the wrong notes. His fiery riffs were gone, replaced by guitar playing that was tentative, repetitious, and lacking emotion.

In January 1997, Slatus booked Derringer as the opener for Johnny's shows in Detroit, Milwaukee, and Chicago. Those shows rejuvenated Johnny's playing, but ended Derringer's relationship with Slatus.

"It brought Johnny back to life," Derringer told writer/guitarist Tom Guerra, who interviewed him for *Vintage Guitar* in 2000. "Those shows allowed Johnny to hear me out there trying to do the best I could, every night before he went on. I'm a pretty competitive guy and Johnny responded. Each night, his solos got a little hotter and he got a little more energetic. It worked out really well. But it ended up with Teddy and I parting ways because Teddy saw Johnny getting more life. I don't think that's the direction Teddy wanted to see Johnny going in. We also saw some things backstage, saw money changing hands; saw a lot of stuff Teddy didn't want us to see. That caused a bunch of problems between me and Teddy and we parted ways."

Derringer, like so many others who cared about Johnny, was appalled and felt helpless as he watched Johnny sink into a medicated haze. He blamed Slatus for Johnny's overmedication and questioned his motivation.

"I don't think Teddy wants to see Johnny getting healthier; he wants to see him dying," Derringer told Guerra. "Frankly, I don't want to see Johnny dying. I don't want to see him being cheated; I want to see Johnny getting everything he's earned. I want to see him getting healthier and stronger—he's not an old man and I don't want to see the record business taking advantage of Johnny. I have a suspicion Teddy wants just the opposite of me. He wants to manipulate, he owns all the powers of attorney, all the rights to everything Johnny does. Johnny's one of those guys whose stuff is going to skyrocket when he dies and Teddy is going to reap all the benefits."

Whether Slatus actually wanted Johnny dead is still up for debate. But he was well aware that Johnny's overmedication affected his health and his performance, and did nothing to help. Johnny's friends, who wanted him off of the drugs and questioned why he was still working with Slatus, were not allowed access to their old friend.

"Johnny needs to get off methadone once and for all," said Derringer. "The sad part about it is, I can't talk to Teddy about that. You can't talk to Johnny because he's inside it; he needs somebody to help him. He's still Johnny Winter. When you go to hear him play, part of you goes, 'Oh man, what happened?' and 'This is sad.' But the other half of you sees between the cracks and sees Johnny still inside there. And here's this music creeping out, even though there's only a little bit of it. 'Oh man, this is still Johnny Winter; he is still just as great as ever.' All he needs to do is check himself into the hospital for about six months and come out once and for all clean. It'll help his health, his music, everything. Teddy doesn't seem to encourage that. Somebody with the power has to be able to, but nobody else has the power to do that."

Johnny's overmedication didn't surprise Epstein. "You can see why he was on a lot of drugs because he is naturally a very nervous guy," he said. "He would always say, 'I'm vibrating right out of my skin.' He is a nervous guy. It's just a matter of how you deal with that. You're talking about somebody who is -holic by nature; he doesn't know how to do anything halfway. He can't take a sip or take one pill; he's got to have fifty."

As Slatus's alcoholism continued to escalate, Johnny's dependence on prescription drugs continued to diminish the quality and number of his shows. Slatus tried to cover up Johnny's health problems by shutting off media access, and verbally attacking writers who tried to set up interviews. Josh Alan Friedman, a musician and writer for the *Dallas Observer*, experienced Slatus's wrath. "I told Slatus Johnny Winter was my all-time number-one guitar hero, and I wanted to do a cover story for the *Dallas Observer*," said Friedman. "But then I casually inquired about Winter's health. Suddenly, like a psychopath, Slatus turned abusive over the phone—screaming, cursing, threatening—it was such an outrageous turn. Teddy Slatus was a monster. There's no telling what damage he did to Winter's career."

"Teddy had quite a temper and a hair trigger," said Epstein. "If he was in a foul mood, it wouldn't take much to set him off. Teddy was kind of psycho, you never knew. He used it to his advantage. You tried not to piss him off, because when he went off, it was just so ugly."

Epstein thought Slatus's personality played into Johnny's over-medication. "Teddy was an enabler," he said. "He wasn't the kind of guy that would say, 'No, Johnny. No more of this, get your shit together.' If Johnny felt bad, he would take him to another doctor."

Although Johnny was still under contract to Virgin/Pointblank, Slatus wanted to increase his own cut by starting his own label. In October 1996, he distributed a press release entitled Blues Legend Johnny Winter and Manager Teddy Slatus Launching CPW Records with his First Recording in Three Years. Slatus distributed the press release at Johnny's gig at the Bottom Line in March 1997, a month before he was scheduled to record two live shows at that club for the Virgin/Pointblank label.

"It was always Teddy's thing to do an imprint label—like the Blue Sky deal with CBS," said John Wooler of Pointblank Records. "But he couldn't leave Virgin and start his own label for Johnny Winter. He legally had to provide an album for me, so that never happened."

Johnny was scheduled to play two consecutive shows at the Bottom Line, but the first show was rescheduled due to numbness in his right hand. "Johnny's health wasn't great," said Epstein. "I think his numbness problem was leading up to the radial nerve palsy. His health always fluctuated. He had nights when he couldn't make his hands work as well as he'd like. But he was never mentally at a loss onstage. Johnny is completely fearless, no matter what condition he's in. He would musically jump off a cliff, go for it, and trust you are there. He's a master, one of the most gifted guys I played with, who knew exactly when to do what to make the crowd go nuts."

*Johnny Winter Live in New York City '97*, released in 1998, was produced by Dick Shurman, and included Epstein on bass and Compton on drums. Slatus claimed the song list was generated by requests from fans, but, in reality, it was the same set the band was playing on the road. Although that CD generated mixed reviews and speculation about Johnny's health, Johnny ignored the bad press. "The record got a pretty good reception," he says. "I thought it was a good showpiece of what we were doing at the time. We chose the Bottom Line because we'd played there a lot and the acoustics sound better in a small club. We recorded two shows and played the same songs every night, so we'd make sure we got something good out of the bunch."

Johnny's relationship with Slatus, both personal and business, was a convoluted one that almost cost Johnny his career and his life. Unlike a professional arrangement where the artist and manager discuss options and make a mutual decision, Johnny called the shots. Slatus worked around that by lying to him, making decisions behind his back, and withholding information.

Hiring Slatus, who had been a doorman and bartender at the Scene, and Johnny's gofer and valet when working as his road manager, ensured it wouldn't be an equal relationship. He pegged Slatus as "Steve Paul's yes-man" when he met him, and wanted a manager who would do what he wanted. Even Johnny's knowledge of Slatus's bizarre behavior when the Scene closed, and his inability to be honest, didn't seem to affect their relationship.

"When Teddy started first going on the road, he was still putting on shows at the Scene, which had closed, with bands that were just in his mind," says Johnny. "He was in his house in Manhattan and would bring on the band that wasn't there, for the people that weren't there. He was real crazy. He wanted to keep it going the way it always had been. When Teddy became my road manager—he didn't have any confidence at all because he didn't know what he was supposed to do. He really had a hard time. He didn't want to tell me if he was making any mistakes, so he was lying about them. It was three or four months before he knew what he was doing."

Another aspect that kept it unequal, and fueled Johnny's isolation, was Slatus's devotion to Johnny's needs and his belief in a hierarchy in the music business.

"Teddy was never a friend; he always treated me like a star," says Johnny. "Sometimes that gets to be a real drag too. You'd like to be treated as a person, but Teddy thought there was a hierarchy; a class thing in music. He shouldn't be going out and having dinner with me because he was working for me, and the people that worked for me shouldn't be friends with me. You weren't supposed to be friends with anybody."

Part of that star treatment was fussing over Johnny's meals, a ritual that is still played out when Johnny is on the road. "Teddy used to make the crew nuts, because he would have them being valets and butlers to Johnny, which really isn't crew work," said Epstein. "Teddy always made such a huge production out of Johnny's dinner, and he'd have the crew guys going mental about getting everything."

Johnny finally started thinking of Slatus as a friend, rather than just a manager, when he helped him during his breakdowns in the early 1990s. He was especially pleased when Slatus identified himself as Johnny's friend when he took him to the doctor. Years later, when Johnny questioned the amount of money he was earning, Slatus used that act of friendship to his advantage.

"I trusted him at first, but sometimes, I haven't been sure," says Johnny. "I remember telling him I didn't trust him once and he said, 'Well, I took care of you when you weren't sure what you wanted to do with Susan and the other girlfriend in Texas. I always helped you, so I don't see how you could think I would do anything against you.' I agreed he was right. But then I wasn't sure because I wasn't making as much money as I thought I should."

Although Johnny met with Slatus once a week about business matters, and received profit and loss statements from his accountant, his failing vision and overmedication ensured that he accepted what he was told at face value. In 2003, when asked if he thought Slatus was ripping him off, Johnny hesitated before answering the question. "I wondered—I wasn't sure, sometimes," he said. "He gets a percentage of everything. Now, I feel like he's doing the best he can. If I'm behind on my statements, and don't have enough money to pay for everything, he lends me money from his account, and gets it back whenever I'm making some money. He's real good about that. During the period I wasn't working [because of my breakdown] he was paying for that with his own money.

"Teddy does what I want him to do and that's important. When I broke my hip, he made sure I had somebody to come over to help me. When I got radial nerve palsy, he took me to the doctors and stayed in my corner. He's been there for me. When I went crazy, he went to the hospital with me and paid for everything till I could afford to pay for it. He's always stuck by me when I went nuts. The last time I went crazy [1994], he paid for the original costs to get me in the hospital."

Because of his problems with managers in the past, Johnny practiced the "better the devil you know than the devil you don't" philosophy with Slatus. "There's so many bad ones out there, I'd hate to think about trying to get a new one," he said. Johnny acknowledged Slatus kept him in the dark about a lot of dealings, and kept him away from reporters, filmmakers, and even his band mates.

"That's a drag," he said. "Sometimes I talk to him about it but he says he's just trying to do the best for me. He tries to keep people away from me that he doesn't think should be around me. Sometimes I don't agree with that, but in most cases, I think he's right. I know Teddy overdoes that sometimes—keeping people away. That's just Teddy."

"Getting together with Johnny was like having an audience with the Pope," said Ganz. "It was, 'You have to wait here, you have to do this, you can't go here.' Then Johnny says to me, 'That's ridiculous, come on.'"

Keeping Johnny isolated went beyond star treatment; it was Slatus's way of ensuring control and limiting information flow. By 2001, the band and crew weren't allowed to see Johnny, unless it was a band rehearsal or a gig. Slatus totally controlled access to Johnny, and fired anyone who tried to work around him.

Compton, who left the band in 1998, was another casualty of Slatus. He was replaced by Vito Liuzzi, a Connecticut drummer who had begun filling in for Compton at rehearsals the previous year. "Tom and Teddy had a falling out of some kind," says Johnny.

"Teddy wanted to get rid of Tom and Tom got tired of fighting it. It was too bad."

Although Johnny could have fought Slatus's decisions, he never did. "Johnny's relationship with Teddy was a marriage; it was way beyond business," said Epstein. "They go back so far, they've been doing this dance for so long. It wasn't just Teddy running Johnny around; Johnny had to give him permission to do it because he could ultimately say no at any moment. I think Teddy cared about Johnny on some level, but not in a selfless way. Take Johnny away from Teddy and he crumbled. He wanted to be Johnny. When he walked him on the stage... a lot of people in the music business who aren't musicians are feeding off that same energy. They'd sure love to be [the artist]; that's why they're drawn to the whole scene."

Val Minett, who worked for Slatus from 1998 to 2002, agreed. "In Teddy's mind, Teddy was the star," she said. "Anybody he worked with, he only did things for them so he would look good. When we would go to Johnny's house for meetings, he would say, 'Look what I did for you!'"

Although Johnny never said anything in public or on the record about Slatus's misdealings, Epstein said he was well aware of what Slatus was doing.

"Johnny knew what was going on the whole time—he wasn't in the dark," said Epstein. "In terms of when he was being taken advantage of, and any of the things Teddy was doing that Johnny didn't want to happen. Johnny knew. He might not have been feeling up to making a change, but he knew. We caught Teddy in some lies and Johnny told me—and this is a quote—'Teddy has a problem with the truth.' Johnny is cagey. He's not gonna let on what he knows, or even a tenth of what he knows. He doesn't say much, but he doesn't miss anything."

By the late 1990s, Slatus's alcoholism spiraled out of control. Johnny no longer saw him socially because he hated to see him drunk and listen to his apology the following day. "He says he's sorry and that he wishes he didn't start doing those things," says Johnny. "Then he says, 'Well, you drink too.' I said, 'Yeah, Teddy, but I don't try to kill people and fire everybody when I drink. I don't overdo it like you do.' He can't stop. He's fired a lot of different people."

"Teddy told me I was fired once or twice," said Epstein. "I just laughed. The bottom line was Johnny hired me, not Teddy. Johnny was the only one that can fire me or hire me. As far as the rest of the crew, Teddy was a very abusive guy. If he didn't get his way, he would go ballistic. He thought nothing of making you feel as bad as he could, sometimes he enjoyed it. Everyone had their run-ins with Teddy. My attitude was: I'm not going to glorify it or take it seriously. Managers just work for the artist like the band does. They can make your life miserable, but don't have the power they think they wield."

Like many people who didn't see Slatus on a daily basis, Epstein initially wasn't aware of his drinking problem. "When I met Teddy, he seemed totally sober," Epstein said. "I didn't notice him drinking till '98 or '99 on one of our European trips. When I showed up in Copenhagen, I bumped into Teddy in the hotel and he was very drunk. I had never seen him that drunk before. The next day, he wouldn't come out of the room. We used a local road manager and did the tour without him.

"Johnny basically hoped Teddy wouldn't fall off the wagon but didn't seem preoccupied about Teddy's drinking. Johnny was pretty self-absorbed most of the time. He was more concerned with what's for dinner and that he got to do whatever he wanted to do when he wanted to do it."

A creature of habit, Johnny doesn't like to alter his routine. He has a set schedule and nothing short of an act of God is about to make him change it, whether it's eating a particular food at a specific time, sleeping during the day and staying up all night, or not giving interviews earlier than 9 PM.

"There's something with food with Johnny that happens with everybody," said Epstein with a laugh. "I've been good friends with Jon Paris for a long time, and we always joke about that. You call Johnny up after six months, you have this great conversation, and halfway through some sentence, he says, 'I gotta eat dinner, got to go, bye.' Click. It's always food . . . or his pills. He had a schedule and it had to be adhered to."

Johnny loved eating and traveling on a tour bus. "It's expensive, but you have everything there, and can sleep on the way to the next gig," he says.

"We always traveled at night because it's easier," said Epstein. "We'd eat dinner, hang out, have a couple of beers, and one by one, people would crash. Johnny would be up all night long. We had satellite TV with music stations, but Johnny would just want the blues station on all the time. It drove us nuts because you hear the same stuff over and over again. We didn't watch movies; we didn't watch TV; it was just the blues station. He'd be up all night long, so there was no relief," Epstein added with a laugh.

In 1998, Slatus moved into a bed-and-breakfast in Colchester, Connecticut and met Betty Ann Johnston, who owned and operated the property. Slatus claimed he moved to Connecticut because Derringer needed financial help; Johnny says Slatus could no longer afford his New York apartment. It was the beginning of his personal and professional relationship with Johnston, who worked her way into his management company. Johnston's blatant dislike and contempt for Johnny (who she blamed for Slatus's drinking), teamed with her manipulative behavior, didn't bode well. She would eventually help Slatus increase his share of Johnny's earnings, and make it easier for him to manipulate and control Johnny and his wife.

Like the star he wanted to be, Slatus is highly visible in the footage of Johnny's May 1998 induction into the Rock Walk on Hollywood's Sunset Strip. Johnny laughs about the day his handprints and signature were immortalized in cement.

"I remember having gooey hands," says Johnny. "They took a lot of pictures, and I donated a guitar." Johnny usually donated cheaper models when asked for memorabilia, and was surprised to learn he had donated a Firebird to the Rock Walk Museum. "That was stupid," he says laughing. "I must have wanted that award awful bad."

Later that year, Slatus hired Val Minett, who managed singer/songwriter Loretta Hagen, to create and maintain Johnny's website. Slatus wanted to manage Hagen and claimed he could get her a record deal. It was the beginning of a four-year business relationship that Minett described as "a weird time that felt like twenty years," and ended with a lawsuit.

Rumors about Johnny's health continued to fly. Even diehard fans thrilled that he was touring, were appalled by his frail appearance and seeing him being led onto the stage, too weak to pick up his guitar. Johnny had lost the edge in his voice and the dexterity in his fingers. Many fans, as well as music critics, questioned why Slatus was keeping him on the road in that condition. To Minett, the answer was obvious.

"Teddy needed the money," she said. "Teddy treated it like a circus. He had his sideshow and that's the way he treated Johnny. Whenever his money started to get down, he would call Bruce [Houghton of Skyline Music] and say we need some gigs."

Earlier that year, Solow Management Corp., the landlord of Johnny's penthouse, sent him a notice of nonrenewal of the lease. Although Johnny had lived in the rent-stabilized apartment since September 1974 and never missed a rent payment, he had listed his corporation Ole Pa Enterprises as the tenant for thirteen subsequent leases. The realty company sued Johnny's corporation, claiming "neither Ole Pa nor Johnny Winter was entitled to renewal." The suit argued that Johnny was a subtenant of Ole Pa, and a corporation cannot use its premises as a primary residence.

Johnny and Susan stayed in the apartment for ten months without a lease (December 1998–September 1999) while the case was pending and Susan looked for a house in Connecticut.

"We were pretty much forced out of the apartment in New York because they kept suing us and evicting us," said Susan. "We were spending so much money on lawyers. I said, 'Let's just get a house and get out of this.'"

Johnston, who began making inroads as a friend and confidant, accompanied Susan when she found and fell in love with an eleven-room house in Fairfield County. Living in a two-story house soon proved to have a downside. In October 2000, Johnny got up in the middle of the night, and half asleep, thought he was in his New York apartment. Thinking he was walking down his old hallway, he stepped out into space and fell down a flight of stairs.

"I screamed," says Johnny, laughing at the memory. "I landed all over—on my ass, my back; and I screamed at Susan to help me get up. I tried to make it up the stairs but I knew something was wrong. I waited about three days before I went to the hospital. I thought it might get better but it got worse. I knew I had to go to the hospital and face the fact I had broken my hip."

Johnston knew a doctor at St. Francis Hospital in Hartford, so Slatus had Johnny taken there instead of to an emergency room. X-rays confirmed a broken hip. Surgeons inserted a plate and four screws to hold the hip together. Johnny stayed in the hospital for four days, and then recuperated at home, forcing the cancellation of an extensive November tour of the Midwest, Northwest, and western Canada.

His bad luck was just beginning. Two months later, his father died in Beaumont at the age of ninety-one, and Johnny was in no shape to fly to Texas for the funeral. "He had broken his hip too, strangely enough," says Johnny. "He fell down in the street—the wind knocked him over. He was real weak and he just got weaker and weaker. I saw him just a few months before he died. He was walking with a walker. I'm glad I went to see him before he died. He was a good person who lived a good life. Even up until his death, he went to choir practice once a week and taught Sunday school."

Although Johnny's hip should have been healing, his problems were far from over. A year after the first surgery, he was still in pain and unable to play standing up. X-rays revealed the metal plate had broken in his hip, and he needed another operation.

When Johnny returned to the stage, he walked with a cane and played sitting down. "It's a drag to have to sit down," says Johnny. "I thought there'd be a lot of rumors about me being too messed up to stand up, but I didn't hear anything. There are always rumors because I had that problem with heroin in the early '70s. People think I'm going back to heroin for some reason. I hate that."

In February 2001, Johnny released a video compilation entitled *Pieces & Bits* with concert footage, TV clips, and personal photos. The video got poor reviews for the "grainy clips and bad sound," with one reviewer calling it a "nothing but a big money grab by

Teddy Slatus." When it was released on DVD that December, fans who purchased both formats complained the DVD version wasn't as good as the video. The reason was obvious. Slatus didn't want to invest any money in the project so asked Minett, who produced it, to ask fans for footage via Johnny's website. Fans obliged but the footage was copies of copies of copies—much of it fifth-generation.

•◆•

In May 2001, a devastating outbreak of Mad Cow Disease cancelled Johnny's plans for a European tour, which included headlining the Bishopstock Blues Festival in England. When he embarked on a month-long tour of the Midwest, Northwest, and western Canada to make up the dates he canceled when he broke his hip, Johnny and his entourage came down with the flu. Worried about his reputation, Johnny performed anyway. "I had a hard time singing, but I wasn't gonna stop just because of the flu," he says. "I didn't want to get the reputation of a band that cancels every time the wind blows the wrong way."

With Johnny's health issues and a sporadic touring schedule, Johnny's band fell to the wayside. Epstein moved to Hawaii, making it too expensive to fly him in for gigs. Whether it was over financial matters or because Epstein and Liuzzi had seen too much (which often predicated a change of lineup), Slatus convinced Johnny to hire new musicians.

"Mark wanted more money and Vito wanted more money, and I just couldn't afford them," says Johnny. "I hated losing Mark and Vito because I thought they were real good. Teddy didn't—he didn't think they were as good as they should be."

Although the Pointblank label had disbanded, Virgin agreed to pick up Johnny's option for one more CD. Slatus, still eager to get a crossover hit, enlisted Tom Hambridge to produce *I'm a Bluesman.* Hambridge, the writer, producer, and drummer who produced Susan Tedeschi's Grammy-nominated *Just Won't Burn* CD, wrote two songs for Johnny, recorded them in Boston, and sent the tapes to Johnny.

"Dick's a good producer but Tom was more commercial," says Johnny. "Tom wrote 'Lone Wolf' and 'Cheatin' Blues'—they were a little more commercial, more rock flavor. I did guitar and vocals over the tracks his band played on. Tom was a good drummer and the bass player [Tommy McDonald] played real nice too."

While dubbing the tracks with Hambridge at the Carriage House Recording Studios in Stamford, Connecticut, Johnny met a guitar player who would turn his life around. Paul Nelson had just finished cutting tracks for the XFL, the professional American football league created as a joint venture between NBC and the World Wrestling Federation that only played for one season. Nelson had studied with Steve Vai at the Berklee College of Music and played with Liege Lord, a heavy metal band that released two recordings on Metal Blade Records in the late 1980s. Slatus was impressed with his musical and technical knowledge and told Nelson he wanted him to be Johnny's second guitarist. Because of Johnny's resistance to having another guitar player in his band, Slatus said he would work him in slowly and tell Johnny he had been hired as his guitar tech. Nelson flew to England with the band the following week. He quickly expanded his role by co-writing three songs with bassist Scott Spray for the CD, and playing rhythm guitar on five tracks.

Slatus hired Hambridge and McDonald as Johnny's rhythm section for the rescheduled Bishopstock Blues Festival in August. The CD was scheduled to be recorded between tours in 2001, but fate has other plans. When Johnny tried to sign a work permit in the airport in London, he had no feeling in his right hand.

"I couldn't move my right hand; it was just hanging down limp from the wrist down," says Johnny. "It was completely numb. I thought it would be okay the next day, and it wasn't, so I went to see a doctor in Bishopstock. He said it was radial nerve palsy and would last about six weeks. If it hadn't healed by then, I'd have to have an operation. It just happens, there's no reason for it. We'd flown all the way over there, and to get off the plane and find out your hand doesn't work—it was real tough."

Rather than letting the promoter break the news to the 5,000 fans waiting to hear him perform, Johnny stepped onstage to announce the cancellation before heading to the doctor. He felt his fans deserved a personal message, and Slatus wanted the audience to know Johnny could walk and talk, and thus quell rumors he had a stroke.

"That was a hard decision to make," Johnny says. "I told everybody I was sorry; that I wanted to play for them, but I couldn't. I was afraid I was going to get booed and have people throw things at me. But they clapped and gave me a standing ovation. It was great."

Despite the damage control, losing feeling in his hand and canceling that gig was another rough blow. "It was a pretty big financial loss," says Johnny. "They were going to pay us pretty well. You have to give back the advance; you have to pay for the rooms and the flights. I lost a lot of money."

When Johnny returned to Connecticut, he went back into the studio with Hambridge, who recorded and dubbed Johnny's vocals on several additional songs. Slatus immediately posted photos of those sessions on Johnny's website to show the label, promoters, and fans it was business as usual.

Yet being unable to play guitar and wondering if he'd need another operation took its toll on Johnny. Doug Brockie, his second guitar player from 1973–1974, traveled from New Jersey to visit him every week, offering moral support and massaging essential oils into his hand.

"I don't know if that helped or not, but I was willing to try anything," says Johnny. "I was afraid I might have to have an operation, and I sure didn't want that. I hated it—I can't even imagine what it would be like not to be able to play guitar. I thought what in the world will happen if I can never play guitar again? I tried not to think about it. I believe in God, and I believe God can do anything for you that you need done. I prayed a lot and it worked."

Johnny wore a leather cast and an Ace bandage, which gave him minimal use of his fingers. "I could use my fingers to smoke or get an iced tea, but it was hard to eat with a bandage," he says. He did exercises every day, and the feeling gradually returned. Within six weeks, he was able to strum his Lazer guitar. Encouraged by his progress, he practiced an hour every day. Within several weeks—

which seemed like months—he regained his picking ability and could play both the Lazer and the Firebird.

•◆•

Meanwhile, Val Minett was learning firsthand about Slatus's deceptive business practices and alcoholic episodes. Lured by the offer of a fulltime salaried job, she had left Tennessee and bought a house in Connecticut, but it wasn't long before she regretted her decision.

"I didn't know Teddy had drinking issues," she said. "The only time I realized I had seen him drunk so many times was the first time I saw him sober. It was an awakening. When I still lived in Tennessee, he would call me all hours of the night with, 'I got this idea. What do you think of this?' 'Let's do that.' He always had a lot of good ideas but he never followed through."

One of the things Slatus never followed through on was paying her a salary. He had a reputation of exploiting people without compensation, and Minett was one of dozens lured into his trap with promises of future projects and eventual payment.

"Almost as soon as I moved up here, their attitude started to change," said Minett. "I noticed just how controlling Betty Ann was and how drunk he was all the time. He would go through periods of sobriety, and always fall back in. I think at times he had Johnny's best interests at heart, but he was a very tortured man."

Minett became increasingly concerned about Johnny's overmedicated state, and the number of prescriptions he got from his doctor, who also kept Slatus supplied with pills. "Betty Ann called him [Johnny's physician] Dr. Pill," said Minett. "Even when Teddy was out of his mind, he made sure Johnny had his medicine. Maybe it was his way of making sure Johnny didn't know how badly Teddy was doing."

Slatus was in and out of rehab in 2001 and 2002, but couldn't stay sober. "Teddy kept falling off the wagon," Minett said. "I was doing everything: arranging the tour, setting up interviews, and going to the gigs. Teddy started crying one day, saying, 'You're Johnny's manager now.' Teddy would fall off the wagon every time something bad happened or something good happened; whenever there was any type of pressure. Two days before they went to Europe, he fell off and Betty Ann had to go to Europe."

In late 2001, when Slatus had a meeting in New York with Sony Music executives to discuss the upcoming release of *Best of Johnny Winter*, he asked Minett to accompany him. When it was time to go to the meeting, he wouldn't come out of his hotel room.

"He answered the door crocked out of his mind in his dress shirt and underwear," Minett said. "I told him we had a meeting, and he told me to change it. I could see the bottle of scotch, and he was trying to not let me walk in the room, pushing me back saying, 'Don't come in here.' Finally he said, 'I'm not alone,' and I saw a prostitute on the bed."

Minett returned to her room to regroup, but the drama has just begun. She got a call from Johnston, who told her to get Slatus's wallet when she heard he was drinking. "I asked how I was going to get his wallet away from him," said Minett. "She says it's in his pants pocket, and I said he wasn't wearing any."

Torn between leaving a bizarre situation, and looking out for Johnny's interests, Minett returned to Slatus's room, but he wouldn't answer the door. When he finally answered his phone, he told her to go without him. She met with the Sony executives and returned to Connecticut that same day. Slatus was missing for a week. To finance his binge and penchant for prostitutes, he ran up $40,000 worth of charges on his American Express card, which Johnston later disputed as fraudulent, claiming the card was stolen.

"It was all to an escort service tagged as Hampton Bay's Antiques," said Minett. "When Teddy did come back, he was still out of his mind. Betty Ann made it like he was trying to break in and tried to hit her. I don't know if it's true, but I can't imagine it. She had him taken away by the police, and then had him put away into a detox place."

Slatus's relationship with Johnston was mutually codependent—she needed him for financial reasons, he needed her to run the business, work as tour manager when he was drunk or in rehab, and convince Susan and Johnny he was looking out for their interests.

She told women they were married. Slatus told women the relationship was strictly business.

"They both hated each other equally," said Minett. "They were both so manipulative; I had a hard time figuring out who was the worst of the evils. If they got you by yourself, they would have you believing the other one was the devil on Earth."

Slatus became an easy mark for the friends he made in rehab. He hired Ricky, a former heroin addict who didn't stay clean, to do odd jobs around his house. When Johnston was away for a few days, Ricky stopped by with several bottles of scotch. They had a couple of drinks together, and before long, Slatus signed over $5,000 worth of checks to his rehab buddy.

"Teddy got so bad sometimes," said Minett. "Betty Ann and I would be working and need Teddy's signature for checks. I would have to go up to his room, where he had pissed and shit all over himself in bed, wake him up, prop him up, and tell him I need his signature. There were many times I had to void checks, because he had signed all over the place. That was his life."

In March 2002, Johnny returned to Carriage House to record guitar parts for three more songs recorded and produced by Hambridge in Boston. Two months later, Johnny started rehearsals with a new lineup that included legendary blues harp player James Montgomery, bassist Scott Spray, and drummer Wayne June. Scott played in Edgar's band, and had filled in for Epstein at rehearsals since 2000. They played three gigs in June, including a show at B. B. King's in New York, followed by six blues festivals in France. Reviews of those shows were mixed; loyal fans were thrilled to see him back onstage, while others were dismayed by his frail appearance and the diminished capacity of his vocals and dexterity on the guitar. Concerned that Johnny only had a forty-five-minute window when he could perform, Slatus hired Montgomery to share frontman duties and infuse energy into the show.

"I was hired to distract from Johnny's health," said Montgomery. "Teddy and Bruce Houghton [Johnny's booking agent] said they needed someone that looks lively, can carry part of the show so the audience isn't saying, 'Look how bad Johnny looks.' I'm a pretty animated performer. Johnny wouldn't have a guitar player up there, but because Muddy worked with harmonica players all the time, it was alright."

Montgomery was dismayed when he began rehearsing with Johnny, wondering how the band—with Johnny in his diminished capacity—could ever play in front of a live audience. "The first rehearsal with Johnny, I was going oh . . . my . . . God. We're going to put this show on the road?" said Montgomery. "Our first show was at a club called Stash's in New London, Connecticut. I'm onstage thinking, this is not working, but the crowd was going nuts. A light bulb went off above my head like in the cartoons. It doesn't matter. They love Johnny. We're going to go over big, we're going to get an encore, they're going to love this show. He has a strong following that is loyal."

Buoyed by the audience reaction, the band rehearsed weekly, playing the same songs at every gig and rehearsal. "Eventually through repetitiveness and rote, we put together a pretty solid show," said Montgomery. "Johnny would still have flashes where you could see he is one of the greatest blues guitarists who ever lived. If he'd been handled differently over the years, he'd be bigger than Eric Clapton."

Johnny's handling was far from professional. Slatus continued to make business decisions that sabotaged Johnny's career. When Robert Gordon, author of the 2002 biography of Muddy Waters, teamed up with Morgan Neville to film a documentary on Waters for the PBS American Masters series, he contacted Slatus to set up an interview with Johnny for the film. When Gordon and crew flew in to interview both Johnny and Keith Richards, who also lives in Connecticut, Slatus cancelled the interview, saying Johnny had a rehearsal for an upcoming tour.

Meanwhile, Slatus's continually underhanded dealings with Minett had reached the breaking point. She told him she couldn't work for him any longer. Johnston called the next day and demanded she return merchandise stored at her house and sign off on the *Pieces & Bits* video. Minett still hadn't received the monies designated by the contract she had with Slatus, but when she called the bank, he had withdrawn the money and closed the *Pieces & Bits* account. She sued, but by the time the courts allocated her the agreed-upon fifty percent, DVD sales had slowed considerably. Minett still hadn't been paid for tour work and maintaining Johnny's website for a year, so she retaliated by blocking access to the website, posting bold black letters on a bright red background proclaiming CLOSED DUE TO NONPAYMENT. It was hardly a victory. She returned to Tennessee, still concerned about Johnny's welfare, and disgusted by the way she had been treated.

"Once they have all your ideas, you've got things running, and you've seen too much, then they're done," she said. "Once they drain you dry, they're done with you."

# 14

# Free at Last

When Slatus discovered the website after returning from a European tour, he put the blame on Minett. He couldn't account for all the money during that tour, so he claimed the bus driver overcharged him $10,000, and the crew had stolen money. Yet the band had seen several—often more than one at a time—well-dressed prostitutes going in or out of his hotel room. More than likely, that's where the money went. In January 2003, when the band embarked on a West Coast tour, Slatus made Montgomery the scapegoat for his out-of-control drinking, charging his liquor to the harp player's hotel room. "In Santa Cruz, Teddy was ordering booze like it was going out of style and saying, 'My God, Montgomery sure is drinking a lot," said Montgomery. "He had a $600 bar bill for six days. They took him right from that hotel and sent him to rehab again."

When Slatus checked into a rehab center in California, he appointed Paul Nelson as tour manager, admonishing, "Don't stab me in the back." Nelson, who already had misgivings about Slatus's financial practices, soon realized Slatus had behind the scenes deals with various club owners. That practice had been going on for decades. One scam was demanding more money (that Johnny never received) on the night of the show. That con became so common, one promoter built it into the budget.

Although that promoter requested anonymity, he shared his experiences with Montgomery. "He would tell the club owner, 'I'm going to book Johnny for $7,000 and tell Teddy I could only get $6,000," said Montgomery. "I want you to take the other $1,000 and put it into stacks of $500 cash.' Later, Teddy would come in just before the show, say, 'Look at this place, its packed. Give me $500 cash or Johnny's not going on.' The club owner would pretend to be surprised and give him the $500. Just before Johnny was about to go on, Teddy would say, 'I need another $500.' The club owner would say, 'You're beating me up, but here's the $500.' It was planned in advance because the guy knew Teddy was going to come in and take that money."

Gonzo journalist Hunter S. Thompson's quote—"The music business is a cruel and shallow money trench, a long plastic hallway where thieves and pimps run free, and good men die like dogs. There's also a negative side."—described Slatus perfectly. His dishonesty ran deep; he considered it business as usual in the music industry.

"Teddy bragged about being a busboy in the Catskills and coming home with more money than the maître d'," said Montgomery. "Teddy was a wheeler-dealer from day one. What he learned in the borscht belt and learned working for Steve Paul was what he thought life was all about. You wheel and deal, you try to get what you can. If there is a little bit of cheating to make sure you get ahead, that's life."

Susan and Johnny suspected financial discrepancies in the late 1990s, but couldn't get out from under Slatus's thumb. In 1997, Edgar and Johnny's mother Edwina joined forces to call Johnny and try to convince him to find another manager.

"Edgar told me Teddy wasn't being honest," says Johnny. "Momma didn't trust Teddy either. Edgar had worked with Teddy but quit working with him because he didn't trust him. That's why Rick Derringer left Teddy too. When Edgar stopped working with Teddy, he told me that he didn't trust him. When I talked to Teddy about it, he'd get real mad. Every time I would accuse him of anything, he'd get really pissed off."

Although Johnny usually let the subject drop after Slatus got indignant, at the urging of Edgar and Edwina, he and Susan asked to have the books audited. Slatus responded by quitting the day before Johnny was scheduled to go on tour.

"He went nuts," said Susan. "'How dare you even think I would do anything like that?' He went crazy, so we backed off. I talked to Murray [their accountant] and tried to go over the financials to try to figure out where things were going. It looked like it was about right. I didn't have any way of knowing otherwise and I didn't want to accuse him unless I really knew. I always thought something was wrong, but I had no way to tell."

When Slatus couldn't go on the road without drinking, Johnston became road manager. She had no knowledge of the music industry and little respect for Johnny and the band, which she considered "a ragtag group of weirdos."

When Johnny confronted him about his drinking in 2003, he said he could quit without any outside help. "Teddy just doesn't want to quit—that's the whole thing," said Johnny during that time frame. "He's got to want to quit before it's gonna work. Teddy has gone to four or five programs for drinking, but none of them have helped. At the last one, all they did was dry him out."

Slatus was drunk when he met Virgin Record executives at Johnny's June SummerStage concert in Central Park. Bouncers at B. B. King's in Manhattan threw him out of Johnny's August performance, which was taped for the *Johnny Winter: Live in Times Square* video. "Teddy was too fucked up that night," says Johnny. "One of my drivers had to take him home and then come back to get us."

Unhappy with the quality of his performance at the B. B. King show, Johnny told Slatus not to release the video. Slatus agreed but released it anyway. Meanwhile, Bob Margolin, Muddy Waters's guitarist, began a project at Sony to produce reissues of the Waters Blue Sky LPs that Johnny produced in the late '70s. Slatus supplied the masters from the Blue Sky sessions, but Johnny knew nothing about the project until I told him about it during one of our interviews. "I'm surprised Johnny didn't know because Teddy Slatus has been involved with all this from the start and recently provided a lot of the original multi-track recordings," said Margolin. "I hope there's nothing weird going on."

Despite Slatus's behind-the-scenes manipulations and rip-offs, he continued to play the gofer, catering to Johnny's every whim. A creature of habit, Johnny wanted what he wanted, when he wanted it. Slatus did what he could to keep him happy. The band and crew spent eight hours in Paris looking for Ocean Spray cranberry juice, and they drove hours out of their way to find Johnny's favorite Jell-O, yogurt (Yoplait with the gold top), and Pop Tarts; they also used a GPS to locate a White Castle or a Taco Bell, which make the only burgers and tacos Johnny will eat.

"It was important for Teddy to have this schedule for Johnny so he could control everything," said Montgomery. "Making sure he had what he wanted, rather than saying no. It was an unreal world where you had a guy who was overmedicated making decisions, and a manager who wasn't making any career decisions at all. Nothing to further his career—just let's keep him on the road, keep him on the medication. It was a bizarre scene."

Even more bizarre was Johnston's role as road manager, which she overplayed to make up for her lack of knowledge and experience. Pushy, overbearing, and sometimes belligerent, she made ridiculous demands for Johnny just to throw her weight around. She flattered Johnny and bought him gifts; but behind his back, she called him a "burnout like Ozzy Osbourne." Smarter than Slatus, especially in his compromised condition, she helped him pad bills for anything and everything; a ninety-dollar car-cleaning bill doubled by the time they sent it to Susan.

"With Teddy, it was twenty dollars here, eighty dollars there, fifty dollars there—the same way he operated in the Catskills as a busboy," said Montgomery. "Teddy thought because he was working so hard for Johnny that he deserved it. My impression was the two of them didn't have a problem with skimming money off the top, because they felt they deserved it for taking care of this poor fucked-up musician. But he was in shambles because of the way they handled his career and the medications they let him do."

During Johnny's 2003 European tour, Johnston's belligerent behavior resulted in lost dates, lost gigs and merchandising income, and a lawsuit. The original itinerary had blues festivals in Norway and Italy. Slatus revised the itinerary a month before the tour began, dropping those festivals and a club in Germany, and adding six new German dates. The tour started with blues festivals in Switzerland and Austria, followed by a show in Leipzig, Germany. After that sold-out performance, Johnston accepted the final advance from Fabulous German Entertainment GmbH, the German promoter. Unhappy with the tour bus they provided, she hired a new bus and, together with the band and crew, skipped town in the middle of the night. Johnston was able to rebook the festivals in Norway and Italy, but it didn't make up for the damage caused by her knee-jerk reaction. Johnny lost seven gigs, had thirteen extra free days in a twenty-three-day tour, and was sued by the promoter, who distributed the following press release:

We are very sorry that Johnny Winter's German tour was cancelled in such a mysterious way, but all our efforts fell on the deaf ears of the US manager Teddy Slatus and actually peaked in an eruption of cursing, which only documents the unprofessional business conduct of this man. . . . At no time during the preparation of the tour was our work effort criticized or dressed down by the US management. Accordingly we simply cannot understand the nightly departure from Leipzig for an unknown destination using an unknown bus.

"Betty Ann talked us into quitting the job," says Johnny. "I thought it was the right thing to do too. We had a really bad bus. The bathroom stunk and there wasn't a bed for me. I wanted a bed in the back for me but it just had narrow couches you couldn't sleep on. And we had two long drives from country to country that ended up being twelve hours and fourteen hours. It was really a drag."

Montgomery, who had fronted his own band since 1970, knew how to save the tour, but neither Slatus nor Johnston would listen to his advice. The entire entourage enjoyed an impromptu European vacation. Johnny's fondest memories were visits to two hash bars in Amsterdam.

"We went into Amsterdam for four days and I smoked myself silly," says Johnny with a laugh. "Hash bars, where they smoke grass too. They have all different kinds of grass that they sell in the bars. The hash was good; long and stringy, real gooey. People mix it up with tobacco and smoke it in the bar. It's legal over there. It's lovely. Going to Amsterdam was definitely worth not doing the gigs. I loved it. Did it all night. The Bulldog was a lot of tourists but there were other places like the Green House where people from Amsterdam went. It was amazing. The Bulldog was a disco. Smokin' and watchin' people in a disco was hilarious."

Fresh from his European tour/vacation, Johnny returned to the studio in July and September to finish *I'm a Bluesman.* Nominated for a Grammy and finally released on Virgin in June 2004, the CD garnered mixed reviews, many commenting on Johnny's diminished vocals. Clueless about Johnny's condition, Slatus told Shurman Johnny should have gotten closer to the microphone.

Blaming the fiasco in Germany on Bruce Houghton and Skyline Music, Slatus began booking Johnny locally in fall 2003 and shopping for a new agency. He told Johnny he had several conversations with ABC (Associated Booking Corp.), but they passed because *Johnny* was too difficult to work with. In early 2004, he signed with the William Morris Agency, but that relationship was short-lived. Montgomery remembers Slatus being "in outer space" when Virgin and William Morris were trying to promote *I'm a Bluesman,* and thinks that impacted Johnny's future at that agency.

"If you're William Morris with a stable of some of the biggest acts in show business, and you call the manager and are getting gibberish on the other end of the phone, how much time and energy are you going to spend on the act?" said Montgomery.

With his manager out of control, Johnny coped as best he could, relying on vodka, pot, and denial to get him through. As long as he was living comfortably, his bills were paid, and he could make a living playing the music he loved, he still gave Slatus free rein. It went beyond his business affairs; Slatus was like a socialist state that took care of all of Johnny's needs. He hired a driver to take him where he needed to go, paid all of Johnny's household and business bills, and set up his doctor, dentist, and methadone appointments.

"Most people are only on methadone for short period of time; whereas thirty years later, Johnny is still on methadone," said Montgomery. "That was just another way Teddy was able to build up all these habits, and for Johnny to feel that, without Teddy, he couldn't make a decision or do anything in his life.'

"In those days, when you talked to musicians, the word on the street was Teddy is really loyal to Johnny. In retrospect, it wasn't loyalty as much as a symbiotic relationship, two codependents. One guy depending on Johnny for all of his income; Johnny depending on Teddy for all his decisions; and the two of them thinking, without the other one I can't go forward. Teddy always thought he was doing the right thing for Johnny. But there were so many wrong things that were done, and so many things in Johnny's career that should have happened and didn't."

To heighten Johnny's dependence, Slatus continued to keep him isolated from friends and family. He referred to Slatus Management as "the organization," and ran it as such. Anyone who saw too much or got too close was fired or denied access. Johnston used her friendship with Susan to find out who had called or stopped by.

Fearful of what Johnny had told me during a year of interviews while Slatus was drunk or in rehab, and especially concerned about our growing friendship, Slatus cut off access and instructed Johnny and Susan to do the same. As much as he wanted his story to be told, Johnny was too medicated and dependent to defy Slatus's demand.

Meanwhile, Montgomery and Nelson, appalled by the amount of medication Johnny was taking, took him to Montgomery's doctor. "There was a brown bag that traveled on the road with us that was like the Holy Grail," Montgomery said. "It was full of pills and methadone. Every day, at this time, we had to pull over to take these, and take these and those. After a year and a half, I started thinking, 'Something's wrong here. Nobody has to take twenty pills a day, I don't care who you are.'"

As president of the New England Blues Society (NEBS), Montgomery had founded a medical program for musicians without health insurance. That program spun off of the blues society to become the DeviBlue Foundation, an organization dedicated to providing free and low-cost health care to musicians throughout New England. Montgomery hooked Johnny up with two of the doctors: Dr. Lawrence S. Hotes, Chief Medical Officer at New England Sinai Hospital in Stoughton, Massachusetts, and Dr. Gerald T. Rosenberg, a physical therapist in Providence, Rhode Island.

"Larry Hotes and Gerry Rosenberg looked at the medications Johnny was taking and said, 'You got to be shittin' me," said Montgomery. "Hotes was shocked. He couldn't believe one patient had been prescribed all this medicine."

Nelson followed up with Dr. Hotes and devised a plan to wean Johnny off of the medication while Slatus was in rehab. It took almost a year for Johnny to be completely free of his daily doses of Klonopin and Risperdal he had been taking for nearly eleven years.

"I had just dropped Teddy off at the clinic, where he was going to be for two months," said Nelson. "I told Dr. Hotes, 'I bring Johnny to a weekly dentist appointment in New York City every Wednesday. Can we start lowering him on these pills? I'll tell you how he feels by our long drives to the dentist.' We start lowering them, with no side effects. His voice got better, his playing got better, and he became more talkative."

Johnny is grateful for Nelson's role in his recovery, as well as Montgomery's role in finding him a new doctor. "James thought I needed to come off those pills and he got the doctor to help me," says Johnny. "Dr. Hotes convinced me I could stop. It was real easy, so I just quit. I quit drinking too. Now I feel great. The pills made me feel messed up—they affected my health, my playing, everything."

Although Slatus always told associates he was weaning Johnny off the medication, nothing could be further from the truth. He initially agreed with Johnny seeing a new doctor, but as Johnny's mind cleared, he began to panic. "Teddy hated it when Johnny came off the pills," said Susan. "Teddy actually called the doctor and told him to put Johnny back on the pills because he was asking too many questions."

Getting Johnny off the meds was step one; once he had cleared that hurdle, Nelson decided it was time for him to get rid of Slatus. Night after night, he reiterated the ways Johnny's manager had hurt his career, and shared his concerns with Susan. The rest of the band helped to convince Johnny that Slatus wasn't looking out for his best interests.

"Me, Paul, Scott, and Wayne formed a team," said Montgomery. "Whoever was up with Johnny late at night, that's all we talked about. 'You can't let this happen; you shouldn't be doing this, you should be doing that.' We didn't care if we got fired. Our mission became: here is one of the greatest blues artists that ever lived, let's make sure he goes out—the last ten, fifteen, twenty, or thirty years—playing and performing with dignity at the top of his potential, getting the full respect he has earned and so richly deserves."

Montgomery didn't mince words when he talked to Johnny about Slatus. "James told me he hated Teddy," says Johnny. "He thought Teddy was doing a horrible job. I thought he was doing okay. I'd been with him for years and I trusted him.

Johnny signed with Piedmont Talent Inc. at the end of 2004, but by then the carpal tunnel syndrome in his right hand had gotten progressively worse. Slatus cancelled his gigs for early 2005 and Montgomery set up an appointment with Dr. Rosenberg, who stabilized Johnny's hand with a splint and brace and hooked him up with a surgeon, who operated on April 7. By now, Johnny was totally off his anti-anxiety medication and seeing the situation a lot clearer. When Shurman called to ask about the surgery, Johnny told him Teddy "screwed up my career."

Slatus cleared Johnny's calendar in early April for eight weeks, but Johnny's hand remained numb throughout June. By July, his playing window was only ten minutes long. Slatus visited him twice while he was healing, but Johnny refused to see him for more than ten minutes. Feeling disgusted with the way Slatus had managed his career, Johnny dragged out his recovery period, while Nelson devised a plan to make Slatus quit.

"We told Teddy we weren't sure if Johnny ever could play again and that we'd move down to North Carolina and get involved in my sister's restaurant," said Susan. "He said, 'You're going to take Johnny with you?' I started laughing and said, 'Of course, do you think I'm going to leave him here?' That shocked the hell out of him. He got real scared that it might actually be over."

That wasn't the only shock Slatus would have to bear. Early on the morning of July 11, Johnston died unexpectedly from an aneurism at the age of fifty-one. Ironically, Johnston had married Slatus less than a month before she passed. Their lawyer had advised them to get married to protect their financial interests if either one died. But there was a more pressing motive for the June wedding. The lawsuit against Slatus by the German promoter had a court date in September. Johnston's quick marriage to Slatus would prevent her from testifying against him.

Slatus missed Johnston's funeral service and was so drunk at the cemetery that two men had to hold him up. His continual blabbering at the gravesite caused the funeral director to take him aside so he wouldn't disrupt the service. Both Susan and Nelson attended the services. When they stopped by Slatus's home after the funeral, Susan watched her husband's business being conducted by Slatus's cleaning lady and the woman who walked his dogs.

Nelson used the opportunity to fully expose the financial discrepancies he has witnessed and documented during the past three years.

"Paul told me all about it the day of Betty Ann's funeral," Susan said. "He had been giving me hints. 'Why don't you ask Teddy about this?' When I would, they would get all upset—what's she doing asking? He let me know Betty Ann was helping Teddy, which made me start wondering. Was she my friend? Wasn't she? Teddy would get her to explain things to me so I would believe it. If I was upset about something, he would ask her to take me antiquing, or she would call me to go to lunch and ask me questions.

"Finding out was difficult. I thought in the beginning she was my friend. But she heard so much of Teddy's crap of how we did this to him, we did that to him, that she started believing him and helping him. But she wasn't faking the friendship at first."

Slatus often called up band members from rehab in a drunken stupor, and left insulting messages on their answering machines; a favorite was, "You guys are losers." Nelson taped a drunken Slatus, slurring "Fuck Johnny" and calling him a "meal ticket"—and played it for Johnny and Susan. They both took it hard. "It was horrible," said Susan. "It sounded like he hated us. Teddy blamed his drinking on Johnny; he blamed everything on Johnny. He really resented Johnny for everything he had. He felt like everything we had belonged to him, and he just started taking it."

When Nelson presented them with proof of Slatus's dishonesty, Susan and Johnny, who trusted and respected him, asked him to become Johnny's manager. Not wanting to kick Slatus when he was down, they waited six weeks after Johnston's death to make it official. On August 25, Johnny hired Nelson as his new manager and fired Slatus, his attorney, and his accountant.

•◆•

When Johnny talks about discovering that Slatus was stealing from him and had been for years, the hurt and betrayal is palpable. "I felt terrible," he says. "It was worse because of all the years. It's hard that I trusted him. Everybody tried to convince me he was a bad person. I should have listened but I didn't want to believe it."

Slatus's reaction to the fax that fired him made it clear that Johnny had made the right decision. "He called that whole day and you could tell he had started drinking," said Susan. "First it was, 'How could you do this to me?' Then it was, 'Why did you do this to me?' Then, 'How dare you do this to me.' He said, 'Is it about the *Pieces & Bits* DVD? If it is, I have $19,000 in an account for that for you.' Of course, before that, when I asked, he said, 'There's no money,' and the accountant said the same thing. We never got a cent. The calls got worse and worse as the night went on. Then he stopped calling and we never talked to him again."

When Susan and Nelson started going through her records, they discovered financial discrepancies that began when Johnny was hospitalized in 1993. "We have proof for the last ten to twelve years, and I'm sure it went a ways before that," she said. "I had all my statements and Paul started looking at them. 'I know the promoters paid for that, but he made you pay for it. I know how much this cost and he charged you too much.' I have records as far back as 1993 where I can prove he overcharged, and charged ridiculous things that I would ask questions about and get the runaround. They didn't think I had any business questioning them about finances."

"Those bills gave the story," said Nelson. "They showed they were being charged for paying their utilities (Slatus added fifteen percent to utility and mortgage payments as a bill-paying fee), paying extra on merchandise bills, it got worse and worse. It was all there—it was blatant thievery."

Determined to rebuild bridges Slatus had burned, as well as Johnny's reputation, Nelson worked feverishly to put Johnny back in the spotlight with an ever increasing schedule of gigs, preceded by interviews with Johnny in the local press. Unlike Slatus, he had a game plan for building Johnny's career.

"Ninety percent of his income was touring; at his age that's sad," said Nelson. "I made a twenty-point list; number one was health, and it had things like the band, bootlegs, appearance, endorsements, equipment, promoter, booking agent, attorneys, and accountants. I knew there were tons of bootlegs and I went onto eBay and started purchasing DVDs and CDs, and also contacted the traders that collected Johnny. I asked them to send me copies of the bar codes, the lot numbers, and the record companies of all the bootlegs. I made a tree of all the companies and submitted it to the attorneys."

Serendipitously, when Johnny played a gig in Texas, a fan told him his original contract with Roy Ames was displayed in a local museum. Nelson gave a copy to Johnny's attorneys. He also contacted BMI to try to increase Johnny's royalty revenue stream.

"BMI attorneys sent letters to all the writers listed," said Nelson. "If they don't respond in a month, full ownership of the song goes back to the artists. We worked that out; now we're checking all the original major record deals. I also got all the rights to the footage. But I couldn't do any of this if Johnny wasn't healthy and didn't have his business matters back on track."

Nelson also set up reunion shows with Rick Derringer and Edgar Winter, who were both thrilled to see Slatus out of the picture. The first Johnny and Edgar reunion show was a "Still Alive and Well Homecoming Benefit" for the Southeast Texas Food Bank at the Beaumont Civic Center on November 17. The following day, Johnny and Edgar would be inducted into the Southeast Texas "Walk of Fame" in their home town for their contributions to music and career accomplishments.

On October 31, less than three weeks before that show, Johnny fell and broke his other hip. This time, he couldn't afford a year-long recovery. Johnny went straight to the hospital, where doctors set it with pins. He was in the hospital for three days, went to rehab for two weeks, and then had therapy at home three days a week. Determined to play the gig despite his pain, and without igniting further rumors about his health, Johnny agreed to Nelson's plan to carry him onto the stage with the house lights down.

"Paul made it so nobody knew," said Susan. "We were afraid it would domino if we canceled one gig. We had already canceled gigs because of his hand, so he went ahead and played."

Despite the respect and camaraderie he shared with Nelson, Johnny felt guilty about firing his former friend and longtime manager, wondering if he'd done the right thing. Less than seven weeks after he let Slatus go, fate—or perhaps karma—closed the door on any second thoughts he may have had.

Three days after Johnny fell and broke his hip, an inebriated Slatus tumbled down the stairs of his home. According to the police report, when Kent Illausky, Slatus's live-in handyman, woke him around 7 AM that morning, an already-drunken Slatus demanded another bottle of Johnny Walker Red. Illausky returned with a bottle, had a drink with Slatus, and went out to work in the yard. When Frances Brown, the woman who cared for Slatus's dogs and birds, later looked in on him, she found him in bed "drunker than I had ever seen him." When Illausky checked on him around 10 AM, Slatus was lying with his head on the stairwell, his legs up the stairs. Illausky called 911, and when police arrived, they found Slatus smelling of alcohol, with injuries to his head and right hand, and cuts and bruises on the left side of his face and forehead. He died shortly after at the Middlesex Medical Center in Marlborough; the official cause of death was "ischemic heart disease."

After Johnston died, Slatus changed his will designating John Johnston III, Johnston's brother, and Diane Oliver (who he also gave power of attorney), as equal beneficiaries. Hired as his cleaning lady in 2001, Oliver became his caretaker and started running the business after Johnston died. At Slatus's funeral, she said she had been Johnston's personal assistant for four years, and although she didn't know what she was doing, she took over all aspects of the business when Johnston died.

Slatus's funeral service was reminiscent of that of Ebenezer Scrooge—there were no friends to mourn him, just a handful of local businessmen. The rabbi read from the newspaper obituary, which said he became "performance manager" for Johnny Winter in 1966—two years before Steve Paul brought Johnny to the Scene. It was obvious no one knew him or how he had spent his life. Instead of displaying his pride and joy—the life-sized framed photo of Slatus proudly standing beside Muddy Waters seated in the ornate carved chair that graces the cover of *King Bee*—his memorabilia table, put together by Oliver and Brown, displayed a photo of Slatus with his mother, several wedding photos, and pictures of him with his cockatiels and dogs. The prayer card photo depicted a pensive gray-haired Slatus lying back with his dogs.

Johnny's oft-quoted reaction to Slatus's death—"Are we having tacos tonight?"—was a way to shield his feelings. Underneath the Texas bravado, Johnny has always been a sensitive man. One can't have a business and personal relationship with someone for thirty-six years without feeling pain at their passing.

Neither Johnny nor Susan attended Slatus's funeral. Susan wanted to pay her respects, but due to the Winters' lawsuit to recoup their losses from his estate, her lawyers advised her against it. Johnny felt differently.

"I just didn't want to go," says Johnny. "I didn't care about him at that point. I was almost glad [he died]. I hate to say that but . . . "

When asked if he felt any sorrow over Slatus's passing, Johnny's initial response was "No, I'm just glad." Yet his words were betrayed by the sadness in his voice. When pressed, it was difficult for him to separate sorrow from his feelings of betrayal.

"I guess I do [feel sorrow]," he says softly. "It pisses me off that I was that dumb; that I let him get away with it. He was so close to me for years, but he was still unfair to me. I can't believe he did that. It's hard to believe he was that bad, and everybody else saw it but me."

"We could never get back what Teddy took," said Susan. "We find out almost every day something else that Teddy's done. Paul made sure everything comes to us now and I have control of all bank accounts. I see what he spends; I control everything. With Teddy, we had an accountant who didn't care about receipts or invoices."

Despite the betrayal and the enormous financial hits, including attorneys' fees for the lawsuits filed by the German promoter and against Slatus's estate, both Susan and Johnny are happy that what one music writer called the "Slatus Death Ride" is over. "Johnny's doing so much better," said Susan. "It's like a big cloud went away."

# 15
# Full Circle

Fully aware that Johnny had been his own worst enemy in terms of career decisions, Paul Nelson made it clear at the onset that Johnny would have to follow his directives. Rather than allowing Johnny to "worry" himself out of doing interviews or playing with other artists, Nelson waits until the last minute to discuss it with him.

"What I do with Johnny is—and he knows I do this—I tell him everything two minutes before he's supposed to do it," said Nelson. "He's accepted me as manager, and I've accepted the responsibility to do the right thing. I know if it's a huge interview, if I tell him in advance, he's going to worry about it, stew over it, brood over it, and eventually cancel it. So I don't give him that opportunity. Every time, he always says, 'I'm so glad I did that—this is great.'"

Johnny's renewed health and busy touring schedule left no room for Montgomery to further his career with his own band, so he left and Nelson joined the lineup.

Johnny's career has experienced a renaissance under Nelson, who rebuilt bridges Slatus burned, got him endorsement deals for a Gibson Custom Shop Johnny Winter Signature Firebird V, a re-creation of Johnny's 1963/1964 Firebird (when Gibson analyzed Johnny's Firebird at the Custom Shop in Nashville, they found a serial number on the headstock and were able to date the neck as 1964, and the body design as 1963), the Dunlop "Texas Slider," a pinky slide modeled after Johnny's slide, and D'Addario strings. He is back in the headlines with stories in *Guitar World, Vintage Guitar,*

*Goldmine, Modern Guitars, Blues Matters, Blues Revue, Penthouse,* and the *AARP Bulletin,* which recognized his achievements on his sixtieth birthday.

Fans can still buy music new to their ears: *Breakin' It Up, Breakin' It Down,* a live recording of formerly unreleased material with Johnny, Muddy Waters, and James Cotton, was released in June 2007. That CD won "Historical Album of the Year" in the 2008 Blues Music Awards presented by the Blues Foundation in Memphis. *Live Bootleg Series Volume 1, Volume 2, Volume 3, Volume 4,* and *Volume 5,* authorized bootlegs of live archival material, were released in October 2007, March 2008, July 2008, February 2009, and June 2009 respectively, generating brisk sales and rave reviews from fans.

Johnny played guest DJ on Bill Wax's Bluesville program on XM satellite radio, and does interviews with newspapers on tours across the U.S., Canada, and Europe that keep him playing three to five nights a week. He began with an average of 120 to 140 gigs a year; by summer 2008, his price had increased so he could cut down to one hundred gigs without losing any income.

For the first time in thirty-seven years, Johnny performed with the Allman Brothers Band. He joined them for three songs on April 8, 2007 during their sold-out run at the Beacon Theater in New York. Allman Brothers' guitarist Warren Haynes, who caught one of Johnny's shows and visited him in his bus, invited him to that show.

"I told Johnny the day before the gig, but I had already agreed with the Allman Brothers that it was gonna happen," said Nelson with a laugh. "When musicians ask, 'Is Johnny excited about playing with us?' I have to say something like 'Words can't describe his feelings,' because he doesn't know yet."

Rather than bear the exorbitant expense of the tour bus that Johnny loves, Nelson found a less expense mode of transportation with a similar set up. The same model is available throughout the U.S., so Johnny, whose vision is greatly diminished, doesn't have to adjust to a new layout in every city. He still stays up all night listening to the blues, but now it is on an iPod that Nelson has loaded with 10,332 blues songs, including Johnny's entire catalogue.

The highest visibility gig of Johnny's renaissance in 2007 was his performance with the Derek Trucks Band at the Crossroads Concert in Chicago on July 28. Crossroads generated a spread in *Rolling Stone* titled "Clapton's Guitar Summit," that included a photo of Eric Clapton and Johnny, with the caption Blues Brothers Clapton with Johnny Winter, who rocked a ten-minute slide version of Dylan's "Highway 61 Revisited." According to writer David Fricke, "The show's first highlight came during Derek Trucks's set, which peaked during his version of 'Highway 61 Revisited' with Johnny Winter." Johnny also joined Clapton, Buddy Guy, John Mayer, Hubert Sumlin, Robert Cray, and Jimmie Vaughan on "Sweet Home Chicago" during the all-star jam.

It was Nelson's perseverance and quick thinking that got Johnny that gig and coerced him to hang around for the jam. Knowing Johnny wouldn't play in the daytime, Nelson waited until the day of the concert to tell Johnny he went on at 1:30 PM. Getting Johnny to hang around till the 11 PM jam took a stroke of genius.

"After Johnny did the show with Trucks, he wanted to go back to the hotel," said Nelson. "I said hold on, went outside, and saw B. B. King. I told him Johnny Winter wants to say hello to you and he said great. I asked him to wait a minute, and told Johnny, B. B. King wants to say hello to you. I sent him in the bus, and he was in there for half an hour. Then I thought, how many musicians will it take for Johnny to meet to kill enough time to make him sit in this bus until the all-star jam? So I went out and did that to Vince Gill, Hubert Sumlin, Los Lobos, John Mayer, Robert Randolph, Stevie Winwood. I told him each one wanted to meet him, brought them on the bus, and by the time it was done, it was thirty minutes before show time. The jam became the last song on the [2007 *Crossroads*] DVD and was all over PBS. It was a hit, it showed him healthy, and Johnny's price went up for all his gigs. I got a letter from Clapton, saying thank you very much; we'd love to have you again in three years."

Professionally, Crossroads was a high point, but the close-up shots of Johnny during that performance depict a man who looks like he lost his best friend. And he did. Uncle John Turner, his closest friend, and the man who convinced him to take a chance on playing the blues, died in Austin on July 26, two days before the concert.

One of Johnny's deepest regrets, one that has stayed with him, was firing Turner and Shannon, who believed in him before he became famous and were willing to take a financial hit to play the music he loved. Following the directive of his manager to let them go with a severance payment of $2,000 each still bothered him, although both had forgiven him and never let it affect the friendship. When he discovered Stevie Ray Vaughan has generously shared his success with Shannon by giving him "points" or a percentage of profits from the recordings they made together, he felt even worse.

In November 2006, Johnny called them onstage to play "Johnny Guitar" at a gig at La Zona Rosa in Austin. It was the first time they had performed live together since 1970. The audience surprised Turner and Shannon with a rousing cheer when they walked onstage and a standing ovation when they finished. But Johnny, who has become quite taciturn due to a decade of overmedication, didn't have much to say when they visited him after the show. The reunion they had longed for was hardly the heartfelt moment they had hoped it would be.

"It was bittersweet," said Shannon. "It was a lot of fun playing; the chemistry was just like the old days, like we never lost anything. But it brought back a lot of memories, including the pain of when Uncle John and I left."

"It was fun—it had been a long time," Turner said in March 2007. "I went early and chatted with Johnny a little bit before the show. He doesn't have much to say to anybody anymore, so I just chat a little bit and get out of the way. I wish we could've got to play some more. That's probably the last time we'll take a stage together. I'd play with him again when he came back to town, but—to tell you the truth—I doubt if we'll ever do that."

Turner was right. Less than three months after he spoke those words, Turner was hospitalized for complications due to Hepatitis C. He had been accepted on the University of Texas Health Science Center's liver-transplant list in December 2006 and had been moved up in April 2007. In May, Austin musicians Carolyn Wonderland and Erin Jaimes began planning benefits to help with medical costs. By June, Shannon's wife Kumi Smedley, club owner Susan Antone, and booking agent/web designer Beverly Howell joined the team. They wanted to ask Johnny to headline Uncathons in Austin and San Antonio, but Turner refused to violate his friend's privacy by giving out his home phone number. They contacted Johnny through Nelson, and when Johnny called to say he'd be coming down to play the benefits, Turner was thrilled.

"You cannot believe how happy and relieved Unc was when he found out Johnny was actually coming," said his wife Morgan. "He thought maybe Johnny and Paul could come down but he never dreamed Johnny would come with his full band. He was really humbled that Johnny was coming. I don't believe he ever thought it would be possible, and when he found out it was, then it was a big emotional sigh of relief. It was the last time I ever saw him really happy. He even planned out where he was going to sit during the performance and how he would be able to get to talk to Johnny. By this time he was in a wheelchair. At first he felt bad about the chair, but decided that the important thing was that his old friend was coming down to support him, and nothing else mattered. He knew Johnny's presence was going to make a big difference in attendance and the money, and boy did it, but the most important thing to him was Johnny."

Although Turner didn't live long enough to see his old friend again, Morgan met with Johnny in his bus before the Antone's benefit in Austin on August 1, 2007. It was an emotional moment for both of them.

"I sat with Johnny for a while before the performance and he was crying," she said. "That made it harder but I loved him for it. He said Unc had been his best friend and he was going to miss him very much. I was so moved that he cried in front of me. Tears just rolled down his cheeks. He was completely broken up and told me he had hoped that he would get to Austin in time to see Unc again.

"When Unc and I had come earlier to a concert, they talked for quite a long time. Unc was the only person he wanted to talk to. He asked Unc all kinds of questions about how he was feeling and what he needed. He asked about the transplant and Unc's symptoms. They were both so earnest and talked for a long time."

When Johnny played the Uncathon at Antone's, the line snaked in front of the club and down Fifth Street for several blocks. Tickets sold out before the benefit; scores of people had to be turned away.

"Susan Antone told me it was the biggest benefit that Antone's had ever held," said Morgan. "It was more than sold out. There was an incredible crush of people and you could hardly walk through the crowd. People went wild. When Erin and Carolyn started in the early summer, they were told they'd be lucky to get $5,000 from the benefit. It turned out that from tickets, donations, and the silent auction, we received over $40,000 just from Antone's.

"It was all because of Johnny's performance. The media had been all over Unc's death—even to a crawl during the ABC news—and it had been in every paper and on the front page of the *Austin American Statesman*. Everyone knew Johnny was coming down to honor his old friend. It was such an emotional thing that it became the event of the summer."

Pinetop Perkins was at Antone's that night, as was harp legend James Cotton, who sat in on "Hoochie Coochie Man." Shannon joined Johnny onstage for "Johnny Guitar," and the two men shared a heartfelt embrace on the way back to the dressing room. It was an evening Shannon called "magical." No matter how painful their breakup had been, there was no doubting the love the former band mates still shared.

•◆•

Now that he's in his sixties, Johnny can look back on all the twists and turns and reflect on his life's journey. Although many artists would shy away from exposing the underbelly of their life story, Johnny is an honest man who believes it's time for his story to be told.

"I've made enough mistakes, where I think it's important for people to know my mistakes, why they happened, and how I got out of it," he says. "Who knows better than I do? I'm the only one that really knows what happened. All they know is that I had a problem. It's important that they know the truth."

From the time he was a child, Johnny always believed he'd be a successful musician; there was never a doubt in his mind. When asked if it was fate or free will that brought him success, he ponders the question before answering. "I think you have a lot to do with your fate," he says. "You can't say its fate and leave it up to that; you've got to work out your own fate. Everything I wanted, I always got. I feel like it was something I had to keep working at, but I knew I was going to be successful. I was determined to get what I wanted and knew I would eventually. It didn't surprise me when it happened; I just was surprised it took so long."

Looking back over a career that has spanned five decades, Johnny feels his biggest mistake was losing his faith in a higher power. "The toughest lesson I ever had to learn was that there was something else up there in control," says Johnny. "That I couldn't make things happen on my own completely—it was very important that I believed in God. I think God is involved in everybody's life; that He is an important part of everybody's life. I don't know exactly why or how, but when I quit believing in God, I got miserable, very unhappy. I stopped believing in God when I thought for a while that I was so cool that I could make anything happen on my own. And it made me realize that you can't do it on your own; you definitely need some help from God. When I asked God for help, I always got it. When I was on heroin, I promised Him that if He could help me get off drugs, I would never disbelieve in Him again. And I never did because He did help me get off drugs and I couldn't do it on my own."

If he had his life to live over again, Johnny wouldn't change a thing. "When I look back on it, I've learned from everything that's happened to me," he says. "I think everything has a reason to happen. Sometimes you don't know what the reason is, but I believe there is always a reason. Setbacks happen to everybody. They make it harder for you, but they're an important part of life and living. And I think they make you stronger.

"Sometimes I wish I hadn't signed with Steve Paul. I thought he was just using me for what he wanted and not really helping. I guess that's just about my only regret. I wish I hadn't taken drugs, but at the same time, I always wanted to know what they were like, so I can't say that I'm sorry I did it. It was something I always wanted to try, so I can't say that's something I would have changed. I've done just about everything I wanted to do and I've been lucky enough to travel just about every place I wanted to travel."

One of the things he has finally learned is to appreciate Susan, and the impact she has had on the quality of his life. "Having Susan in my life—she's made it better in so many ways that I can't even imagine what it would be like without her," he says. "She's done things for me I could never do for myself. She's made me feel useful and is an important part of my life."

Being recognized as a musician all over the world is a heady feeling, and Johnny plans to continue playing the blues as long as he can. "If I hadn't been a musician, I can't imagine being anything else," he says. "It was something I've loved to do all my life. I can't imagine taking it away; being a musician is part of me."

Like most baby boomers, Johnny isn't looking forward to aging, even though longevity runs in his family. When he was fifty-nine, Johnny didn't like approaching the big six-o. "It's scary," he says. "I'm scared of old age. I don't want to be older. To me, I figure sixty is entering old age. I didn't know if I'd make it this far, but I sure hoped I would. I used to say I wanted to be playing the blues when I'm eighty. Now I'd like to go a lot further than eighty. Eighty's nothing now; I'd like to go to one hundred."

When asked how he would like to be remembered, he doesn't think twice.

"As a good blues player," he says with a smile.

# Discography

## AUTHORIZED RELEASES: ALBUMS

*Johnny Winter*, Columbia, 1969
*Progressive Blues Experiment*, Imperial/United Artists, 1969
*Second Winter*, Columbia, 1969
*Johnny Winter And*, Columbia, 1970
*Johnny Winter and Live*, Columbia, 1971
*Still Alive and Well*, Columbia, 1973
*Saints and Sinners*, Columbia, 1974
*John Dawson Winter III*, Blue Sky, 1974
*Captured Live!*, Blue Sky, 1976
*Edgar and Johnny Winter Together*, Blue Sky, 1976
*Nothin' But the Blues*, Blue Sky, 1977
*White, Hot & Blue*, Blue Sky, 1978
*Raisin' Cain*, Blue Sky, 1980
*The Johnny Winter Story*, CBS, 1980 (double LP)
*Raised on Rock*, CBS, 1980 (double LP; same recording as above)
*Guitar Slinger*, Alligator, 1984
*Serious Business*, Alligator, 1985
*Third Degree*, Alligator, 1986
*The Winter of '88*, MCA/Voyager, 1988
*Let Me In*, Point Blank, 1991
*"Hey, Where's Your Brother?"*, Point Blank, 1992
*Scorchin' Blues*, Sony, 1992 (Columbia compilation)
*A Rock N' Roll Collection*, Sony, 1994 (two-CD Columbia compilation)
*Anthology*, Sony, 1995
*White Hot Blues*, Sony, 1997

*Live in NYC '97*, Virgin, 1998
*Return of Johnny Guitar*, Empire Music Collection, 2000
*Deluxe Edition*, Alligator, 2001
*The Best of Johnny Winter*, Sony Legacy, 2002
*I'm a Bluesman*, Virgin, 2004
*Live Bootleg Series, Volume 1*, Friday Music, 2007
*Live Bootleg Series, Volume 2*, Friday Music, 2008
*Live Bootleg Series, Volume 3*, Friday Music, 2008
*Live Bootleg Series, Volume 4*, Friday Music, 2009
*Live Bootleg Series, Volume 5*, Friday Music, 2009
*Johnny Winter: The Woodstock Experience*, Sony Legacy, 2009

### PRODUCED AND/OR PLAYED ON WITH MUDDY WATERS

*Hard Again*, Blue Sky, 1977
*I'm Ready*, Blue Sky, 1978
*Muddy "Mississippi" Waters Live*, Blue Sky, 1979
*King Bee*, Blue Sky, 1981
*Breakin' It Up & Breakin' It Down*, Sony Legacy, 2007

### PRODUCED AND PLAYED ON WITH SONNY TERRY

*Whoopin'*, Alligator, 1984

## AUTHORIZED RELEASES: SINGLES

"School Day Blues"/"You Know I Love You," Dart Records, 1959
"Creepy"/"Oh My Darling," KRCO, 1960
"Hey, Hey, Hey"/"One Night of Love," KRCO, 1960
"Shed So Many Tears"/"That's What Love Does," Frolic Records, 1961
"Voodoo Twist"/"Ease My Pain," Frolic Records, 1962
"Broke and Lonely"/"Crying in My Heart" (under the artist name "Texas Guitar Slim"), Diamond Records; then leased to Jin Records, 1963
"Roadrunner"/"The Guy You Left Behind," Todd Records, 1963
"Gangster of Love"/"Eternally," Frolic Records, 1963
"Eternally"/"You'll Be the Death of Me," Atlantic Records, 1964
"Gone for Bad"/"I Won't Believe It," Frolic Records; then leased to MGM, 1964
"Please Come Home for Christmas"/"Out of Sight" (under the artist name "Insight"), Cascade Records, 1966
"Birds Can't Row Boats"/"Leavin' Blues," Pacemaker Records, 1967

"Comin' Up Fast (Part 1)"/"Comin' Up Fast (Part 2)" (with the Great Believers), Cascade Records, 1967

"Tramp"/"Parchman Farm" (with the Traits), Universal, 1967

## RELEASES BY OR WITH OTHER ARTISTS

### GREGG ALLMAN

*One More Try: An Anthology*, Polygram, 1997. Johnny plays slide on "Wasted Words," recorded at a jam in August 1972 that also included Buddy Miles and Berry Oakley.

### ALLMAN BROTHERS

*Welcome to Hollywood*, Archivio, 1994. A bootleg of the Allman Brothers concert at the Hollywood Bowl on August 6, 1972. Johnny plays "Johnny B. Goode" during the encore, and jams with the band on Robert Johnson's "Dust My Broom."

*The Allman Brothers Band Live at the Atlanta International Pop Festival—July 3 & 5, 1970*, Epic/Legacy, 2003. Features Johnny on "Mountain Jam."

### MIKE BLOOMFIELD AND AL KOOPER

*Fillmore East: The Lost Concert Tapes 12/13/68*, Columbia/Legacy, 2003. Johnny makes his Fillmore East debut playing "It's My Own Fault."

### LONNIE BROOKS

*Wound Up Tight*, Alligator, 1986. Johnny plays guitar on "Got Lucky Last Night" and "Wound Up Tight."

### CANNED HEAT, JOHN MAYALL, AND WALTER TROUT

*The Secret Jam—Live at the Lone Star in New York City 10/12/83*. Bootleg recording of the *Tribute to Muddy* show. Johnny plays guitar and sings with Canned Heat and Trout on "I'm Tired of Living," "On the Road Again," "Lovin' With a Feeling," "Baby, Please Don't Go," "Shake That Boogie," and "I Can't See the Justice."

### JAMES COTTON

*Taking Care of Business*, Capital, 1970. Johnny plays acoustic slide on "She Moves Me," and joins Michael Bloomfield on guitar on "Georgia Swing."

**RICK DERRINGER**

*Spring Fever*, Blue Sky, 1975. Johnny plays slide guitar.

**BOB DYLAN**

*30th Anniversary Concert Celebration*, Sony, 1993. Johnny plays his fiery rendition of "Highway 61 Revisited" at the Madison Square Garden tribute show to Bob Dylan.

**BUDDY GUY**

*Messin' with the Blues*, VSP (Italy), 1994. Live shows with Buddy Guy recorded at the Cubby Bear (March 23) and Vic Theater (December) in Chicago in 1991.

**BUGS HENDERSON**

*American Music*, Bingo Pajama Records, 1988; Flat Canyon Records, 1993. Johnny plays a guitar solo on an eight-minute version of "Honky Tonky" during a jam with Henderson, Jimmy Vaughan, Willie Nelson, and other Texas guitarists.

*Legendary Jams—1976 to 1980*, Taxim Records, 1997. Jams include Henderson, Roy Buchanan, Freddie King, Ted Nugent, and Johnny Winter. Johnny sings and plays guitar on "Talk to Your Daughter" and "It's My Own Fault," both recorded live at the Palladium in Dallas, Texas in 1979.

**JIMI HENDRIX**

*Lifelines: The Jimi Hendrix Story*, Reprise, 1990. Johnny plays on "Things I Used to Do," recorded at a late night jam at the Record Plant.

**ROCKY HILL** (late guitarist and brother of ZZ Top bassist Dusty Hill)

*Texas Shuffle*, Tomato Records, 1982. Johnny added guitar and vocals to "Hootchie Cootchie Man" [sic], "Bad Girl Blues," and "Red Rooster Jam."

**JOHN LEE HOOKER**

*Mr. Lucky*, Virgin, 1991. Johnny and his band—bassist Jeff Ganz and drummer Tom Compton—accompany Hooker on "Susie."

*Face to Face*, Eagle Records, 2003. Johnny and Jefferson Airplane and Hot Tuna bassist Jack Casady accompany Hooker on "Face to Face."

### ROBERT PALMER

*Ridin' High*, EMI/Capital, 1992. Johnny sings and plays guitar on "Hard Head."

### OTIS RUSH

*Take a Look Behind*, Weeping Goat label. Audience recording of the July 4, 1978 Village Vanguard show. Johnny plays with Rush and his band on "Every Day I Have the Blues" and "Take a Look Behind." Cover photo is of Otis Rush; the back photo is a shot of Johnny and Luther Allison.

### ERIC SARDINAS

*Treat Me Right*, Evidence, 1999. Johnny sings and plays guitar on "Tired of Tryin'."

### JEREMY STEIG

*Temple at Birth*, Columbia, 1975. Steig played on *Still Alive and Well* in 1973, and Johnny returns the favor. He played acoustic and electric guitar with the improvisational jazz flutist on "King Tut Strut," "Ouanga," and "Mountain Dew Blues."

### ISAAC PAYTON SWEAT (IKEY SWEAT)—*unauthorized releases by Roy Ames after Sweat's death*

*Texas Honky Tonk Dreams*, Collectables, 1994.

*Cotton Eyed Joe*, M. I. L. Multimedia, 1997. Photo of Johnny and Ikey on cover with promo "featuring Johnny Winter."

### UNCLE JOHN TURNER

*Johnny Winter and Uncle John Turner*, Thunderbolt Records, 1989; released as *Back in Beaumont* on the Magnum label in 1990. Johnny plays lead guitar and harp in the 1981 sessions as a favor to his former drummer. Both were upset when it was released with Johnny's photo on the cover.

### BRUCE WILLIS

*If It Don't Kill You, It Just Makes You Stronger*, Motown Records, 1989. Johnny plays slide guitar on "Here Comes Trouble Again."

### EDGAR WINTER

*Entrance*, Epic, 1970. Edgar and Johnny co-wrote eight songs; Edgar wrote the music and Johnny wrote the lyrics. Johnny plays guitar on "Tobacco Road," and harmonica on several cuts.

*Edgar Winter's White Trash*, Epic, 1971. Johnny plays slide on "I've Got News for You."

*Roadwork*, Epic, 1972. Johnny plays guitar on "Rock and Roll Hoochie Koo."

*Johnny and Edgar Winter Discussing Together*, Blue Sky Records, 1976.

*Winter Blues*, Rhino/WEA, 1999. Johnny plays slide guitar on "On the Tip of My Tongue."

## SELECTED BOOTLEG RELEASES

This is a sampling of unauthorized CDs. When I went over the list with Johnny, he was shocked by the number of bootlegs. He knew that Ken Ritter, his manager from 1960 to 1964, and Roy Ames, who managed him from 1966 to 1968, had released numerous bootlegs of the singles they had produced for him. But he had no idea there were so many. The song lists were even more surprising. Most consist of a selection from twenty to thirty of Johnny's early singles, listed in varying order, packaged with different cover photography, and released under different names on a variety of labels. Johnny's Houston shows with Willie Dixon and the Chicago All Stars, and with Jimmy Reed, were also released by Ames under a number of titles.

*39-32-29 Blues*, Go label, 2002

*About Blues*, Janus, 1970

*Austin, Texas*, United Artists, 1974; Phantom, date unknown (reissue of *Progressive Blues Experiment*)

*Back in Beaumont*, Thunderbolt, 1996, 2000 (Winter and Uncle John Turner)

*Before the Storm*, Janus, 1971

*Best of Live*, Thunderbolt, 2000

*Birds Can't Row Boats*, Relix, 1991 (original release date: 1988)

*Black Cat Bone*, Thunderbolt, 1999

*Blue Suede Shoes*, Thunderbolt, 1996

*Blues in a Box*, M. I. L. Multimedia, 1998 (poor-quality box set)

*Blues to the Bone*, Relix, 1995

*Blues to the Bone*, Collectables, 1996; also released as *Raw to the Bone*, Thunderbolt, 2002 (recorded with Calvin "Loudmouth" Johnson)

*Broke and Lonely*, Magnum, 1996; Thunderbolt, 2001

*Can't Loose the Blues* [sic], Not Guilty (bootleg of 1991 live show at Ventura Concert Theater), date unknown

*Collectors Box Set*, Past & Present, 2003 (four discs; original release date: 2000)

*Crying the Blues: Late '60s Concert at Liberty Hall—Houston, Texas*, Collectables, 1996 (Johnny and Willie Dixon)

*Crying the Blues: Live in Concert*, Thunderbolt, 1996 (Johnny and Willie Dixon)

*Early Heat*, Special Music, 1995 (original release date: 1990)

*Early Times*, Janus, 1970

*Early Winter*, Griffin Records, 1996; President Records, 2003 (original release date: 1977)

*Early Winter/Johnny Winter*, President Records, 2003

*Ease My Pain*, Sundazed, 1997 (original release date: March 12, 1996)

*Electric Blues Man*, Magnum, 1996

*Electric Man Blues*, Thunderbolt, 1996, 1999 (two discs)

*Eternally/The Johnny Winter Story, Volume 2*, P-Vine (Japan), date unknown (photo of Johnny and Ikey Sweat on cover)

*First Winter/The Original Album*, Disky, 1991

*Five After Four AM*, TKO Magnum Midline, 2002

*Gangster of Love*, Collectables, 1992

*Golden Days of Rock and Roll*, Pulsar, 1992 ('70s and '80s material)

*Hard at Work*, Phantom, 2000

*History of the Blues*, Rock Dreams, 1978; also released as *Live at the Texas Opry House* on Thunderbolt in 2002

*Hits You Remember*, Madacy Records, 2000 (two-disc CD set—one Johnny and one Edgar)

*Hot*, Pigs Eye, date unknown (August 1, 1969 show at the Hollywood Bowl)

*Houston Sessions*, Catfish (UK), 2002

*An Introduction to Johnny Winter*, Fuel, 2006

*Jack Daniels Kind of Day*, Thunderbolt, 1996

*Johnny B. Goode—18 Electrifying Songs*, Disky, 1997

*Johnny Winter*, Phantom, 2001 (UK budget-priced compilation)

*Johnny Winter Box Set*, Relix, 2000 (three studio discs and a live disc)

*The Johnny Winter Story*, GRT, 1969

*The Johnny Winter Story*, P-Vine (Japan), date unknown

*Leavin' Blues*, Music Mirror, date unknown
*Liberty Hall Sessions*, Magnum, 1996
*Liberty Hall Sessions Live*, TKO Magnum Midline, 2002 (Johnny and Jimmy Reed)
*Liberty Hall Sessions/Live at the Texas Opry House*, Thunderbolt, 2001 (two discs)
*Live at Liberty Hall 1972*, Last Call Records, 2002
*Live at the Texas Opry House*, Thunderbolt, 2002
*Live in Houston/Busted in Austin*, Thunderbolt, 1991, 1996
*Live in Houston/No Time to Live*, Thunderbolt, 2002 (two discs)
*Livin' the Blues*, Phantom, 1996 (Danish budget-priced compilation)
*Living in the Blues*, Thunderbolt, 1996; Sundazed, 1997; Disky, 1998
*A Lone Star Kind of Day*, Relix, 1991
*Lone Star Shootout*, Varese Records, 2001 (compilation of '60s and '70s live shows without recording dates or locations; includes Jimmy Reed on "Big Boss Man" and Willie Dixon on "Spoonful")
*Masters*, Eagle, 1998
*Nightrider*, Relix, 1991 (original release date: 1974)
*No Time to Live*, Magnum Midline, 2001; Thunderbolt, 2002
*Original Winter: The Sixties Sessions*, Thunderbolt, 2001
*Platinum Series*, D-3 Entertainment, 2000
*Raised on Rock*, Prestige, Elite, 2002
*Ready for Winter*, Accord Records, 1994
*Relix Records Best of Blues, Volume 2*, Relix, 1997
*Relix Records Best of Blues, Volume 3*, Relix, 1997
*Roadrunner*, Babylon, 1992
*Rock & Pop Legends*, Disky, 1995
*Rock & Roll*, KRB Music Companies, 1999
*Rock N Roll Hoochie Coo*, Phantom, 2000
*Rock N' Roll People*, Silver Star, 2001
*School Day Blues*, Collectables, 1996
*Sideman*, Collectables, 1996 (a bootleg CD of songs that Ames produced and Johnny played on as a sideman)
*Still Alive and Well/Captured Live!*, BGO (Beat Goes On), 2002
*Stranger in Your Eye + 1*, Phantom, 2002; also released as *Before the Storm* in 1971
*Suicide Won't Satisfy*, Phantom, 1988
*Suicide Won't Satisfy*, Thunderbolt, 1998
*Suicide Won't Satisfy/Black Cat Bone*, Thunderbolt, 2002 (two discs)

*Texas Blues*, Recall Records, 1998 (two discs)
*Texas Tornado*, Charly Records (UK), 1993; Charly Budget (UK), 1994; Griffin Records, 1995
*Ultimate Collection (Slim Package)*, Madacy Records, 2002 (two-disc CD set—one Johnny and one Edgar)
*Walking by Myself (Live)*, Relix, 1992 (1977 concert in Hempstead, New York)
*White Heat*, M. I. L. Multimedia, 1998
*White Lightning*, Magnum, 1996; Thunderbolt, 1996
*White Lightning/Broke & Lonely*, Thunderbolt, 2000 (two discs)
*Winter Blues*, Castle Communications, 1997
*Winter Essentials 1960–1967 (Original Recording Remastered)*, Fuel Records, 2003
*Winter Heat (Extra Tracks)*, M. I. L. Multimedia, 1998
*Winter's Scene*, Pair, 1990 (original release date: 1972)

Special thanks to Jim Geuther, webmaster of http://www.yee.ch/winter, for his meticulous research on Johnny's recordings.

# Bibliography

Aledort, Andy. Liner notes. *Second Winter*, Sony/Legacy, 2004.

Brown, Thomas F. "Deep Politics in Jefferson County During the Mid-Twentieth Century," paper presented at meeting of the Beaumont Historical Society, January 2006.

"Champagne Breakfast with Muddy." *Creem*, June 1977.

"Chicken-Soup Freak." *Time*, February 28, 1969.

Dann, Laurel. "A Winter's Tale." *Rock*, August 27, 1973.

Dolgikh, Eugene. "Bruce Iglauer: Alligator Forever." http://home.nestor .minsk.by/jazz/articles/2005/05/0027.html. June 14, 2005.

Flippo, Chet. "Just Act Like I'm a Person, Dammit!" *Rolling Stone*, July 6, 1972.

Friedman, Josh Alan. "The Beautiful Loser." *Dallas Observer*, 1996.

Guerra, Tom. "Thoughts on Johnny Winter: Luther Nallie." *Vintage Guitar*, November 2001.

____. "Rick Derringer—Thoughts on Johnny Winter." *Vintage Guitar*, November 2001.

Hickey, Dennis. "The Complete Illustrated List of Vulcan Gas Company Posters and Handbills." http://www.faculty.missouristate.edu/d/dvh804f/vulcan.htm.

Hodenfield, Jan. "Steve Paul Splits the Scene." *Rolling Stone*, September 6, 1969.

"Hot Prospect: Columbia's Bid Bags Johnny Winter." *Rolling Stone*, March 1, 1969.

"An Interview with Johnny Winter and Rick Derringer. *Creem*, August 1970.

Jacobson, Nels. "The Maverick Tradition: Postering in Austin, Texas." *OFFtheWALL*, 1991/Volume No. 1/Issue No. 2; 1992/Volume No. 1/ Issue No. 3.

Jahn, Mike. "Chicago, Winter at Fillmore East." *New York Times*, November 16, 1969.

*Johnny and Edgar Winter Discussing Together*, Blue Sky Records, ASZ 242, 1976.

"Johnny Winter: It's Just Bad Music." *Rolling Stone*, April 16, 1970.

"Johnny Winter: Still Alive and Well," *Play:Back*, published by Columbia, Epic, and Columbia Custom Labels, 1973.

Kahn, Ashley. "Johnny Winter Back to the Blues—His Early Years (Part 1)." *Goldmine*, March 28, 1986.

Lomax, John Nova. "Good Riddance to Bad Rubbish—Roy Ames, child pornographer and record producer, dies at 66." *Houston Press*, August 28, 2003.

Morthland, John. "Johnny Winter on Music, Hype and Happiness." *Rolling Stone*, October 15, 1970.

Muise, Dan. *Gallagher, Marriott, Derringer & Trower: Their Lives and Music.* Milwaukee: Hal Leonard Corporation, 2002.

Nelson, Paul. "Johnny Winter Fiasco Goes On." *Rolling Stone*, May 3, 1969.

Pareles, Jon. "Review/Blues: Low-Key Tribute to John Lee Hooker." *New York Times*, October 21, 1990.

Pisaretz, Jim. "Rockin' Tattoo Blues." *Easy Riders: Tattoo Magazine of Skin Art*, Summer 1989.

"Research Report Series," National Institute on Drug Abuse. http://www.nida.nih.gov/ResearchReports/Heroin/heroin3.html.

"Rock Stars Hoping to Get Last Laugh in Comic Book Case." *Intellectual Property Litigation Reporter*, July 9, 2002, Vol. 9; No.4: 9 (LexisNexis).

Sepulvado, Larry & John Burks. "Texas." *Rolling Stone*, December 7, 1968.

Sherman, Jim. "Texas Rip-Off: It's the Roy Ames Way." *Blues Access*, Volume 20, Winter 1995.

*Strangers in Town*, VHS documentary, directed by Lois Siegel (Montreal, Quebec, Canada: Lois Siegel Productions, 1988).

Swensen, John. "Nothin' But the Blues, Johnny Winter." *Rolling Stone*, August 25, 1977.

Trynka, Paul. *Iggy Pop: Open Up and Bleed.* New York: Broadway Books, 2007.

Wheeler, Tom. "Waters/Winter Interview." *Guitar Player*, August 1983.

Wild, David. Liner notes. *Bob Dylan: 30th Anniversary Concert Celebration*, Columbia, 1993.

Zackon, Fred. *Heroin: The Street Narcotic*, edited by Solomon H. Snyder. New York: Chelsea House Publications, 1992.

# Index

www.ingramcontent.com/pod-product-compliance
Lightning Source LLC
LaVergne TN
LVHW010533100826
845148LV00001B/169